Lecture Notes in Computer Science   10215

Commenced Publication in 1973
Founding and Former Series Editors:
Gerhard Goos, Juris Hartmanis, and Jan van Leeuwen

Editorial Board

David Hutchison
  Lancaster University, Lancaster, UK
Takeo Kanade
  Carnegie Mellon University, Pittsburgh, PA, USA
Josef Kittler
  University of Surrey, Guildford, UK
Jon M. Kleinberg
  Cornell University, Ithaca, NY, USA
Friedemann Mattern
  ETH Zurich, Zurich, Switzerland
John C. Mitchell
  Stanford University, Stanford, CA, USA
Moni Naor
  Weizmann Institute of Science, Rehovot, Israel
C. Pandu Rangan
  Indian Institute of Technology, Madras, India
Bernhard Steffen
  TU Dortmund University, Dortmund, Germany
Demetri Terzopoulos
  University of California, Los Angeles, CA, USA
Doug Tygar
  University of California, Berkeley, CA, USA
Gerhard Weikum
  Max Planck Institute for Informatics, Saarbrücken, Germany

More information about this series at http://www.springer.com/series/7408

Jonathan P. Bowen · Zhiming Liu
Zili Zhang (Eds.)

Engineering Trustworthy Software Systems

Second International School, SETSS 2016
Chongqing, China, March 28 – April 2, 2016
Tutorial Lectures

 Springer

Editors
Jonathan P. Bowen
London South Bank University
London
UK

Zili Zhang
Southwest University
Chongqing
China

Zhiming Liu
Southwest University
Chongqing
China

ISSN 0302-9743   ISSN 1611-3349   (electronic)
Lecture Notes in Computer Science
ISBN 978-3-319-56840-9   ISBN 978-3-319-56841-6   (eBook)
DOI 10.1007/978-3-319-56841-6

Library of Congress Control Number: 2017936652

LNCS Sublibrary: SL2 – Programming and Software Engineering

Printed on acid-free paper

This Springer imprint is published by Springer Nature
The registered company is Springer International Publishing AG
The registered company address is: Gewerbestrasse 11, 6330 Cham, Switzerland

Preface

The Second School on Engineering Trustworthy Software Systems (SETSS 2016) was held from March 28 to April 2, 2016, at Southwest University, Chongqing, China. It was aimed at PhD and master's students in particular, from around China, as well as being suitable for university researchers and industry software engineers. The first 50 participants accepted for the school received free places. This volume contains a record of some of the lectures and seminars delivered at the school.

The school was held when Southwest University was celebrating its 110th anniversary. It was organized by the School of Computer and Information Science at Southwest University, providing lectures on leading-edge research in methods as well as tools for use in computer system engineering. The school aimed to enable participants to learn about state-of-the-art software engineering methods and technology advances from experts in the field.

An opening address was delivered by the Vice President of Southwest University, Professor Yanqiang Cui, followed by an introduction to SETSS 2016 by Prof. Zhiming Liu. Sessions at the school were chaired by Professors Zili Zhang, Jonathan Bowen, Zhiming Liu, and Jim Woodcock.

The following lectures (four 90-min lecture sessions each) were delivered during the school:

- Tao Xie: "Parameterized Unit Testing: Theory and Practice"
- Michael Butler: "Modelling and Verification in Event-B"
- Martin Leucker: "Runtime Verification"
- Yifeng Chen: "Parallel Programming Today"
- Jim Woodcock: "Semantics of Reactive Systems"
- Alvaro Miyazawa: "Java in the Safety-Critical Domain – A Refinement Approach"

In addition, there were two 120-min evening seminars on related subject areas:

- Jonathan P. Bowen: "Alan Turing: Founder of Computer Science"
- Zhilin Wu: "Formal Reasoning About Infinite Data Values: An Ongoing Quest"

These additional presentations complemented the longer lecture courses.

Courses

Modelling and Verification in Event-B

Lecturer: Prof. Michael Butler, University of Southampton, UK

Biography: Michael Butler is Professor of Computer Science at Southampton University. He is internationally recognized as a leading expert in refinement-based formal methods. He holds a PhD (Computation) from the University of Oxford. His research work encompasses applications, tools, and methodology for formal methods, especially refinement-based method such as B and Event-B. He has made key methodological contributions to the Event-B formal method, especially around model composition and decomposition. He plays a leading role in the development of several tools for B and Event-B, especially the Rodin toolset. Butler has a strong track record of collaboration with industry on the deployment of formal methods.

Overview: Formal modelling and verification lead to deeper understanding and higher consistency of specification and design than informal or semi-formal methods. A refinement approach means that models represent different abstraction levels of system design; consistency between abstraction levels is ensured by formal verification. These lectures provided an introduction to modelling and verification using Event-B offering guidance on the appropriate use of set theory for domain modelling, use of refinement to represent systems at different abstraction levels, and use of mathematical proof to verify the consistency between refinement levels.

Parallel Programming Today

Lecturer: Prof. Yifeng Chen, Peking University, China

Biography: Yifeng Chen is a research professor at the School of Electronics Engineering and Computer Science at Peking University and Vice Head, Department of Computer Science and Technology. He is a member of the Software Institute and the theory group. His main research interests include parallel programming model for multi-core and many-core architectures and parallel computing, (imperative, parallel, object-oriented, and probabilistic) programming languages, and programming theory. His research activities include serving as a PC member for conferences such as lCTAC, UTP, lFM, IPDPS, SC, PPoPP, and CCGrid.

Overview: Today's parallel computer systems are diverse. This lecture presented several lower-level tools of parallel programming and explained how to lift the level of programming in algebraic structures. The parallel programming paradigms of this lecture included the CUDA parallel computing platform for programming the General-Purpose Graphics Processor Unit that powers the Tianhe-1A supercomputer,

OpenMP Offload for programming Intel's MIC (Many Integrated Core) Architecture that powers Tianhe 2 supercomputer, and MPI (Message Passing Interface) for programming a cluster of servers connected with a high-speed network.

Runtime Verification

Lecturer: Prof. Martin Leucker, University of Lübeck, Germany

Biography: Martin Leucker is Director of the Institute for Software Engineering and Programming Languages at the University of Lübeck, Germany. He obtained his Habilitation at TU München (awarded in 2007) while being a member of Manfred Broy's group on Software and Systems Engineering. At TU Munich, he also worked as a Professor of Theoretical Computer Science and Software Reliability. Martin Leucker is the author of more than 100 reviewed conference and journal papers in software engineering, formal methods, and theoretical computer science. He is frequently a PC member of top-ranked conferences and has been the principal investigator in several research projects with industry participation, especially in the medical devices, automotive, and energy domains.

Overview: This tutorial course gave an introduction to the field of runtime verification. More specifically, it presented a comprehensive and coherent assessment to linear temporal logic-based monitor synthesis approaches. Both rewriting and automata-based techniques, each from a propositional as well as from a data perspective, were covered. Beyond a formal account, applications, especially in the area of testing, were presented. To this end, a practical introduction to the tool JUnitRV, which combines traditional unit testing for Java with runtime verification techniques, was included.

Java in the Safety-Critical Domain – A Refinement Approach

Lecturer: Dr. Alvaro Miyazawa, University of York, UK

Biography: Alvaro Miyazawa is a research associate in the High Integrity Systems Engineering Group at the University of York. His doctoral work formalized the semantics of Stateflow charts and defined a refinement strategy for the verification of sequential and parallel implementations. Since then, he has worked on the COMPASS project developing a comprehensive and integrated formal semantics for SysML with particular emphasis on state machine, block definition, and internal block diagrams, and on the hiJaC project, extending the formal semantics of Safety Critical Java and refinement strategies for verification and generation of SCJ programs. He has been working on the RoboCalc project, developing a formal state machine notation tailored for the design and analysis of robotic applications.

Overview: Safety Critical Java (SCJ) is a version of Java designed for programming real-time and safety-critical systems that require certification. A group at the University of York is working with members of the Open Group committee that is defining a standard for SCJ to outline techniques for verification of programs. This course presented SCJ, the challenges involved in verifying SCJ programs, and the approach used for this. New modelling languages and techniques for automatic generation and verification of models were also covered.

Semantics of Reactive Systems

Lecturer: Prof. Jim Woodcock, University of York, UK

Biography: Jim Woodcock is Professor of Software Engineering and Head of the Department of Computer Science at the University of York in England. His main research interests are in the industrial applications of software engineering, formal verification, programming language semantics, and cyber-physical systems. The research team he previous led at Oxford University won the Queen's Award for Technological Achievement for its work on the formal development of smart cards. He is a Fellow of the UK Royal Academy of Engineering.

Overview: Unifying Theories of Programming (UTP) provides a foundation for compositional semantics for a variety of different language paradigms. This course showed how to give semantics to imperative programs, pointer-rich programs, reactive programs with concurrency and communication, and reactive programs with mobile channels. It also demonstrated how these different paradigms can be composed to create a powerful programming language with stateful, reactive, reconfigurable processes.

Parameterized Unit Testing: Theory and Practice

Lecturer: Prof. Tao Xie, University of Illinois at Urbana-Champaign, USA

Biography: Tao Xie is Associate Professor and Willett Faculty Scholar in the Department of Computer Science at the University of Illinois at Urbana-Champaign, USA. His research interests are in software engineering and software security, with a focus on software testing, software analytics, and educational software engineering. He was ACM Distinguished Speaker and is an IEEE Computer Society Distinguished Visitor. He received an NSF CAREER Award in 2009. In addition, he received a 2014 Google Faculty Research Award, a 2011 Microsoft Research Software Engineering Innovation Foundation (SEIF) Award, the 2008, 2009, and 2010 IBM Faculty Awards, and a 2008 IBM Jazz Innovation Award. He was the program chair of ISSTA 2015.

Overview: This course presented the latest research and practice on principles, techniques, and applications of parameterized unit testing in practice, highlighting success stories, research and education achievements, and future research directions in developer testing. The course helped improve developer skills and knowledge for writing PUTs and gave an overview of tool automation in supporting PUTs. Attendees acquired the skills and knowledge needed to perform research or conduct practice in the field of developer testing and to integrate developer testing techniques in their own research, practice, and education.

Seminars

Alan Turing: Founder of Computer Science

Lecturer: Prof. Jonathan P. Bowen, London South Bank University, UK

Biography: Jonathan Bowen, FBCS FRSA, is Chairman of Museophile Limited (founded in 2002) and Emeritus Professor at London South Bank University, where he established and headed the Centre for Applied Formal Methods in 2000. During 2013–2015, he was Professor of Computer Science at Birmingham City University. His interests have ranged from formal methods, safety-critical systems, the Z notation, provably correct systems, rapid prototyping using logic programming, decompilation, hardware compilation, software/hardware co-design, linking semantics, and software testing, to the history of computing, museum informatics, and virtual communities.

Overview: Alan Turing (1912–1954) has been increasingly recognized as an important mathematician and philosopher, who despite his short life developed ideas that have led to foundational aspects of computer science and related fields. This seminar talk provided an overview of the diverse aspects related to Turing's remarkable achievements, with respect to the production of a book, *The Turing Guide*, a collected volume of 42 chapters, published by Oxford University Press in 2017. Although the story of Turing can be seen as one of tragedy, with his life cut short while still at the height of his intellectual powers, just short of his 42nd birthday, from a historical viewpoint Turing's contribution to humankind has been triumphant.

Formal Reasoning About Infinite Data Values: An Ongoing Quest

Lecturer: Dr. Zhilin Wu, Institute of Software, Chinese Academy of Sciences, China

Biography: Zhilin Wu is an associate research professor at the State Key Laboratory of Computer Science, Institute of Software, Chinese Academy of Sciences. His main research interests include program analysis and verification, computational logic, automata theory, and database theory.

Overview: Infinite data values are pervasive in computer systems, e.g., process identifiers, file names, integer or floating variables in programs, data parameters in network messages, records in databases, etc. Nevertheless, reasoning about them formally is notoriously difficult, since the infinity of data domains easily induces the undecidability of the reasoning tasks. The usual practice in most of the current approaches or tools is to ignore or abstract away the data infinity. A long-term goal is to show that in many scenarios, proper formalisms can be found, so that on the one hand the infinite data values, instead of being abstracted away, can be handled directly and explicitly, and on the other hand, the reasoning process can still be largely automated and made efficient. In this seminar, a summary of efforts toward this goal over the previous five years was given.

From the lectures and seminars, a record of the school has been distilled in six chapters in this volume as follows:

- Jonathan P. Bowen: "Alan Turing: Founder of Computer Science"
- Jim Woodcock and Simon Foster: "UTP by Example: Designs"
- Michael Butler: "Reasoned Modelling with Event-B"
- Ana Cavalcanti, Alvaro Miyazawa, Andy Wellings, Jim Woodcock,
  and Shuai Zhao: "Java in the Safety-Critical Domain"
- Martin Leucker: "Runtime Verification for Linear-Time Temporal Logic"
- Taolue Chen, Fu Song, and Zhilin Wu: "Formal Reasoning on Infinite Data Values:
  An Ongoing Quest"

We would like to thank the lecturers and their coauthors for their professional commitment and effort, the strong support of Southwest University, and the enthusiastic work of the local organization team, without whom SETSS 2016 would not have been possible. Thank you to Xin Chen (Nanjing University) for help with assembling the proceedings. We are grateful for the support of Alfred Hofmann and Anna Kramer of Springer *Lecture Notes in Computer Science* in the publication of this volume.

February 2017   Jonathan P. Bowen
                                                                Zhiming Liu
                                                                 Zili Zhang

Attendees, organizers, and lecturers at SETSS 2016. Front row, left to right: Tao Xie, Michael Butler, Jonathan Bowen, Yanqiang Cui, Zili Zhang, Guoqiang Xiao, Zhiming Liu.

Organization

Program Committee

Jonathan P. Bowen	London South Bank University, UK
Michael Butler	University of Southampton, UK
Ana Cavalcanti	University of York, UK
Yifeng Chen	Peking University, China
Martin Leucker	University of Lübeck, Germany
Bo Liu	Southwest University, China
Zhiming Liu	Southwest University, China
Jim Woodcock	University of York, UK
Zhilin Wu	Institute of Software, CAS, China
Tao Xie	University of Illinois at Urbana-Champaign, USA
Zili Zhang	Southwest University, China

Contents

Alan Turing: Founder of Computer Science

Jonathan P. Bowen[1,2](✉)

[1] Division of Computer Science and Informatics, School of Engineering,
London South Bank University, Borough Road, London SE1 0AA, UK
jonathan.bowen@lsbu.ac.uk
http://www.jpbowen.com
[2] Museophile Limited, Oxford, UK

Abstract. In this paper, a biographical overview of Alan Turing, the
20th century mathematician, philosopher and early computer scientist,
is presented. Turing has a rightful claim to the title of 'Father of modern
computing'. He laid the theoretical groundwork for a universal machine
that models a computer in its most general form before World War II.
During the war, Turing was instrumental in developing and influencing
practical computing devices that have been said to have shortened the
war by up to two years by decoding encrypted enemy messages that were
generally believed to be unbreakable. After the war, he was involved with
the design and programming of early computers. He also wrote foundational papers in the areas of what are now known as Artificial Intelligence
(AI) and mathematical biology shortly before his untimely death. The
paper also considers Turing's subsequent influence, both scientifically
and culturally.

1 Prologue

Alan Mathison Turing [8,23,33] was born in London, England, on 23 June 1912.
Educated at Sherborne School in Dorset, southern England, and at King's College, Cambridge, he graduated in 1934 with a degree in mathematics. Twenty
years later, after a short but exceptional career, he died on 7 June 1954 in
mysterious circumstances. He is lauded by mathematicians, philosophers, and
computer sciences, as well as increasingly the public in general.

Unlike some theorists, Turing was willing to be involved with practical aspects
and was as happy to wield a soldering iron as he was to wrestle with a mathematical problem, normally from a unique angle. With hindsight, Turing's 1936
seminal paper on computable numbers foretold the capabilities of the modern
computer. World War II (1939–45) then brought about a radical, but perhaps
fortuitous, change of direction in Turing's career, as his unique mathematical
abilities were recognized during his time at Cambridge and he was invited to
join Bletchley Park, the centre of the United Kingdom's efforts to break German
secret codes. Decryption was laborious to do by hand in the time needed and
Turing recognized that machines, together with great human ingenuity, could
tackle the problem far more quickly and reliably.

© Springer International Publishing AG 2017
J.P. Bowen et al. (Eds.): SETSS 2016, LNCS 10215, pp. 1–15, 2017.
DOI: 10.1007/978-3-319-56841-6_1

In 1999, *Time* magazine listed Turing among the 20th century's one hundred greatest minds [47], along with the DNA discoverers Crick and Watson, the physicist Albert Einstein, Alexander Fleming, the discoverer of penicillin, and the flying pioneers, the Wright brothers. Turing's achievements during his short lifetime were extensive. Best known as the genius who broke Germany's most secret codes during the Second World War, Turing was also the founding 'father of computer science' [5,8,9]. A search of "father of computer science" and "Alan Turing" together on Google gives over 57,000 results. Today, all who use information technology are familiar with the impact of his original ideas [17,18].

Turing proposed the insightful innovation of storing applications, and the other programs necessary for computers to perform for us, inside the computer's memory, ready to be opened whenever desired. At a time when the term 'computer' meant nothing more than a human clerk who sat at a desk doing calculations by hand, Turing envisaged a 'universal computing machine' [48] whose function could easily be transformed from acting as a word processor, to a desk calculator, to an automated chess opponent – or to anything else that can be formulated as an algorithmic software program. Like many significant ideas, this now seems as obvious as the arch or the wheel, but with this single invention of the stored program universal computer, Turing transformed the world.

In 1945, Turing went on to start the design of a stored-program electronic computer called the Automatic Computing Engine – or ACE. The name was in homage to the 19th-century computing pioneer Charles Babbage who proposed large mechanical calculating 'engines'. Turing's sophisticated ACE design saw wider success later in form of the English Electric Company's DEUCE computer, one of the earliest electronic computers to be available commercially. The DEUCE became an early success for the developing computer industry in the United Kingdom and, together with a small number of other computers, all greatly influenced by Turing's ideas, the DEUCE helped propel the UK into the age of the computer.

Turing also contributed to advances at the University of Manchester, where the engineers Sir Frederic Williams (1911–1977) and his student and then colleague Tom Kilburn (1921–2001) built the first universal Turing machine to be realized in electronic hardware. Their 'Baby', which can be considered as the world's earliest modern computer, first ran in June 1948, the same year that Turing joined the Computing Machine Laboratory at Manchester. He remained there for the rest of his life.

In addition to his exceptional theoretical and practical contributions with respect to the development of the computer, not to mention the new science of computer programming, Turing was the first pioneer of the areas of computing now known as Artificial Intelligence (AI) [52]. He also made important contributions to mathematics, logic, philosophy, theoretical biology, and the study of the mind. Mathematicians, philosophers, and computer scientists all claim Turing as their own as a result.

2 Biography

2.1 Youth and Pre-war

Alan Turing [22] was the son of an British civil servant who worked in India [33]. In 1912, his parents returned to England for his birth in Maida Vale, west London, at what is now the Colonnade Hotel [55]. At the age of 14, he was sent to Sherborne School, a traditional British public school in Dorset in southern England. In 1926, on crossing the English Channel from France where his family was living at the time, and arriving at Southampton for his first term at school, he found that the General Strike was under way and that no trains were running. He took the initiative and cycled the significant distance from Southampton to Sherborne, staying the night at Blandford Forum on the way (see Fig. 1), demonstrating his determination when faced with a practical problem even at this age.

Fig. 1. The Crown hotel at Blandford Forum, Dorset, where Turing stayed during his 1926 cycle ride to Sherborne School. (Photograph by Jonathan Bowen.)

Turing's interest in science was noted by his schoolteachers, but was not particularly encouraged at such a conservative establishment. He was able to solve advanced problems from first principles, for example without having been taught calculus. By the age of 16, he had encountered and understood the work of Albert Einstein (1879–1955). While at school Turing formed a close friendship with a fellow scientifically minded student, Christopher Morcom, who tragically died in 1930 during his last term at Sherborne. This had a traumatic effect on Turing and any religious leanings that Turing may have had were affected, subsequently making him more atheistic in his outlook, but possibly increasing his interest in the working of the mind.

Turing went on to study mathematics at King's College, Cambridge, from 1931 to 1934, graduating with a first-class degree; he was subsequently elected at a remarkably young age to be a Fellow of the College in 1935. At Cambridge, the direction of his research was influenced by the lectures of Max Newman (1897–1984), one of his few academic collaborators. In 1936, he submitted his groundbreaking paper on computable numbers [48] that was to form the cornerstone for the rest of his career; this presented the concept of a computing machine, and in particular a 'universal machine' capable of computing a wide class of numbers. Newman recognized the importance of the work and encouraged Turing for much of his subsequent career. Turing's notion of universality was what is thought of as 'programmability' in computers today. As he stated in a paper in the context of a human computer, "a man provided with paper, pencil, and rubber, and subject to strict discipline, is in effect a universal machine" [29,50].

Turing's efforts developed the 1931 research of the German mathematician Kurt Gödel (1906–1978) and have led to the use of the term 'Turing machine' for his universal machine: he demonstrated that any mathematical calculation that can be represented as an algorithm can be performed by such a machine. The *Entscheidungsproblem* (or 'decision problem') was a mathematical challenge posed by David Hilbert (1862–1943) in 1928 as to whether is there always an algorithm to determine the truth or falsity of a mathematical statement. Turing also demonstrated the insolubility of the problem by first showing that it is impossible to decide algorithmically whether a given Turing machine is satisfactory. This is now known as the halting problem and the issue was a vexing one to mathematicians. Turing machines remain a very important concept in the theory of computation and computability to this day [24].

From 1936 to 1938, Turing studied for a PhD degree at Princeton University in the USA under the American mathematician Alonzo Church (1903–1995), obtaining his doctorate in a remarkably short period [1,49]. Earlier, they had independently developed the Church–Turing thesis, characterizing the nature of computation and stating that every effectively calculable function produced by any means is also computable using a Turing machine. Although the thesis cannot be proved, it is almost universally accepted by mathematicians and theoretical computer scientists.

Turing later returned to Cambridge and attended lectures by the philosopher Ludwig Wittgenstein (1889–1951) about mathematical foundations. Wittgenstein argued that mathematicians invented (rather than discovered) truth, but Turing disagreed.

2.2 World War II

Turing was recruited to Bletchley Park (or 'Station X') [32,45], after working part-time for the Government Code and Cypher School (now known as the Government Communications Headquarters, or GCHQ). Before World War II, he had already contributed ideas on breaking the German Enigma machine (see Fig. 2) for encrypting messages. This meant that within weeks of joining Bletchley Park he had specified a machine that could be used to help decode

Enigma messages [46]. This was named the 'bombe' after an earlier and less efficient Polish-designed machine, the 'bomba'.

Fig. 2. A German Enigma machine (left) and the Turing Bombe rebuild project (right) at Bletchley Park. (Photographs by Jonathan Bowen.)

The bombe worked by taking a piece of probable plain text from the original message (known as a 'crib') and working through combinations of the Enigma machine's rotors and plugboard settings. Most possible settings would quickly produce contradictions, allowing them to be eliminated and leaving only a few combinations to be investigated in greater depth. The machine effectively undertook a mathematical proof mechanically, far more quickly and reliably than a human (or even a team of humans) was able to do so.

Turing chose to work on naval Enigma decryption because, as he said, "no one else was doing anything about it and I could have it to myself". This was typical of Turing, although he collaborated well with others at Bletchley Park. During his time there, he developed a number of novel decryption techniques and devices, which were often given playful slang terms. One of these, developed in 1942, was 'Turingery' or 'Turingismus', a hand technique for finding patterns in the Lorenz cipher wheel cams. It was especially useful because the information remained valid for a significant period.

Some of Turing's eccentricities were evident while he worked at Bletchley Park. He chained his cup to his radiator in his office within the unprepossessing Hut 6 (see Fig. 3) to avoid it being lost or stolen. He was also known to wear his gas mask while cycling to work, not because of fear of being gassed, but to avoid hay fever.

Turing was not averse to dealing with administrative issues when necessary. At one point when Turing could not obtain the personnel he needed, he and others at Bletchley Park contacted Winston Churchill about the urgency of the

Fig. 3. Hut 6 at Bletchley Park, now restored. (Photograph by Jonathan Bowen.)

matter. This elicited the response "Action this day" [46] from Churchill, who well understood the importance of the work undertaken at Bletchley Park.

Although not directly involved in its design, Turing's influence on work at Bletchley Park helped in the development of the world's first programmable digital electronic computer there, the Colossus [26], designed by Tommy Flowers (1905–1998). Turing was awarded the OBE (Officer of the Order of the British Empire) in 1945 for his war work, but his actual contribution remained secret for many years afterwards.

2.3   Post-war

After World War II, from 1945 to 1947, Turing worked at the National Physical Laboratory (NPL), west of London [57]. Here, influenced by his experience at Bletchley Park, he worked on the design of the very fast Automatic Computing Engine (ACE), an early computer [20,25]. Unfortunately, delays (partly due to bureaucracy) meant that Turing became frustrated with the project, and even the cut-down Pilot ACE was not built until after he left NPL to return to Cambridge for a sabbatical year. Turing never returned to work at NPL.

In 1948, he joined the mathematics department at the University of Manchester, where his earlier mentor from Cambridge, Max Newman, was now based [42]. He was appointed the Deputy Director of the University's computing laboratory, working on software for the Manchester Mark 1 'Baby', an early stored-program computer [37]. Turing worked on software for the Mark 1 and even produced what may have been the first proof of correctness for a program [51]. Although this had little influence at the time, its importance in the field of formal methods [6,15] was realised much later [11,41].

In 1950, Turing published a seminal paper on the subject of machine intelligence, later known as Artificial Intelligence, in the journal *Mind* [52]. He devised what became known as the 'Turing test' to provide a possible demonstration of machine intelligence. To pass the test, a computing machine must appear human when interacting with a person in such a way that it is indistinguishable from a real human being. Such a feat has still not been achieved fully, although it is deemed to be a viable aim and remains relevant to this day. There are now many variants for the test.

Towards the end of his life until his early and inadequately explained death in 1954, Turing worked in the interdisciplinary area of mathematical biology – and specifically, morphogenesis, the process that allows organisms to generate their shape. In 1952, he published a paper, *The chemical basis of morphogenesis* [53], which demonstrated that simple mathematical equations can produce complex patterns; this paper has subsequently been very influential as a foundational work in the field of computational biology, but much of his work in this area was not published until his *Collected Papers* appeared much later [19].

3   Influence

3.1   Coined Terms

Turing's name is associated with a significant number of different concepts coined by others and related directly or indirectly to his original ideas. Many can be found on Wikipedia [56]. Two of the most well-known are Turing's abstract concept of a computing device, now known as a 'Turing machine', and his idea of a test for machine intelligence in comparison with a human, the 'Turing test'. There are also more specialized versions of these concepts, such as a 'symmetric Turing machine', the 'reverse Turing test' where a human attempts to mimic being a computer, and a 'visual Turing test' for computer vision systems.

The 'Church–Turing thesis' (aka 'Turing's thesis') is a hypothesis about computable functions named after mathematician and Turings PhD supervisor Turing himself. The idea was conceived separately and using different approaches by both of them in the 1930s. Later in 1985, David Deutsch formulated a stronger physical version of the Church–Turing thesis, the 'Church–Turing–Deutsch principle' [28].

In computability theory, 'Turing reduction' is an algorithm that transforms one problem into another problem using a function that is computable by an oracle machine, a Turing machine connected to an 'oracle' that is able to provide a solution for a given computational problem. 'Turing equivalence' means that the reduction is possible in both directions. 'Turing computability' is the main form of computability used in recursion theory. The 'Turing degree', or degree of unsolvability of a set of natural numbers, gives a measure for the level of the set's algorithmic unsolvability.

The term 'Turing tarpit' (or tar-pit) was coined by the American computer scientist Alan Perlis (1922–1990) in 1982. It is a term for a computer interface or programming language that is flexible in the facilities provided, but is hard to learn in general due to the lack of support for its more widely used features.

There is even a programming language named 'Turing', developed in 1982 as a teaching language in the standard imperative programming style. Further related languages include 'Turing+', introduced in 1987 for programming concurrent systems, and 'Object-Oriented Turing', developed in 1991 as a replacement for Turing+, providing object-oriented programming features.

Recently, the term 'Alan Turing law' entered general use to describe United Kingdom legislation proposed in 2016 for an amnesty law to pardon homosexual men retrospectively [2]. This passed into UK law in 2017 [3].

3.2 Online Resources

There is a significant amount of material relating to Turing that is accessible online. Some of the leading websites in this regard include [10]:

- *Alan Turing: The Enigma* (http://www.turing.org.uk) [12], maintained by Turing's definitive biographer, Andrew Hodges [33];
- *The Turing Digital Archive* (http://www.turingarchive.org), provided by Turing's college, King's College, Cambridge, with nearly 3,000 images;
- *The Turing Archive for the History of Computing* (http://www.alanturing. net), digital facsimiles by Jack Copeland, a leading Turing scholar [19,21], and Diane Proudfoot, from Canterbury Christ Church University in New Zealand;
- *The Alan Turing Year* (http://www.turingcentenary.eu), celebrating Turing's 2012 centenary of his birth, with various events around the world [18].

Google Scholar (http://scholar.google.com) provides information about academic publications written by researchers around the world, including an entry for Turing [30] (see Fig. 4). Turing's three most cited papers have been foundational for three important fields of study.

Google Scholar also presents the number of citations per year for a given author. Citations to Turing's work have grown exponentially over the years in general, with relatively few still at the time of the Hodges biography in 1983 [33] and far more by the time of his 2012 centenary (see Fig. 5). There are now around six citations a day to Turing's work in scientific publications around the world.

Microsoft Academic Search, generated by a research project at Microsoft Research in Beijing, until recently provided similar facilities to Google Scholar, although with a smaller number of publications that were no longer being updated in recent years. It did however have better graphical visualization presentation of coauthors, citing authors, and transitive coauthorship links between any two authors [10]. It included an entry for Alan Turing. More recently, Microsoft has launched a new facility, *Microsoft Academic* (http://academic. microsoft.com), with a better corpus of publications but without the same visualization facilities. E.g., for Turing's entry, see [40].

The *Mathematics Genealogy Project* is a web-based resource providing access to a database (http://genealogy.math.ndsu.nodak.edu) of mathematically

Title 1–20		Cited by	Year
The chemical basis of morphogenesis AM Turing Bulletin of Mathematical Biology 52 (1), 153-197	Mathematical biology	9966 *	1952
On computable numbers, with an application to the Entscheidungsproblem AM Turing Proceedings of the London Mathematical Society 42 (2), 230-265	Theoretical computer science 9096		1936
Computing machinery and intelligence AM Turing Mind 59 (236), 433-460	Artificial Intelligence	9095	1950
Systems of logic based on ordinals AM Turing Proceedings of the London Mathematical Society 2 (1), 161-228		973	1939
Intelligent machinery AM Turing The Essential Turing, 395-432		916 *	1948
Computing machinery and intelligence AM Turing Computers & Thought, 11-35		665	1995
Rounding-off errors in matrix processes AM Turing The Quarterly Journal of Mechanics and Applied Mathematics 1 (1), 287-308		621	1948
Computability and λ-definability AM Turing The Journal of Symbolic Logic 2 (4), 153-163		534	1948
Checking a large routine AM Turing The early British computer conferences, 70-72		488 *	1948
Digital computers applied to games AM Turing, MA Bates, BV Bowden, C Strachey Faster than thought 101		397	1953

Fig. 4. Alan Turing's most cited papers on Google Scholar [30]

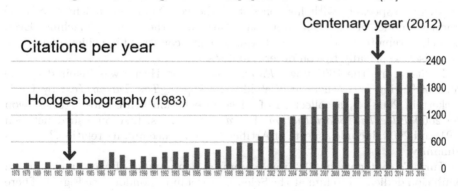

Fig. 5. Citations to Alan Turing's publications by year on Google Scholar [30].

related PhD supervisors and their students. Turing's PhD supervisor, the Princeton University mathematician Alonzo Church, has an entry that includes Turing [39]. Turing himself only had one PhD student, the mathematician Robin Gandy (1919–1995) at the University of Cambridge, who was subsequently an academic at the University of Oxford.

3.3 Cultural Influence

Turing has had a very significant scientific influence historically [7], but his now iconic status has also influenced more mainstream culture too, partly due to his treatment as a homosexual, now considered unjust, and his short life, most likely due to his resulting suicide. In theatre for example, *Breaking the Code* was a 1986 play by Hugh Whitemore [34], based on Turing's life and specifically the biography by Andrew Hodges [33]. It was performed in London's West End and later in 1988 on Broadway in New York, starring the British actor Derek Jacobi in the lead role of Turing on both occasions. In 1996, the play appeared as a BBC television film, also with Jacobi as Turing.

There have been a number of sculptures dedicated to the memory of Alan Turing in the UK and elsewhere. In 2001, a memorial to Turing was installed in Sackville Park, Manchester, where he worked at the end of his life. This is in the form of a bronze sculpture of Turing sitting on a bench and holding an apple. It was widely believed that Turing committed suicide due to biting a cyanide-laced apple. The monument was unveiled on 23 June, Turing's birthday. It was inspired by the play *Breaking the Code.*

A unique slate sculpture of Turing with an Enigma machine by Stephen Kettle is now on display at Bletchley Park [36]. The slate selected was from North Wales, which Turing visited both as a child and adult. There are other memorial sculptures and busts of Turing around the world. For example, at Southwest University in Chongqing, China, there is a bust outside the computer science department (see Fig. 6), along with the American mathematician and computing pioneer John von Neumann (1903–1957), who was himself influenced by Turing, especially with his concept of the von Neumann machine, a more practical model of the computer than Turing's earlier Turing machine. Even in such a remote location from Turing's home country, his achievements are recognised, especially by computer scientists.

In literature, the 1995 novel *Enigma* by Robert Harris was inspired by the work of Turing and others at Bletchley Park [31]. *The Turing Test* by Chris Beckett in 2008 [4], a collection of 14 science fiction genre short stories, won the 2009 *Edge Hill Short Fiction Award.* The stories, first published between 1991 and 2006, include aspects of Artificial Intelligence and its relationship with humanity.

Turing's centenary in 2012 was celebrated in a number of ways, including an exhibition dedicated to him at the Science Museum in London (see Fig. 7). There were also a number of Turing-related meetings at Bletchley Park, Cambridge, Manchester, Oxford, and elsewhere [13,18].

In popular music, the musical duo known as the Pet Shop Boys were inspired by a 2011 UK television documentary on Turing and then the Hodges biography [33] to write the musical work *A Man for the Future*, based on the life of Alan Turing. This included read passages from the Hodges biography, chosen with the help of Hodges himself. The operatic work, in eight movements, was premiered in a BBC PROM concert at the Royal Albert Hall in London on 29 July 2014, including extensive choral contributions by the BBC Singers, and received a standing ovation.

Fig. 6. Busts of Alan Turing (left) and John von Neumann (right) on the campus of Southwest University, Chongqing, China. (Photographs by Jonathan Bowen.)

Fig. 7. The entrance of an exhibition on Alan Turing at the Science Museum, London, for his centenary in 2012. (Photograph by Jonathan Bowen.)

In film, *The Imitation Game* of 2014 [35] was an American Hollywood production of a historical drama, loosely based on Turing's life and incorporating much fictional dramatic licence, with Andrew Hodges as a consultant. The film starred the leading film actors Benedict Cumberbatch as Turing and Keira Knightley as Joan Clarke MBE (1917–1996), his fellow cryptanalyst at Bletchley Park, to whom Turing proposed marriage in early 1941.

In art, the Lumen Prize winner Andy Lomas has been inspired by morphogenesis to combine his mathematical, programming, and artistic abilities to produce pseudo-living organisms at the cellular level in 2D, 3D and moving forms [10, 38]. There has also been influence of the Turing test on poetry [16]. No doubt Turing's ideas and increasing fame will continue to inspire the arts for the future too.

4   Epilogue

Turing was a homosexual at the time when homosexuality was illegal in the United Kingdom. He was charged with gross indecency in 1952, losing his security clearance as a result, and was forced to take female hormones in an attempt to 'cure' him if he wished to avoid imprisonment. On 8 June 1954, his cleaner found him dead at his home in Wilmslow, Cheshire. The cause of death was certainly cyanide poisoning, believed to be from a half-eaten apple found by his bed, but this was never tested. It was determined that he had committed suicide, although it is possible that his death was an accident since he experimented with cyanide at home. A verdict in today's courts would undoubtedly be less decisive from the evidence available [21].

Earlier that year, in a postcard to his friend, the Cambridge and Oxford mathematician Robin Gandy, Turing had written a short poem:

Hyperboloids of wondrous Light;
Rolling for aye through Space and Time;
Harbour those Waves which somehow Might;
Play out God's holy pantomime

– an apposite epitaph for someone who moved from religious belief to disbelief during his lifetime [33]. Geoffrey Jefferson, Professor of Neurosurgery at the University of Manchester, aptly described Turing as "a sort of scientific Shelley" [54, 55]. Both Turing and the poet Percy Bysshe Shelley (1792–1822) were somewhat maverick and individualistic geniuses who died before their time.

Turing was elected a Fellow of the Royal Society (FRS) in 1951 [42], an indication of the esteem held for him by scientists in the United Kingdom, but wider recognition of his contributions came long after his death with the development of computer science [27] and as the truth of his crucial wartime role at Bletchley Park began to be revealed [32]. It is notable that Turing's three most cited papers by far (currently around 9–10,000 citations each on Google Scholar [30]) (see also Fig. 4) were published in 1936, 1950, and 1952 [48, 52, 53]; each of these was foundational in subsequent fields: theoretical computer science, artificial intelligence, and mathematical biology. Given Turing's premature death in 1954, within four year of the publication of two of his three most significant papers, it is very likely that he would have gone on to produce further inspirational work had he lived longer.

The 2012 book *The Scientists* [43] included Alan Turing as one of the top 43 scientists of all time [8]. Turing is increasingly remembered by the public at large as well as by scientists. There is now a memorial statue in Manchester and a unique slate statue is on view at Bletchley Park, as previously mentioned. There are blue plaques marking his London birthplace, the home where he died in Cheshire, and elsewhere. In 2009, there was even a UK government apology by the Prime Minister, Gordon Brown, for his official treatment, followed by a Royal Pardon by Queen Elizabeth II in 2013 [13].

Perhaps most fittingly, the nearest equivalent to the Nobel Prize, given annually to an outstanding computer scientist by computing's international professional body, the Association for Computing Machinery (ACM), is known as the *A. M. Turing Award* (http://amturing.acm.org). Turing's legacy is explored further in [13]. Despite his untimely death at only 41, Alan Turing's influence will live on in the field of computing, mathematics, and philosophy.

Acknowledgements. Thank you to my good colleague Prof. Zhiming Liu for academic support over the years and financial support provided through Southwest University in Chongqing, China. Thank you as well to my coauthors, Prof. Jack Copeland et al., on *The Turing Guide* [23,44]. Parts of this paper have been adapted and updated from [8], with permission of the editor, and from a talk at Gresham College in London [9].

References

1. Appel, A.W. (ed.): Alan Turing's systems of logic. The Princeton thesis, Princeton University Press (2014)
2. BBC: 'Alan Turing law': thousands of gay men to be pardoned. BBC News, 20 October 2016. http://www.bbc.co.uk/news/uk-37711518
3. BBC: Thousands of gay men pardoned for past convictions. BBC News, 31 January 2017. http://www.bbc.co.uk/news/uk-38814338
4. Beckett, C.: The Turing Test. Elastic Press (2008/2012)
5. Bernhard, C.: Turing's Vision: The Birth of Computer Science. MIT Press, Cambridge (2016)
6. Boca, P.P., Bowen, J.P., Siddiqi, J. (eds.): Formal Methods: State of the Art and New Directions. Springer, London (2010)
7. Bowen, J.P.: A brief history of algebra and computing: an eclectic Oxonian view. IMA Bull. **31**(1/2), 6–9 (1995)
8. Bowen, J.P.: Alan Turing. In: Robinson [43], pp. 270–275
9. Bowen, J.P.: Alan Turing: the founder of computer science. Gresham College, 31 October 2013. http://www.gresham.ac.uk/lectures-and-events/alan-turing-the-founder-of-computer-science
10. Bowen, J.P.: Alan Turing: virtuosity and visualisation. In: Bowen et al. [14], pp. 197–204. http://dx.doi.org/10.14236/ewic/EVA2016.40

11. Bowen, J.P.: The Z notation: whence the cause and whither the course? In: Liu, Z., Zhang, Z. (eds.) SETSS 2014. LNCS, vol. 9506, pp. 103–151. Springer, Cham (2016). doi:10.1007/978-3-319-29628-9_3

12. Bowen, J.P., Angus, J., Borda, A., Beler, A., Hodges, A., Filippini-Fantoni, S.: The development of science museum websites: case studies. In: Hin, L.T.W., Subramaniam, R. (eds.) E-Learning and Virtual Science Centers, chap. XVIII, sect. 3, Case Studies, pp. 366–392. Idea Group Publishing, Hershey (2005)

13. Bowen, J.P., Copeland, B.J.: Turing's legacy. In: Copeland et al. [23], chap. 42

14. Bowen, J.P., Diprose, G., Lambert, N. (eds.): EVA London 2016: Electronic Visualisation and the Arts. Electronic Workshops in Computing, BCS (2016). http://www.bcs.org/ewic/eva2016

15. Bowen, J.P., Hinchey, M.G.: Formal methods. In: Gonzalez, T.F., Diaz-Herrera, J., Tucker, A.B. (eds.) Computing Handbook, chap. 71, vol. 1, 3rd edn, pp. 1–25. CRC Press, Boca Raton (2014)

16. Clements, W.: Poetry beyond the Turing test. In: Bowen et al. [14], pp. 213–219. http://dx.doi.org/10.14236/ewic/EVA2016.42

17. Cooper, S.B., Hodges, A. (eds.): The Once and Future Turing: Computing the World. Cambridge University Press, Cambridge (2016)

18. Cooper, S.B., van Leeuwen, J. (eds.): Alan Turing: His Work and Impact. Elsevier Science, Amsterdam (2013)

19. Copeland, B.J. (ed.): The Essential Turing. Oxford University Press, Oxford (2004)

20. Copeland, B.J. (ed.): Alan Turing's Automatic Computing Engine: The Master Codebreaker's Struggle to Build the Modern Computer. Oxford University Press, Oxford (2005)

21. Copeland, B.J.: Turing: Pioneer of the Information Age. Oxford University Press, Oxford (2012)

22. Copeland, B.J., Bowen, J.P.: Life and work. In: Copeland et al. [23], chap. 1

23. Copeland, B.J., Bowen, J.P., Sprevak, M., Wilson, R.J., et al.: The Turing Guide. Oxford University Press, Oxford (2017)

24. Copeland, B.J., Posy, C.J., Shagrir, O.: Computability: Turing, Gödel, Church, and Beyond. MIT Press, Cambridge (2013)

25. Copeland, B.J., et al.: Alan Turing's Electronic Brain. Oxford University Press (2005/2012)

26. Copeland, B.J., et al.: Colossus: The Secrets of Bletchley Park's Codebreaking Computers. Oxford University Press, Oxford (2006)

27. Dasgupta, S.: It Began with Babbage: The Genesis of Computer Science. Oxford University Press, Oxford (2014)

28. Deutsch, D.: Quantum theory, the Church-Turing principle and the universal quantum computer. Proc. R. Soc. **440**(1818), 97–117 (1985). http://dx.doi.org/10.1098/rspa.1985.0070

29. Evans, C.R., Robertson, A.D.J. (eds.): Key Papers: Cybernetics. Butterworths, London (1968)

30. Google Scholar: Alan Turing. Google (2017). http://scholar.google.com/citations?user=VWCHlwkAAAAJ

31. Harris, R.: Enigma. Hutchinson, London (1995)

32. Hinsley, F.H., Stripp, A. (eds.): Code Breakers: The Inside Story of Bletchley Park. Oxford University Press, Oxford (1993)

33. Hodges, A.: Alan Turing: The Enigma. Simon and Schuster/Princeton University Press (1983/2012)

34. IMDb: Breaking the Code. Internet Movie Database (1996). http://ww.imdb.com/title/tt0115749

35. IMDb: The Imitation Game. Internet Movie Database (2014). http://imdb.com/title/tt2084970
36. Kettle, S.: Alan Turing. Stephen Kettle (2012). http://www.stephenkettle.co.uk/turing.html
37. Lavington, S. (ed.): Alan Turing and His Contemporaries: Building the World's First Computers. BCS - The Chartered Institute for IT, Swindon (2012)
38. Lomas, A.: Species explorer: an interface for artistic exploration of multi-dimensional parameter spaces. In: Bowen et al. [14], pp. 95–102. http://dx.doi.org/10.14236/ewic/EVA2016.23
39. Mathematics Genealogy Project: Alonzo Church. Department of Mathematics, North Dakota State University (2017). http://genealogy.math.ndsu.nodak.edu/id.php?id=8011
40. Microsoft Academic: A.M. Turing. Microsoft (2017). http://academic.microsoft.com/#/detail/664303655
41. Morris, F.L., Jones, C.B.: An early program proof by Alan Turing. IEEE Ann. Hist. Comput. 6(2), 139–143 (1984). http://dx.doi.org/10.1109/MAHC.1984.10017
42. Newman, M.H.A.: Alan Mathison Turing, 1912–1954. Biogr. Mem. Fellows R. Soc. 1, 253–263 (1955). http://dx.doi.org/10.1098/rsbm.1955.0019
43. Robinson, A. (ed.): The Scientists: An Epic of Discovery. Thames and Hudson, London (2012)
44. Robinson, A.: All around Turing. New Sci. 3107, 42–43 (2017)
45. Smith, M.: Station X: The Codebreakers of Bletchley Park. Channel 4 Books, London (1998)
46. Smith, M., Erskine, R. (eds.): Action this Day: Bletchley Park from the Breaking of the Enigma Code to the Birth of the Modern Computer. Bantam Press, London (2001)
47. Time: The great minds of the century. Time 153(12), 29 March 1999. http://content.time.com/time/magazine/article/0,9171,990608,00.html
48. Turing, A.M.: On computable numbers with an application to the Entscheidungsproblem. Proc. Lond. Math. Soc. 2(42), 230–265 (1936/7). http://dx.doi.org/10.1112/plms/s2-42.1.230
49. Turing, A.M.: Systems of logic based on ordinals: a dissertation. Ph.D. thesis, Princeton University, USA (1938)
50. Turing, A.M.: Intelligent machinery: a report. Technical report, National Physical Laboratory, UK (1948). http://www.alanturing.net/intelligent_machinery. (also in [29])
51. Turing, A.M.: Checking a large routine. In: Campbell-Kelly, M. (ed.) The Early British Computer Conferences, pp. 70–72. MIT Press, Cambridge (1949/1989)
52. Turing, A.M.: Computing machinery and intelligence. Mind 5(236), 433–460 (1950). http://dx.doi.org/10.1093/mind/LIX.236.433
53. Turing, A.M.: The chemical basis of morphogenesis. Philos. Trans. R. Soc. Lond. 237(641), 37–72 (1952). http://dx.doi.org/10.1098/rstb.1952.0012
54. Turing, D.: Prof. Alan Turing Decoded. The History Press, Stroud (2015)
55. Turing, S.: Alan M. Turing. W. Heffer & Sons/Cambridge University Press (1959/2012)
56. Wikipedia: Category: Alan Turing. Wikipedia (2017). http://en.wikipedia.org/wiki/Category:Alan_Turing
57. Yates, D.M.: Turing's Legacy: A History of the National Physical Laboratory 1945–1995. Science Museum, London (1997)

UTP by Example: Designs

Jim Woodcock[✉] and Simon Foster

University of York, York, UK
jim.woodcock@york.ac.uk

Abstract. We present a tutorial introduction to the semantics of a basic nondeterministic imperative programming language in Unifying Theories of Programming (UTP). First, we give a simple relational semantics that accounts for a theory of partial correctness. Second, we give a semantics based on the theory of precondition-postcondition pairs, known in UTP as designs. This paper should be read in conjunction with the UTP book by Hoare & He. Our contribution lies in the large number of examples we introduce.

1 Introduction

A seminal paper by Hoare and his colleagues [49] describes programming language design as the task of a mathematical engineer, and the algebraic laws of programming as the interface with the language user. This paper is a tutorial introduction to the Hoare & He approach to programming language semantics, known as Unifying Theories of Programming (UTP). Our objective is to introduce the topic through a series of examples, showing how UTP is used to give the denotational semantics of a simple programming language, and how that semantics supports a rich set of algebraic laws for reasoning about programs and their specifications. We restrict ourselves here to a nondeterministic programming language, but we do supply an extensive set of references to the large number of different programming paradigms now addressed by UTP.

Our paper is structured as follows. We give an overview of UTP in Sect. 2. We illustrate the ideas by constructing a UTP theory to capture Boyle's Law, which describes the relationship between the temperature, volume, and pressure of an ideal gas. We describe the meta-language used in UTP in Sect. 3. It is a point-wise variant of Tarski's alphabetised relational calculus. We introduce our nondeterministic imperative programming language in Sect. 4. We describe the semantics of the assignment, conditional, nondeterministic choice, and sequential composition statements. Before we can give a meaning to iteration and recursion, we need to cover some basic theory that underpins these constructs. In Sect. 5, we give an introduction to lattice theory, before returning in Sect. 6 to discuss recursion. We conclude our discussion of partial correctness in Sect. 7, by describing how the axioms of Hoare logic and the weakest precondition calculus can be validated by proving them as theorems in our relational semantics.

The second half of the paper deals with the specification of total correctness of a program. Section 8 introduces the notion of a design: a precondition-postcondition pair embedded in the larger theory of relations. In Sect. 9,

J.P. Bowen et al. (Eds.): SETSS 2016, LNCS 10215, pp. 16–50, 2017.
DOI: 10.1007/978-3-319-56841-6_2

we describe the complete lattice of designs. We connect our two theories, relations and designs, by exhibiting in Sect. 10 a Galois connection that maps between them. Finally, we return to the theory of designs in Sect. 11, and show the two principal healthiness conditions that characterise the lattice.

In all these sections, we illustrate the ideas with a large number of examples.

2 Unifying Theories of Programming (UTP)

UTP is Hoare & He's long-term research agenda to provide a common basis for understanding the semantics of the modelling notations and programming languages used in describing the behaviour of computer-based systems [50]. The technique they employ is to describe different modelling and programming paradigms in a common semantic setting: the alphabetised relational calculus. They isolate individual features of these languages in order to be able to emphasise commonalities and differences. They record formal links between the resulting theories, so that predicates from one theory can be translated into another, often as approximations. These links can also be used to translate specifications into designs and programs as part of a program development method.

UTP has been used to describe a wide variety of programming theories. In [50], Hoare & He formalise theories of sequential programming, with assertional reasoning techniques for both partial and total correctness; a theory of correct compilation; concurrent computation with reactive processes and communications; higher-order logic programming; and theories that link denotational, algebraic, and operational semantics.

Other contributions to UTP theories of programming language semantics, including: angelic nondeterminism [24,25,63]; aspect-oriented programming [27]; component systems [81]; event-driven programming [52,82,85]; lazy evaluation semantics [39]; object-oriented programming [20,64,68]; pointer-based programming [41]; probabilistic programming [9,44,47,69,84]; real-time programming [42, 46]; reversible computation [69,70]; timed reactive programming [65–67,71,74]; and transaction programming [43,44]. Individual programming languages have been given semantics in UTP. This includes the hardware description languages Handel-C [60,61] and Verilog [83]; the multi-paradigm languages *Circus* [14,57,58, 71,79] and CML [75,78]; Safety-Critical Java [21–23,26,59]; and Simulink [19]. A wide variety of programming theories have been formalised in UTP, including confidentiality [6,7]; general correctness [29,32,33,40]; theories of testing [17,18,72]; hybrid systems; theories of flash memory [13,15]; and theories of undefinedness [5,76]. These are complemented by a collection of meta-theory, including work on higher-order UTP [80]; UTP and temporal-logic model checking [2]; and CSP as a retract of CCS [45].

Mechanisation is a key aspect of any formalisation, and UTP has been embedded in a variety of theorem provers, notably in ProofPower-Z and Isabelle [10,12,28,35,37,38,55,56,79]. This allows a theory engineer to mechanically construct UTP theories, experiment with them, prove properties, and eventually deploy them for use in program verification. In these notes we focus on our Isabelle embedding of the UTP called Isabelle/UTP [36].

UTP has its origins in the work on predicative programming, which was started by Hehner; see [48] for a summary. The UTP research agenda has as its ultimate goal to cover all the interesting paradigms of computing, including both declarative and procedural, hardware and software. It presents a theoretical foundation for understanding software and systems engineering, and has already been exploited in areas such as hardware [61,85], hardware/software co-design [8] and component-based systems [81]. But it also presents an opportunity when constructing new languages, especially ones with heterogeneous paradigms and techniques.

Having studied the variety of existing programming languages and identified the major components of programming languages and theories, we can select theories for new, perhaps special-purpose languages. The analogy here is of a theory supermarket, where you shop for exactly those features you need while being confident that the theories plug-and-play together nicely.

Hoare & He define three axes for their classification of language semantics: (a) The first is by computational model, such as programming in the following styles: imperative, functional, logical, object-based, real-time, concurrent, or probabilistic. (b) The second is by level of abstraction, with requirements orientation at the very highest level, through architectural and algorithmic levels, down to platform dependence and hardware specificities at the lowest level. (c) The third axis is in the method of the presentation of semantics, such as denotational, operational, algebraic, or axiomatic. Language semantics are usually structured as complete lattices of predicates linked by Galois connections.

Example 1 (UTP theory: Boyle's Law). Building a UTP theorem is not unlike describing a physical phenomenon in physics or chemistry, and so we take as our first example modelling the behaviour of gas with varying volume and pressure. This is a physical phenomenon subject to Boyle's Law, which states

> "For a fixed amount of an ideal gas kept at a fixed temperature k, p (pressure), and V (volume) are inversely proportional (while one doubles, the other halves)."

Suppose that we want to build a computer simulation of this physical phenomenon. We need to decide what we can observe in this electronic experiment. Fortunately, the statement of Boyle's Law tells us which observations we can make in an experiment: the temperature k, the pressure p, and the volume V. These three variables form the alphabet of predicates of interest: the state of the system. In fact, they are real-world observations, and this is the model-based agenda: k, p, and V are all variables shared with real world. There is another observation hidden in the statement of Boyle's Law: the fixed amount of the gas. In a perfect world, we could count n, the number of molecules of the gas, for that is what we mean by stating that we have a fixed amount of it. But this observation is finessed by the implicit assumption that the gas is perfectly confined. If ϕ is a condition in our theory, then its alphabet is given by $\alpha(\phi) = \{p, V, k\}$; if it is a relation, then its alphabet is given by $\alpha(\phi) = \{p, V, k, p', V', k'\}$.

Having fixed on an alphabet for our theory of ideal gases, our next task is to decide on its signature: the syntax for denoting objects of the theory. Here, this will comprise three operations on the state of the system: initialisation and the manipulation of the volume and pressure of the gas. There is no call for an operation to change the temperature.

The next task is to define some healthiness conditions for predicates in our theory. These can be thought of as enforcing state and dynamic invariants, and the statement of Boyle's Law suggests one of each type. The static invariant applies to conditions on states and requires that V and p are inversely proportional: $p * V = k$. The dynamic invariant applies to relations describing state transitions and requires that k must be constant: $k' = k$.

In UTP, the technique for dealing with invariants is to create a function that enforces the invariant. Define the function $\textbf{\textit{B}}$ on predicates as follows:

$$\textbf{\textit{B}}(\phi) \;=\; (\exists\, k \bullet \phi) \wedge (k = p * V)$$

In this definition, we preserve the values of the pressure and volume and create a possibly new temperature that is in the right relationship to p and V. So, regardless of whether or not ϕ was healthy before application of $\textbf{\textit{B}}$, it certainly is afterwards. For example, suppose that we have

$$\phi \;=\; (p = 10) \wedge (V = 5) \wedge (k = 100)$$

then we have the following derivation

$$
\begin{aligned}
\textbf{\textit{B}}(\phi) &= (\exists\, k \bullet \phi) \wedge (k = p * V) \\
&= (\exists\, k \bullet (p = 10) \wedge (V = 5) \wedge (k = 100)) \wedge (k = p * V) \\
&= (p = 10) \wedge (V = 5) \wedge (k = p * V) \\
&= (p = 10) \wedge (V = 5) \wedge (k = 50)
\end{aligned}
$$

An obvious and very desirable property is that $\textbf{\textit{B}}$ is idempotent: $\textbf{\textit{B}}(\textbf{\textit{B}}(\phi)) = \textbf{\textit{B}}(\phi)$. This means that taking the medicine twice leaves you as healthy as taking it once (no overdoses). This gives us a simple test for healthiness. A predicate ϕ is already healthy if applying $\textbf{\textit{B}}$ leaves it unchanged: $\phi = \textbf{\textit{B}}(\phi)$. So, in UTP, the healthy predicates of a theory are the fixed points of idempotent functions, such as $\textbf{\textit{B}}$.

Now suppose that we know that the pressure of the gas is somewhere between 10 and 20 Pa; this is recorded by the predicate ψ:

$$\psi \;=\; (p \in 10 \mathbin{..} 20) \wedge (V = 5)$$

The predicate ψ is rather weak in that it describes a variety of valid states (p and k are loosely constrained), as well as invalid states where the state invariant doesn't hold. In particular, ψ is satisfied by our other predicate ϕ:

$$\phi \Rightarrow \psi$$

Notice that this is still true if we make both predicates healthy with $\textbf{\textit{B}}$:

$$\textbf{\textit{B}}(\phi) \Rightarrow \textbf{\textit{B}}(\psi)$$

$$(p = 10) \wedge (V = 5) \wedge (k = 50) \Rightarrow (p \in 10 \mathbin{..} 20) \wedge (V = 5) \wedge (p * V = k)$$

In this way, **B** is monotonic with respect to the lattice ordering. □

3   Relational Calculus

As we saw in Example 1, UTP is based on an alphabetised version of the relational calculus. Relations are written pointwise, as predicates on free variables, each of which must be in the alphabet of the relation. For example, as we'll find out below, the assignment $P = (x := x + y)$ has semantics $x' = x + y \wedge y' = y$. It is a relation between two states. The value of the programming variables x and x in the after-state are denoted by x' and y', respectively; the values of x and y in the before-state are denoted by x and y, respectively. These four variables must all be in the alphabet of the relation P: $\alpha P = \{x, y, x', y'\}$. It is not possible to determine the exact alphabet of a relation simply from its free variables, even though they must be included. For this reason, alphabets should be specified separately. The alphabet is partitioned between before-variables ($in\alpha P$) and after-variables ($out\alpha P$). A relation with an empty output alphabet is called a condition.

The principal operators of the relational calculus are:

Operator	Syntax	Operator	Syntax
conjunction	$P \wedge Q$	disjunction	$P \vee Q$
negation	$\neg\, P$	implication	$P \Rightarrow Q$
universal quantification	$\forall x \bullet P$	existential quantification	$\exists x \bullet P$
relational composition	$P \mathbin{;} Q$		

When two relations P and Q are used to specify programs, there is a correctness relation between them, the former viewed as a specification and the latter as an implementation. Suppose that both relations are on a vector of program variable x, then they each relate the values of the variables in this vector in the states before and after their execution; we denote these values by x and x', respectively. If every pair (x, x') that satisfies Q also satisfies P, then Q is said to be a refinement of P. To formalise this, we introduce the universal closure of a predicate

$$[\, P \,] \;=\; \forall x, y, \mathbin{..} z \bullet P \qquad\qquad\qquad [\textit{for } \alpha P = \{x, y, \mathbin{..} z\}]$$

Refinement is then universal inverse implication:

$$P \sqsubseteq Q \;\textbf{iff}\; [\, Q \Rightarrow P \,]$$

An important law for reasoning about existential quantification is the one-point rule:

$$(\exists x : T \bullet P \wedge (x = e)) \;=\; e \in T \wedge P[e/x] \qquad [\text{providing } x \text{ is not free in } e]$$

4   Nondeterministic Imperative Programming Language

We now consider a simple nondeterministic programming language with the following syntax:

$$Prog ::= I\!I \mid x := e \mid P \lhd b \rhd Q \mid P \sqcap Q \mid \textbf{while } b \textbf{ do } P$$

The syntax is the signature of the theory of nondeterministic imperative programming. The alphabet of predicates in this theory consists of a vector of the programming variables in scope. If P is a condition, then its alphabet is $\{v\}$ and if it is a relation, then $\{v, v'\}$. We now give the semantics for each of the program constructs.

4.1   Skip

The program $I\!I$ (skip) does nothing (many programming languages have such a no-op instruction). Suppose that the program state consists of a vector of variables v, then this vector is unchanged by the execution of the program:

$$I\!I_{\{v\}} \mathrel{\widehat{=}} (v' = v) \qquad\qquad \alpha I\!I_{\{v\}} \mathrel{\widehat{=}} \{v, v'\}$$

Skip plays an important role in the algebra of programs, since as shown below, it is both a left and a right unit for sequential composition.

$$P \mathbin{;} I\!I_{\alpha P} = P = I\!I_{\alpha P} \mathbin{;} P$$

4.2   Conditional

The conditional program is written in an infix notation:

$$P \lhd b \rhd Q \mathrel{\widehat{=}} (b \wedge P) \vee (\neg\, b \wedge Q) \qquad\qquad \alpha(P \lhd b \rhd Q) \mathrel{\widehat{=}} \alpha P$$

The condition b constrains the common before-state; the two relations P and Q must have the same alphabet:

$$\alpha b \subseteq \alpha P = \alpha Q$$

The infix notation is chosen so as to make the algebraic properties of conditional more apparent. The following laws of the conditional are familiar algebraic properties.

$$P \lhd b \rhd P = P \qquad\qquad\qquad\qquad\qquad\qquad\qquad \text{idempotence}$$
$$P \lhd b \rhd Q = Q \lhd \neg\, b \rhd P \qquad\qquad\qquad\qquad\qquad \text{commutativity}$$
$$(P \lhd b \rhd Q) \lhd c \rhd R = P \lhd b \wedge c \rhd (Q \lhd c \rhd R) \qquad\quad \text{associativity}$$
$$P \lhd b \rhd (Q \lhd c \rhd R) = (P \lhd b \rhd Q) \lhd c \rhd (P \lhd b \rhd R) \quad \text{distributivity}$$
$$P \lhd true \rhd Q = P = Q \lhd false \rhd P \qquad\qquad\qquad\qquad\quad \text{unit}$$

The next two examples are laws that simplify the conditional when one of its operands is either **true** or **false**.

Example 2 (Conditional).

$$(P \lhd b \rhd \textbf{true}) = (b \Rightarrow P) \qquad\qquad [\textit{conditional-right-true}]$$

Proof.

$$
\begin{aligned}
&(P \lhd b \rhd \textbf{true}) \\
=\ &\{ \text{ conditional } \} \\
&(b \wedge P) \vee (\neg\, b \wedge \textbf{true}) \\
=\ &\{ \text{ and-unit } \} \\
&(b \wedge P) \vee \neg\, b \\
=\ &\{ \text{ absorption } \} \\
&P \vee \neg\, b \\
=\ &\{ \text{ implication } \} \\
&b \Rightarrow P
\end{aligned}
$$

Example 3 (Conditional).

$$(P \lhd b \rhd \textbf{false}) = (b \wedge P) \qquad\qquad [\textit{conditional-right-false}]$$

Proof.

$$
\begin{aligned}
&(P \lhd b \rhd \textbf{false}) \\
=\ &\{ \text{ conditional } \} \\
&(b \wedge P) \vee (\neg\, b \wedge \textbf{false}) \\
=\ &\{ \text{ and-zero } \} \\
&(b \wedge P) \vee \textbf{false} \\
=\ &\{ \text{ or-unit } \} \\
&b \wedge P
\end{aligned}
$$

The next law imports the condition into its left-hand operand.

Example 4 (Conditional).

$$(P \lhd b \rhd Q) = ((b \wedge P) \lhd b \rhd Q) \qquad\qquad [\textit{left-condition}]$$

Proof.

$$
\begin{aligned}
&(P \lhd b \rhd Q) \\
=\ &\{ \text{ conditional } \} \\
&(b \wedge P) \vee (\neg\, b \wedge Q) \\
=\ &\{ \text{ idempotence of conjunction } \} \\
&(b \wedge b \wedge P) \vee (\neg\, b \wedge Q) \\
=\ &\{ \text{ conditional } \} \\
&(b \wedge P) \lhd b \rhd Q
\end{aligned}
$$

Our next law is reminiscent of modus ponens: it allows us to simplify the conditional if we know the condition is true.

Example 5 (Conditional).

$$b \wedge (P \triangleleft b \triangleright Q) = (b \wedge P) \qquad\qquad [\textit{left-simplification-1}]$$

Proof.

$$
\begin{aligned}
& b \wedge (P \triangleleft b \triangleright Q) \\
={}& \{ \text{ conditional-conjunction } \} \\
& b \wedge P \triangleleft b \triangleright b \wedge Q \\
={}& \{ \text{ right-condition } \} \\
& b \wedge P \triangleleft b \triangleright \neg\, b \wedge b \wedge Q \\
={}& \{ \text{ contradiction } \} \\
& b \wedge P \triangleleft b \triangleright \textbf{false} \\
={}& \{ \text{ conditional-right-false } \} \\
& b \wedge P
\end{aligned}
$$

The next law demonstrates that the conditional is associative, taking the encapsulated conditions into account.

Example 6 (Conditional).

$$(P \triangleleft b \triangleright Q) \triangleleft c \triangleright R = P \triangleleft b \wedge c \triangleright (Q \triangleleft c \triangleright R) \qquad [\textit{associativity}]$$

Proof.

$$
\begin{aligned}
& P \triangleleft b \wedge c \triangleright (Q \triangleleft c \triangleright R) \\
={}& \{ \text{ conditional } \} \\
& (b \wedge c \wedge P) \vee ((\neg\, b \vee \neg\, c) \wedge (Q \triangleleft c \triangleright R)) \\
={}& \{ \text{ and-or-dist. } \} \\
& (b \wedge c \wedge P) \vee (\neg\, b \wedge (Q \triangleleft c \triangleright R)) \vee (\neg\, c \wedge (Q \triangleleft c \triangleright R)) \\
={}& \{ \text{ right-simpl. } \} \\
& (b \wedge c \wedge P) \vee (\neg\, b \wedge (Q \triangleleft c \triangleright R)) \vee (\neg\, c \wedge R) \\
={}& \{ \text{ conditional } \} \\
& (b \wedge c \wedge P) \vee (\neg\, b \wedge c \wedge Q) \vee (\neg\, b \wedge \neg\, c \wedge R) \vee (\neg\, c \wedge R) \\
={}& \{ \text{ absorption } \} \\
& (b \wedge c \wedge P) \vee (\neg\, b \wedge c \wedge Q) \vee (\neg\, c \wedge R) \\
={}& \{ \text{ and-or-dist } \} \\
& (c \wedge ((b \wedge P) \vee (\neg\, b \wedge Q))) \vee (\neg\, c \wedge R) \\
={}& \{ \text{ conditional } \} \\
& ((b \wedge P) \vee (\neg\, b \wedge Q)) \triangleleft c \triangleright R \\
={}& \{ \text{ conditional } \} \\
& (P \triangleleft b \triangleright Q) \triangleleft c \triangleright R
\end{aligned}
$$

Our final example in this section is taken from [50]. It expresses in a general way the relationship between the conditional and any truth functional operator. A logical operator is truth-functional if the truth-value of a compound predicate is a function of the truth-value of its component predicates. A key fact about truth-functional operators is that substitution distributes through them.

Example 7 (Conditional).

$$(P \odot Q) \lhd b \rhd (R \odot S) = (P \lhd b \rhd R) \odot (Q \lhd b \rhd S) \qquad \text{[exchange]}$$

where $\odot$ is any truth-functional operator.

Proof.

$\quad (P \lhd b \rhd R) \odot (Q \lhd b \rhd S)$
$= \{ \text{ propositional calculus: excluded middle } \}$
$\quad (b \vee \neg b) \wedge ((P \lhd b \rhd R) \odot (Q \lhd b \rhd S))$
$= \{ \text{ and-or-distribution } \}$
$\quad (b \wedge ((P \lhd b \rhd R) \odot (Q \lhd b \rhd S))) \vee (\neg b \wedge ((P \lhd b \rhd R) \odot (Q \lhd b \rhd S)))$
$= \{ \text{ Leibniz } \}$
$\quad (b \wedge ((P[\textbf{true}/b] \lhd \textbf{true} \rhd R[\textbf{true}/b]) \odot (Q[\textbf{true}/b] \lhd \textbf{true} \rhd S[\textbf{true}/b])))$
$\quad \vee (\neg b \wedge ((P[\textbf{false}/b] \lhd \textbf{false} \rhd R[\textbf{false}/b]) \odot (Q[\textbf{false}/b] \lhd \textbf{false} \rhd S[\textbf{false}/b])))$
$= \{ \text{ conditional-unit } \}$
$\quad (b \wedge (P[\textbf{true}/b] \odot Q[\textbf{true}/b])) \vee (\neg b \wedge (R[\textbf{false}/b] \odot S[\textbf{false}/b]))$
$= \{ \text{ Leibniz } \}$
$\quad (b \wedge (P \odot Q)) \vee (\neg b \wedge (R \odot S))$
$= \{ \text{ conditional } \}$
$\quad (P \odot Q) \lhd b \rhd (R \odot S)$

4.3   Sequential Composition

The composition of two programs $(P \,;\, Q)$ first executes P, and then executes Q on the result of P. If $out\alpha P = in\alpha Q' = \{v'\}$, then

$$P \,;\, Q \; \hat{=} \; \exists v_0 \bullet P[v_0/v'] \wedge Q[v_0/v]$$

$$in\alpha(P \,;\, Q) \; \hat{=} \; in\alpha P \qquad out\alpha(P \,;\, Q) \; \hat{=} \; out\alpha Q$$

Sequential composition is associative and distributes leftwards into the conditional.

$$P \,;\, (Q \,;\, R) = (P \,;\, Q) \,;\, R \qquad\qquad\qquad \text{associativity}$$
$$(P \lhd b \rhd Q) \,;\, R = (P \,;\, R) \lhd b \rhd (Q \,;\, R) \qquad\qquad \text{left distributivity}$$

The following trading law allows us to move a condition from the after-state of P to the before-state of Q.

Example 8 (Sequential composition).

$$(P \wedge b') \,;\, Q \; = \; P \,;\, (b \wedge Q) \qquad\qquad \text{[trading]}$$

Proof.

$$(P \wedge b') \; ; Q$$
$$= \{ \text{ sequence } \}$$
$$\exists v_0 \bullet P[v_0/v'] \wedge b'[v_0/v'] \wedge Q[v_0/v]$$
$$= \{ \text{ decoration } \}$$
$$\exists v_0 \bullet P[v_0/v'] \wedge b[v_0/v] \wedge Q[v_0/v]$$
$$= \{ \text{ sequence } \}$$
$$P \; ; (b \wedge Q)$$

A special case of the last example is a one-point rule for sequential composition.

Example 9 (Sequential composition). For constant k and x' not free in P:

$$(P \wedge x' = k) \; ; Q \;\; = \;\; P \; ; Q[k/x] \hspace{2cm} [\textit{left one-point}]$$

Proof.

$$(P \wedge x' = k) \; ; Q$$
$$= \{ \text{ sequence } \}$$
$$\exists v_0, x_0 \bullet P[v_0/v'] \wedge x_0 = k \wedge Q[v_0, x_0/v, x]$$
$$= \{ \text{ one-point rule } \}$$
$$\exists v_0 \bullet P[v_0/v'] \wedge Q[v_0, k/v, x]$$
$$= \{ \text{ sequence } \}$$
$$P \; ; Q[k/x]$$

A similar one-point rule exists for moving in the other direction:

$$P \; ; (x = k \wedge Q) \;\; = \;\; P[k/x'] \; ; Q$$

4.4   Assignment

The assignment $(x :=_A e)$ relates two states with alphabet A and A', respectively, which together include x, x', and the free variables of e. It changes x to take the value e, keeping all other variables constant. For $A = \{x, y, \ldots, z\}$ and $\alpha e \subseteq A$, we have

$$x :=_A e \;\; \widehat{=} \;\; (x' = e \wedge y' = y \wedge \cdots \wedge z' = z) \hspace{1.5cm} \alpha(x :=_A e) \;\; \widehat{=} \;\; A \cup A'$$

The subscript to the assignment operator is omitted when it can be inferred from context.

$$(x := e) = (x, y := e, y) \hspace{3cm} \text{contract frame}$$
$$(x, y, z := e, f, g) = (y, x, z := f, e, g) \hspace{2cm} \text{commutativity}$$
$$(x := e \; ; x := f(x)) = (x := f(e)) \hspace{1cm} \text{assignment-conditional distributivity}$$

A leading assignment can be pushed into a following conditional.

Example 10 (Sequential composition).

$$(x := e \,;\, (P \lhd b(x) \rhd Q)) \qquad\qquad \textit{[left-assignment-conditional]}$$
$$= ((x := e \,;\, P) \lhd b(e) \rhd (x := e \,;\, Q))$$

Proof.

$$x := e \,;\, (P \lhd b(x) \rhd Q)$$
$$= \{ \text{ assignment } \}$$
$$(x' = e \land v' = v) \,;\, (P \lhd b(x) \rhd Q)$$
$$= \{ \text{ left-one-point, twice } \}$$
$$(P[e/x] \lhd b(e) \rhd Q[e/x])$$
$$= \{ \text{ left-one-point, twice } \}$$
$$((x' = e \land v' = v) \,;\, P) \lhd b(e) \rhd ((x' = e \land v' = v) \,;\, Q)$$
$$= \{ \text{ assignment } \}$$
$$(x := e \,;\, P) \lhd b(e) \rhd (x := e \,;\, Q)$$

Notice how this proof is entirely algebraic.

4.5   Nondeterministic Choice

The nondeterministic choice $P \sqcap Q$ behaves either like P or like Q:

$$P \sqcap Q \;\hat=\; P \lor Q$$

$$P \sqcap P = P \qquad\qquad\qquad\qquad\qquad\qquad \text{idempotence}$$
$$P \sqcap Q = Q \sqcap P \qquad\qquad\qquad\qquad\qquad \text{commutativity}$$
$$P \sqcap (Q \sqcap R) = (P \sqcap Q) \sqcap R \qquad\qquad\qquad \text{associativity}$$
$$P \lhd b \rhd (Q \sqcap R) = (P \lhd b \rhd Q) \sqcap (P \lhd b \rhd R) \qquad \lhd \rhd\text{-}\sqcap \text{ distributivity}$$
$$P \sqcap (Q \lhd b \rhd R) = (P \sqcap Q) \lhd b \rhd (P \sqcap R) \qquad \sqcap\text{-}\lhd \rhd \text{ distributivity}$$
$$(P \sqcap Q) \,;\, R = (P \,;\, R) \sqcap (Q \,;\, R) \qquad\qquad \text{sequence disjunctivity}$$
$$P \,;\, (Q \sqcap R) = (P \,;\, Q) \sqcap (P \,;\, R)\text{‘} \qquad\qquad \text{sequence disjunctivity}$$

5   Lattices

Let $(L, \sqsubseteq)$ be a partially ordered set and let a and b be any pair of elements in L. The meet of a and b, the lattice operator denoted by $a \sqcap b$, is the greatest lower-bound of a and b:

$$a \sqcap b \;\hat=\; \max \{ c : L \mid c \sqsubseteq a \land c \sqsubseteq b \}$$

The join of a and b, denoted by $a \sqcup b$, is the least upper-bound of a and b:

$$a \sqcup b \;\hat=\; \min \{ c : L \mid a \sqsubseteq c \land b \sqsubseteq c \}$$

Both operators are idempotent, commutative, and associative, and satisfy a pair of absorption laws:

$a \sqcap a = a$	$\sqcap$-idempotent
$a \sqcap b = b \sqcap a$	$\sqcap$-commutative
$a \sqcap (b \sqcap c) = (a \sqcap b) \sqcap c$	$\sqcap$-associative
$a \sqcup a = a$	$\sqcup$-idempotent
$a \sqcup b = b \sqcup a$	$\sqcup$-commutative
$a \sqcup (b \sqcup c) = (a \sqcup b) \sqcup c$	$\sqcup$-associative
$a \sqcup (a \sqcap b) = a$	$\sqcup$-$\sqcap$-absorption
$a \sqcap (a \sqcup b) = a$	$\sqcap$-$\sqcup$-absorption

A lattice consists of a partially set $(L, \sqsubseteq)$, such that any two elements have both a meet and a join. L is a complete lattice if every subset A of L has both a meet and a join. The greatest lower-bound of the whole of L is the bottom element $\bot$; the least upper-bound of the whole of L is the top element $\top$.

Example 11 (Powerset lattice). The powerset of S ordered by inclusion is a lattice. The empty set is the least element and S is the greatest element. Intersection is the meet operation and union is the join. Figure 1 depicts the lattice $(\{0, 1, 2\}, \subseteq)$.

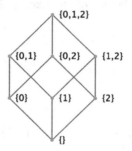

Fig. 1. The lattice $(\{0, 1, 2\}, \subseteq)$.

Example 12 (Divisibility lattice). The natural numbers ordered by divisibility form a partial order. Divisibility is defined as follows:

$$m \text{ divides } n \;\; \widehat{=} \;\; \exists k \bullet k * m = n$$

The natural number 1 is the bottom element: it exactly divides every other number. The natural number 0 is the top element: it can be divided exactly by every other number. Figure 2 depicts the lattice $(0 .. 8, \text{divides})$.

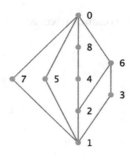

Fig. 2. The lattice $(0 \mathinner{.\,.} 8, \text{divides})$.

A function f is monotonic with respect to an ordering $\sqsubseteq$, providing that

$$\forall\, x, y : \operatorname{dom} f \bullet x \sqsubseteq y \Rightarrow f(x) \sqsubseteq f(y)$$

Now we come to the theorem that justifies our interest in complete lattices. Tarski's fixed-point theorem states the following:

> Let L be a complete lattice and let $f : L \to L$ be a monotonic function; then the set of fixed points of f in L is also a complete lattice.

Example 13 (Fixed points in Powerset lattice). Let $f : \mathbb{P}\{0, 1, 2\} \to \mathbb{P}\{0, 1, 2\}$ be defined as $f(s) = s \cup \{0\}$. Clearly, f is monotonic with respect to the subset ordering. Figure 3 depicts the lattice of the fixed points of f.

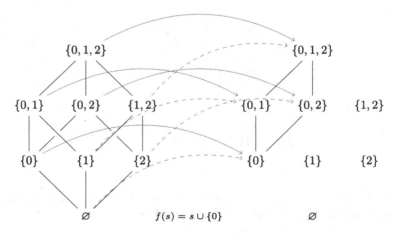

Fig. 3. Fixed points of $f(s) = s \cup \{0\}$.

Tarski's theorem is interesting for us, since we want to give semantics to iteration and recursion in terms of fixed points. The theorem guarantees the existence of

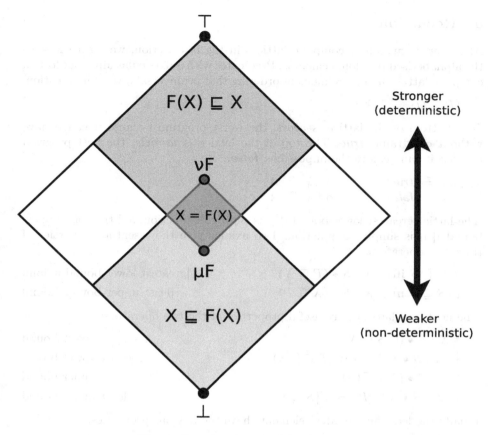

Fig. 4. Complete lattice of fixed points.

a fixed point, so long as the body of the iteration or recursion is monotonic. Furthermore, it helps us to choose which fixed point to use, by guaranteeing the arrangement of all fixed points in a lattice. The bottom element of the fixed-point lattice is conventionally denoted by μF and the top element by νF. The former is the weakest fixed-point of F and the latter the strongest fixed-point of F. Figure 4 shows the complete lattice of fixed points of a function F. The diagram also shows how the lattice of fixed points can be defined using the order relation on the lattice, since

$$(X = F(X)) = (X \sqsubseteq F(X)) \wedge (F(X) \sqsubseteq X)$$

A pre-fixed point of F is any X such that $F(X) \sqsubseteq X$; a post-fixed point of F is any X such that $X \sqsubseteq F(X)$. Now, another way to express Tarski's fixed-point theorem is

A monotonic function on a complete lattice has a weakest fixed-point that coincides with its weakest pre-fixed-point; its strongest fixed-point coincides with its strongest post-fixed-point.

6   Recursion

After our discussion of complete lattices in the last section, we return now to
the alphabetised relational calculus. Predicates with a particular alphabet form a
complete lattice under a refinement ordering that is universal inverse implication

$$(P \sqsubseteq Q) = [Q \Rightarrow P]$$

The bottom of the lattice is *abort*, the worst program because it can behave
without constraint: **true**. The top of the lattice is *miracle*, the best program
because it can achieve the impossible: **false**.

$$\bot_A \mathrel{\widehat{=}} \textbf{true} \qquad \alpha \bot_A \mathrel{\widehat{=}} A$$
$$\top_A \mathrel{\widehat{=}} \textbf{false} \qquad \alpha \top_A \mathrel{\widehat{=}} A$$

The lattice greatest lower-bound ($\sqcap$) is simply disjunction and the least upper-
bound ($\sqcup$) is simply conjunction. Two axioms give the essential properties of
these two operators.

$$P \sqsubseteq \bigsqcap S \text{ iff } \forall X : S \bullet (P \sqsubseteq X) \qquad \text{[greatest lower-bound axiom]}$$
$$\bigsqcap S \sqsubseteq P \text{ iff } \forall X : S \bullet (X \sqsubseteq P) \qquad \text{[least upper-bound axiom]}$$

The next four laws specify useful properties of the two operators:

$$\forall X : S \bullet (\bigsqcap S \sqsubseteq X) \qquad\qquad\qquad \text{lower bound}$$
$$(\forall X : S \bullet P \sqsubseteq X) \Rightarrow (P \sqsubseteq \bigsqcap S) \qquad\qquad \text{greatest lower-bound}$$
$$\forall X : S \bullet (X \sqsubseteq \bigsqcap S) \qquad\qquad\qquad \text{upper bound}$$
$$(\forall X : S \bullet X \sqsubseteq P) \Rightarrow (\bigsqcap S \sqsubseteq P) \qquad\qquad \text{least upper-bound}$$

Finally the least and greatest elements have the obvious properties:

$$\bot \sqsubseteq P \qquad\qquad\qquad\qquad\qquad\qquad\qquad \text{bottom element}$$
$$P \sqsubseteq \top \qquad\qquad\qquad\qquad\qquad\qquad\qquad\qquad \text{top element}$$

In this setting, recursion is given a semantics as the strongest fixed-point,
the least upper bound of all the post-fixed points of the recursive function.

$$\nu F \mathrel{\widehat{=}} \bigsqcup \{ X \mid X \sqsubseteq F(X) \}$$

The weakest fixed-point has the dual definition:

$$\mu F \mathrel{\widehat{=}} \bigsqcap \{ X \mid F(X) \sqsubseteq X \}$$

These two operators have the following characteristic properties:

$$(F(Y) \sqsubseteq Y) \Rightarrow (\mu F \sqsubseteq Y) \qquad\qquad\qquad \text{weakest fixed-point}$$
$$\mu F = F(\mu F) \qquad\qquad\qquad\qquad\qquad\qquad \text{fixed point}$$
$$(S \sqsubseteq F(S)) \Rightarrow (S \sqsubseteq \nu F) \qquad\qquad\qquad \text{strongest fixed-point}$$
$$\nu F = F(\nu F) \qquad\qquad\qquad\qquad\qquad\qquad \text{fixed point}$$

Example 14 (Hoare logic for while loop). Strongest fixed-point semantics leads to a simple rule for reasoning about iteration, which is defined in terms of recursion.

$$\frac{\{\,b \wedge c\,\}\ P\ \{\,c\,\}}{\{\,b \wedge c\,\}\ \textbf{\textit{while}}\ b\ \textbf{\textit{do}}\ P\ \{\,\neg\,b \wedge c\,\}}$$

The validity of this rule depends on the strongest fixed-point law:

$$(S \sqsubseteq F(S)) \Rightarrow (S \sqsubseteq \nu F)$$

This allows us to reason about a recursive implementation, at the risk of producing an infeasible program: the miracle is always a correct implementation. Of course, since it is the predicate **false**, it has no behaviour, and in particular, cannot be guaranteed to terminate. So the simplicity of the rule must be balanced by proving termination separately.

In contrast, the weakest fixed-point law doesn't allow us to reason about a recursive implementation, but instead about a recursive specification, since the fixed-point operator is on the left of the refinement, which is not useful here:

$$(F(Y) \sqsubseteq Y) \Rightarrow (\mu F \sqsubseteq Y)$$

If we can show that the recursive program terminates, then the weakest and strongest fixed-points actually coincide.

Our next law shows how to unfold a weakest fixed-point involving the composition of two functions. This is known as the rolling rule.

Example 15 (Fixed points).

$$\mu X \bullet F(G(X))\ =\ F(\mu X \bullet G(F(X)))$$

Proof. We prove this by mutual refinement.

1. ($\sqsubseteq$)

$$
\begin{aligned}
&\mu X \bullet F(G(X)) \sqsubseteq F(\mu X \bullet G(F(X))) \\
=\ &\{\ \text{weakest fixed-point}\ \} \\
&\textstyle\bigsqcap\{\,X \mid F(G(X)) \sqsubseteq X\,\} \sqsubseteq F(\mu X \bullet G(F(X))) \\
\Leftarrow\ &\{\ \text{lower bound}\ \} \\
&F(\mu X \bullet G(F(X))) \in \{\,X \mid F(G(X)) \sqsubseteq X\,\} \\
\Leftarrow\ &\{\ \text{comprehension}\ \} \\
&F(G(F(\mu X \bullet G(F(X))))) \sqsubseteq F(\mu X \bullet G(F(X))) \\
=\ &\{\ \text{fixed point}\ \} \\
&F(\mu X \bullet G(F(X))) \sqsubseteq F(\mu X \bullet G(F(X))) \\
=\ &\{\ \text{refinement reflexive}\ \} \\
&true
\end{aligned}
$$

2. ($\sqsupseteq$) Suppose by hypothesis that $F(G(X)) \sqsubseteq X$.

$$F(G(X)) \sqsubseteq X$$
$\Rightarrow \{ \ G \text{ monotonic } \}$
$$G(F(G(X))) \sqsubseteq G(X)$$
$= \{ \text{ comprehension } \}$
$$G(X) \in \{ X \mid G(F(X)) \sqsubseteq X \}$$
$\Rightarrow \{ \text{ lower bound } \}$
$$\textstyle\bigsqcap\{ X \mid G(F(X)) \sqsubseteq X \} \sqsubseteq G(X)$$
$= \{ \text{ weakest fixed-point } \}$
$$\mu X \bullet G(F(X)) \sqsubseteq G(X)$$
$\Rightarrow \{ \ F \text{ monotonic } \}$
$$F(\mu X \bullet G(F(X))) \sqsubseteq F(G(X))$$
$\Rightarrow \{ \text{ monotonicity of refinement, hypothesis } \}$
$$F(\mu X \bullet G(F(X))) \sqsubseteq X$$

Therefore,

$$\forall X \in \{ X \mid F(G(X)) \sqsubseteq X \} \bullet F(\mu X \bullet G(F(X))) \sqsubseteq X$$

and so by the definition of least upper-bound, we have

$$F(\mu X \bullet G(F(X))) \sqsubseteq \textstyle\bigsqcap\{ X \mid F(G(X)) \sqsubseteq X \}$$

and so by the definition of weakest fixed-point we have

$$F(\mu X \bullet G(F(X))) \sqsubseteq \mu X \bullet F(G(X))$$

Example 16. Haskell B. Curry's **Y** combinator is a higher-order function that computes a fixed point of other functions.

$$\boldsymbol{Y} \ \widehat{=} \ \lambda G \bullet (\lambda g \bullet G(g\,g))(\lambda g \bullet G(g\,g))$$

We prove that $\boldsymbol{Y} F$ really is a fixed point of F.

Proof.

$\boldsymbol{Y} F$
$= \{ \ \boldsymbol{Y} \text{ definition } \}$
$$(\lambda G \bullet (\lambda g \bullet G(g\,g))(\lambda g \bullet G(g\,g)))\, F$$
$= \{ \text{ reduction } \}$
$$(\lambda g \bullet F(g\,g))(\lambda g \bullet F(g\,g))$$
$= \{ \text{ above } \}$
$$(\lambda g \bullet F(g\,g))(\lambda g \bullet F(g\,g))$$
$= \{ \text{ reduction } \}$
$$F((\lambda g \bullet F(g\,g))(\lambda g \bullet F(g\,g)))$$
$= \{ \text{ above } \}$
$$F(\boldsymbol{Y} F)$$

Example 17. Define the body of a function that calculates factorials as follows:

$$F \; \widehat{=} \; \lambda f \bullet \lambda x \bullet (1 \lhd x = 0 \rhd x * f(x-1))$$

Calculate the value of $(\boldsymbol{Y}F)(n)$ in terms of $(\boldsymbol{Y}F)(n-1)$.

$(\boldsymbol{Y}F)(n)$
$= \{ \;$ $\boldsymbol{Y}$ is a fixed point of F $\; \}$
$(F(\boldsymbol{Y}F))(n)$
$= \{ \;$ F definition $\; \}$
$(\lambda x \bullet (1 \lhd x = 0 \rhd x * (\boldsymbol{Y}F)(x-1)))(n)$
$= \{ \;$ β reduction $\; \}$
$1 \lhd n = 0 \rhd n * (\boldsymbol{Y}F)(n-1)$

Example 18 (Lattices). Suppose that we know that a function F has a unique fixed-point, modulo C.

$$(C \wedge \mu F) = (C \wedge \nu F)$$

Suppose in addition that C is itself a fixed-point of F. Prove that F has an unconditional unique fixed-point. That is, the weakest and strongest fixed-points are equal, modulo C. But C is also a fixed point. The last two facts mean that the strongest fixed-point is actually C.

$C \wedge \mu F = C \wedge \nu F$
$= \{ \;$ predicate calculus $\; \}$
$[\, C \Rightarrow (\mu F = \nu F) \,]$
$\Rightarrow \{ \;$ C is a fixed point of F $\; \}$
$[\, C \Rightarrow (\mu F = \nu F) \wedge \mu F \sqsubseteq C \sqsubseteq \nu F \,]$
$= \{ \;$ Leibniz $\; \}$
$[\, C \Rightarrow (\mu F = \nu F) \wedge \nu F \sqsubseteq C \sqsubseteq \nu F \,]$
$\Rightarrow \{ \;$ propositional calculus $\; \}$
$[\, C \Rightarrow (\nu F \sqsubseteq C) \,]$
$\Rightarrow \{ \;$ refinement $\; \}$
$[\, C \Rightarrow [\, C \Rightarrow \nu F \,] \,]$
$\Rightarrow \{ \;$ propositional calculus $\; \}$
$[\, C \Rightarrow \nu F \,]$
$= \{ \;$ refinement $\; \}$
$\nu F \sqsubseteq C$
$= \{ \;$ νF is strongest fixed-point, so $C \sqsubseteq \nu F$, equality $\; \}$
$\nu F = C$

7 Assertional Reasoning

Hoare logic is a system for reasoning about computer programs, in this case, about programs written in the nondeterministic programming language we have introduced. In this kind of program logic, each syntactic construct in the language's signature is provided with an introduction rule that can be used to reason about this construct.

The key notion in Hoare logic is the Hoare triple $\{p\}\, Q\, \{r\}$:
If precondition p holds of the state before the execution of program Q,
then, if Q terminates, postcondition r will hold afterwards.

Notice that this is a statement of partial correctness. The Hoare triple is defined in UTP as follows:

$$\{p\}\, Q\, \{r\} \;\widehat{=}\; (p \Rightarrow r') \sqsubseteq Q$$

The definition constructs a relational specification from the precondition p and postcondition r as an implication: $p \Rightarrow r'$. (Note how the postcondition must be decorated as a predicate on the after-state to distinguish it from the precondition, which is a predicate on the before-state.) If the precondition doesn't hold, then this is simply **true**, which is the semantics of the *abort* program, which is the bottom of the refinement lattice and Q automatically refines it.

The rules of Hoare logic can now all be proved valid as theorems from the definition of the Hoare triple.

L1   if $\{p\}\, Q\, \{r\}$ and $\{p\}\, Q\, \{s\}$ then $\{p\}\, Q\, \{r \wedge s\}$
L2   if $\{p\}\, Q\, \{r\}$ and $\{q\}\, Q\, \{r\}$ then $\{p \vee q\}\, Q\, \{r\}$
L3   if $\{p\}\, Q\, \{r\}$ then $\{p \wedge q\}\, Q\, \{r \vee s\}$

L4 $\{\, r[e/x]\, \}\, x := e\, \{\, r\, \}$
L5   if $\{p \wedge b\}\, Q_1\, \{r\}$ and $\{p \wedge \neg\, b\}\, Q_2\, \{r\}$
     then $\{\, p\, \}\, Q_1 \vartriangleleft b \vartriangleright Q_2\, \{\, r\, \}$
L6   if $\{p\}\, Q_1\, \{s\}$ and $\{s\}\, Q_2\, \{r\}$ then $\{p\}\, Q_1 \,;\, Q_2\, \{r\}$

L7   if $\{p\}\, Q_1\, \{r\}$ and $\{p\}\, Q_2\, \{r\}$ then $\{p\}\, Q_1 \sqcap Q_2\, \{r\}$
L8   if $\{b \wedge c\}\, Q\, \{c\}$
     then $\{\, c\, \}\, \nu X \bullet (Q\, ;\, X) \vartriangleleft b \vartriangleright I\!I\, \{\, \neg\, b \wedge c\, \}$
L9 $\{false\}\, Q\, \{r\}$ and $\{p\}\, Q\, \{true\}$
     and $\{p\}\, \textbf{false}\, \{false\}$ and $\{p\}\, I\!I\, \{p\}$

We prove the axiom for reasoning about the conditional as a theorem in the underlying semantics of Hoare logic.

Example 19 (Hoare logic).

   if $\{p\}\, Q\, \{r\}$ **and** $\{q\}\, Q\, \{r\}$ **then** $\{(p \vee q)\}\, Q\, \{r\}$

Proof.

$$\{(p \lor q)\} \, Q \, \{r\}$$
$= \{$ Hoare triple $\}$
$\quad [\, Q \Rightarrow ((p \lor q) \Rightarrow r')\,]$
$= \{$ collecting antecedents $\}$
$\quad [\, Q \land (p \lor q) \Rightarrow r'\,]$
$= \{$ and-or-distribution $\}$
$\quad [\, (Q \land p) \lor (Q \land q) \Rightarrow r'\,]$
$= \{$ or-implies $\}$
$\quad [\, (Q \land p \Rightarrow r') \land (Q \land q \Rightarrow r')\,]$
$= \{$ for-all-associativity $\}$
$\quad [\, Q \land p \Rightarrow r'\,] \land [\, Q \land q \Rightarrow r'\,]$
$= \{$ collecting antecedents $\}$
$\quad [\, Q \Rightarrow (p \Rightarrow r')\,] \land [\, Q \Rightarrow (q \Rightarrow r')\,]$
$= \{$ Hoare triple $\}$
$\quad (\{p\} \, Q \, \{r\}) \land (\{q\} \, Q \, \{r\})$

Next, we prove the rule for reasoning about assignment.

Example 20 (Assignment rule).

$$\{r[e/x]\} \, x := e \, \{r\}$$

Proof.

$$\{r[e/x]\} \, x := e \, \{r(x)\}$$
$= \{$ Hoare triple $\}$
$\quad [\, x := e \Rightarrow (r[e/x] \Rightarrow r[x'/x])\,]$
$= \{$ assignment $\}$
$\quad [\, x' = e \land v' = v \Rightarrow (r[e/x] \Rightarrow r[x'/x])\,]$
$= \{$ universal one-point rule $\}$
$\quad [\, (r[e/x] \Rightarrow r[x'/x][e/x'])\,]$
$= \{$ substitution, implication $\}$
$\quad [\, \textbf{true}\,]$
$= \{$ universal quantification $\}$
$\quad true$

The Hoare triple $\{p\} \, Q \, \{r\}$ is a tertiary relation between a precondition p, postcondition r and program Q. If we fix any two of these, then we can find solutions for the third. The weakest precondition calculus is based on this idea: it fixes the program Q and a postcondition r and provides the weakest solution for p [30,31].

Example 21 (Weakest precondition derivation).

$$\{\, p \,\} \, Q \, \{\, r \,\}$$
$$= \{\text{ Hoare triple }\}$$
$$[\, Q \Rightarrow (\, p \Rightarrow r' \,) \,]$$
$$= \{\text{ implication }\}$$
$$[\, p \Rightarrow (\, Q \Rightarrow r' \,) \,]$$
$$= \{\text{ universal closure } (v' \text{ in the alphabet) }\}$$
$$[\, p \Rightarrow (\forall\, v' \bullet Q \Rightarrow r' \,) \,]$$
$$= \{\text{ De Morgan's law }\}$$
$$[\, p \Rightarrow \neg\, (\exists\, v' \bullet Q \wedge \neg\, r' \,) \,]$$
$$= \{\text{ change of bound variable (fresh } v_0) \,\}$$
$$[\, p \Rightarrow \neg\, (\exists\, v_0 \bullet Q[v_0/v'] \wedge \neg\, r_0 \,) \,]$$
$$= \{\text{ sequential composition }\}$$
$$[\, p \Rightarrow \neg\, (\, Q \,;\, \neg\, r \,) \,]$$

The final line of this derivation suggests the weakest solution for Q to guarantee r: p can be equal to any predicate that satisfies this expression, but it cannot be weaker than $\neg\, (\, Q \,;\, \neg\, r \,)$. That is, the behaviours other than those where Q violates the postcondition r. This leads us to the definition:

$$Q \ \textbf{wp} \ r \ \mathrel{\widehat{=}} \ \neg\, (\, Q \,;\, \neg\, r \,)$$

We now use this definition to prove some of the laws of the weakest precondition calculus as theorems of the relational theory.

Example 22 (Weakest precondition for sequential composition).

$$((P \,;\, Q) \ \textbf{wp} \ r) = (P \ \textbf{wp} \ (Q \ \textbf{wp} \ r))$$

Proof.

$$((P \,;\, Q) \ \textbf{wp} \ r)$$
$$= \{\ \textbf{wp} \ \}$$
$$\neg\, ((P \,;\, Q) \,;\, \neg\, r)$$
$$= \{\text{ sequence }\}$$
$$\neg\, (\exists\, v_0 \bullet (P \,;\, Q[v_0/v']) \wedge \neg\, r_0)$$
$$= \{\text{ sequence }\}$$
$$\neg\, (\exists\, v_0 \bullet (\exists\, v_1 \bullet P[v_1/v'] \wedge Q[v_1, v_0/v, v']) \wedge \neg\, r_0)$$
$$= \{\text{ expand scope }\}$$
$$\neg\, (\exists\, v_1, v_0 \bullet P[v_1/v'] \wedge Q[v_1, v_0/v, v'] \wedge \neg\, r_0)$$
$$= \{\text{ restrict scope }\}$$
$$\neg\, (\exists\, v_1 \bullet P[v_1/v'] \wedge (\exists\, v_0 \bullet Q[v_1, v_0/v, v'] \wedge \neg\, r_0))$$
$$= \{\text{ sequence }\}$$

$$\neg \, (\exists \, v_1 \bullet P[v_1/v'] \wedge (Q[v_1/v] \, ; \neg \, r))$$
$$= \{ \text{ double negation } \}$$
$$\neg \, (\exists \, v_1 \bullet P[v_1/v'] \wedge \neg \, \neg \, (Q[v_1/v] \, ; \neg \, r))$$
$$= \{ \ \textbf{wp} \ \}$$
$$\neg \, (\exists \, v_1 \bullet P[v_1/v'] \wedge \neg \, (Q[v_1/v] \ \textbf{wp} \ r))$$
$$= \{ \text{ sequence } \}$$
$$\neg \, (P \, ; \neg \, (Q \ \textbf{wp} \ r))$$
$$= \{ \ \textbf{wp} \ \}$$
$$(P \ \textbf{wp} \ (Q \ \textbf{wp} \ r))$$

Example 23 (Weakest precondition conjunctive).

$$(Q \ \textbf{wp} \ (\textstyle\bigwedge R)) = \textstyle\bigwedge \{ (Q \ \textbf{wp} \ r) \mid r \in R \}$$

Proof.

$$Q \ \textbf{wp} \ (\textstyle\bigwedge R)$$
$$= \{ \ \textbf{wp} \ \}$$
$$\neg \, (Q \, ; \neg \, (\textstyle\bigwedge R))$$
$$= \{ \text{ duality } \}$$
$$\neg \, (Q \, ; \textstyle\bigvee \{ \neg \, r \mid r \in R \})$$
$$= \{ \text{ sequence disjunction } \}$$
$$\neg \, (\textstyle\bigvee \{ Q \, ; \neg \, r \mid r \in R \})$$
$$= \{ \text{ duality } \}$$
$$\textstyle\bigwedge \{ \neg \, (Q \, ; \neg \, r) \mid r \in R \}$$
$$= \{ \ \textbf{wp} \ \}$$
$$\textstyle\bigwedge \{ Q \ \textbf{wp} \ r) \mid r \in R \}$$

8   Designs

We now turn to an important theory in UTP that describes the semantics of our nondeterministic imperative programming once more, but this time in a theory of total correctness. Termination is captured in the semantics by using assumption-commitment pairs. This gives a way of specifying behaviour that is similar to VDM [51], B [1], and the refinement calculus [3,53,54].

The theory of designs involves two boolean observations: ok, which signals that the program has started; and ok', which signals that the program has terminated. The use of these two observations allows us to encode the precondition and postcondition as a single relation:

$$(P \vdash Q) \ \widehat{=} \ (ok \wedge P \Rightarrow ok' \wedge Q)$$

for P and Q not containing ok or ok'. This definition can be read as

"If the program has started (ok) and the precondition P holds, then it must terminate (ok') in a state where the postcondition Q holds."

Example 24 (Search with sentinel). Suppose that we want to specify a program that searches an *array* for an element x, and that we assume that x is somewhere in the array (maybe in multiple occurrences). We can arrange for this assumption to hold by extending the array by one element and inserting x at the end (Dijkstra's "sentinel"). We model the array as a function from indexes to elements. Here is our specification:

$$x \in \text{ran } array \vdash array' = array \wedge i' \in \text{dom } array \wedge array(i') = x$$

The precondition states that we can assume $x \in \text{ran } array$. The postcondition states that the array isn't changed by this operation $array' = array$, that the index ends up pointing to an element of the array $i' \in \text{dom } array$, and that it ends up pointing to an occurrence of x in the array $array(i') = x$.

We now re-express the semantics of the nondeterministic programming language in terms of designs.

8.1   Skip

Skip still does nothing, as before, but we must add a precondition to insist that it always terminates:

$$\mathbb{II}_D \mathrel{\widehat{=}} (\textbf{true} \vdash \mathbb{II})$$

8.2   Conditional

In design semantics, the conditional is a choice between two designs. The result is, of course, a design:

$$(P_1 \vdash P_2) \lhd b \rhd (Q_1 \vdash Q_2) = (P_1 \lhd b \rhd Q_1) \vdash (P_2 \lhd b \rhd Q_2)$$

Actually, this is not a definition, but a theorem that relies on the previous definition of the conditional and on the definition of a design.

8.3   Sequential Composition

For the sequential composition operator, we have another theorem:

$$(p_1 \vdash P_2) \mathbin{;} (Q_1 \vdash Q_2) = (p_1 \wedge (P_2 \textbf{ wp } Q_1) \vdash P_2 \mathbin{;} Q_2)$$

The meaning of the sequential composition augments this precondition by the weakest precondition for the first postcondition to establish the second precondition. This guarantees that control can be passed successfully from the first design to the second. Finally, the overall postcondition is simply the relational composition of the individual postconditions.

8.4 Assignment

For the design assignment, we need to consider a precondition that guarantees that the assignment will not abort. In the case of $(x := 1/y)$, the precondition establishes the definedness of the expression $1/y$, which includes $y \neq 0$, as well as considerations of overflow and underflow. In this paper, we assume that the expression is well-defined, without these problems. As a result, we simply lift the semantics of the relational assignment:

$$x := e \; \widehat{=} \; (\textbf{\textit{true}} \vdash x := e)$$

8.5 Nondeterministic Choice

For nondeterministic choice, we have another theorem:

$$(P_1 \vdash P_2) \sqcap (Q_1 \vdash Q_2) \; = \; (P_1 \wedge Q_1 \vdash P_2 \vee Q_2)$$

The resulting design must satisfy the assumptions of both designs, but need establish the postcondition of only one of them.

9 The Complete Lattice of Designs

The greatest lower-bound of a set of designs has a similar form to the binary case for nondeterministic choice. Since we don't know which design will be selected, all the preconditions must hold in advance of the selection. The postcondition is nondeterministically selected.

$$\textstyle\bigsqcap_i (P_i \vdash Q_i) \; \widehat{=} \; (\bigwedge_i P_i) \vdash (\bigvee_i Q_i)$$

The least upper-bound of a set of designs has a weaker precondition than each individual design (see the discussion on refinement, below). But at the same time, since it is the least upper-bound, this precondition needs to be as strong as possible. Thus, the actual precondition is $(\bigvee_i P_i)$. The postcondition is the conjunction of all the individual postconditions, each modified to assume its individual precondition.

$$\textstyle\bigsqcup_i (P_i \vdash Q_i) \; \widehat{=} \; (\bigvee_i P_i) \vdash (\bigwedge_i P_i \Rightarrow Q_i)$$

To exemplify this, we show how to construct an operation to take the absolute value of an integer from the least upper bound of the positive and negative cases.

Example 25 (Least upper-bound of designs).

$$\begin{aligned}
&(x \geq 0 \vdash x' = x) \sqcap (x \leq 0 \vdash x' = -x) \\
&= (x \geq 0 \vee x \leq 0 \vdash (x \geq 0 \Rightarrow x' = x) \wedge (x \leq 0 \Rightarrow x' = -x)) \\
&= (\textbf{\textit{true}} \vdash x' = |x|)
\end{aligned}$$

With these definitions, designs form a complete lattice. The bottom of the lattice is abort

$$\bot_D \ \widehat{=} \ \textbf{\textit{false}} \vdash \textbf{\textit{true}}$$

The definition of a design allows us to simplify this to **true**. The top of the lattice is miracle:

$$\top_D \ \widehat{=} \ \textbf{\textit{true}} \vdash \textbf{\textit{false}}$$

Again, we can simplify this, and we obtain $\neg \ ok$. So, the program that can achieve the impossible is the program that cannot be started.

9.1   Recursion

Recursion means exactly the same in the theory of designs as it did in the simpler theory of relations

$$\mu F \ \widehat{=} \ \bigsqcap \{ \, X \mid F(X) \sqsubseteq X \, \}$$

Consider a function F expressed using the other program operators. Since the lattice of designs is closed under all these operators, we can always express F as a precondition-postcondition pair: a design. Since μF is expressed using the lattice operator $\bigsqcap$, it is also a design, and so, the theory of designs is closed under the least fixed-point operator. Hoare & give a theorem to show how to calculate the explicit precondition and postcondition of a recursively defined design [50, p. 81].

A refinement calculus, such as those in [3,53,54], must give ways of implementing such recursively defined designs. Hoare & He's weakest fixed-point lemma [50, p. 62] is the foundation of a general condition for proving the termination of a recursively defined program. We leave the details to the next tutorial.

10   Galois Connections

In UTP, the links between different theories are expressed as Galois connections. Backhouse [4] introduces a useful example, which we adopt here.

Example 26 (The floor function). The floor function is defined informally as follows:

For all real numbers x, the floor of x is the greatest integer that is at most x.

More formally, the floor function is an extreme solution for n in the following equivalence:

$$real(n) \leq x \ \textbf{iff} \ n \leq floor(x)$$

Where $real : \int \to$ is a function that casts an integer to its real number representation. It should be noted that we're overloading the inequality relation. On one side of the equivalence, it is inequality between two real numbers, whilst on the other side, it is inequality between integers.

Example 27 (Floor rounds downwards). Instantiating n to $floor(x)$, our equivalence gives us

$$real(floor(x)) \leq x \text{ iff } floor(x) \leq floor(x)$$

which simplifies to $real(floor(x)) \leq x$. So, we now know that the floor function rounds downwards.

Example 28 (Floor is inverse for real). Instantiating x to $real(n)$, we get

$$real(n) \leq real(n) \text{ iff } n \leq floor(real(n))$$

which simplifies to $n \leq floor(real(n))$. Now, using our previous result, with x instantiated to $real(n)$, we have the conjunction

$$n \leq floor(real(n)) \wedge real(floor(real(n))) \leq real(n)$$

Next, the function that maps an integer to its real representation is injective, so we have

$$n \leq floor(real(n)) \wedge floor(real(n)) \leq n$$

which is equivalent to

$$n = floor(real(n))$$

So, *floor* is an exact inverse for *real*.

Example 29 (Floor brackets real). Let's take the contrapositive of the equivalence defining the floor function:

$$real(n) \leq x \text{ iff } n \leq floor(x)$$
$= \{ \text{ contraposition } \}$
$$\neg (real(n) \leq x) \text{ iff } \neg (n \leq floor(x))$$
$= \{ \text{ arithmetic } \}$
$$x < real(n) \text{ iff } floor(x) < n$$
$= \{ \text{ arithmetic } \}$
$$x < real(n) \text{ iff } floor(x) + 1 \leq n$$

Now, instantiate n with $floor(x) + 1$:

$$x < real(floor(x) + 1) \text{ iff } floor(x) + 1 \leq floor(x) + 1$$

But we already know that $floor(x) \leq x$, so we have

$$floor(x) \leq x \leq floor(x) + 1$$

Example 30 (Floor monotonic). We want to prove that

$$x \leq y \;\Rightarrow\; floor(x) \leq floor(y)$$

First, we specialise the definition of the Galois connection between *real* and *floor*:

$$real(n) \leq x \text{ iff } n \leq floor(x)$$
$$\Rightarrow \{ \text{ specialisation with x,n := y,floor(x) } \}$$
$$real(floor(x)) \leq y = floor(x) \leq floor(y)$$

Now we can use this result to prove the monotonicity of *floor*:

$$floor(x) \leq floor(y)$$
$$= \{ \text{ above } \}$$
$$real(floor(x)) \leq y$$
$$\Leftarrow \{ \text{ transitivity of } \leq \}$$
$$real(floor(x)) \leq x \leq y$$
$$= \{ \text{ since } floor(x) \leq x \}$$
$$x \leq y$$

What we have achieved in the last example is to prove that *real* and *floor* form a Galois connection between the real numbers and the integers and to explore some of the consequences of this result. Specifically, the *floor* function provides the best approximation of a real number as an integer. We now describe the notion of Galois connections more generally.

Let **S** and **T** both be complete lattices. Let L be a function from **S** to **T**. Let R be a function from **T** to **S**. The pair (L, R) is a Galois connection if

$$\text{for all } X \in \mathbf{S} \text{ and } Y \in \mathbf{T}:$$
$$L(X) \sqsupseteq Y \quad \text{iff} \quad X \sqsupseteq R(Y)$$

R is a weak inverse of L (right adjoint); L is a strong inverse of R (left adjoint).

Example 31 (Galois connection: relational theory and designs). There is a Galois connection between the two semantics that we have provided for the nondeterministic imperative programming language.

The left adjoint, which we'll call $Des(R)$, maps a plain relation R to a design. The relation comes from the theory of partial correctness, where we assume that a relational program R terminates. We record this assumption by adding the precondition **true** when we map to the design **true** $\vdash R$.

The right adjoint, which we'll call *Rel*, maps a design back to a plain relation. In the theory of designs, we can observe the start and termination of execution, but these observations cannot be made in the theory of relations. So we must assume initiation and termination by setting ok and ok' both the **true**. Thus we have $Rel(D) = D[\textbf{true}, \textbf{true}/ok, ok']$.

We introduce the abbreviations: $D^b = D[b/ok']$, $D^t = D^{\textbf{true}}$, $D^f = D^{\textbf{false}}$.

Example 32 (Des is the inverse of Rel).

Proof.

$$Des \circ Rel(P \vdash Q)$$
$$= \{ \text{ definition of } Rel \ \}$$
$$Des((P \vdash Q)^t[\textbf{\textit{true}}/ok])$$
$$= \{ \text{ substitution } \}$$
$$Des(P \Rightarrow Q)$$
$$= \{ \text{ definition of } Des \ \}$$
$$= \textbf{\textit{true}} \vdash P \Rightarrow Q$$
$$= \{ \text{ definition of design, propositional calculus } \}$$
$$= P \vdash Q$$

Example 33 (Extraction of precondition and postcondition). Every design D can be expressed as $(\neg D^f \vdash D^t)$. Without loss of generality, we exploit the fact that we have characterised designs syntactically. So it is sufficient to prove that

$$P \vdash Q \ = \ \neg (P \vdash Q)^f \vdash (P \vdash Q)^t$$

Proof.

$$\neg (P \vdash Q)^f \vdash (P \vdash Q)^t$$
$$= \{ \text{ definition of design, substitution } \}$$
$$\neg (ok \wedge P \Rightarrow false \wedge Q) \vdash ok \wedge P \Rightarrow true \wedge Q$$
$$= \{ \text{ propositional calculus } \}$$
$$ok \wedge P \vdash ok \wedge P \Rightarrow Q$$
$$= \{ \text{ definition of design } \}$$
$$ok \wedge P \Rightarrow ok' \wedge (ok \wedge P \Rightarrow Q)$$
$$= \{ \text{ propositional calculus } \}$$
$$ok \wedge P \Rightarrow ok' \wedge Q$$
$$= \{ \text{ definition of design } \}$$
$$P \vdash Q$$

This example allows us to write the following equation for *Rel*:

$$Rel(D) = (\neg D^f \Rightarrow D^t)$$

Example 34 (Refinement for designs). Recall the definition of refinement for relations:

$$P \sqsubseteq Q \ = \ [Q \Rightarrow P]$$

We keep the same order relation on designs; after all, a design is a rather special kind of relation. In VDM and B, refinement is usually expressed through the two slogans:

Weaken the precondition, strengthen the postcondition.

More formally,

$$(P_1 \vdash P_2) \sqsubseteq (Q_1 \vdash Q_2) \;=\; [\, P_1 \Rightarrow Q_1 \,] \wedge [\, P_1 \wedge Q_2 \Rightarrow Q_1 \,]$$

We show that the VDM/B slogan is a consequence of the relational view of refinement. That is,

$$((P_1 \vdash P_2) \sqsubseteq (Q_1 \vdash Q_2)) \;=\; [\, P_1 \wedge Q_2 \Rightarrow P_2 \,] \wedge [\, P_1 \Rightarrow Q_1 \,]$$

Proof.

$$
\begin{aligned}
&(P_1 \vdash P_2) \sqsubseteq (Q_1 \vdash Q_2) \\
={}& \{ \text{ definition of refinement } \} \\
&[\, (Q_1 \vdash Q_2) \Rightarrow (P_1 \vdash P_2) \,] \\
={}& \{ \text{ universal closure } \} \\
&[\, (Q_1 \vdash Q_2)[true/ok] \Rightarrow (P_1 \vdash P_2)[true/ok] \,] \\
&\wedge [\, (Q_1 \vdash Q_2)[false/ok] \Rightarrow (P_1 \vdash P_2)[false/ok] \,] \\
={}& \{ \text{ definition of design } \} \\
&[\, (Q_1 \Rightarrow ok' \wedge Q_2) \Rightarrow (P_1 \Rightarrow ok' \wedge P_2) \,] \\
={}& \{ \text{ universal closure } \} \\
&[\, (Q_1 \Rightarrow ok' \wedge Q_2)[true/ok'] \Rightarrow (P_1 \Rightarrow ok' \wedge P_2)[true/ok'] \,] \\
&\wedge [\, (Q_1 \Rightarrow ok' \wedge Q_2)[false/ok'] \Rightarrow (P_1 \Rightarrow ok' \wedge P_2)[false/ok'] \,] \\
={}& \{ \text{ propositional calculus } \} \\
&[\, (Q_1 \Rightarrow Q_2) \Rightarrow (P_1 \Rightarrow P_2) \,] \wedge [\, \neg\, Q_1 \Rightarrow \neg\, P_1 \,] \\
={}& \{ \text{ propositional calculus } \} \\
&[\, P_1 \wedge (Q_1 \Rightarrow Q_2) \Rightarrow P_2 \,] \wedge [\, P_1 \Rightarrow Q_1 \,] \\
={}& \{ \text{ predicate calculus } \} \\
&[\, P_1 \wedge Q_2 \Rightarrow P_2 \,] \wedge [\, P_1 \Rightarrow Q_1 \,]
\end{aligned}
$$

Finally, we use this result to show that *Des* and *Rel* form a Galois connection.

Example 35 ((Des, Rel) is a Galois connection).

Proof.

$$
\begin{aligned}
&Des(R) \sqsupseteq D \\
={}& \{ \text{ definition of } Des \} \\
&(\textbf{true} \vdash R) \sqsupseteq D \\
={}& \{ \text{ refinement of designs } \} \\
&[\, \neg\, D^f \Rightarrow \textbf{true} \,] \wedge [\, \neg\, D^f \wedge R \neg D^t \,] \\
={}& \{ \text{ propositional calculus } \} \\
&[\, \neg\, D^f \wedge R \neg D^t \,] \\
={}& \{ \text{ propositional calculus } \} \\
&[\, R \Rightarrow (\neg\, D^f \neg D^t) \,] \\
={}& \{ \text{ refinement of relations } \} \\
&R \sqsupseteq (\neg\, D^f \neg D^t) \\
={}& \{ \text{ definition of } Rel \} \\
&R \sqsupseteq Rel(D)
\end{aligned}
$$

11   Design Healthiness Conditions

There are two principal healthiness conditions for design-hood: one for ok and one for ok'.

The first concerns starting programs: no observation can be made before the program starts.

$$\textbf{H1}(P) \;=\; ok \Rightarrow P$$

The second concerns terminating programs: anything is better than nontermination

$$\textbf{H2} : [\, P[\textbf{false}/ok'] \Rightarrow P[\textbf{true}/ok'] \,]$$

This healthiness condition states that you mustn't require nontermination as a property of a program.

*Example 36 (**H2** as a monotonic idempotent).* We've expressed **H2** as a property, but it can also be expressed as a monotonic idempotent function. The **H2** property that we've specified requires a predicate to be monotonic in ok'. We can introduce a pseudo-identity to capture this:

$$J \;=\; (ok \Rightarrow ok') \wedge \mathbb{I}(v)$$

and then redefine **H2** as a function:

$$\textbf{H2}(P) \;=\; P \; ; \; J$$

This leads to a useful lemma, for a **H2**-healthy predicate P:

$$P \;=\; P^f \vee (ok' \wedge P^t)$$

Proof.

$$
\begin{aligned}
&\quad P \\
&= \{\ P \text{ is } \textbf{H2}\ \} \\
&\quad P \; ; \; J \\
&= \{\ \text{propositional calculus}\ \} \\
&\quad P \; ; \; (\neg\, ok \vee ok') \wedge \mathbb{I}(v) \\
&= \{\ \text{relational calculus}\ \} \\
&\quad (P \; ; \neg\, ok \wedge \mathbb{I}(v)) \vee (P \; ; \; ok' \wedge \mathbb{I}(v)) \\
&= \{\ \text{relational calculus}\ \} \\
&\quad (P^f \; ; \mathbb{I}(v)) \vee ((P \; ; \mathbb{I}(v)) \wedge ok') \\
&= \{\ \text{relational unit (alphabets match)}\ \} \\
&\quad P^f \vee ((P \; ; \mathbb{I}(v)) \wedge ok') \\
&= \{\ \text{relational calculus}\ \} \\
&\quad P^f \vee ((\exists\, ok' \bullet P) \wedge ok') \\
&= \{\ \text{case enumeration } (ok' \text{ is boolean})\ \} \\
&\quad P^f \vee ((P^t \vee P^f) \wedge ok') \\
&= \{\ \text{propositional calculus}\ \} \\
&\quad P^f \vee (P^t \wedge ok') \vee (P^f \wedge ok') \\
&= \{\ \text{absorption}\ \} \\
&\quad P^f \vee (P^t \wedge ok')
\end{aligned}
$$

This is known as *J*-splitting, and it emphasises the asymmetry in the use of ok': you can observe when a program terminates, but not when it doesn't.

Example 37 (H1 relations). We give four examples of **H1** relations.

1. The bottom of the design lattice is **false** ⊢ **true**, which is equivalent to **true**, which, by the propositional calculus, is a fixed point of the **H1** healthiness condition: $(ok \Rightarrow \textbf{true}) = \textbf{true}$.
2. The top of the design lattice is **true** ⊢ **false**, which is equivalent to $\neg\ ok$, which, by the propositional calculus, is also a fixed point of the **H1** healthiness condition: $(ok \Rightarrow \neg\ ok) = \neg\ ok$.
3. A property of implication means that any predicate with ok as an implicative antecedent must be **H1**-healthy. For example: $(ok \wedge x \neq 0 \Rightarrow x' < x)$.
4. Finally, every design must be **H1**-healthy, since ok is an implicit assumption. For example: $(x \neq 0 \vdash x' < x)$.

Example 38 (H2 predicates). We give four examples of **H2** relations.

1. The bottom of the design lattice is **H2**-healthy:

$$\perp_D^f$$
$$= \textbf{true}^f$$
$$= \textbf{true}$$
$$= \textbf{true}^t$$
$$= \perp_D^t$$

2. The top of the design lattice is also **H2**-healthy:

$$\top_D^f$$
$$= (\neg\ ok)^f$$
$$= \neg\ ok$$
$$= (\neg\ ok)^t$$
$$= \top_D^t$$

3. Any predicate that insists on termination is **H2**-healthy. For example:

$$(ok' \wedge (x' = 0))^f$$
$$= \textbf{false}$$
$$\Rightarrow (x' = 0)$$
$$= (ok' \wedge x' = 0)^t$$

4. Finally, any design is **H2**-healthy. For example:

$$(x \neq 0 \vdash x' < x)^f$$
$$= (ok \wedge x \neq 0 \Rightarrow ok' \wedge x' < x)^f$$
$$= (ok \wedge x \neq 0 \Rightarrow \textbf{false})$$
$$\Rightarrow (ok \wedge x \neq 0 \Rightarrow x' < x)$$
$$= (ok \wedge x \neq 0 \Rightarrow ok' \wedge x' < x)^t$$
$$= (x \neq 0 \vdash x' < x)^t$$

12   In Conclusion

This concludes our tutorial introduction to the theories of relations and designs in UTP. Other tutorial introductions may be found in [16,77]. Of course, the interested reader is encouraged to go back to the source of the ideas and read the book.

References

1. Abrial, J.-R.: The B Book - Assigning Programs to Meanings. Cambridge University Press, Cambridge (1996)
2. Anderson, H., Ciobanu, G., Freitas, L.: UTP and temporal logic model checking. In: [11], pp. 22–41 (2008)
3. Back, R.-J., Wright, J.: Refinement Calculus: A Systematic Introduction. Graduate Texts in Computer Science. Springer, Heidelberg (1998)
4. Backhouse, R.: Galois connections and fixed point calculus. In: Backhouse, R., Crole, R., Gibbons, J. (eds.) Algebraic and Coalgebraic Methods in the Mathematics of Program Construction. LNCS, vol. 2297, pp. 89–150. Springer, Heidelberg (2002). doi:10.1007/3-540-47797-7_4
5. Bandur, V., Woodcock, J.: Unifying theories of logic and specification. In: Iyoda, J., Moura, L. (eds.) SBMF 2013. LNCS, vol. 8195, pp. 18–33. Springer, Heidelberg (2013). doi:10.1007/978-3-642-41071-0_3
6. Banks, M.J., Jacob, J.L.: On modelling user observations in the UTP. In: [62], pp. 101–119 (2010)
7. Banks, M.J., Jacob, J.L.: Unifying theories of confidentiality. In: [62], pp. 120–136 (2010)
8. Beg, A., Butterfield, A.: Linking a state-rich process algebra to a state-free algebra to verify software/hardware implementation. In: FIT, Proceedings of the 8th International Conference on Frontiers of Information Technology (2010)
9. Bresciani, R., Butterfield, A.: A probabilistic theory of designs based on distributions. In: [73], pp. 105–123 (2012)
10. Butterfield, A.: Saoithín: a theorem prover for UTP. In: [62], pp. 137–156 (2010)
11. Butterfield, A. (ed.): UTP 2008. LNCS, vol. 5713. Springer, Heidelberg (2010). doi:10.1007/978-3-642-14521-6
12. Butterfield, A.: The logic of $U \cdot (TP)^2$. In: [73], pp. 124–143 (2012)
13. Butterfield, A., Freitas, L., Woodcock, J.: Mechanising a formal model of flash memory. Sci. Comput. Program. **74**(4), 219–237 (2009)
14. Butterfield, A., Sherif, A., Woodcock, J.: Slotted-circus. In: Davies, J., Gibbons, J. (eds.) IFM 2007. LNCS, vol. 4591, pp. 75–97. Springer, Heidelberg (2007). doi:10.1007/978-3-540-73210-5_5
15. Butterfield, A., Woodcock, J., Formalising flash memory: first steps. In: 12th International Conference on Engineering of Complex Computer Systems (ICECCS 2007), 10–14 July 2007, Auckland, New Zealand, pp. 251–260. IEEE Computer Society (2007)
16. Cavalcanti, A., Woodcock, J.: A tutorial introduction to CSP in Unifying Theories of Programming. In: Cavalcanti, A., Sampaio, A., Woodcock, J. (eds.) PSSE 2004. LNCS, vol. 3167, pp. 220–268. Springer, Heidelberg (2006). doi:10.1007/11889229_6
17. Cavalcanti, A., Gaudel, M.-C.: A note on traces refinement and the *conf* relation in the unifying theories of programming. In: [11], pp. 42–61 (2008)

18. Cavalcanti, A., Gaudel, M.-C.: Specification coverage for testing in Circus. In: [62], pp. 1–45 (2010)
19. Cavalcanti, A., Mota, A., Woodcock, J.: Simulink timed models for program verification. In: Liu, Z., Woodcock, J., Zhu, H. (eds.) Theories of Programming and Formal Methods. LNCS, vol. 8051, pp. 82–99. Springer, Heidelberg (2013). doi:10. 1007/978-3-642-39698-4_6
20. Cavalcanti, A., Sampaio, A., Woodcock, J.: Unifying classes and processes. Softw. Syst. Model. 4(3), 277–296 (2005)
21. Cavalcanti, A., Wellings, A., Woodcock, J.: The safety-critical Java memory model: a formal account. In: Butler, M., Schulte, W. (eds.) FM 2011. LNCS, vol. 6664, pp. 246–261. Springer, Heidelberg (2011). doi:10.1007/978-3-642-21437-0_20
22. Cavalcanti, A., Wellings, A.J., Woodcock, J.: The safety-critical Java memory model formalised. Formal Asp. Comput. 25(1), 37–57 (2013)
23. Cavalcanti, A., Wellings, A.J., Woodcock, J., Wei, K., Zeyda, F.: Safety-critical Java in circus. In: Wellings, A.J., Ravn, A.P. (eds.) The 9th International Workshop on Java Technologies for Real-time and Embedded Systems, JTRES 2011, York, 26–28 September 2011, pp. 20–29. ACM (2011)
24. Cavalcanti, A., Woodcock, J.: Angelic nondeterminism and unifying theories of programming. Electr. Notes Theor. Comput. Sci. 137(2), 45–66 (2005)
25. Cavalcanti, A., Woodcock, J., Dunne, S.: Angelic nondeterminism in the unifying theories of programming. Formal Asp. Comput. 18(3), 288–307 (2006)
26. Cavalcanti, A., Zeyda, F., Wellings, A.J., Woodcock, J., Wei, K.: Safety-critical Java programs from circus models. Real-Time Syst. 49(5), 614–667 (2013)
27. Chen, X., Ye, N., Ding, W.: A formal approach to analyzing interference problems in aspect-oriented designs. In: [62], pp. 157–171 (2010)
28. Chen, Y.: Programmable verifiers in imperative programming. In: [62], pp. 172–187 (2010)
29. Deutsch, M., Henson, M.C.: A relational investigation of UTP designs and prescriptions. In: [34], pp. 101–122 (2006)
30. Dijkstra, E.W.: Guarded commands, nondeterminacy and formal derivation of programs. Commun. ACM 18(8), 453–457 (1975)
31. Dijkstra, E.W.: A Discipline of Programming. Prentice-Hall, Upper Saddle River (1976)
32. Dunne, S.: Conscriptions: a new relational model for sequential computations. In: [73], pp. 144–163 (2012)
33. Dunne, S.E., Hayes, I.J., Galloway, A.J.: Reasoning about loops in total and general correctness. In: [11], pp. 62–81 (2008)
34. Dunne, S., Stoddart, B. (eds.): UTP 2006. LNCS, vol. 4010. Springer, Heidelberg (2006)
35. Feliachi, A., Gaudel, M.-C., Wolff, B.: Unifying theories in Isabelle/HOL. In: [62], pp. 188–206 (2010)
36. Foster, S., Zeyda, F., Woodcock, J.: Isabelle/UTP: a mechanised theory engineering framework. In: Naumann, D. (ed.) UTP 2014. LNCS, vol. 8963, pp. 21–41. Springer, Heidelberg (2015). doi:10.1007/978-3-319-14806-9_2
37. Foster, S., Woodcock, J.: Unifying theories of programming in Isabelle. In: Liu, Z., Woodcock, J., Zhu, H. (eds.) Unifying Theories of Programming and Formal Engineering Methods. LNCS, vol. 8050, pp. 109–155. Springer, Heidelberg (2013). doi:10.1007/978-3-642-39721-9_3
38. Foster, S., Zeyda, F., Woodcock, J.: Unifying heterogeneous state-spaces with lenses. In: Sampaio, A., Wang, F. (eds.) ICTAC 2016. LNCS, vol. 9965, pp. 295–314. Springer, Heidelberg (2016). doi:10.1007/978-3-319-46750-4_17

39. Guttmann, W.: Lazy UTP. In: [11], pp. 82–101 (2008)
40. Guttmann, W.: Unifying recursion in partial, total and general correctness. In: [62], pp. 207–225 (2010)
41. Harwood, W., Cavalcanti, A., Woodcock, J.: A theory of pointers for the UTP. In: Fitzgerald, J.S., Haxthausen, A.E., Yenigun, H. (eds.) ICTAC 2008. LNCS, vol. 5160, pp. 141–155. Springer, Heidelberg (2008). doi:10.1007/978-3-540-85762-4_10
42. Hayes, I.J.: Termination of real-time programs: definitely, definitely not, or maybe. In: [34], pp. 141–154 (2006)
43. Jifeng, H.: Transaction calculus. In: [11], pp. 2–21 (2008)
44. Jifeng, H.: A probabilistic BPEL-like language. In: [62], pp. 74–100 (2010)
45. He, J., Hoare, T.: Csp is a retract of CCS. In: [34], pp. 38–62 (2006)
46. He, J., Qin, S., Sherif, A.: Constructing property-oriented models for verification. In: [34], pp. 85–100 (2006)
47. He, J., Sanders, J.W.: Unifying probability. In: [34], pp. 173–199 (2006)
48. Hehner, E.: Retrospective and prospective for unifying theories of programming. In: [34], pp. 1–17 (2006)
49. Hoare, C.A.R., Hayes, I.J., Jifeng, H., Morgan, C., Roscoe, A.W., Sanders, J.W., Sørensen, I.H., Spivey, J.M., Sufrin, B.: Laws of programming. Commun. ACM 30(8), 672–686 (1987)
50. Hoare, C.A.R., Jifeng, H.: Unifying Theories of Programming. Prentice Hall, Upper Saddle River (1998)
51. Jones, C.B.: Systematic Software Development Using VDM. Prentice-Hall International, Upper Saddle River (1986)
52. McEwan, A.A., Woodcock, J.: Unifying theories of interrupts. In: [11], pp. 122–141 (2008)
53. Morgan, C.: Programming from Specifications, 2nd edn. Prentice-Hall International, Upper Saddle River (1994)
54. Morris, J.M.: A theoretical basis for stepwise refinement and the programming calculus. Sci. Comput. Program. 9, 287–306 (1987)
55. Nuka, G., Woodcock, J.: Mechanising a unifying theory. In: [34], pp. 217–235 (2006)
56. Oliveira, M., Cavalcanti, A., Woodcock, J.: Unifying theories in ProofPower-Z. In: [34], pp. 123–140 (2006)
57. Oliveira, M., Cavalcanti, A., Woodcock, J.: A denotational semantics for circus. Electr. Notes Theor. Comput. Sci. 187, 107–123 (2007)
58. Oliveira, M., Cavalcanti, A., Woodcock, J.: A UTP semantics for circus. Formal Asp. Comput. 21(1–2), 3–32 (2009)
59. Oliveira, M., Cavalcanti, A., Woodcock, J.: Unifying theories in ProofPower-Z. Formal Asp. Comput. 25(1), 133–158 (2013)
60. Perna, J.I., Woodcock, J.: A denotational semantics for Handel-C hardware compilation. In: Butler, M., Hinchey, M.G., Larrondo-Petrie, M.M. (eds.) ICFEM 2007. LNCS, vol. 4789, pp. 266–285. Springer, Heidelberg (2007). doi:10.1007/978-3-540-76650-6_16
61. Perna, J.I., Woodcock, J.: UTP semantics for Handel-C. In: [11], pp. 142–160 (2008)
62. Qin, S. (ed.): UTP 2010. LNCS, vol. 6445. Springer, Heidelberg (2010)
63. Ribeiro, P., Cavalcanti, A.: Designs with angelic nondeterminism. In: Seventh International Symposium on Theoretical Aspects of Software Engineering, TASE 2013, 1–3 July 2013, Birmingham, pp. 71–78. IEEE (2013)
64. Santos, T., Cavalcanti, A., Sampaio, A.: Object-orientation in the UTP. In: [34], pp. 18–37 (2006)

65. Sherif, A., Cavalcanti, A., He, J., Sampaio, A.: A process algebraic framework for specification and validation of real-time systems. Formal Asp. Comput. **22**(2), 153–191 (2010)
66. Sherif, A., Jifeng, H.: Towards a time model for *Circus*. In: George, C., Miao, H. (eds.) ICFEM 2002. LNCS, vol. 2495, pp. 613–624. Springer, Heidelberg (2002). doi:10.1007/3-540-36103-0_62
67. Sherif, A., Jifeng, H., Cavalcanti, A., Sampaio, A.: A framework for specification and validation of real-time systems using circus actions. In: Liu, Z., Araki, K. (eds.) ICTAC 2004. LNCS, vol. 3407, pp. 478–493. Springer, Heidelberg (2005). doi:10.1007/978-3-540-31862-0_34
68. Smith, M.A., Gibbons, J.: Unifying theories of locations. In: [11], pp. 161–180 (2008)
69. Stoddart, B., Bell, P.: Probabilistic choice, reversibility, loops, and miracles. In: [62], pp. 253–270 (2010)
70. Stoddart, B., Zeyda, F., Lynas, R.: A design-based model of reversible computation. In: [34], pp. 63–83 (2006)
71. Wei, K., Woodcock, J., Cavalcanti, A.: Circus time with reactive designs. In: [73], pp. 68–87 (2012)
72. Weiglhofer, M., Aichernig, B.K.: Unifying input output conformance. In: [11], pp. 181–201 (2008)
73. Wolff, B., Gaudel, M.-C., Feliachi, A. (eds.): UTP 2012. LNCS, vol. 7681. Springer, Heidelberg (2013)
74. Woodcock, J.: The miracle of reactive programming. In: [11], pp. 202–217 (2008)
75. Woodcock, J.: Engineering UToPiA. In: Jones, C., Pihlajasaari, P., Sun, J. (eds.) FM 2014. LNCS, vol. 8442, pp. 22–41. Springer, Heidelberg (2014). doi:10.1007/978-3-319-06410-9_3
76. Woodcock, J., Bandur, V.: Unifying theories of undefinedness in UTP. In: [73], pp. 1–22 (2012)
77. Woodcock, J., Cavalcanti, A.: A tutorial introduction to designs in unifying theories of programming. In: Boiten, E.A., Derrick, J., Smith, G. (eds.) IFM 2004. LNCS, vol. 2999, pp. 40–66. Springer, Heidelberg (2004). doi:10.1007/978-3-540-24756-2_4
78. Woodcock, J., Cavalcanti, A., Fitzgerald, J.S., Larsen, P.G., Miyazawa, A., Perry, S.: Features of CML: a formal modelling language for systems of systems. In: 7th International Conference on System of Systems Engineering, SoSE 2012, Genova, 16–19 July 2012, pp. 445–450. IEEE (2012)
79. Zeyda, F., Cavalcanti, A.: Encoding Circus programs in ProofPowerZ. In: [11], pp. 218–237 (2008)
80. Zeyda, F., Cavalcanti, A.: Higher-order UTP for a theory of methods. In: [73], pp. 204–223 (2012)
81. Zhan, N., Kang, E.Y., Liu, Z.: Component publications and compositions. In: [11], pp. 238–257 (2008)
82. Zhu, H., He, J., Peng, X., Jin, N.: Denotational approach to an event-driven system-level language. In: [11], pp. 258–278 (2008)
83. Zhu, H., Liu, P., He, J., Qin, S.: Mechanical approach to linking operational semantics and algebraic semantics for Verilog using Maude. In: [73], pp. 164–185 (2012)
84. Zhu, H., Sanders, J.W., He, J., Qin, S.: Denotational semantics for a probabilistic timed shared-variable language. In: [73], pp. 224–247 (2012)
85. Zhu, H., Yang, F., He, J.: Generating denotational semantics from algebraic semantics for event-driven system-level language. In: [62], pp. 286–308 (2010)

Reasoned Modelling with Event-B

Michael Butler[(✉)]

University of Southampton, Southampton, UK
mjb@ecs.soton.ac.uk

Abstract. This paper provides an overview of how the Event-B language and verification method can be used to model and reason about system behaviour. Formal modelling and reasoning help to increase understanding and reduce defects in requirements specification. Sets and relations play a key role in modelling as do operators on these structures. Precise definitions and rules are provided in order to help the reader gain a strong understanding of the mathematical operators for sets and relations. While the emphasis is on mathematical reasoning, particularly through invariant proofs, the paper also covers less formal reasoning such as identification of problem entities supported by class diagrams and validation of formal models against informal requirements. The use of tools for animation, model checking and proof is also outlined.

1 Introduction

This paper provides an introduction to formal modelling using the Event-B language and method [1]. We make no strong assumptions about the existing knowledge of the reader other than in interest in learning about the approach and a willingness to start to put it into practice.

It is useful to motivate the role and value of the formal methods that we are outlining and advocating in this paper. Essentially it is about improving the processes that are used to engineer software-based systems so that specification and design errors are identified and rectified as soon as possible in the system development cycle. From the earliest days of software engineering it has been recognised that the cost of fixing a specification or design error is higher the later in the development that error is identified. This is summarised by the following observation about software development by Boehm [2]:

Boehm's First Law: *Errors are more frequent during requirements and design activities and are more expensive the later they are removed.*

This observation is bourne out by many studies of software engineering projects. For example, a 2013 report from the Carnegie-Mellon Software Engineering Institute (SEI) highlights studies showing that requirements and architecture defects make up approximately 70% of all system defects and that 80% of these defects are discovered late in the development life cycle [3].

© Springer International Publishing AG 2017
J.P. Bowen et al. (Eds.): SETSS 2016, LNCS 10215, pp. 51–109, 2017.
DOI: 10.1007/978-3-319-56841-6_3

Early Identification of Errors Through Formal Modelling

Clearly, identifying errors at the point at which they have become expensive to fix, long after they were introduced, is undesirable. More desirable would be to discover errors as soon as possible when they are less expensive to fix. So, why is it difficult to achieve this ideal profile in practice? Common errors introduced in the early stages of development are errors in understanding the system requirements and errors in writing the system specification. Without a rigorous approach to understanding requirements and constructing specifications, it can be very difficult to uncover such errors other than through testing of the software product after a lot of development has already been undertaken. Why is it difficult to identify errors that are introduced early in the development cycle? One reason is lack of precision in formulating specifications resulting in ambiguities and inconsistencies that are difficult to detect and may store up problems for later. Another reason is too much complexity, whether it is complexity of requirements, complexity of the operating environment of a system or complexity of the design of a system.

To overcome the problem of lack of precision, we advocate the use of *formal modelling*. As well as encouraging precise descriptions, formal modelling languages are supported by verification methods that support the discovery and elimination of inconsistencies in models. But precision on its own does not address the problem of complex requirements and operating environments. Complexity cannot be eliminated but we can try to master it. To master complexity, we advocate the use of *abstraction*. Abstraction is about simplifying our understanding of a system to arrive at a model that is focused on what we judge to be the key or critical features of a system. A good abstraction will focus on the purpose of a system and will ignore details of how that purpose is achieved. We do not ignore the complexity indefinitely: instead, through incremental modelling and analysis, we can layer our understanding and analysis of a system. This incremental treatment of complexity is the other side of the coin to abstraction, namely, *refinement*.

The Event-B modelling approach is intended for early stage analysis of computer systems. It provides a rich modelling language, based on set theory, that allows precise descriptions of intended system behaviour (models) to be written in an abstract way. It provides a mathematical notion of consistency together with techniques for identifying inconsistencies or verifying consistency within a model. It also provides a notion of refinement of models together with a notion of consistency between a model and its refinement. By abstracting and modelling system behaviour in Event-B, it is possible to identify and fix requirements ambiguities and inconsistencies at the specification phase, much earlier in the development cycle than system testing. In this way, rather than having an error-discovery profile in which most errors are discovered during system testing, we would arrive at an ideal profile in which more errors are discovered as soon as they are introduced. This paper will focus on precision and verification of consistencies in abstract specifications and does not cover refinement of models. Section 13 points to some further reading on refinement.

Requirements and Formal Models

We assume that the results of any requirements analysis phase is a requirements document written in natural language. There remains a potentially large gap between these informal requirements and a formal model. In this paper we will touch on this gap but not address it in any comprehensive way. In the context of a system development that involves both informal requirements and formal specification, it is useful to distinguish two notions of validation as follows:

- *Requirements validation* involves analysing the extent to which the (informal) requirements satisfy the needs of the stakeholders.
- *Model validation* involves analysing the extent to which the (formal) model accurately captures the (informal) requirements.

Both of these forms of validation require the use of human judgement, ideally by a range of stakeholders. In addition, we can perform mathematical judgements on a formal model. We refer to this use of mathematical judgements are *model verification*, that is, the extent to which a model satisfies a given set of mathematical judgements. Key to the effective use of model verification is strong tool support that automates the verification effort as much as possible. Arriving at good abstractions, formalising them, enriching models through refinement and making mathematical judgements all require skill and effort. This upfront effort is sometimes referred to as *front-loading*: putting more effort than is usual into the early development stages in order to save test and fix effort later.

Overview of Paper

Logic and set theory are the mathematical basis of Event-B. In this paper we explain how these mathematical concepts are used to write precise specifications in the form of Event-B models and how we reason about such models using mathematics. We use *sets* as a form of abstract data structure to model collections of entities that have a certain status and we define *events* that specify ways in which these sets may be manipulated to represent changes in the status of entities. For example, Sect. 2 shows how a set is used to model collections of users who have permission to be in a building and presents events for adding users to this set when they are registered and for removing users from this set when they are de-registered. Mathematical operators on sets allow us to easily specify manipulations of sets and Sect. 3 provides a brief overview of the set operators used throughout this paper while Sect. 5, covers issues that arise with finiteness of sets and determining the size of sets.

Sets are used to model collections of entities of the same kind. When we want to model connections between different kinds of entities, we use *relations* which are covered in Sects. 6 and 7.

The main unit of specification in Event-B is a *machine* and this is introduced in Sect. 4. A machine contains a list of variables and a list of events that modify the variables in precisely defined ways. A machine also contains a list of *invariants* that describe desired properties of the variables of a machine, e.g., *users inside the building must have permission to be there*.

Many set operators are defined using mathematical logic. For example, *intersection* of sets is defined in terms of *logical conjunction*: an element x is in the intersection of sets S and T if x is in S *and* x is in T. Section 3 gives a brief overview of the main logical operators used and the connection between logic and sets. At various stages in the paper additional mathematical operators are introduced to support the required modelling. Mathematical definitions are provided to help the reader's understanding of the operators and to support mathematical reasoning. Logic allows us to reason about machines, in particular, it allows us to prove that events of a machine preserve constraints specified by invariants and this is covered in several places in the paper.

We use several case studies to illustrate the use of the modelling and reasoning concepts of Event-B. Sections 2–4 use a simple example of a system for controlling access to a building. This case study is used to in illustrate the use of sets as abstract data structures and the use of invariants for specifying desired properties of structures. The case study is also used to provide the initial illustration of the use of mathematical reasoning to verify properties of a machine. In Sects. 8 and 9 we use a generalisation of the access control system that manages access to a collection of buildings rather than a single building. This case study is used to illustrate the use of relations (e.g., between users and buildings) and to consolidate the concepts from the earlier sections. A *function* is a special case of a relation and we use an example of a simple banking system to illustrate the use of functions in modelling in Sect. 10.

While reading and understanding a specification written in a language such as Event-B requires a relatively small amount of training, the ability to write a formal specification requires more skill and, as with programming, that skill is best developed through practice. Using the access control example, Sects. 8 and 9 provide guidelines on how an Event-B model can be constructed from a list of informal system requirements. The author has found that the use of class diagrams provides a useful initial bridge between informal requirements and formal models involving relations and functions. Class diagrams help to identify in a graphical way the various entities appropriate for a system model and the various connections between the different kinds of entities. For example, in an access control model, *users* and *buildings* are two relevant entities and the access rights are represented by an association between those entities.

A key advantage of Event-B is the availability of tool support for reasoning about formal models. Sections 11 and 12 provide an overview of tool support (animation, model checking, proof obligation generation and automated proof) that is available to support model validation and verification.

Section 13 briefly overviews some material that provides a deeper treatment of Event-B than this paper and also overviews other related formal modelling and analysis methods.

2   Modelling with Sets and Invariants

We illustrate modelling with sets through an example of access control to a building. The system should allow only registered users to enter the building and should keep track of which users are inside the building. We start by considering two sets, *in*, representing the users who are inside the building and *out*, representing the users who are outside the building. The two sets are illustrated by the Venn diagram in Fig. 1.

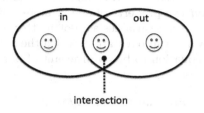

Fig. 1. Venn diagram for *in* and *out*

The diagram illustrates that we might have users in the overlapping area between the two sets (the intersection) and users in the non-overlapping areas. However, for this particular example, we would not expect any users to be both inside and outside the building so we would like to rule this possibility out as illustrated in Fig. 2. When the intersection of two sets is empty, we say the sets are *disjoint* and disjointness is illustrated in Fig. 3 by having no overlap between the sets. This disjointness property may be represented by the following mathematical equation:

$$in \cap out = \varnothing$$

The equation says that the intersection of the two sets ($in \cap out$) is empty ($\varnothing$).

The system we are modelling is dynamic in that users may enter or leave the building. In our model, this will be reflected by changes to the sets *in* and *out*.

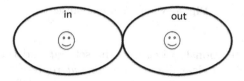

Fig. 2. Venn diagram: empty intersection

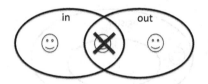

Fig. 3. Venn diagram: disjoint sets

Thus we treat *in* and *out* as *variables* whose values may be changed. We make the following declaration:

$$\textbf{variables} \quad in, out$$

While the values of the variables may change, the disjointness property should remain true. An *invariant* is a property of one or more variables that should be preserved by an changes to the variables so, not matter what changes occur in the system, it should never get into a state in which the invariant is falsified. We require the disjointness equation to be an invariant of our access control model so we declare:

$$\textbf{invariant} \quad in \cap out = \varnothing$$

We mentioned the concept of registered users at the beginning of this section so we introduce a set, called *register*, representing registered users. We will allow the set of registered user to change, e.g., by adding a new user to the register, so we declare *register* to be a variable:

$$\textbf{variable} \quad register$$

Only registered users should be allowed in the building and we model this property by requiring *in* to be contained entirely within *register* as illustrated in Fig. 4. As the diagram illustrates, a user who is in the building must also be registered. The diagram also illustrates that some users may be registered without being in the building. We say that *in* is a *subset* of *register*, written in mathematical notation as: $in \subseteq register$. We declare this subset property on *in* and *register* as an invariant:

$$\textbf{invariant} \quad in \subseteq register$$

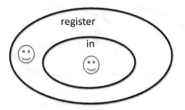

Fig. 4. Venn diagram: subset

What about the relationship between the set *out* and the set *register*? Up to now we have not been clear about whether *out* represents all possible users including those that are not registered. Let us make a modelling decision that *out* represents exactly those users who are registered and are outside the building.

Fig. 5. Venn diagram: set union

Thus registered users are either in or out. This is illustrated by Fig. 5 which shows that *register* is the *union* of *in* and *out*. Mathematically, the union is written as $in \cup out$ and we declare the union property as an invariant:

$$\textbf{invariant}\quad register = in \cup out$$

We can add behaviours to the model, such as a user entering the building or leaving the building, by specifying *events*. An event defines an atomic transition on states, that is, it defines a relationship between a state before the event is executed and the resulting state after the event is executed. An atomic transition representing a user entering the building is illustrated by Fig. 6. This shows Venn diagrams for the variables *in* and *out* both before and after execution of the *Enter* event. In the before state, user u is in the set *out* while in the after state u is in the set *in*, i.e., the *Enter* event moves user u from *out* to *in*. As shown in Fig. 6, the specification of the *Enter* event has three parts:

- *parameter u* representing the user who is entering the building
- a *guard* requiring that the user is in the set *out*
- an *action* that moves u from *out* to *in*,

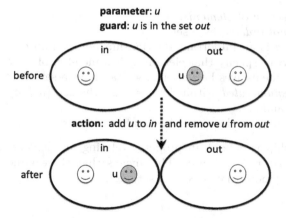

Fig. 6. Illustrating the *Enter* event

The *Enter* event is specified in Event-B notation as follows (including comments):

$Enter \ \hat{=}$
    any u **where**
        grd1: $u \in out$ // u must be registered and outside
    then
        act1: $in := in \cup \{u\}$ // add u to in
        act2: $out := out \setminus \{u\}$ // remove u from out
    end

Here the keyword **any** indicates that u is a parameter. The guard of the event appears between the **where** and **then** keywords while the actions appears between the **then** and **end** keywords. The guard labelled $grd1$ requires that u is in the set out, written $u \in out$. The actions of the event specify *assignments* that modify some of the variables of the model, e.g., the action labelled $act1$ assigns the value $in \cup \{u\}$ to the variable in. The action labelled $act2$ uses *set difference* to remove u from out: $s \setminus t$ is the difference between sets s and t, i.e., the set elements of s that are not in t.

Although the $Enter$ event contains several actions, the order in which the actions appear does not matter as all of the actions are executed together, not in series.

The syntax for specifying events will be described systematically in Sect. 4. Before presenting further details of the model of the building access control we give a quick overview, in the next section, of the key concepts of set theory that are important in the Event-B notation.

3   Overview of Set Theory

Here we list some key features of sets:

- A *set* is a collection of *elements*.
- Elements are *not ordered* by a set.
- Set *membership* is an important relationship between an element and a set. We write $x \in S$ to specify that element x is a member of set S.
- Elements may themselves be sets, i.e., we can have a set of sets.
- Sets may be *enumerated* within braces, e.g., the set $\{a, b, c\}$ contains three elements, a, b and c.
- The set containing no elements, the *empty* set, is written $\varnothing$.

Set membership is a boolean property relating an element and a set, i.e., either x is in S or x is not in S. This means that there is no concept of an element occurring more that once in a set, e.g.,

$$\{a, a, b, c\} \ = \ \{a, b, c\}.$$

Set membership says nothing about the relationship between the elements of a set other than that they are members of the same set. This means that the order in which we enumerate a set is not significant, e.g.,

$$\{a, b, c\} \ = \ \{b, a, c\}.$$

These two characteristics distinguish sets from data structures such as lists or arrays where elements appear in order and the same element my occur multiple times.

3.1   Typing and Powersets

All the elements of a set must have the same *type* where a type is a special kind of set known as a *carrier set*. Figure 7 illustrates that the variables *register*, *in* and *out* are all subsets of the carrier set *USER*. In Event-B we use an invariant to define the carrier set of a variable, e.g.,

$$\textbf{invariant} \quad register \subseteq USER$$

This declaration means that all the elements of the set *register* have the type *USER*. If we also have the invariant $register = in \cup out$, the elements of *in* and *out* must have the same type as the elements of *register*. That is, the type of *in* and *out* can be inferred from the type of *register* because of the invariant $register = in \cup out$. All the elements of a set must have the same type.

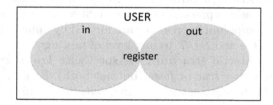

Fig. 7. Carrier set *USER*

A carrier set is maximal in that it is not a subset of any other set. A model may contain several carrier sets and these are implicitly disjoint from each other. For example, we could have a model that contains two carrier sets *USER* and *BUILDING*. We cannot combine carrier sets using set union, intersection or difference, e.g., $USER \cup BUILDING$ is invalid. In Sect. 6 we will see that we can combine carrier sets in another way to form relations. A carrier set remains fixed during the execution of a model, i.e., actions of an event cannot assign to a carrier set.

Suppose C is a carrier set. To define the type of an element x to be C, we simply declare $x \in C$. If S is not a carrier set and $S \subseteq C$, then the declaration $x \in S$ means that the type of x is C.

The Event-B notation has an in-built carrier set representing integers, written $\mathbb{Z}$. Elements of this set can be written using the usual literals, e.g., 1, 2, 3. The Event-B notation supports the usual arithmetic operators for integers such as addition and multiplication.

A *powerset* of a set is the set of all subsets of that set. For set S, we write $\mathbb{P}(S)$ for the powerset of S. For example,

$$\mathbb{P}(\{a, b, c\}) = \{\varnothing, \{a\}, \{b\}, \{c\}, \{a,b\}, \{a,c\}, \{b,c\}, \{a,b,c\}\}$$

Note that both the empty set and the set itself are contained within a set's powerset.

Up to now we have referred to the type of the elements of a set, e.g., all the elements of *register* have type *USER*. What about the type of the set itself (as opposed to the elements of the set)? We use the powerset operator to define the type of the set itself:

> If the elements of a set S are of type C then the type of S is $\mathbb{P}(C)$.

For example, we have:

- the type of the set *register* is $\mathbb{P}(USER)$
- the type of the set $\{1, 2, 3\}$ is $\mathbb{P}(\mathbb{Z})$

3.2   Expressions and Predicates

Expressions are syntactic structures for specifying values (elements or sets). Literals (e.g., 3, $\varnothing$) are basic expressions as are variables (e.g., *register*) and carrier sets (e.g., *USER*). Compound expressions are formed by applying expressions to operators such as $x + y$ and $S \cup T$ to any level of nesting.

Predicates are syntactic structures for specifying *logical* statements, i.e., statements that are either *true* or *false* (but not both). Equality of expressions is an example predicate, e.g., *register* $=$ *in* $\cup$ *out*. Set membership and subset relations are other examples. For integer elements we can write ordering predicates such as $x \leq y$. Assume that a, S, T, x and y are expressions (S and T are set expressions while x and y are integer expressions). We have available the following basic predicates:

Basic Predicates: $a \in S$, $S \subseteq T$, $S = T$, $x = y$, $x < y$, $x \leq y$

Predicate Operators: Compound predicates are formed using the standard logical operators listed in the following table (assume P and Q are predicates):

Name	Predicate	Definition
Negation	$\neg P$	P does *not* hold
Conjunction	$P \wedge Q$	Both P *and* Q hold
Disjunction	$P \vee Q$	Either P holds *or* Q holds
Implication	$P \Rightarrow Q$	If P holds, then Q holds

Quantified Predicates: We have seen that a predicate P may refer to one or more variables, e.g., $x \leq y$. We can quantify over a variable of a predicate universally or existentially:

Name	Predicate	Definition
Universal quantification	$\forall x \cdot P$	P holds for *all* x
Existential quantification	$\exists x \cdot P$	P holds for *some* x

In the predicate $\forall x \cdot P$ the quantification is over all possible values in the type of the variable x. Typically we constrain the range of values using implication, e.g., we could specify that every element of the set *in* is also an element of the set *register*:

$$\forall u \cdot u \in in \implies u \in register$$

In the case of existential quantification we typically constraint the range of values using conjunction, e.g., we could specify that integer z has a positive square root as follows:

$$\exists y \cdot 0 \leq y \wedge y \times y = z$$

Free and Bound Variables: A variable that is universally or existentially quantified in a predicate is said to be a *bound* variable. A variable referenced in a predicate that is not bound variable is called a *free* variable. For example, in the above predicate, y is bound while z is free.

Predicates on sets can be defined in terms of the logical operators as follows:

Name	Predicate	Definition
Subset	$S \subseteq T$	$\forall x \cdot x \in S \implies x \in T$
Set equality	$S = T$	$S \subseteq T \wedge T \subseteq S$

3.3   Set Operators

We already used expression operators on sets such as union and intersection. We now defines these operators more precisely using predicates. A predicate provides a way of defining a set: the set of elements that satisfy the predicate. Consider the union $S \cup T$. The elements of the union are those elements that are either in S or in T. More precisely, the set $S \cup T$ is defined by the set of elements x satisfying the predicate $x \in S \vee x \in T$. The following table provides definitions of the set operators using logical operators:

Name	Predicate	Definition
Union	$x \in S \cup T$	$x \in S \quad \vee \quad x \in T$
Intersection	$x \in S \cap T$	$x \in S \quad \wedge \quad x \in T$
Difference	$x \in S \setminus T$	$x \in S \quad \wedge \quad x \notin T$
Powerset	$x \in \mathbb{P}(S)$	$x \subseteq S$
Empty set	$x \in \varnothing$	*False*

Note that $x \notin T$ is a shorthand for $\neg(x \in T)$. Similarly we can use the shorthand $S \neq T$ for $\neg(S = T)$.

4 Structuring Models with Machines

We have already introduced several Event-B constructs such as carrier sets, variables, invariants and events. So is there a way of packaging these into components? A *machine* is an Event-B component in which the variables, invariants, and events are placed. Carrier sets that are required by a machine are placed in a separate component called a *context*. An Event-B context can also contain constants and axioms. The axioms are predicates that define properties of the carrier sets and the constants. For example, for our building access control example, we might want to model a capacity constraint on the building. We could do this by introducing a constant *max_capacity* and an axiom stating that *max_capacity* is greater than zero.

4.1 Context

A context with name $C1$ has the following form:

---

context $C1$

sets   ⟨*list of carrier sets*⟩

constants   ⟨*list of constants*⟩

axioms   ⟨*list of labelled axioms*⟩

end

The following example is a context for the building access model which introduces a carrier set and a constant:

context   *BuildingContext*
sets   *USER*
constants   *max_capacity*
axioms
    axm1: $max\_capacity \in \mathbb{Z}$
    axm2: $max\_capacity > 0$
end

Each axiom in the context is a predicate. For traceability purposes, each axiom in a context is given a unique label (e.g., axm1). The axioms in this context specify that *max_capacity* is an integer (axm1) whose value is assumed to be greater than zero (axm2).

4.2 Machine

In Event-B, a machine defines the dynamic behaviour of a model through events that are guarded by and act on the variables. The events are expected to maintain the invariants; we will see later how this is verified. A machine may *see* one or more contexts which provide the carrier sets, constants and axioms to be used by the machine. A machine with name M has the following form:

> **machine** $M1$
>
> **sees** ⟨*list of context names*⟩
>
> **variables** ⟨*list of variables*⟩
>
> **invariants** ⟨*list of labelled invariants*⟩
>
> **events** ⟨*list of events*⟩
>
> **end**

For example, part of the machine for the building access is specified as follows:

machine *Building*
sees *BuildingContext*
variables *register, in, out*
invariants
    inv1: $register \subseteq USER$
    inv2: $register = in \cup out$
    inv3: $in \cap out = \varnothing$
events ...

This machine is named *Building*; it sees the previously defined *BuildingContext* and it contains three variables. *register, in* and *out*. As discussed previously, the invariants specify that registered users are of type *USER* (inv1), registered users are either inside or outside (inv2) and no user is both inside and outside (inv3).

We postpone treatment of any building capacity constraint to later.

In Sect. 2 we showed the *Enter* event which models a user entering the building. Here we present the general syntax of event definitions. Each event of a machine has a name, a list of parameters, a list of guards and a list of actions structured as follows:

    ⟨*name*⟩ $\hat{=}$
        any ⟨*list of parameters*⟩ **where**
        ⟨*list of labelled guards*⟩
        then
        ⟨*list of labelled actions*⟩
        end

Guards are predicates that specify conditions on the machine variables and the event parameters. Each action assigns a value to a machine variable and has the form:

$$\langle variable \rangle \; := \; \langle expression \rangle$$

For example, here is the *Enter* event again:

Enter $\;\hat{=}$
 any u **where**
  grd1: $u \in out$
 then
  act1: $in := in \cup \{u\}$
  act2: $out := out \setminus \{u\}$
 end

An event may be executed for particular values of the parameters when all its guards are satisfied. When an event is executed, all of the actions of that event are performed simultaneously. Because of the simultaneity, it is not allowed for two different actions in an event to assign to the same variable as this would lead to conflicting updates. As with invariants, the guards and actions are labelled.

4.3   Preserving Invariants

When specifying an event, it is important to ensure that the invariants are preserved by its actions. We can assume that the invariants are satisfied prior to execution of the event and we need to demonstrate that the actions do not result in any invariant being violated.

Let us consider whether the *Enter* event preserves the invariants of the access control model. Invariant $inv1$ refers to the *register* variable only and, since none of the actions modify *register*, this invariant is trivially preserved. Invariant $inv2$ is an equation specifying that *register* is the union of *in* and *out*:

$$register \; = \; in \cup out \qquad (1)$$

The actions of the *Enter* event modify the variables in right-hand side of the equation but not the left-hand side. However since u is moved from *out* to *in*, the overall value on the right-hand side remains unchanged and the equation remains valid. More precisely, the effect of the actions of the *Enter* event on the invariant can be represented by replacing each variable in the invariant by the expression on the right-hand side of the assignment to that variable, i.e., replace *in* by $in \cup \{u\}$ and *out* by $out \setminus \{u\}$, giving:

$$register \; = \; \underline{(in \cup \{u\})} \; \cup \; \underline{(out \setminus \{u\})} \qquad (2)$$

The result of replacing *in* and *out* are underlined in Eq. (2). We say that invariant $inv2$ is preserved when Eq. (2) follows from Eq. (1) and the guard of *Enter*, that is, when proving Eq. (2), we can assume that Eq. (1) holds and that the guards of the *Enter* event hold. The proof is as follows:

$$(in \cup \{u\}) \cup (out \setminus \{u\})$$

$$= \quad \text{``} \cup \text{ is associative and commutative''}$$

$$in \cup (out \setminus \{u\}) \cup \{u\}$$

$$= \quad \text{``} grd1 : \text{ u} \in out\text{''}$$

$$in \cup out$$

$$= \quad \text{``} inv2\text{''}$$

$$register$$

Each step in the simple proof is justified either by appealing to a rule of set theory (the first step), by appealing to an event guard (the second step) or to the invariant $inv2$ (the third step) with the justification indicated by "inverted commas". Both union and intersection are associative and commutative as captured in this table:

Description	Rule
Union associative	$(s \cup t) \cup u = s \cup (t \cup u)$
Union commutative	$s \cup t = t \cup s$
Intersection associative	$(s \cap t) \cap u = s \cap (t \cap u)$
Intersection commutative	$s \cap t = t \cap s$

The second step in the above proof of Eq. (2) relies on the following simplification rule for sets which states that if x is in set s, then subtracting x from s and adding x to the result yields s:

Description	Rule
Simplify	$x \in s \implies (s \setminus \{x\}) \cup \{x\} = s$

An advantage of the actions of an event being executed simultaneously is that we do not need to consider intermediate states in which invariants might be violated. For example, if $act1$ and $act2$ were executed sequentially, $inv2$ would be violated in between $act1$ and $act2$ before being re-established by $act2$. To re-iterate: the actions within an event are always executed simultaneously and not sequentially.

We have shown that the *Enter* event maintains $inv1$ and $inv2$. We now consider the remaining invariant, $inv3$. Invariant $inv3$ specifies that in and out are disjoint. If we removed action $act2$ from the *Enter* event, this would lead to a violation of $inv2$ as u would end up both in and out. However, since both actions together move u from out to in, their disjointness is preserved. Let us prove this mathematically. Invariant $inv2$ is:

$$in \cap out = \varnothing \tag{3}$$

As we have seen, the effect of the actions of the *Enter* event on the invariant can be represented by replacing each variable in the invariant by the expression on the right-hand side of the assignment to that variable, i.e., replace in by $in \cup \{u\}$ and out by $out \setminus \{u\}$, giving:

$$(in \cup \{u\}) \cap (out \setminus \{u\}) = \varnothing \qquad (4)$$

The proof of this is captured by the following general rule about sets which states that if two sets are disjoint then removing elements from one and adding them to the other maintains the disjointness:

Description	Rule
Keep disjoint	$s \cap t = \varnothing \quad \Rightarrow \quad (s \setminus r) \cap (t \cup r) = \varnothing$

4.4 Machine Initialisation

Every machine has a special event (named **initialisation**) that initialises the machine variables. The acccess control machine is initialised by setting all three variables to be empty:

initialisation $\hat{=}$
    act1: $in := \varnothing$
    act2: $out := \varnothing$
    act3: $register := \varnothing$

An initialisation event has no guards nor parameters and the assignment expressions (right-hand side) cannot refer to the machine variables. This is because no assumptions can be made about the values of the variables prior to initialisation. The initialisation should *establish* the invariant, i.e., the values assigned to the variables together should satisfy the invariants. In this case, all three invariants are trivially established, i.e.,

$\varnothing \subseteq USER$
$\varnothing \cap \varnothing = \varnothing$
$\varnothing = \varnothing \cup \varnothing$

4.5 Other Access Control Events

We now look at some of the other events for access control: exiting the building, registering a new user and de-registering a user. The *Exit* event is the opposite of the *Enter* event: the user should be in the building and is moved from *in* to *out*:

$Exit$ $\hat{=}$
    any u **where**
        grd1: $u \in in$
    then
        act1: $in := in \setminus \{u\}$
        act2: $out := out \cup \{u\}$
    end

This event maintains the invariants based on similar arguments that we used previously for the *Enter* event.

When registering a user, we need a 'fresh' value to represent the new user, i.e., a value that is not already in the set *register*. This fresh value is then added to the set of registered users. The event could be specified as follows:

$RegisterUser1 \quad \hat{=}$
   any *u* **where**
      grd1: $u \in USER$
      grd2: $u \notin register$
   then
      act1: $register := register \cup \{u\}$
   end

The first guard gives a type to *u* while the second guard ensures that *u* is fresh. Let us consider whether the action violates any invariants. It turns out that the action violates the equation of *inv2* ($register = in \cup out$): it expands the left-hand side without expanding the right-hand side. We can resolve this by adding an action that also expands the right-hand side of the equation. We can do this by adding *u* to *in* or to *out*. In this case, it makes more sense to add *u* to *out* rather than *in*, as we would not expect that the new user would end up inside the building immediately at the point at which they are registered. Thus, an improved version of the event is specified as follows:

$RegisterUser2 \quad \hat{=}$
   any *u* **where**
      grd1: $u \in USER$
      grd2: $u \notin register$
   then
      act1: $register := register \cup \{u\}$
      act2: $out := out \cup \{u\}$
   end

This specification of the user registration does maintain *inv3*. Let us prove this mathematically. Invariant *inv3* is:

$$register \; = \; in \; \cup \; out \qquad (5)$$

The actions of the event modify this to the following equation:

$$\underline{register \cup \{u\}} \; = \; in \; \cup \; \underline{(out \cup \{u\})} \qquad (6)$$

We prove that this equation follows from the invariant:

$$register \cup \{u\}$$
$$= \quad \text{``}inv3\text{''}$$
$$(in \; \cup \; out) \cup \{u\}$$
$$= \quad \text{``}\cup \text{ is associative''}$$
$$in \cup (out \cup \{u\})$$

A user who is already registered may be de-registered by removing them from *register*. Removing u from *register* without removing u from *in* or *out* will lead to a violation of *inv2*. One solution is to remove u from both *in* and *out* leading to the following specification of the event for de-registering:

$DeRegisterUser1$ $\;\widehat{=}\;$
    any u **where**
        grd1: $u \in register$
    then
        act1: $register := register \setminus \{u\}$
        act2: $out := out \setminus \{u\}$
        act3: $in := in \setminus \{u\}$
    end

This specification will preserve *inv2* since u is removed from both sides of the equation. This event is applicable whether registered user u is inside or outside the building. However, if we consider a building access control system, it probably does not make sense to de-register a user while they are inside the building so we strengthen the guard to specify that u is outside (and registered):

$DeRegisterUser2$ $\;\widehat{=}\;$
    any u **where**
        grd1: $u \in out$
    then
        act1: $register := register \setminus \{u\}$
        act2: $out := out \setminus \{u\}$
    end

Note that this version does not modify *in*. If u was a member of *in*, this would result in a violation of *inv2*. However, from the guard of the event we know that u is an element of *out* and, since *in* and *out* are disjoint (*inv3*), we know that u cannot be an element of *in*. Thus it is sufficient to remove u from *out* in order to maintain *inv2*.

We leave it as an exercise for the reader to prove that *DeRegisterUser2* preserves the invariants. The following rules are used in the proofs:

Description	Rule
Distribute difference	$(s \cup t) \setminus r \;=\; (s \setminus r) \;\cup\; (t \setminus r)$
Simplify	$x \notin s \;\Rightarrow\; s \setminus \{x\} \;=\; s$
Keep disjoint	$s \cap t = \varnothing \;\Rightarrow\; (s \setminus r) \cap t \;=\; \varnothing$

4.6   Machine Behaviour and Nondeterminism

A simple way of thinking about the behaviour of an Event-B machine is as a *transition system* that moves from one state to another through execution of events. The states of a machine are represented by the different configurations of values for the variables. The variables of a machine are initialised by execution of the special **initialisation** event. An event is enabled in some state for some parameter values if all of the guards of the event are satisfied. For example, the *Enter* event in the access control model is enabled for parameter value $u1$ in any state in which $u1$ is an element of the variable *out*.

In any state that a machine can reach, an enabled event is chosen to be executed to define the next transition. If several events are enabled in a state, then the choice of which event occurs is nondeterministic. Also, if an event is enabled for several different parameter values, the choice of value for the parameters is nondeterministic – the choice just needs to satisfy the event guards. For example, in the *RegisterUser2* event, the choice of value for parameter u is nondeterministic, with the choice of value being constrained by the guards of the event to ensure that it is a fresh value.

Treating the choice of event and parameter values as nondeterministic is an abstraction of different ways in which the choice might be made in an implementation of the model. For example, if it is an interactive system, the choice might be offered to a user via a graphical interface. If it is an information processing system, the choice might be made by some scheduler. If the machine reaches a state in which no event is enabled, then it is said to be *deadlocked*.

5   Finiteness, Cardinality and Well-Definedness

Previously we considered the possibility of placing a constraint on the the the number of users allowed inside the building at any one time. We could represent this as an invariant specifying that the number of elements in the set *in* is bounded by the constant *max_capacity*. In set theory, the number of elements in a set is called its *cardinality* and in Event-B this is written as $card(S)$. For example,

$$card(\{a, b, c\}) = 3.$$

However a word of caution: cardinality is only defined for finite sets. If S is an infinite set, then $card(S)$ is undefined. Whenever we use the *card* operator, we must ensure that it is only applied to a finite set. This issue of *well-definedness* applies to some other operators as well. For example, division by zero is not well-defined and when using division we must ensure that the divisor is not zero.

As is standard in set theory, sets in Event-B may be finite or infinite. For example, the set of integers is infinite. A carrier set defined in a context is infinite unless we explicitly specify that it is finite. Naturally, an enumerated set, e.g., $S = \{a, b, c\}$, is finite. We can specify that a set S is finite using the predicate *finite(S)*. In the building access system, we would expect the set of people who are inside the building to be finite which we write as *finite(in)*. Initially *in* is empty and thus finite. The only way of expanding the set *in* is through the *Enter* event which adds one user at a time. Thus the set *in* can never become infinite.

To model the finiteness and capacity constraints on the access control, we extend the set of invariants of the machine as follows:

invariants

...
  inv4: $finite(in)$
  inv5: $card(in) \leq max\_capacity$

In $inv5$, $card(in)$ is well-defined since we know that in is finite from $inv4$. Considering preservation of $inv4$, the only event that expands in is the *Enter* event and it maintains the finiteness of in ($inv4$) by the argument outlined above. For $inv5$, $max\_capacity$ is a constant so cannot decrease during execution of the machine so we only need to consider events that might cause $card(in)$ to increase. As we have already said, *Enter* is the only event that expands in and thus increases $card(in)$. The *Enter* event as previoulsy specified places no constraint on the number of people already in the building so we need to strengthen it by adding guard $grd2$ as follows:

$Enter2 \;\; \widehat{=}$
  any u **where**
    grd1: $u \in out$
    grd2: $card(in) < max\_capacity$
  then
    act1: $in := in \cup \{u\}$
    act2: $out := out \setminus \{u\}$
  end

Note that $grd2$ requires $card(in)$ to be strictly less that $max\_capacity$ in order to ensure that the size of the resulting value for in is less than or equal to $max\_capacity$.

The following table summaries the finiteness and cardinality operators we have just introduced. The table also includes a column to indicate when a predicate or expression is well-defined:

Name	Operator	Meaning	Well-definedness
Finite	$finite(S)$	Set S is finite	*True*
Cardinality	$card(S)$	Number of elements in set S	$finite(S)$

Note that some of our definition tables do not have a well-definedness column. In these cases the predicate or expression is always well-defined.

The following rules about finiteness and cardinality are used to prove that $inv4$ and $inv5$ are preserved by the events:

Description	Rule
Finite union	$finite(s) \wedge finite(t) \implies finite(s \cup t)$
Finite difference	$finite(s) \implies finite(s \setminus t)$
Increase card	$x \notin s \implies card(s \cup \{x\}) = card(s) + 1$
Decrease card	$x \in s \implies card(s \setminus \{x\}) = card(s) - 1$

6   Introducing Relations

We have seen how sets can be used to model access control for a building. We introduced a carrier set to represent users but we did not introduce a carrier set to represent buildings. The reason for not introducing buildings is that our model was intended for a single building and the identity of that building was implicit. Let us consider generalising our modelling of access control to a system with multiple buildings. For this we introduce a carrier set representing buildings so that we can distinguish different buildings. Figure 8 illustrates the two distinct carrier sets, one for users and the other for buildings.

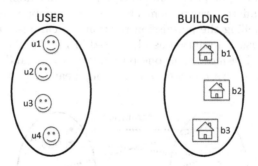

Fig. 8. Distinct carrier sets

Rather than allowing registered users to enter any building, we would like to model a more fine-grained control over which buildings a user is allowed to enter. This is illustrated in Fig. 9 which represents a permission relation between users and buildings. An arrow from a user to a building indicates that particular user has permission to enter that building. For example, in Fig. 9, user $u1$ has permission to enter two of the buildings, $b1$ and $b2$. Figure 9 represents three different sets: a set of *users*, a set of *buildings* and a set of *arrows* between users and buildings. Mathematically an arrow from user u to building b is represented by a *pair* of elements, written $u \mapsto b$. A *relation* is represented by a set of pairs, for example, the permission relation of Fig. 9 is represented by the following set P of pairs:

$$P = \{u1 \mapsto b1, \quad u1 \mapsto b2, \quad u2 \mapsto b1, \quad u2 \mapsto b3, \quad u4 \mapsto b2, \quad u4 \mapsto b3\}$$

The permission model demonstrates that a relation allows us to connect distinct carrier sets. Management of relationships between different kinds of entities is a key role of many computerised systems, including access control, business systems, information systems and communications systems. Thus relations are a useful mathematical structure for modelling such systems.

A pair $u \mapsto b$ has a *first* element u and a *second* element b. Given a set of pairs, it is useful to refer to the set of the first elements of all pairs, called the *domain*, and the set of second elements, called the *range*. For the example relation P above, we have

$$dom(P) = \{u1, u2, u4\}$$
$$ran(P) = \{b1, b2, b3\}$$

Here, $dom(P)$ represents the set of users who have permission to enter some building while $ran(P)$ represents the set of buildings for which some user has permission to enter.

Figure 9 labels the permission relation as *many-to-many*. This means that many different domain elements can be mapped to the same range element, e.g., $u1$ and $u2$ are both mapped to $b1$, and also that the same domain element can be mapped to many different range elements, e.g., $u1$ is mapped to both $b1$ and $b2$.

As well as modelling the permission relation, we can also model the current location of a user using a relation as illustrated in Fig. 10. We would not expect a user to be located in more than one building at a time and thus the location relation is required to be a *many-to-one* relation, meaning that a domain element

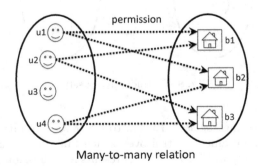

Many-to-many relation

Fig. 9. Permission relation

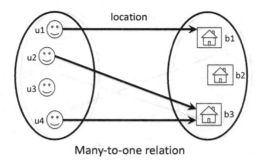

Fig. 10. Location relation

can be mapped to exactly one range element rather than many. A many-to-one relation still allows many different domain elements to be mapped to the same range element, e.g., $u2$ and $u4$ are both located in the same building in Fig. 10. Many-to-one relations are also called *functions* and are covered in more detail in Sect. 7.3.

Since the permission and location relations are themselves sets, we can formulate a connection between them. For an access control system we require that if a user is located in a building, then they have permission to be in that building. This requirement is represented by specifying that *location* is a subset of *permission*, i.e., any pair in the *location* relation is also a pair of the *permission* relation. The connection between the two relations is illustrated in Fig. 11 where *location* is clearly a subset of *permission*.

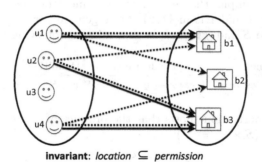

Fig. 11. Location satisfies permission

A many-to-one relation is a special case of a many-to-many relation. A further special case is a *one-to-one* relation in which each domain element is related to exactly one range element and each range element is related to exactly one domain element. This is illustrated in Fig. 12 where the *location* relation is such that users are mapped one-to-one with buildings, i.e., no two users are located in the same building. If we required single occupancy for the buildings, then we could represent this with an invariant specifying that *location* is one-to-one.

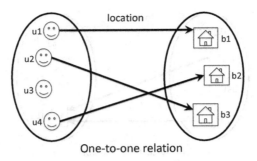

One-to-one relation

Fig. 12. Location with single occupancy

7   Cartesian Products and Relations

We have seen that an ordered pair is an element consisting of two parts, a *first* part and a *second* part, and is written as $x \mapsto y$. Given two sets S and T, we can form what is called their *Cartesian product*. This is the set of all those pairs whose first component is in S and second component is in T. The Cartesian product of S with T is written $S \times T$. For example, the Cartesian product of $\{a, b, c\}$ with $\{1, 2\}$ is expanded to a set of pairs as follows:

$$\{a, b, c\} \times \{1, 2\} = \{a \mapsto 1, \ a \mapsto 2,$$
$$b \mapsto 1, \ b \mapsto 2,$$
$$c \mapsto 1, \ c \mapsto 2\}$$

Here we see, for example, that $a \mapsto 1$ is an element of the Cartesian product since a is in $\{a, b, c\}$ and 1 is in $\{1, 2\}$. More generally $x \mapsto y$ is an element of $S \times T$ when x is in S and y is in T as shown in the following table:

Name	Predicate	Definition
Cartesian product	$x \mapsto y \ \in \ S \times T$	$x \in S \ \wedge \ y \in T$

The following derivation shows that the product of any set with the empty set is itself empty $(S \times \varnothing = \varnothing)$:

$$x \mapsto y \in S \times \varnothing$$
$$= \quad \text{``Definition of } \times \text{''}$$
$$x \in S \ \wedge \ y \in \varnothing$$
$$= \quad \text{``Definition of } \varnothing \text{''}$$
$$x \in S \ \wedge \ false$$
$$= \quad \text{``Logic''}$$
$$false$$
$$= \quad \text{``Definition of } \varnothing \text{''}$$
$$x \mapsto y \in \varnothing$$

7.1 Type Constructors and Structured Types

In Sect. 3.1, we saw that the powerset operator is used to define the type of a set. The powerset operator can be used to construct a type $\mathbb{P}(T)$ from a type T so we refer to it as a *type constructor*. Similarly, Cartesian product is a type constructor: the type $S \times T$ is constructed from the types S and T. A *structured type* is a type formed using a type constructor such as $\mathbb{P}$ or $\times$.

- Powerset ($\mathbb{P}$) is the type constructor for sets.
- Cartesian product ($\times$) is the type constructor for ordered pairs.

In Event-B, constants, variables, parameter and expressions have a type and these types come in three forms

- Basic type: integer ($\mathbb{Z}$), Boolean.
- Carrier set, e.g., *USER, BUILDING*.
- Structured type: $\mathbb{P}(S)$, $S \times T$.

The type constructors can be nested and combined to form more complex structured types such as:

- Set of sets: $\mathbb{P}(\mathbb{P}(T))$
- Set of pairs: $\mathbb{P}(S \times T)$
- Pair of sets: $\mathbb{P}(S) \times \mathbb{P}(T)$, $S \times \mathbb{P}(T)$, $\mathbb{P}(S) \times T$

The following table presents some example expressions and their corresponding structured type:

Expression	Type
$\{5,6,3\}$	$\mathbb{P}(\mathbb{Z})$
$4 \mapsto 7$	$\mathbb{Z} \times \mathbb{Z}$
$\{5,6,3\} \mapsto 7$	$\mathbb{P}(\mathbb{Z}) \times \mathbb{Z}$
$\{4 \mapsto 8,\ 3 \mapsto 0,\ 2 \mapsto 9\}$	$\mathbb{P}(\mathbb{Z} \times \mathbb{Z})$

7.2 Relations

Through the permission example (Fig. 9) we have seen that a relation is modelled as a set of pairs, i.e., a structured type formed using both the $\times$ and $\mathbb{P}$ constructors. Because this structured type is a useful modelling construct, it is given its own symbol in Event-B: we write $S \leftrightarrow T$ as a shorthand for $\mathbb{P}(S \times T)$. The following table provides the definition of the relation arrow:

Name	Predicate	Definition
Relation	$r \in S \leftrightarrow T$	$r \in \mathbb{P}(S \times T)$

For the access control example, we may specify that the *permission* variable is a (many-to-many) relation with the following invariant:

invariant $permission \in USER \leftrightarrow BUILDING$

Here is another example of a relation, named *directory*, that relates people to phone numbers:

invariant $directory \in PERSON \leftrightarrow NUMBER$

A possible value for the directory is as follows:

$$directory = \{mary \mapsto 287573,$$
$$mary \mapsto 398620,$$
$$john \mapsto 829483,$$
$$jim \mapsto 398620\}$$

It is worth pointing out the difference between the two arrow symbols used in representing relations:

$\leftrightarrow$ combines *two sets* to form a *set*.
$\mapsto$ combines *two elements* to form an *ordered pair*.

We already introduced the domain and range of a relation. These are defined by the following table:

Name	Predicate	Definition
Domain	$x \in dom(R)$	$\exists y \cdot\ x \mapsto y \in R$
Range	$y \in ran(R)$	$\exists x \cdot\ x \mapsto y \in R$

For the example directory shown above, we have:

$$\text{dom}(directory) = \{mary, john, jim\}$$
$$\text{ran}(directory) = \{287573, 398620, 829483\}$$

Note that when we declare a constant or variable to be a relation between two sets, as well as defining its type, we are implicitly constraining the domain and range of the relation: Suppose we have $s \subseteq S$ and $t \subseteq T$ and we declare $r \in s \leftrightarrow t$, then it follows that

$$r \in \mathbb{P}(S \times T)$$
$$dom(r) \subseteq s$$
$$ran(r) \subseteq t$$

7.3 Functions

From Fig. 10 we saw that the *location* relation should be a many-to-one relation, i.e., each user is located in at most one building at any moment. The many-to-one property means that if a user u is in the domain of *location*, then that user is mapped to a single building by the location relation. In that case, we can write *location*(u) to refer to the building that u is located in. For example, from Fig. 10, we have:

$$location(u1) = b1$$
$$location(u2) = b3$$
$$location(u4) = b3$$

If a user u is not in the domain of *location*, then *location*(u) is not well-defined. For example, from Fig. 10, $u3$ is not in the domain of *location* therefore *location*($u3$) is not well-defined.

In general, a many-to-one relation f is said to be *functional*. This is written as $f \in S \nrightarrow T$ and means that every element in the domain of f is mapped to exactly one element in the range. The functionality property is specified mathematically by stating that if a domain value x is mapped to range value y, then x cannot be mapped to any other range value y'. This is shown in the following table:

Name	Predicate	Definition
Partial function	$f \in S \nrightarrow T$	$f \in S \leftrightarrow T \;\wedge$ $\forall x, y, y' \cdot\; x \mapsto y \in f \;\wedge\; y' \neq y$ $\Rightarrow\; x \mapsto y' \notin f$

Note that when we declare $f \in S \nrightarrow T$ we say that f is a *partial* function. It is said to be partial because there may be values in the set S that are not in the domain of f. For example, from Fig. 10, $u3$ is in *USER* but is not in the domain of *location*. A relation is said to be a *total* function from S to T when it is a partial function and its domain is exactly S:

Name	Predicate	Definition
Total function	$f \in S \rightarrow T$	$f \in S \nrightarrow T \;\wedge\; dom(f) = S$

We have seen that we can write *location*($u1$) since *location* is functional. In general, when a relation f is functional, we can treat it as a mathematical function and write $f(x)$ for the value that x is mapped to. For $f(x)$ to be well-defined, two conditions must hold: f must be functional and x must be in the domain of f. This is shown in the following definition:

Name	Expression	Meaning	Well-definedness
Function application	$f(x)$	$f(x) = y$ $\Leftrightarrow x \mapsto y \in f$	$f \in S \nrightarrow T \;\wedge$ $x \in dom(f)$

This definition uses the *if and only if* ($\Leftrightarrow$) logical operator: $P \Leftrightarrow Q$ is short for $P \Rightarrow Q \;\wedge\; Q \Rightarrow P$.

8   Access Control Specification

Now that we have explained relations and functions, we will make use of them to construct an Event-B specification of access control for multiple buildings. We start by presenting the high-level requirements in an informal way. As already stated, computer-based system is designed to satisfy some requirements in the real world and it is usual to express system requirements in natural language. Documentation of the requirements in natural language will guide the construction of the Event-B specification and will also provide a form of "sanity check" against which to validate the Event-B specification. It helps understanding if we try to describe the intended purpose of the system being designed in a concise way. For the access control system this is as follows:

> **Purpose:** The purpose of the access control system is to ensure that users may be in a building only if they have permission to be in that building.

We provide a more detailed list of requirements, giving each one a label so that we can refer to it later. In each of the following requirements "the system" refers to the access control system:

- **FUN1:** The system shall maintain a register of recognised users and shall provide operations for managing the user register.
- **FUN2:** The system shall maintain a register of protected buildings and shall provide operations for managing the building register.
- **FUN3:** The system shall maintain the permissions for each user, determining the building they are allowed to enter, and shall provide operations for managing the permissions.
- **FUN4:** The system shall allow a user to enter a building provided they have permission.
- **FUN5:** The system shall allow a user to exit a building without constraint.
- **ASM1:** A user will be in at most one building at any time.
- **ASM2:** A user cannot move directly from one building to another building.

Most of these requirements are *functional requirements*[1], that is, requirements defining the intended function of the system. The last requirements in the list are *assumptions* about the environment in which the system is operating, e.g.,

---

[1] Not to be confused with a functional (many-to-one) relation!

we assume that there is a physical constraint on users which means they cannot be in more than one building at any time.

We referrred to the requirements as *high-level*. By this we mean there is not necessarily enough detail in the requirements to build the system. For example, **FUN4** does not provide detail on how a user would enter a building or how they might be prevented from entering. Nonetheless, we will see that it is still feasible and useful to make a formal analysis of the high-level requirements in Event-B.

8.1 Set and Relations for Access Control

From the requirements **FUN1** and **FUN2** we identify two kinds of entity in the system, users and buildings. These give rise to two carrier sets for our specification of the system as defined in the following context:

> **context** *BuildingAccessContext*
> **sets**   *USER, BUILDING*
> **end**

Having identified the carrier sets, we consider what set variables to include in the model, i.e., variables that are subsets of a carrier set. Looking at **FUN1**, we see that a variable set of registered users is required. We will call this variable *user*, where *user* ⊆ *USER*. Similarly, **FUN2** suggests a variable set of buildings so we introduce a variable *building* ⊆ *BUILDING*. These two set variables are specified in an Event-B machine as follows:

> **machine** *BuildingAccess*
> **sees** *BuildingAccessContext*
> **variables**   *user, building, ...*
> **invariants**
> 　　inv1:   *user* ⊆ *USER*
> 　　inv2:   *building* ⊆ *BUILDING*

Naming Convention: Although it is not required by the Event-B language, we will use all UPPER case letters for names of carrier sets. When a model has multiple carrier sets representing different kinds of entity, we will use a lower case version of a carrier set name for the variable corresponding to the set of instances of that entity. For example, the user entity is represented by the carrier set *USER* and the set of instances (i.e., the register users) is represented by the variable *user*. While the carrier set is fixed, the instance set may be expanded or reduced through execution of events.

We also want to identify any required relational variables for our specification. **FUN3** suggests a relation to represent user permissions, while **FUN4** suggests a relation to represent user location. The diagrams in Figs. 9 and 10 illustrate the permission and location relations between users and buildings. These diagrams are useful for illustrating specific instances of relations but they do not provide a general representation. To illustrate relations between sets more generally we use

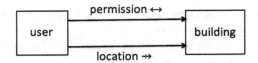

Fig. 13. Relations for access control

the class diagram shown in Fig. 13. A *class diagram* is a construct from object oriented design that is used to represent classes and associations between classes. In Fig. 13, the sets are represented as classes (the boxes) while the relations are presented as associations (the arrows). An association represents a relation between the indicated sets. We place the relevant mathematical symbol next to the name of the relation to indicate its nature (many-to-many, many-to-one, etc.). Thus Fig. 13 indicates that *permission* is a relation between *user* and *building*:

$$permission \in user \leftrightarrow building$$

Because of **ASM1**, Fig. 13 indicates that *location* is a partial function from *user* to *building*, giving rise to the following mathematical specification:

$$location \in user \nrightarrow building$$

From the requirements, and with the aid of a class diagram, we have identified two kinds of variables for our Event-B specification:

- Set variables: *user*, *building*
- Relation variables: *permission*, *location*

The full list of variables and corresponding invariants is specified as follows:

> **variables**   *user*, *building*, *location*, *permission*
> **invariants**
> > inv1: $user \subseteq USER$
> > inv2: $building \subseteq BUILDING$
> > inv3: $permission \in user \leftrightarrow building$
> > inv4: $location \in user \nrightarrow building$

It is important to observe that invariants *inv3* and *inv4* specify constraints between multiple variables (as well as defining the types of the relation variables). For example, included in *inv3* is the constraint that the domain of *permission* is included in *user*. This means that the system only maintains permission information for registered users. The range of *permission* is constrained to be included in *building* which means that any permissions that a user has can only be for registered buildings. Requirement **FUN3** does not precisely state these two constraints though **FUN3** could be interpreted as requiring that permission is only between registered users and registered buildings. In the mathematical representation, the constraints are specified precisely. Similarly, $inv4$ specifies that only registered users may be located in buildings and those buildings must be registered.

Our access control specification contains two relation variables and we consider whether we can identify an invariant that constrains the connection between these two variables. In fact we have already identified such an invariant in Fig. 11 where $location$ is required to be included in $permission$. Thus our model has one additional invariant:

invariants
$\quad \ldots$

$\quad inv5: \quad location \subseteq permission$

Invariant $inv5$ addresses **FUN4**, the main access control requirement.

The list of invariants for the $BuildingAccess$ machine may be classified into three kinds:

1. Constraints between set variables ($inv1$, $inv2$).
2. Constraints between a relational variable and set variables ($inv3$, $inv4$).
3. Constraints between relational variables ($inv5$).

The first two kinds of invariant can often be easily identified from a class diagram derived from the requirements. The class diagram is constructed by identifying the main entities suggested by the requirements (e.g., $USER$ and $BUILDING$) and the relevant relationships between them (e.g. $permission$ and $location$). The third kind of invariant does not always follow directly from a class diagram and may come directly from the requirements. In Fig. 13, because $permission$ and $location$ have the same source and target, the question of whether one is a subset of the other is suggested.

From the requirements, we have identified carrier sets, variables and invariants but the requirements also suggest events to be included in the Event-B specification. Here we identify a list of events by systematically reviewing each requirement:

- **FUN1:** Suggests $RegisterUser$ and $DeRegisterUser$ events.
- **FUN2:** $RegisterBuilding$ and $DeRegisterBuilding$.
- **FUN3:** $AddPermission$ and $RemovePermission$.
- **FUN4:** $EnterBuilding$.
- **FUN5:** $ExitBuilding$.
- **ASM1:** $EnterBuilding$.
- **ASM2:** $EnterBuilding$.

As can be seen with the $EnterBuilding$ event, it is sometimes the case that different requirements will give rise to the same event. This is because the requirements may describe different aspects of the behaviour represented by the event. For example, both **FUN4** and **ASM1** put constraints on when a user may enter a building.

8.2   Expansion Events

When a specification involves sets, it is common to have events for expanding sets (e.g., *RegisterUser*) and reducing sets (e.g., *DeRegisterUser*). We look at the expansion events first. Events to specify registration of users and buildings are similar to the registration event presented in Sect. 4.5:

$RegisterUser$ $\hat{=}$
    any u **where**
        grd1: $u \notin user$
    then
        act1: $user := user \cup \{u\}$
    end

$RegisterBuilding$ $\hat{=}$
    any b **where**
        grd1: $u \notin building$
    then
        act1: $building := building \cup \{u\}$
    end

Notice that we omitted a guard specifying that parameter b is an element of $BUILDING$. This is because the type of b can be inferred from $grd1$ since the set $building$ has type $\mathbb{P}(BUILDING)$. Similarly for the *RegisterUser* event.

The *AddPermission* event gives a registered user b permission to enter a registered building b by adding the ordered pair $u \mapsto b$ to the *permission* relation:

$AddPermission$ $\hat{=}$
    any u, b **where**
        grd1: $u \in user$
        grd2: $b \in building$
    then
        act1: $permission := permission \cup \{u \mapsto b\}$
    end

The guards of this event are required in order to preserve invariant $inv3$ which constrains the domain and range of the *permission* relation. For example, if $grd1$ was $u \in USER$ instead then the event might violate the invariant by giving permission to a non-registered user.

Here is an alternative version of the event that adds a set of buildings bs to the users permission rather than a single building:

$AddMultiPermission$ $\hat{=}$
    any u, bs **where**
        grd1: $u \in user$
        grd2: $bs \subseteq building$
    then
        act1: $permission := permission \cup (\{u\} \times bs)$
    end

The expression $\{u\} \times bs$ defines a relation that maps u to each element in bs. The following rules are used to prove that $inv3$ is preserved:

Description	Rule
Product relation	$s \subseteq S \;\wedge$ $t \subseteq T$ $\qquad \Rightarrow \quad s \times t \;\in\; S \leftrightarrow T$
Union relation	$q \in S \leftrightarrow T \;\wedge$ $r \in S \leftrightarrow T$ $\qquad \Rightarrow \quad (q \cup r) \;\in\; S \leftrightarrow T$

The event modelling a user entering a building is parameterised by the entering user and the building they are entering:

$EnterBuilding \;\;\hat{=}$
    any u, b **where**
        grd1: $u \notin dom(location)$
        grd2: $u \mapsto b \in permission$
    then
        act1: $location := location \cup \{u \mapsto b\}$
    end

From **ASM2** we expect that a user is not located in any building when they try to enter a building hence $grd1$ which specifies that u is not in the domain of $location$. From **FUN4**, we identify $grd2$ which specifies that u has permission to enter b. The effect of $act1$ is to add the ordered pair $u \mapsto b$ to $location$.

The invariants that the $EnterBuilding$ event affects are $inv4$ and $inv5$. Invariant $inv5$, which specifies that $location$ is included in $permission$, is maintained because of $grd2$. Invariant $inv4$ specifies that $location$ is functional. Adding a mapping for u to $location$ maintains the functionality of $location$ because $grd1$ specifies that u is not already mapped to any buildings. Without $grd1$, the event could violate the functionality as u might end up being mapped to more than one building in $location$. The following rule about expanding a partial function captures this property. It states that if f is functional and x is not in the domain of f, then $f \cup \{x \mapsto y\}$ is also functional:

Description	Rule
Function extension	$f \in S \nrightarrow T \;\wedge$ $x \notin dom(f) \;\wedge$ $x \mapsto y \in S \times T$ $\qquad \Rightarrow \quad (f \cup \{x \mapsto y\}) \;\in\; S \nrightarrow T$

8.3   Reduction Events and Domain Subtraction

We have already seen how we can reduce sets using the set difference operator. We can use this to model a user u exiting a building b as follows:

$ExitBuilding$ $\hat{=}$
  any u, b **where**
    grd1: $u \mapsto b \in location$
  then
    act1: $location := location \setminus \{u \mapsto b\}$
  end

Alternatively, we can use an operator on relations called *domain subtraction* to model a user exiting a building. Domain subtraction, written $A \lhd R$, takes two arguments, a relation a relation $R \in S \leftrightarrow T$ and a set $A \subseteq S$, and removes those pairs from R whose first part is in A. This is illustrated by the following equation which shows the result of domain subtracting a set containing a user from an example of the *location* relation:

$$\{u2\} \lhd \{u1 \mapsto b1,\ u2 \mapsto b3,\ u4 \mapsto b3\} = \{u1 \mapsto b1,\ u4 \mapsto b3\}$$

Here we see that the mapping from $u2$ to $b3$ is removed to give the reduced set on the right-hand side. The general definition of the operator is as follows:

Name	Predicate	Definition
Domain subtraction	$x \mapsto y \in A \lhd R$	$x \mapsto y \in R \ \wedge \ x \notin A$

Here is a specification of the *ExitBuilding* event that has just one parameter, the user u. It removes u from the *location* function using domain subtraction:

$ExitBuilding$ $\hat{=}$
  any u **where**
    grd1: $u \in dom(building)$
  then
    act1: $location := \{u\} \lhd location$
  end

This event preserves the permission invariant ($inv5$) and the functionality of *location* ($inv3$). This follows from the following rules which show that domain subtraction reduces a relation and that inclusion preserves functionality:

Description	Rule
Domain subtract inclusion	$(A \lhd R) \subseteq R$
Inclusion functional	$f \in S \twoheadrightarrow T \ \wedge$ $g \subseteq f$ $\Rightarrow \ g \in S \twoheadrightarrow T$

8.4   Invariant Violation

While exiting a building causes no problems from the point of view of invariant preservation, removing permissions can be problematic. Consider the following specification of an event that removes all permissions for a user u using the domain subtraction operation:

$RemovePermissions1 \ \hat{=}$
   any u **where**
      grd1: $u \in user$
   then
      act1: $permission := \{u\} \lhd permission$
   end

Here is a reminder of the permission inclusion invariant:

$$inv5: \quad location \ \subseteq \ permission$$

Action $act1$ of the $RemovePermissions1$ event results in the following modified version of $inv5$:

$$location \ \subseteq \ \{u\} \lhd permission$$

This does not follow from $inv5$. The problem is that we are reducing the right-hand side of this set inclusion without reducing the left-hand side. If the user u was located in a building and we remove all their permissions, then after executing the $RemovePermissions1$ event, u would still be in a building but they would no longer have permission to be there, thus violating $inv5$!

8.5   Fixing the Violation

One solution to this invariant violation problem would be to add an action to also remove the user from whatever building they are in by removing them from the domain of $location$ as well:

$RemovePermissions2 \ \hat{=}$
   any u **where**
      grd1: $u \in user$
   then
      act1: $permission := \{u\} \lhd permission$
      act2: $location := \{u\} \lhd location$
   end

With this version of the event, the modified invariant becomes:

$$\{u\} \lhd location \ \subseteq \ \{u\} \lhd permission$$

This inclusion follows from invariant $inv5$ which means that $RemovePermissions2$ preserves $inv5$. Mathematically this is because domain subtraction is *monotonic*. In general, an operation op is said to be monotonic when it preserves inclusion between sets:

Name	Definition
Monotonic	$S \subseteq T \;\Rightarrow\; op(S) \subseteq op(T)$

Description	Rule
Domain subtract monotonic	$R \subseteq Q \;\Rightarrow\; A \vartriangleleft R \subseteq A \vartriangleleft Q$

Another way of ensuring that *inv5* is maintained would be to allow permissions for u to be removed only if they are not currently inside a building. Here is a version that only modifies *permission* but has an additional guard, specifying that the user is not located in any building:

RemovePermissions3 $\;\widehat{=}$
    any u **where**
        grd1: $u \in user$
        grd2: $u \notin dom(location)$
    then
        act1: $permission := \{u\} \vartriangleleft permission$
    end

To see why this preserves the permission invariant we make use of the following rule; this states that if x is not in the domain of relation R then removing x from the domain of R has no effect:

Description	Rule
Simplify domain subtract	$x \notin dom(R) \;\Rightarrow\; (\{x\} \vartriangleleft R) = R$

The modified invariant resulting from *RemovePermissions3* is

$$location \;\subseteq\; \underline{\{u\} \vartriangleleft permission}$$

Because of *grd1* we can assume that $u \notin dom(location)$ and therefore that $location = \{u\} \vartriangleleft location$ so this is the same as the following inclusion:

$$\{u\} \vartriangleleft location \;\subseteq\; \{u\} \vartriangleleft permission$$

As before, this inclusion follows from *inv5* by monotonicity.

We have seen that the *RemovePermissions1* event does not preserve the permission inclusion invariant (*inv5*) while the other two versions of permission removal, *RemovePermissions2* and *RemovePermissions3*, do preserve the invariant. Clearly we would want to rule out *RemovePermissions1* since it fails to satisfy a mathematical judgement. Although *RemovePermissions2* preserves the permission inclusion invariant, it does combine two separate functions into one atomic event. At the very least it would be more appropriate to reflect the dual role in the name the event, e.g., *ExitAndRemovePermission*. We note that *location* is a *monitoring* variable that is used to keep track of the physical location of users while *permission* is a *conceptual* variable that models a key concept in access control which does not reflect any physical entities. We prefer to keep changes to monitoring variables (e.g., *location*) separate from changes to conceptual variables (e.g., *permission*) so we use *RemovePermissions3* as our specification of permission removal. This choice does mean that permission cannot be removed from a user for a building they are currently located in until after they exit the building. If it was deemed important, we might have a mechanism to force a user to exit a building but we treat this as out of scope of our analysis. Whenever the construction of the Event-B model raises ambiguities about the requirements (such as whether we can remove permissions for a user who is located in a building), then we should consider asking the system provider (the client) to clarify the requirements.

It is ok to remove permission from a user for a particular building even if they are located in another building? Here is an event that does this:

$RemoveSinglePermission \; \hat{=}$
    any u, b **where**
        grd1: $u \mapsto b \in permission$
        grd2: $u \mapsto b \notin location$
    then
        act1: $permission := permission \setminus \{u \mapsto b\}$
    end

Here *grd2* does not prevent u from being located in some building b' that is different to b. To see why this event preserves *inv5*, consider the effect of the action *act1* on the invariant:

$$location \subseteq permission \setminus \{u \mapsto b\}$$

Because of *grd2*, $location = location \setminus \{u \mapsto b\}$, so this inclusion is the same as

$$location \setminus \{u \mapsto b\} \subseteq permission \setminus \{u \mapsto b\}$$

This inclusion follows from *inv5* by monotonicity of set difference (set difference, set union and set intersection are all monotonic).

8.6 Range Subtraction

The domain subtraction operator ($\lhd$) is used to remove pairs from a relation based a domain set argument. There is also a *range subtraction* operator ($\rhd$) that removes pairs based on a range set argument. For example:

$$\{u1 \mapsto b1, \; u2 \mapsto b3, \; u4 \mapsto b3\} \; \rhd \; \{b1\} = \{u2 \mapsto b3, \; u4 \mapsto b3\}$$

Notice that in the case of domain subtraction, the set argument comes first and the relation comes second ($A \lhd R$) while the arguments are swapped for the range operator ($R \rhd B$). The operator definition is as follows:

Name	Predicate	Definition
Range subtraction	$x \mapsto y \in R \rhd B$	$x \mapsto y \in R \ \wedge \ y \notin B$

The event to remove a building from the registered buildings makes use of range subtraction to remove all permissions associated with that building:

$DeRegisterBuilding \ \widehat{=}$
    any b **where**
        grd1: $b \in building$
        grd2: $b \notin ran(location)$
    then
        act1: $building := building \setminus \{b\}$
        act2: $permission := permission \rhd \{b\}$
    end

While b is removed from *building* by action *act*1, action *act*2 removes any permission associated with b from *permission*. This is required in order preserve invariant *inv*3 which specifies that *permission* is a relation between *user* and *building*. The following rules show how the relational subtraction operators reduce the domain/range of a relation:

Description	Rule
Domain/range *reduction*	$R \in S \leftrightarrow T \ \Rightarrow$ $\quad (A \lhd R) \ \in \ (S \setminus A) \leftrightarrow T$ $\quad (R \rhd B) \ \in \ S \leftrightarrow (T \setminus B)$

Notice that *grd*2 of the *DeRegisterBuilding* event requires that b has no occupants (no users are located in b). This ensures that the event maintains *inv*4 stating that the range of *location* is included in *building* and also maintains the permission inclusion invariant *inv*5 when the permissions for b are removed by *act*2.

The event to de-register a user is specified as follows:

$DeRegisterUser \ \widehat{=}$
    any b **where**
        grd1: $u \in user$
        grd2: $u \notin dom(location)$
    then
        act1: $user := user \setminus \{u\}$
        act2: $permission := \{u\} \lhd permission$
    end

Guard *grd*2 requires that u is not located in a building (preserving *inv*5), while action *act*2 removes all permissions for u (preserving *inv*3).

For both of the de-register events, we required that the building is unoccupied (for *DeRegisterBuilding*) or the user is not in a building (for *DeRegisterUser*). This was to ensure the preservation of the invariant *inv5*. An alternative way of preserving *inv5*, that does not require guards on *location*, would be to reduce *location* as well, as we saw with *Remove Permission2*. As with permission removal, we prefer to keep location changes and user registration changes as separate events. This is again because *location* is a monitoring variable while the property of being registered is conceptual.

9   Query Events

The events we have looked at so far all include actions that change one or more variables. Sometimes we are interested in querying information about a system such as the location of a user. Here is the specification of such an event:

$QueryLocation \ \hat{=}$
    any $u, result$ **where**
        grd1: $u \in dom(location)$
        grd2: $result \in BUILDING$
        grd3: $result = location(u)$
    end

The event has two parameters: u, the user whose location is being queried, and $result$, the result of the query. In this case the result of the query is the location of u. The Event-B language does not have an explicit notion of an output parameter. We adopt the convention of naming a parameter representing an output as $result$. Typically the value of a result parameter will be defined by an exact equation such as $grd3$ above. We refer to an event that specifies a result but does not modify any variables as a *query event*.

The guard that specifies the type of the result in *QueryLocation*, $grd2$, is not strictly necessary since the type can be inferred from the equation in $grd3$. However making the type of $result$ explicit makes the specification clearer.

Another query we could perform on the access control system would be to find out the set of buildings that a particular user has permission to enter. To do that we use the *relational image* operator. Given a relation $R \in S \leftrightarrow T$ and a set $A \subseteq S$, the expression $R[A]$ represents the set of range elements corresponding to some domain element in A. For example, consider again the following simple relation:

$$directory = \{mary \mapsto 287573,$$
$$mary \mapsto 398620,$$
$$john \mapsto 829483,$$
$$jim \mapsto 398620\}$$

If we want to identify the set of numbers that *mary* is mapped to, we write $directory[\{mary\}]$ where

$$directory[\{mary\}] = \{287573, 398620\}$$

Note the argument within the brackets must be a set of domain elements rather than a single element which is why we do not write $directory[mary]$.

In general, a range element y is in the relational image of A under R if there is some element x in A that is mapped to y by R. This specified precisely in the following table:

Name	Predicate	Definition
Relational image	$y \in R[A]$	$\exists x \cdot x \in A \ \wedge \ x \mapsto y \in R$

Suppose there are no elements of A mapped to range elements by R. In that case there is no x in A satisfying $x \mapsto y \in R$ and therefore $R[A]$ will be empty.

The event to query the permissions of a user makes use of relational image:

$QueryPermissions \ \hat{=}$
    any $u, result$ **where**
        grd1: $u \in user$
        grd2: $result \subseteq BUILDING$
        grd3: $result = permission[\{u\}]$
    end

Here the result is specified as the relational image of $\{u\}$ under the permission relation, i.e., the set of buildings for which u has permission. In the case that the user has no permissions, then the result will be the empty set.

We have seen that relational image allows us to specify a query on a relation going from domain elements to range elements. To perform a query in the opposite direction, from range to domain, we can take the *inverse* of a relation, written R^{-1}. The inverse of R is the result of swapping the order of each pair in R. For example, the inverse of the *directory* relation specified above is as follows:

$$directory^{-1} = \{287573 \mapsto mary,$$
$$398620 \mapsto mary,$$
$$829483 \mapsto john,$$
$$398620 \mapsto jim\}$$

We can use this to query the people associated with phone number 398620 as follows:

$$directory^{-1}[\ \{398620\} \ ] = \{mary, jim\}$$

The inverse operator is defined in the following table:

Name	Predicate	Definition
Relational inverse	$y \mapsto x \in R^{-1}$	$x \mapsto y \in R$

Using inverse and image, a query event that provides the set of users who have permission to enter building b is specified as follows:

$QueryBuildingUsers \; \hat{=}$
   any $b, result$ **where**
      grd1: $b \in building$
      grd2: $result \subseteq USER$
      grd3: $result = permission^{-1}[\{b\}]$
   end

We can use a similar query event to provide the set of occupants of a building:

$QueryBuildingOccupants \; \hat{=}$
   any $b, result$ **where**
      grd1: $b \in building$
      grd2: $result \subseteq USER$
      grd3: $result = location^{-1}[\{b\}]$
   end

Note that while *location* is functional, the inverse of *location* might not be. This is illustrated by Fig. 10 where two different users, $u2$ and $u4$ are located in $b3$. This means that in the inverse relation, $b3$ is mapped to two different users and thus $location^{-1}$ is not functional. If a relation is one-to-one, e.g., Fig. 12, then its inverse is also functional. A one-to-one function is also called *injective* and is declared as $f \in S \rightarrowtail T$. An injective function is defined as a function whose inverse is also functional:

Name	Predicate	Definition
Injective function	$f \in S \rightarrowtail T$	$f \in S \nrightarrow T \;\wedge\; f^{-1} \in T \nrightarrow S$

9.1 Requirements Tracing

In order to be systematic about validation of the model against the requirements, we will re-visit the list of requirements and annotate each one with a explanation of how it is represented in the Event-B model. This is a form of *tracing* information: a means of tracing from a requirement through to a part, or parts, of the formal model. This is shown as a table in Fig. 14 where the explanations of how a requirement is represented in the formal model are in shown in the second column. For example, the annotation on **FUN1** provides an explanation of how that requirement is represented in the formal model through the *user* variable and the *RegisterUser* and *UnRegisterUser* events.

10 Simple Bank

We make use of some of the techniques shown so far to develop a model of a simple banking system. This case study emphasises the use of functions and introduces an additional mathematical concept (function override). The case study also serves to re-enforce the steps that may be taken in developing an

Requirement	Representation in model
FUN1	This is represented by the *user* variable modelling registered users (*inv*1) and by the *RegisterUser* and *DeRegisterUser* events.
FUN2	This is represented by the *building* variable modelling registered buildings (*inv*2) and by the *RegisterBuilding* and *DeRegister-Building* events.
FUN3	This is represented by the *permissions* variable (*inv*3) and by the *AddPermission* and *RemovePermission* events.
FUN4	This is represented by the permission invariant (*inv*5) and by the *EnterBuilding* event. Guard *grd*2 of the *EnterBuilding* event ensures that the entering user has permission.
FUN5	This is represented by the *ExitBuilding* event. There is no constraint on this event other than the user is located in a building (*grd*1).
ASM1	This is represented by the location being functional (*inv*4).
ASM2	This is represented by *grd*1 of the *EnterBuilding* event which requires that the entering user is not currently located in any building.

Fig. 14. List of requirement labels with tracing information

Event-B model from a list of requirements including the use of a class diagram to identify the main entities and the relationship between them. Here is a list of functional requirements for the simple bank:

– **FUN1:** The system shall maintain a register of bank **customers** and shall provide operations for managing the customer set.
– **FUN2:** The system shall maintain a **name** and **address** for each customer and shall provide operations for managing these.
– **FUN3:** The system shall allow customers to have several **accounts** and allow customers to share accounts.
– **FUN4:** The system shall provide operations for managing the account set.
– **FUN5:** The system shall maintain a **balance** for each account.
– **FUN6:** The system shall ensure that account balances are never negative.
– **FUN7:** The system shall provide operations for depositing and withdrawing funds to and from an account and for transferring funds between accounts.

10.1 Sets and Relations

The first step in developing the model is to identify some carrier sets. In the functional requirements above we have highlighted some nouns in bold, e.g., **customers** in **FUN1**. Requirement **FUN2** introduces names and addresses at a high level and does not define a specific format. We will treat names and addresses as abstract values and model them using carrier sets. These highlighted nouns suggest the carrier sets shown in Fig. 15. Note that we only highlighted the first occurrence of a noun to avoid duplication. Figure 15 does not identify a carrier set for **balance** in **FUN5**. For simplicity we decide to model the amount of money in an account as an integer value; we could have chosen more detail such as currency units (e.g., euros) and subunits (e.g., cents). Integers are already part of the Event-B language.

Fig. 15. Carrier sets for simple bank

Figure 15 gives rise to the following context for our simple bank model:

context *BankContext*
sets   *ACCOUNT, CUSTOMER, NAME, ADDRESS*
end

Next we identify whether any of the requirements suggest relations between sets. **FUN2** suggests a relation between *CUSTOMER* and *NAME* and between *CUSTOMER* and *ADDRESS*. We name these relations *name* and *address* respectively and they are shown in Fig. 16. **FUN3** suggests a relation between *CUSTOMER* and *ACCOUNT* which we name as *accounts*. **FUN5** suggests a relation between *ACCOUNT* and integers which we name as *balance*.

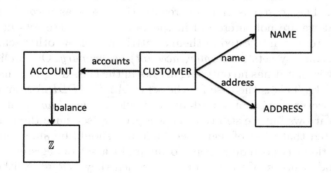

Fig. 16. Adding relations for the bank

Having identified the main sets and required relationships between them, we add a bit more precision to the diagram. For the building access model we distinguished the (fixed) carrier sets for users and buildings from the (variable) registered sets and we do the same for the simple bank. In Fig. 17 we have replaced the *CUSTOMER* and *ACCOUNT* carrier sets by the *customer* and *account* variable sets. The variable sets represent registered customers and accounts respectively and they allow us to represent constraints such as requiring customers to be registered in order to have accounts. In order to avoid confusion with the set *account*, we have changed the name of the relation between *customer* and *account* to *cust_acc* in Fig. 17. The other way in which we finesse the diagram is to determine the nature of each relation (many-to-many, etc.). Since **FUN3** requires that a customers may have multiple accounts, we conclude that *cust_acc* should be a many-to-many relation. From **FUN2** we conclude that each customer has one name and one address hence we conclude that these should be functional. We mark them as *total* functions from *customer* to indicate that each registered customer has a name and an address. Similarly from **FUN5** we conclude that *balance* should be a total function from *account*.

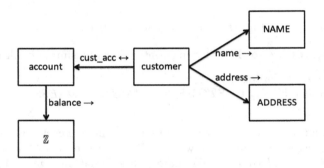

Fig. 17. Finessing the bank model

We have not introduced variable sets corresponding to **NAME** nor **ADDRESS**. The reason is that we regard these sets as *secondary*. By this we mean that we are not interested in the values from these sets in their own right and we are only interested in them as attributes of the other sets. We refer to the non-secondary sets (*customer, account*) as *primary*. One indicator of a secondary set is that it has no outgoing arrows in the class diagram, and only has incoming arrows. This is the case for the sets *NAME, ADDRESS* and indeed $\mathbb{Z}$ in Fig. 17. However this is not a hard-and-fast rule: the *building* set of Fig. 13 has no out-going arrows but we still treat it as a primary set since the requirements explicitly stated that a set of registered buildings should be maintained. In the simple bank there is no requirement to maintain a set of registered addresses and names independent of the customer to which they belong. Neither is there a requirement to maintain a set of balance values independent of the accounts to which they belong.

Construction of the class diagram of Fig. 17 allows to identify the set and relation variables. The primary sets *customer* and *account* become variable sets while the relations *name, address, cust_acc* and *balance* become relation variables:

machine   *Bank*
sees   *BankContext*
variables   *customer, account, name, address, cust_acc, balance*
invariants
    inv1: $customer \subseteq CUSTOMER$
    inv2: $account \subseteq ACCOUNT$
    inv3: $name \in customer \rightarrow NAME$
    inv4: $address \in customer \rightarrow ADDRESS$
    inv5: $cust\_acc \in customer \leftrightarrow account$
    inv6: $balance \in account \rightarrow \mathbb{Z}$

An advantage of having the variable set *customer* in the model is that it allows us to specify that the functions *name* and *address* have exactly the same domain. All of the above invariants are derived directly from Fig. 17 (which in turn was derived from the requirements via the other two class diagrams).

We study the requirements again to check if there are any further invariants we could identify. The only requirement from which we can identify a further invariant is **FUN6** which states that account balances are never negative (a rather conservative requirement for a bank!). We can represent this requirement by strengthening *inv6* to specify that the range of *balance* is the set of naturals rather than integers (naturals are written $\mathbb{N}$ and represent all the non-negative integers, i.e., those $n \in \mathbb{Z}$ where $n \geq 0$):

invariants
    ...
    inv6b: $balance \in account \rightarrow \mathbb{N}$

An alternative formulation of *FUN5* is to specify that the balance of each account is non-negative using universal quantification:

invariants
    ...
    inv6: $balance \in account \rightarrow \mathbb{Z}$
    inv7: $\forall a \cdot a \in account \Rightarrow balance(a) \geq 0$

In *inv7* we restrict the quantification to those a in the set *account*. Since *balance* is total on the set *account*, the expression *balance(a)* is guaranteed to be well-defined.

We are not yet done with identifying invariants. Although we might not be able to identify this explicitly from the requirements, we need to be careful about the domain and range of the *cust_acc* relation. Invariant *inv5* specifies that the domain of *cust_acc* is a subset of *customer* but does not specify that the domain is equal to *customer*. This means we may have customers who have no accounts associated with them. Similarly *inv5* allows for register accounts that have no customers associated with them. The requirements are not clear on this and we now have the opportunity to be more precise.

We decide that we may have a customer who has no accounts, e.g., this might arise when we register a customer before we create any accounts for them. Thus

$dom(cust\_acc)$ does not need to equal *customer* and can be a subset. However, we decide that it is not ok to have an account that has no customers associated with it. We introduce a further invariant to specify that every account is associated with some customer:

invariants
      ...
      inv8: $ran(cust\_acc) = account$

The combination of *inv5* and *inv8* means that each customer has *zero* or more accounts, while each account has *one* or more customers.

10.2 Expansion Events

We introduced a distinction between primary and secondary sets and we identified that *customer* and *account* as the primary sets in Fig. 17. It is for the primary sets that we introduce expansion events (events that expand some set of elements). The *customer* set is expanded by the event for registering a new customer:

$RegisterCustomer \ \hat{=}$
    any c, n, a **where**
        grd1: $c \notin customer$
        grd2: $n \in NAME$
        grd3: $a \in ADDRESS$
    then
        act1: $customer := customer \cup \{c\}$
        act2: $name := name \cup \{c \mapsto n\}$
        act3: $address := address \cup \{c \mapsto a\}$
    end

Similar to registration of new users in the building access example, the new customer c is represented by a 'fresh' value (*grd1*). Since we are expanding *customer* (*act1*), and since *name* and *address* are total functions on *customer*, we also need to expand *name* and *address* (*act2* and *act3*). The values for the name and address of the new customer are provided as parameters n and a.

The following rule shows how extending a total function maintains functionality. It shows that the extended function ($f \cup \{x \mapsto y\}$) is total on an expanded domain ($S \cup \{x\}$).

Description	Rule
Total function extension	$f \in S \rightarrow T \ \wedge$ $x \notin S \ \wedge \ y \in T$ $\Rightarrow \ (f \cup \{x \mapsto y\}) \in (S \cup \{x\}) \rightarrow T$

Our *RegisterCustomer* event does not associate any accounts to the new customer. This does not violate any invariants since we concluded that a customer may have zero or more accounts. Since we also concluded that an account must have at least one associated customer (*inv8*), we need to associate at least one customer with a newly created account. We chose to associate a set of customers with a newly created account and this set will need to be non-empty. Since *balance* is total on *account*, we also need to associate a balance value with the newly created account; we will set the balance to be zero. We specify the event as follows:

$CreateAccount \; \hat{=}$
   any a, cs **where**
      grd1: $a \notin account$
      grd2: $cs \subseteq customer$
      grd3: $cs \neq \varnothing$
   then
      act1: $account := account \cup \{a\}$
      act2: $cust\_acc := cust\_acc \cup (cs \times \{a\})$
      act3: $balance := balance \cup \{a \mapsto 0\}$
   end

A note on the naming of these events: we used 'register' to name expansion event for customers (*RegisterCustomer*) while we used 'create' for accounts (*CreateAccount*). The reason is that values in *customer* correspond to entities that are external to the bank while accounts are entities that are internal to the bank. To use our previously-introduced terminology, *customer* is a monitoring variable while *account* is a conceptual variable. Of course naming is matter of taste and judgement. Our distinction between registration and creation is simply a guideline.

The above expansion events contribute to addressing the requirements for 'managing' the set of accounts (**FUN1**) and the set of accounts (**FUN4**). Both these requirements also suggest reduction events for the primary sets, e.g., *DeRegisterCustomer* and *DeleteAccount*. **FUN4** also suggests events for expanding and reducing the set of customers associated with an account, e.g., *AddAccountCustomer* and *RemoveAccountCustomer*. We leave the specification of these to the reader. As before, care must be taken to ensure that all the invariants are preserved by these reduction events.

10.3   Function Override

Requirement **FUN2** suggests events for modifying the address of a customer and possibly even the name of a customer. **FUN7** suggests events for increasing and decreasing the balance of an account and for transferring funds between accounts. Specification of all of these involve modifying a function so that the range value that some domain element is mapped to is updated, e.g., to withdraw money from account a, the *balance* function gets updated so that the value associated with a is changed to a smaller value. To represent function update mathematically we use the *function override* operator.

We illustrate the use of this operator with an example first. Assume that the *balance* function has the following value:

$$balance = \{a1 \mapsto 100, \ a2 \mapsto 350, \ a3 \mapsto 800, \ a4 \mapsto 50\}$$

If we want to change the balance of account $a2$ to 300, we use function override ($\Leftarrow$) with *balance* as the first argument and a mapping from $a2$ to 300 as the second argument, written $balance \Leftarrow \{a2 \mapsto 300\}$. The following equation shows the result of this overriding:

$$balance \Leftarrow \{a2 \mapsto 300\} = \{a1 \mapsto 100, \ a2 \mapsto \underline{300}, \ a3 \mapsto 800, \ a4 \mapsto 50\}$$

As highlighted in the resulting function on the right-hand side, 350 has been replaced by 300. Function override is a combination of domain subtraction and set union, i.e., $f \Leftarrow \{a \mapsto b\}$ is the same as removing the existing mapping for a from f using domain subtraction and adding the updated mapping using union:

$$f \Leftarrow \{a \mapsto b\} = (\{a\} \lhd\!\!\!- f) \cup \{a \mapsto b\}$$

More generally, the second argument for function override is itself a function, $f \Leftarrow g$, rather than just a singleton mapping $f \Leftarrow \{a \mapsto b\}$. The general definition also uses domain subtraction and set union as shown in the following table:

Name	Expression	Definition
Function override	$f \Leftarrow g$	$(dom(g) \lhd\!\!\!- f) \cup g$

The specification of the event for depositing money in an account, *Increase-Balance*, uses function override to update the value of balance:

$IncreaseBalance \ \widehat{=}$
    any a, m **where**
       grd1: $a \in account$
       grd2: $m > 0$
    then
       act1: $balance := balance \Leftarrow \{a \mapsto balance(a) + m\}$
    end

Here m is the amount to be deposited in account a. We require m to be greater than zero since adding zero would seem rather pointless ($grd2$). In $act1$ the balance of account a is updated to the value $balance(a) + m$.

It is worth noting the difference between extending a function using union and updating a function using function override. Function extension is used when adding a new value to the domain, e.g., expanding the domain of *balance* when creating an account. Function override is used when modifying the range value associated with an existing domain element, e.g., modifying the *balance* of an existing account when depositing money.

The following rules about function override support mathematical reasoning. The first rule shows the conditions under which a function override $(f \nleftarrow \{x \mapsto y\})$ remains a total function. The second rule shows that the result of applying a function override $(f \nleftarrow \{x \mapsto y\})$ to domain value w depends on whether w is the same as or different to x:

Description	Rule
Total *function* *update*	$f \in S \to T \ \wedge$ $x \in S \ \wedge \ y \in T$ $\Rightarrow \ (f \nleftarrow \{x \mapsto y\}) \ \in \ S \to T$
Apply *function* *update*	$f \in S \to T \wedge w \in S \ \Rightarrow$ $w = x \ \Rightarrow \ (f \nleftarrow \{x \mapsto y\})(w) = y$ $w \neq x \ \Rightarrow \ (f \nleftarrow \{x \mapsto y\})(w) = f(w)$

The shape of action *act1* in *IncreaseBalance* is a common one when updating functions at a single domain point, i.e., it has the form $f := f \nleftarrow \{x \mapsto E\}$. Because update of a function at a single point is a common action in Event-B, it may be written in a simple syntactic form $f(x) := E$. This syntactic form is defined by the following table:

Name	Action	Definition
Function single assignment	$f(x) := E$	$f := f \nleftarrow \{x \mapsto E\}$

Using this form, the *IncreaseBalance* event is specified as follows:

$IncreaseBalance \ \hat{=}$
    any a, m **where**
        grd1: $a \in account$
        grd2: $m > 0$
    then
        act1: $balance(a) := balance(a) + m$
    end

The *DecreaseBalance* event is specified in a similar way with the balance being decreased:

$DecreaseBalance \ \hat{=}$
  any a, m **where**
    grd1: $a \in account$
    grd2: $m > 0$
    grd3: $m \leq balance(a)$
  then
    act1: $balance(a) := balance(a) - m$
  end

With this event, the amount to be withdrawn should not exceed the current balance of the account ($grd3$). This is to ensure that the balance does not go negative ($inv7$). Let us reason about this more precisely. Recall that $inv7$ is a quantification over accounts as follows:

$$\text{inv7:} \quad \forall a \cdot a \in account \Rightarrow balance(a) \geq 0$$

Action $act1$ of $DecreaseBalance$ is equivalent to assigning an overridden function to $balance$ and so gives rise to the following modified invariant:

$$\forall a' \cdot a' \in account \ \Rightarrow \ \underline{(balance \mathbin{\lhd\mkern-9mu-} \{a \mapsto balance(a) - m\})(a')} \geq 0 \qquad (7)$$

Note that here we have renamed the quantified variable a to a'. This is to avoid a name clash with the event parameter a. The *Apply Function Update* rule shown above suggests that we reason about (7) by considering two cases: $a = a'$ and $a \neq a'$.

In the case that $a = a'$, (7) is simplified by the *Apply Function Update* rule to the following:

$$\forall a' \cdot a' \in account \wedge a' = a \ \Rightarrow \ balance(a) - m \geq 0 \qquad (8)$$

This is equivalent to $balance(a) \geq m$ which follows from $grd3$ of $DecreaseBalance$.

In the case that $a \neq a'$, (7) is simplified to the following:

$$\forall a' \cdot a' \in account \wedge a' \neq a \ \Rightarrow \ balance(a') \geq 0 \qquad (9)$$

This follows from $inv7$.

Requirement **FUN7** requires an event for transferring money from one account, a, to another account, b. This is specified as follows, and as with the $DecreaseBalance$ event, requires that the amount to be transferred does not exceed the balance of the source account a:

$TransferBalance \ \hat{=}$
    any a, b, m **where**
        grd1: $a \in account$
        grd2: $b \in account$
        grd3: $a \neq b$
        grd4: $m > 0$
        grd5: $m \leq balance(a)$
    then
        act1: $balance := balance \Leftdomres \{\ a \mapsto balance(a) - m,$
                           $b \mapsto balance(b) + m\ \}$
    end

Note that $grd3$ requires that the source and target accounts are distinct (to avoid pointless transfers). The action $act1$ uses function override to update the two account balances simultaneously. We might be tempted to write the actions of $TransferBalance$ as two single updates as follows:

    act1: $balance(a) := balance(a) - m$
    act2: $balance(b) := balance(b) + m$

This is syntactically invalid in Event-B as it involves two actions assigning to the same variable in a single event and so we avoid this form.

    We can introduce event parameters representing values local to the event to increase the readability of the specification of $TransferBalance$:

$TransferBalance \ \hat{=}$
    any a, b, m, na, nb **where**
        grd1: $a \in account$
        grd2: $b \in account$
        grd3: $a \neq b$
        grd4: $m > 0$
        grd5: $m \leq balance(a)$
        grd6: $na = balance(a) - m$
        grd7: $nb = balance(b) + m$
    then
        act1: $balance := balance \Leftdomres \{\ a \mapsto na,\ b \mapsto nb\ \}$
    end

Here na and nb represent the new balances of a and b respectively whose values are defined by $grd6$ and $grd7$.

    Events to update the name or address of a customer can also be specified using function override. We leave these to the reader. The requirements do not explicitly mention queries on the bank data such as the balance of an account or the customers associated with an account. We leave these for the reader to specify.

11   Model Validation Through Animation

A very useful validation technique for Event-B models is to use an animation tool such as ProB [4] or AnimB[2]. With these tools, the carrier sets are instantiated with some illustrative values, e.g., the carrier set *USER* is instantiated with the values *u1*, *u2*, *u3*, and the model can be executed with these values. The execution is driven by the modeller and at each step the state can be inspected. For the purposes of animating our access control model, let us assume that the carrier set *USER* is instantiated with the values $u1, u2, u3$ and that *BUILD-ING* is instantiated with the values $b1, b2, b3$. Figure 18 represents the state that is reached by executing the following sequence of events on our model of the building access control system:

$$initialisation$$
$$RegisterBuilding(b1)$$
$$RegisterBuilding(b2)$$
$$RegisterUser(u1)$$
$$AddPermission(u1, b1)$$
$$EnterBuilding(u1, b1)$$

Figure 18 shows the values of the sets *user* and *building* and the relations *permission* and *location* as tables. The *user* and *building* tables show that there is one registered user and two registered buildings. The *permission* table shows that $u1$ has permission to enter $b1$ while the *location* table shows that $u1$ is located in building $b1$. These values for the variables are what we would expect to see after execution of the given sequence of events. Figure 18 also shows the events that are enabled in the reached state. We see that two more users $(u2, u3)$ and one more building $(b3)$ can be registered. At the bottom of the list of enabled events we see that user $u1$ may leave building $b1$. We can see that the *EnterBuilding* event is not in the list of enabled events. This is as expected since the only

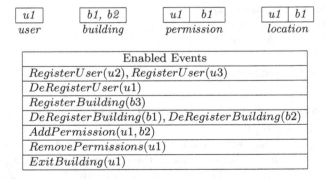

Enabled Events
$RegisterUser(u2), RegisterUser(u3)$
$DeRegisterUser(u1)$
$RegisterBuilding(b3)$
$DeRegisterBuilding(b1), DeRegisterBuilding(b2)$
$AddPermission(u1, b2)$
$RemovePermissions(u1)$
$ExitBuilding(u1)$

Fig. 18. Result of animating model through first sequence of events

---

registered user, $u1$, is currently in building $b1$ and there is no means to directly enter one building from another.

The value of the animation is that it helps us make human judgements about whether the behaviour specified by the model is what we would expect given the informal requirements. In this case we can make a judgement that the values of the tables correspond to what we would expect after the given sequence of event executions is performed. Inspecting the enabled events allows to check that the guards of the events are sufficiently strong, e.g., the fact that *EnterBuilding* is not in the list of enabled events in Fig. 18 helps us to validate the guards specified for that event.

The event sequence above registers two buildings and one user. Here is a second event sequence that continues from the first, adding a second user $u2$, giving that user permissions, entering $u2$ in building $b2$ and exiting user $u1$:

$$RegisterUser(u2)$$
$$AddPermission(u2, b1)$$
$$AddPermission(u2, b2)$$
$$EnterBuilding(u2, b2)$$
$$ExitBuilding(u1)$$

The state resulting from continuing from the state of Fig. 18 is shown in Fig. 19. In this figure, $u2$ has been added to *user*, two rows have been added to *permission* and the *location* table has been updated. We see that an animation tool allows us to execute sequences of events on sample data values and inspect the effect of these on a representation of the state of a machine and on the enabledness of events.

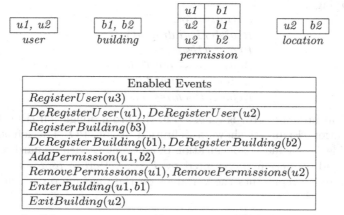

Fig. 19. Result of animating model through second sequence of events

12   Model Verification

Manual inspection of the tables in Figs. 18 and 19 shows that they both represent states satisfying invariants $inv1$ to $inv5$. However, rather than using manual inspection to check for satisfaction of invariants, model verification can be used to do this in a systematic and automated way. Model verification involves making mathematical judgements about the model. The main mathematical judgement we apply to the abstract model is to determine whether the invariants are guaranteed to be maintained by the events. Mathematical judgements are formulated as *proof obligations* (PO). These are mathematical theorems whose proof we attempt to discharge using a deductive proof system. In the Rodin toolset [5] for Event-B, mechanical proof of POs may be complemented by the use of the ProB model checker which searches for invariant violations by exploring the reachable states of a model.

Previously we argued that the *RemovePermissions1* event could violate the permission inclusion invariant ($inv5$). Let us see how this plays out in animation of the model. Consider the state of the access control system shown in Fig. 19. As already explained, this state is reachable by executing a particular sequence of events. In this state, $u2$ is in building $b2$ and has permission to be there. Now if the next event to be performed was $RemovePermissions1(u2)$, the state reached would be as shown in Fig. 20. This new state is an *incorrect* state, that is, it violates the permission inclusion invariant since user $u2$ is still in building $b2$ even though $u2$ not longer has permission to be there. Indeed, ProB can automatically find a sequence of events that lead to an invariant violation (known as a *counterexample*). The counterexample that leads to the state in Fig. 20 is not the shortest possible counterexample. ProB can automatically find a shorter counterexample that leads to violation of the permission inclusion invariant such as the following:

$$initialisation$$
$$Register Building(b1)$$
$$Register User(u1)$$
$$AddPermission(u1, b1)$$
$$EnterBuilding(u1, b1)$$
$$RemovePermissions1(u1)$$

We look at how the error is reflected in the proof obligation (PO) for invariant preservation. Figure 21 shows a definition of this PO. The left side of the figure provides a schematic specification of an event E with a guard represented by $G(p, v)$ and an action represented by $F(p, v)$. Here p represents the event parameters and v represents the variables on the machine on which the event

$u1, u2$	$b1, b2$	$u1$	$b1$	$u2$	$b2$
user	building	permission		location	

Fig. 20. Incorrect state reached when *RemovePermissions1(u2)* is applied to state in Fig. 19

operates. We write $G(p, v)$ to indicate that p and v are free variables of the predicate G. Assuming that $I(v)$ represents a invariant of the machine, the right hand side of Fig. 21 shows the PO used to prove that the invariant is maintained by event E. The PO is in the form of a list of hypotheses and a goal. The PO is discharged by proving that the goal is true assuming that the hypotheses are true. In this case, the hypotheses are the invariant itself (Hyp1) and the guard of the event (Hyp2). The goal is the invariant with the free occurrences of variable v replaced by $F(p, v)$, the value assigned to to v by the action of the event.

$E \;\;\widehat{=}$
   any p **where**
       @*grd* $G(p, v)$
   then
       @*act* $v := F(p, v)$
   end

Invariant Preservation PO:

Hyp1 : $I(v)$

Hyp2 : $G(p, v)$

Goal : $I(\, F(p, v)\,)$

Fig. 21. Invariant preservation proof obligation for an event

The Rodin tool for Event-B generates the invariant preservation POs for all of the events of the access control model and the automated provers of Rodin are able to discharge all of the generated POs except for one: the specification of the *RemovePermissions1* event together with invariant *inv5* give rise to the following PO that cannot be proved:

Hyp1 : *location* $\subseteq$ *permission*

Hyp2 : $u \in$ *user*

Goal : *location* $\subseteq$ $\underline{\{u\} \lhd permission}$

Here, Hyp1 is the invariant to be preserved and Hyp2 is the guard of the event. The event makes an assignment to the *permission* variable and thus the goal is formed by substituting *permission* by $\{u\} \lhd permission$. The result of the substitution is underlined in the goal. The problem here is that the right-hand side of the set inequality in the goal, $\{u\} \lhd permission$, is reduced compared with that in the hypothesis, Hyp1, while the left-had side, *location*, remains unchanged (as discussed in Sect. 8.4).

To address this problem with the *RemovePermissions1* event, we provided two alternative specifications of permission removal. For example, the specification of the *RemovePermissions3* event together with *inv5* gives rise to the following PO that can be proved beause of the additional hypothesis provided by the additional guard:

$$\text{Hyp1} : \quad location \subseteq permission$$
$$\text{Hyp2a} : \quad u \in user$$
$$\text{Hyp2b} : \quad u \notin dom(location)$$
$$\text{Goal} : \quad location \subseteq \{u\} \lhd permission$$

The counterexample generated by the ProB model checker highlighted a problem with the specification of the *RemovePermissions1* event. This stronger condition for removing permission was identified through our attempt to prove that the original specification of the event maintained the permission inclusion invariant, leading to *RemovePermission3*. It is appropriate that we make a (human) judgement about the validity of this stronger specification of removing authorisation. Is it a reasonable constraint? Well, if we expect the access control policy to hold always, we have no choice: without the stronger guard, the event cannot maintain the permission inclusion invariant. We could remove the invariant completely from the model but that seems like an unsatisfactory solution since it would mean we were not addressing the main purpose of access control in our formalisation and would undermine what we can reasonably state in our requirements. For the purposes of this paper, we make the judgement that the invariant should stay and thus the revised version of the event, *RemovePermission3*, with the stronger guards holds.

13   Further Reading

Refinement is a key concept in Event-B and is used for structuring complex specifications and for relating abstract models with more concrete, implementation-oriented models. We have not covered refinement in this paper because of space limitations. For a comprehensive introduction to modelling, refinement and proof in Event-B see Abrial's book on the topic [1]. For an overview of the role and practice of refinement in Event-B see [6]. Event-B evolved from the B Method which was also developed by Abrial [7]. The B Method was developed to model and reason about software systems and has module structuring mechanisms similar to modular programming languages. Event-B was designed to reason about systems that may include hardware and physical components as well as software. Some component-based structuring mechanisms for Event-B are described in [8].

In Sect. 4.6 we saw that the choice of value for a parameter is treated as nondeterministic: any value that satisfies the guards may be chosen. In Event-B, it is also possible to specify nondeterministic actions of the following form [1]:

$$v := v' \mid P(v, v')$$

Here $P(v, v')$ is a predicate that describes a relation between the before and after values of variable v. The nondeterministic action states that v should be assigned a new value v' such that $P(v, v')$ holds. For example, assuming that x is an integer variable, then the following action increases x by a nondeterministic amount:

$$x := x' \mid x < x'$$

Nondeterministic actions have a *feasibility* proof obligation which requires that there exists some value v' satisfying $P(v, v')$ when the invariant and event guards hold [1]. In this paper, we only made use of deterministic actions and used the choice of parameter values to represent nondeterminism within an event. Our reason for using this style is that it allows the nondeterministically chosen value to be available across all of the actions of an event. For example, in the *RegisterUser2* event in Sect. 4.5, the parameter u is used in both actions so that the same nondeterministically chosen value for u is added to *register* and to *out*.

The mathematical language of Event-B (logic and set theory) is similar to the mathematical language of the B Method. These in turn were influenced by the Z notation [9] and VDM [10]. The use of class diagrams to aid the construction of Event-B models, as used in this paper, was inspired by the UML-B notation which provides a graphical syntax for parts of Event-B [11].

For more information on the Rodin tool see [5]. The Rodin tool can be downloaded via the Event-B.org[3] website which also contains a Rodin User Manual[4]. The Atelier B tool[5] supports the B Method. For details of the ProB tool see [4] and the ProB website[6]. ProB is available as a plug-in for Rodin as is the AnimB tool[7].

14   Concluding

This paper provided an overview of how the Event-B language and verification method can be used to model and reason about system behaviour. Reasoning about the system is not just about proving invariant properties. Several different forms of reasoning were deployed in addition to mathematical reasoning: identification of the main purpose of a system, abstraction from design details in requirements, identification of the various entities in the system and their relationships – all of these are forms of reasoning. Constructing the formal model based on the requirements is another form of reasoning as is validation of the model against the requirements through human judgement. All these forms of reasoning complement each other in helping us to understand the purpose of a system and the constraints on the system.

Event-B encourages us to identify the main entities of the problem under consideration and the relationships between those entities. It also encourages us to identify what properties should always hold (invariants), under what conditions system transitions are allowed (guards) and the effect of those transitions on

---

[3]   www.event-b.org.

[4]   www3.hhu.de/stups/handbook/rodin/current/html/index.html.

[5]   www.atelierb.eu/en/outil-atelier-b/.

[6]   www3.hhu.de/stups/prob/index.php/The_ProB_Animator_and_Model_Checker.

[7]   www.animb.org.

the system state (actions). We have seen how the mathematical structures chosen can encourage us to identify different kinds of events such as set expansion events, set reduction events and query events.

This paper emphasised mathematical reasoning as this is a particular strength of a specification language such as Event-B. The paper presented definitions and rules in order to help the reader gain a strong understanding of the mathematical operators and their properties. Understanding the properties of the mathematical operators helps ensure that we are choosing the appropriate operators in order to specify an intended effect. It allows us to check that the mathematics is being used in an appropriate way, both from a validation point of view (is the specification meeting the requirements?) and a correctness point of view (is the specification maintaining invariants?).

Many of the invariants used in this paper were in the form of equations $(E = F)$ and inclusions $(E \subseteq F)$. Typically the actions of an event modify one or both sides of an equation or inclusion. We used two main ways of preserving the equations and inclusions: either adding sufficient actions to ensure both sides of an equation or inclusion are modified in similar ways or using guards and properties of the operators to verify that modifying only one side still preserves the equation or inclusion.

We quoted Boehm's First Law in the introduction. Let us quote Boehm's Second Law [2] in the conclusion:

Boehm's Second Law: *Prototyping significantly reduces requirements and design errors, especially for user errors.*

We would argue that a formal model in a language such as Event-B acts as a form of early prototype allowing us to uncover and fix errors in requirements. Of course, while formal modelling addresses the key concepts in the problem being solved by a software system, it does not deal with the important issue of user interfaces (which can cause the user errors referred to in Boehm's Second Law); a software prototype remains an important tool in uncovering requirements on user interfaces. Formal modelling and reasoning help to uncover conceptual errors in requirements while software prototypes help uncover user interface errors.

We conclude by summarising some key messages:

- The role of problem abstraction and formal modelling is to increase understanding of a problem leading to good quality requirements and design documents with low error rates.
- The role of model validation is to ensure that formal models adequately represent the intended behaviour of a system.
- The role of model verification is to improve the quality of models through formulation of invariants and reasoning about those invariants, including rectifying specifications where appropriate.

References

1. Abrial, J.R.: Modeling in Event-B: System and Software Engineering. Cambridge University Press, Cambridge (2010)
2. Boehm, B.W.: Software Engineering Economics, 1st edn. Prentice Hall PTR, Upper Saddle River (1981)
3. Feiler, P., Goodenough, J., Gurfinkel, A., Weinstock, C., Wrage, L.: Four pillars for improving the quality of safety-critical software-reliant systems. Technical report, Software Engineering Institute, Carnegie-Mellon University (2013). https://resources.sei.cmu.edu/asset_files/WhitePaper/2013_019_001_47803.pdf
4. Leuschel, M., Butler, M.: ProB: an automated analysis toolset for the B Method. Int. J. Softw. Tools Technol. Trans. 10(2), 185–203 (2008). http://eprints.soton.ac.uk/262886/
5. Abrial, J.R., Butler, M., Hallerstede, S., Hoang, T., Mehta, F., Voisin, L.: Rodin: an open toolset for modelling and reasoning in Event-B. STTT 12(6), 447–466 (2010). http://dx.doi.org/10.1007/s10009-010-0145-y
6. Butler, M.: Mastering system analysis and design through abstraction and refinement. In: Engineering Dependable Software Systems. IOS Press (2013). http://eprints.soton.ac.uk/349769/
7. Abrial, J.R.: Modeling in Event-B: System and Software Engineering. Cambridge University Press, Cambridge (1996)
8. Silva, R., Pascal, C., Hoang, T., Butler, M.: Decomposition tool for Event-B. Softw. Pract. Exp. 41(2), 199–208 (2011). http://www.eprints.soton.ac.uk/271714/
9. Woodcock, J., Davies, J.: Using Z - Specification, Refinement, and Proof. Prentice-Hall, Upper Saddle River (1996). http://www.usingz.com
10. Jones, C.: Systematic Software Development using VDM. Prentice Hall, Upper Saddle River (1990)
11. Snook, C., Butler, M.: UML-B: formal modelling and design aided by UML. ACM Trans. Softw. Eng. Methodol. 15(1), 92–122 (2006). http://eprints.soton.ac.uk/260169/

Java in the Safety-Critical Domain

Ana Cavalcanti$^{(\boxtimes)}$, Alvaro Miyazawa, Andy Wellings, Jim Woodcock,
and Shuai Zhao

Department of Computer Science, University of York, York, UK
`Ana.Cavalcanti@york.ac.uk`

Abstract. Safety-Critical Java (SCJ) is an Open Group standard that
defines a novel version of Java suitable for programming systems with
various levels of criticality. SCJ enables real-time programming and certification of safety-critical applications. This tutorial presents SCJ and
an associated verification technique to prove correctness of programs
based on refinement. For modelling, we use the *Circus* family of notations,
which combine Z, CSP, Timed CSP, and object orientation. The technique caters for the specification of functional and timing requirements,
and establishes the correctness of designs based on architectures that
use the structure of missions and event handlers of SCJ. It also considers
the integrated refinement of value-based specifications into class-based
designs using SCJ scoped memory areas. As an example, we use an SCJ
implementation of a widely used leadership-election protocol.

1 Introduction

Java needs no introductions: it has a wide base of programmers, an impressive
collection of libraries, and continues to evolve with the backing of a very large
number of companies. However, it lacks effective support for real-time application
development, in particular it has poor facilities for real-time scheduling and
unpredictable memory management. This has led to the creation of the Real-
Time Specification for Java (RTSJ) [47], which augments the Java platform
to provide a real-time virtual machine and support preemptive priority-based
scheduling and a complementary region-based memory management mechanism.

Java augmented by the RTSJ provides a comprehensive set of facilities suitable for a wide range of real-time applications. Safety-critical applications, however, require the use of a controlled engineering approach, to ensure reliability,
robustness, maintainability, and traceability. Many of them also require certification based on standards before they can be deployed. For these reasons, it is
common to reduce complexity (and with it flexibility) via the adoption of language subsets. Examples are SPARK Ada [3] and MISRA C [37]. In this context,
RTSJ is far too rich: it includes the whole of Java, and more.

SCJ has been designed under the Java Community Process: JSR 302. It
defines a minimal set of capabilities required for safety-critical applications
using Java implementations. As a result of this effort, we have an SCJ specification, a reference implementation, and a technology compatibility kit, which
contains benchmark examples used to confirm that a particular implementation

© Springer International Publishing AG 2017
J.P. Bowen et al. (Eds.): SETSS 2016, LNCS 10215, pp. 110–150, 2017.
DOI: 10.1007/978-3-319-56841-6_4

is compatible with the SCJ specification. The goal is to support certification under, for example, the DO-178 [42]. Nothing is said, however, about design techniques.

As opposed to the RTSJ, SCJ enforces a constrained execution model based on missions, event handlers, and memory areas [46]. SCJ restricts the RTSJ. It prohibits use of the heap and defines a policy for the use of memory areas, which are cleared at specific points of the program flow to avoid the unpredictable garbage collection of the heap. The SCJ design is organised in Levels (0, 1, and 2), with a decreasing amount of restrictions to the execution model.

In this tutorial, we give a detailed description of SCJ and its programming and memory models. For illustration, we use a Level 1 implementation of a leadership-election protocol, which is widely used for coordination of distributed systems. SCJ Level 1 corresponds roughly to the Ravenscar profile for Ada [6].

We also present here a technique for verification by refinement of SCJ Level 1 programs [12]. It uses the *Circus* family of notations [10], which combine constructs from Z [49] for data modelling, CSP [40] for behavioural specification, and standard imperative commands from Morgan's refinement calculus [34]. We cover *Circus Time* [45], with facilities for time modelling from Timed CSP [39], and *OhCircus* [11], based on the Java model of object-orientation. This tutorial gives an overview of *Circus* and its constructs relevant for modelling SCJ designs.

Our technique is based on the stepwise development of SCJ programs based on specification models that do not consider the details of either the SCJ mission or memory models. Development proceeds by model transformation justified by the application of algebraic laws that guarantee that the transformed model is a refinement of the original model. Before, presenting the SCJ refinement technique, we give an overview of algebraic refinement.

The verification technique is a refinement strategy: a procedure for application of algebraic refinement laws. Four *Circus* specifications characterise the major development steps: we call them anchors, as they identify the (intermediate) targets for model transformation and the design aspects treated in each step of development. Each anchor is written using a different combination of the *Circus* family of notations. The first anchor is the abstract specification written in *Circus Time*. The last is written in *SCJ-Circus*; it is so close to an SCJ program as to enable automatic code generation. This tutorial describes this technique using the verification of the leadership-election protocol as an example.

Next, we present the notations used in our work, namely, SCJ, in Sect. 2, and *Circus*, in Sect. 3. Algebraic refinement is the subject of Sect. 4. Finally, Sect. 5 presents our refinement strategy. We draw some conclusions, where we identify open problems on refinement for SCJ, in Sect. 6.

2   Safety-Critical Java

This section provides an introduction to the Safety-Critical Java programming model and gives an example of a simple program that can control several robots. The robots are shown in Fig. 1 and they perform a coordinated dance. One of them is elected the leader robot and initiates the dance routine. The others are

Fig. 1. Dancing robots

followers and perform the actions indicated by the leader. During the dance, robots can fail and, if necessary, a new leader can be elected. An identical SCJ program runs on each robot. We present the overall architecture of the application and then focus on the details of the election algorithm.

An SCJ program is executed under the auspices of an SCJ virtual machine, which provides core Java services and an infrastructure to manage the life-cycle of safety-critical applications. The core services are those typically provided by a standard Java virtual machine and include support for bytecode execution and memory management. The infrastructure is provided in a Java extension library named `javax.safetycritical`. It supports the main programming abstractions defined by SCJ and requires specialised support from the core services, not found in standard Java virtual machines. Typically, an SCJ virtual machine is hosted on a high-integrity operating system (such as Green Hills Integrity real-time operating system), as illustrated in Fig. 2.

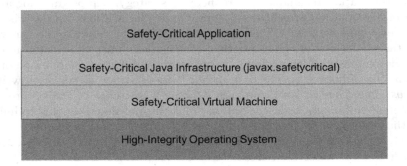

Fig. 2. Safety-critical Java: VM and infrastructure (Color figure online)

In order to understand the SCJ programming model, there are three main topic areas that must be mastered:

1. applications, missions and mission sequencers;
2. concurrency and scheduling; and
3. memory management.

These topics are covered in the next three sections. Throughout, we use the robot leadership-election application as an illustrative example.

2.1 Applications, Missions and Mission Sequencers

An SCJ program is started by invoking the SCJ virtual machine with a parameter that identifies the application's main program. This is called a *safelet* in SCJ, as it is analogous to an applet in which Java code executes in a constrained web-browser environment. The SCJ infrastructure defines the interface to a safelet, and the application must provide a class that implements this interface.

The application itself consists of the execution of a sequence of *missions,* where a mission represents an application's activity that must be completed. For example, a program that controls the flight of an aircraft might have three main missions: one that manages the take-off activity, one that maintains the flight at its cruising altitude, and one that oversees the landing procedures.

In our robot application, there are two missions. During the first mission a leader is elected. Once the election is completed, the robots perform their dance mission. If a failure occurs, the robots return to the election mission.

As illustrated in Fig. 3, each mission has three phases of operation:

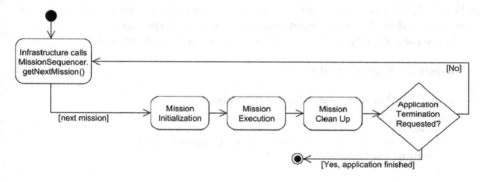

Fig. 3. Safety-critical application phases [29]

1. Initialization – during which the resources needed to complete the mission are acquired and initialised. In our robot application, the initialisation of the election mission acquires access to a wireless network and establishes links with the other robots.
2. Execution – during which the activity of the mission is performed: it starts after the initialization phase has been completed. In our robot application, the execution phase of the election mission implements a communication protocol to elect a new leader robot.
3. Cleanup – starts after completion of the execution phase, and is responsible for returning any resources and performing any other needed finalization

code. In our robot application, all resources are returned automatically to the operating system when the program terminates. Hence, there is no explicit application cleanup code.

The order of execution of missions is controlled by an application-defined *mission sequencer* as also illustrated in Fig. 3.

Hence, the `Safelet` interface contains the following two methods:

```
1   package javax.safetycritical;
2
3   public interface Safelet<M extends Mission<M>> {
4     public void initializeApplication();
5     public MissionSequencer<M> getSequencer();
6     ...
7   }
```

The `initializeApplication` method is called by the SCJ infrastructure after the SCJ virtual machine has been initialised. Following this, it calls the `getSequencer` method to obtain the application mission sequencer that will oversee the sequence of execution of the missions.

As mentioned in the previous section, SCJ has three compliance levels. The SCJ uses Java generics to ensure that a mission sequencer and its missions have been designed for the same compliance level and are type safe.

The structure of the code for the robots example is shown below:

```
1    import javax.safetycritical.*;
2
3    class RobotApp implements Safelet<RobotMission> {
4
5        @Override
6        public MissionSequencer<RobotMission> getSequencer() {
7            return new RobotSequencer(...);
8        }
9
10       @Override
11       public void initializeApplication() {
12           ...
13       }
14   }
```

All missions that are scheduled by an application must have a common super-class. In the robots example, this is called `RobotMission` and appears as the generic parameter at line 2. The `getSequencer` method at line 5 now can only return a mission sequencer that schedules missions of type `RobotMission`.

For this tutorial, we ignore a mission sequencer's parameters and just consider one of its main methods: `getNextMission` on line 10 below. This method is called by the infrastructure to select the initial mission to execute, and subsequently, each time a mission terminates, in order to determine the next mission to execute.

```
1    package javax.safetycritical;
2
3    public abstract class MissionSequencer<M extends Mission<M>>
4            extends ManagedEventHandler {
5
6    /** Construct a MissionSequencer object to oversee
7     * a sequence of mission executions
8     */
9    public MissionSequencer(...) {
10       ...
11   }
12
13   protected abstract M getNextMission() {
14       ...
15   }
16   ...
17 }
```

A mission sequencer is an *asynchronous event handler* (ASEH): it executes in its own thread of control. This is considered in depth in Sect. 2.2.

The structure of the robot mission sequencer can now be given:

```
1    import javax.safetycritical.*;
2
3    class RobotSequencer extends MissionSequencer<RobotMission> {
4
5        private Mission mission;
6        private boolean electing = true;
7
8        public RobotSequencer(...) {
9            super(...); . . .
10       }
11
12       @Override
13       public Mission getNextMission() {
14           if (electing) {
15               return new ElectionMission();
16           } else {
17               return new DanceMission();
18           }
19       }
20
21   }
```

The boolean variable `electing` on line 4 indicates whether a new leader needs to be elected. If it has value true, then the method `getNextMission` in line 12 returns a mission to perform this task: an instance of `ElectionMission`.

The `Mission` class encapsulates the direct infrastructure support for an SCJ mission; its main methods are shown below. The application extends this class and overrides its `initialize` and `cleanUp` methods.

```
1   package javax.safetycritical;
2   public abstract class Mission<M extends Mission<M>> {
3     public Mission() {}
4
5     protected abstract void initialize();
6     protected boolean cleanUp() {...}
7
8     /* Request that this mission be terminated */
9     public final boolean requestTermination() {...}
10
11    /* Is there an outstanding termination request for this mission */
12    public final boolean terminationPending() {...}
13
14    /* Obtain the controlling sequencer */
15    public MissionSequencer<M> getSequencer() {...}
16
17    /* Obtain the current mission.*/
18    public static <M extends Mission<M>> M getMission() {...}
19  }
```

A typical implementation of `initialize` instantiates and registers all the ASEHs that constitute the `Mission`. Besides, `initialize` may also instantiate and initialise mission-level data structures. The infrastructure ensures that ASEHs can only be instantiated and registered during the `initialize` method. The infrastructure also arranges to begin executing the registered ASEHs associated with a particular `Mission` upon return from its `initialize` method.

The `cleanUp` method is called by the infrastructure after all asynchronous event handlers registered with the mission have terminated.

The `requestTermination` method is called by the application to initiate mission termination. When it is called, the infrastructure invokes the method `signalTermination` (see Sect. 2.2) on each ASEH registered in the mission. Additionally, the infrastructure (1) disables all periodic event handlers (PEHs) associated with this `Mission`, so that they experience no further releases; (2) disables all aperiodic event handlers (APEHs), so that no further releases are honoured; (3) clears the pending event (if any) for each event handler (including any one-shot event handlers), so that the event handler can be effectively shut down following completion of any event handling that is currently active; (4) waits for all of the ASEH objects associated with this mission to terminate their execution; (5) invokes the `cleanUp` methods for each of the ASEHs associated with this mission; and (6) invokes the `cleanUp` method associated with this mission.

In our robot example, the `Election` and `Dance` missions have a common superclass: the `RobotMission` class sketched below. Irrespective of the mission's main functionality, it must manage communication between the robots across the wireless network. The common initialization code, therefore, creates and registers two ASEHs. On line 4 below, the `Receiver` class is a PEH. Its goal is to receive communication from the robots.

```
1   public abstract class RobotMission extends Mission<RobotMission> {
2       ...
3       protected void initialize() {
4           Receiver receiver = new Receiver(...);
5           receiver.register();
6
7           Sender sender = new Sender(...);
8           sender.register();
9       }
10  }
```

Similarly on line 7, the `Sender` class is also a PEH. Its goal is to broadcast communication to the other robots. Both of the robot's missions extend this class; for instance, the election mission is given below.

```
1   class ElectionMission extends RobotMission {
2       @Override
3       protected void initialize() {
4           super();
5           Elector elector = new Elector(...);
6           elector.register();
7       }
8       ...
9   }
```

`ElectionMission` creates and registers an additional PEH. Its goal is to use the state of each robot to determine whether it should be a leader or a follower.

2.2 Concurrency and Scheduling

In general, there are two models for creating concurrent programs. The first is a thread-based model in which each concurrent entity is represented by a thread of control. The second is an event-based model, where an event handler executes in direct response to the firing of its associated event. The RTSJ, upon which SCJ is based, supports a rich concurrency model allowing real-time threads and asynchronous events. The SCJ Level 1 concurrency model simplifies this and relies exclusively on asynchronous event handling.

An ASEH executes in response to invocation requests (known as *release events*); the resulting execution of the associated logic is a *release*. Release requests are categorised as follows: periodic, sporadic, or aperiodic. If R_i denote the time at which an ASEH has had the ith release event occur, then:

1. an ASEH is periodic when there exists a value $T > 0$ such that, for all i, $R_{i+1} - R_i = T$, where T is called the period;
2. an ASEH that is not periodic is said to be aperiodic; and

3. an aperiodic ASEH is said to be sporadic when there is a known value $T > 0$ such that for all i, $R_{i+1} - R_i \geq T$. T is then called the minimum interarrival time (MIT).

PEHs are timed triggered in SCJ, which means that they are indirectly released via the passage of time (using a real-time clock). APEHs and sporadic (SEH) handlers can be both timed triggered or released directly from application code.

SCJ specifies a set of constraints on the RTSJ concurrency model. This constrained model is enforced by defining a new set of classes, all of which are implementable using the concurrency constructs defined by the RTSJ. As an example, the following shows the class for a PEH. This class permits the automatic periodic execution of code. The `handleAsyncEvent` method behaves as if the handler were attached to a periodic timer. This method is executed once for every release. The class is abstract; non-abstract sub-classes must override `handleAsyncEvent` and may override the default `cleanUp` method.

```
1    package javax.safetycritical;
2
3    public abstract class PeriodicEventHandler extends ManagedEventHandler
4    {
5        /* Constructs a periodic event handler.
6         * priority: specifies the priority parameters for this periodic event handler.
7         * release: specifies the periodic release parameters, in particular the
8         * start time, period and deadline miss handler.
9         */
10       public PeriodicEventHandler(PriorityParameters priority,
11                               PeriodicParameters release, ...) {...}
12
13       /* Applications override this method to provide
14          the code to be executed on each release */
15       public void handleAsyncEvent() {...}
16
17       /* Register this handler with its mission */
18       public void register() {...}
19
20       /* Called by the infrastructure during the mission cleanup phase *
21       public void cleanUp() {...}
22
23       /* Called by the infrastructure to indicate that the enclosing mission
24        * has been instructed to terminate. SS*/
25       public void signalTermination() {...}
26   }
```

The SCJ supports communication between ASEHs using shared variables, and so requires support for synchronisation and priority-inversion management protocols. On multiprocessor platforms, it is assumed that all processors can access all shared data and resources, although not necessarily with uniform access times. SCJ requires implementations to support priority-ceiling emulation, a particular protocol that allows the synchronisation to be analysed for its timing properties.

Scheduling in SCJ is performed in the context of a *scheduling allocation domain*. The scheduling allocation domain of an ASEH consists of the set of processors on which that schedulable object may be executed. Each ASEH can be scheduled for execution in only one scheduling allocation domain. At Level 1, multiple allocation domains may be supported, but each domain must consist of a single processor. Hence, from a scheduling perspective, a Level 1 system is a fully partitioned system. Within a scheduling allocation domain, multiple ASEHs are scheduled for execution in priority order using a priority-based scheduler. If ASEHs have the same priority, then they are scheduled in a FIFO order, that is, the order in which they become schedulable.

In the robot example, there are several PEHs in each mission. Two handlers are responsible for robot-to-robot communication in each mission. The other ones focus on the main activity of the mission (electing a leader, detecting a change in leadership, and performing the dance). The full software architecture of the program is illustrated in Fig. 4.

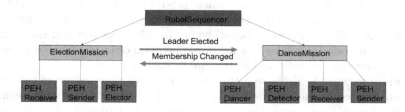

Fig. 4. The architecture of the robots safety-critical application

For small embedded systems, it is often required that we optimise the solution in order to reduce the scheduling overheads. One possibility is to combine the PEHs responsible for communication into one handler. The `Elector` can then be transformed into an APEH which is released on successful receipt of one round of communication. This is illustrated in Fig. 5.

2.3   Memory Management

In standard Java all objects are allocated on a heap. Traditionally, dynamic memory allocation and the resulting heap management (garbage collection) has been vetoed by the authorities who certify safety-critical systems on the grounds

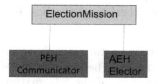

Fig. 5. Optimised architecture of the election mission

that it is too unpredictable. For this reason, the RTSJ introduces the notion of a memory area; this is a chunk of memory from where the memory for object allocation is taken. The Java heap is an example of a memory area.

The RTSJ supports two additional types of memory areas: immortal and scoped memory. Every object allocation is performed with an allocation context. It can change dynamically by a thread of control entering into and exiting from a memory area. The current allocation context at the time an object allocation is requested determines which memory area its space comes from.

Objects created in immortal memory are never collected: once created they exist for the lifetime of the application. Objects in scoped memory areas are automatically freed when no thread of control has an active allocation context for that memory area, that is, it has entered but not exited that memory area.

SCJ constrains the memory model of RTSJ by not allowing the heap memory area. It also distinguishes between scoped memory areas that can be entered by multiple ASEHs (called *mission memory*) and those that are private to an ASEH (called *private memory*). Each mission has a single mission memory. Each ASEH has a single private memory area (called *per-release memory area*), which is entered into automatically when the ASEH is released and exited automatically (and hence has all its objects collected) when the release completes. Each ASEH may also have nested private memories for ephemeral objects. All objects stored in mission memory are collected at the end of each mission.

In addition, all ASEHs have a thread stack where they can store references to objects created in the various memory areas. Figure 6 illustrates the memory hierarchy of an SCJ program. In order to maintain the referential integrity of all objects in SCJ programs, a reference to an object A cannot be assigned in a field of an object B if object A's lifetime is less than object B's lifetime. If allowed, object A could disappear and leave object B with a dangling pointer.

In our robot example, the system state is stored in immortal memory, data that must be communicated between handlers is stored in mission memory, and all other data is stored in private memory areas or on the handlers stack. This is a typical data design for valid and efficient SCJ programs.

2.4   The Election Details

For the election, each robot has the following associated information:

- Id: this uniquely identifies the robot and its IP address;
- Petition: a unique ranking among the robots that indicates how badly the robot wants to be the leader. The robot with the highest petition that is online is elected the leader;
- Status: an indication of whether the robot is the leader, a follower or undecided.

The application maintains in immortal memory an array with this information; it has one position for each robot. The array includes a logical timestamp that indicates the freshness of the state of the information received. The timestamp is incremented by the `Elector` and `Detector` handlers in every period.

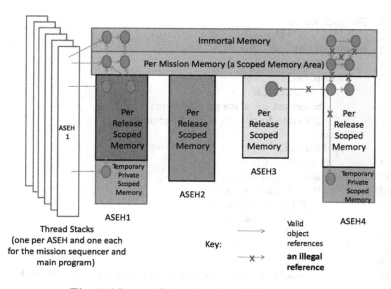

Fig. 6. Memory hierarchy of an SCJ program

The `Sender` PEH broadcasts its robot's state every 500 ms. The `Receiver` PEH receives as many messages as are available every 500 ms. The `Elector` reviews the global state each 3000 ms and decides whether its robot should elect itself as leader or become a follower. When the global state shows that all robots have decided and that there is only one leader, the mission terminates, and the `Dancing` mission is executed. During this mission, the `Detector` continues to monitor the global state every 3000 ms. If the status quo is changed, then the `Dance` mission terminates and a new `Election` mission is executed. The `Dancer` PEH sends and receives dancing commands every 3000 ms depending on whether it is the leader or the follower.

The full code for the leadership-election example that is presented here is at www.cs.york.ac.uk/circus/hijac/code/LeaderElectionPaper.zip. The pseudo code shown Fig. 7 summarises the overall optimized approach.

Essentially there are two parallel activities (the `Communicator` – lines 4–9 and the `Elector` – lines 9–19). The `Communicator` is responsible for periodically sending out a robot's state to its neighbouring robots, and then acquiring their current states. The `Elector` is aperiodic and is released after the `Communicator` has acquired all its neighbours states. It analyses the global state and if a leader has been globally agreed, it requests termination of the current mission. Otherwise, if its petition is the highest among all the robots, then it makes a claim to be the leader, or then it settles for being a follower.

In the next section, we present a formal specification for the robot application. We develop the optimized approach.

```
 1   For each robot:
 2
 3   IN PARALLEL
 4     Communicator:
 5       PERIODIC
 6         IN SEQUENCE
 7           broadcast my state to neighbours
 8           get state from each of my neighbours
 9     Elector:
10       APERIODIC
11         IN SEQUENCE
12           analyse global state
13           IF no leader agreed
14             IF I have highest petition
15               Claim leadership
16             ELSE
17               Claim follower
18           ELSE
19             Request mission termination as leader has been established
```

Fig. 7. Pseudo-code for the optimised leadership-election algorithm

3   Circus

The search for increasing levels of abstraction is a key feature in software engineering, and, particularly, in language design. For example, the concept of class embeds a notion of an abstract data type and allows a structured modelling of real-world entities, capturing both their static and dynamic properties. The notion of process abstracts from low-level control structures, allowing a system architecture to be decomposed into cooperative and active components.

Despite the complementary nature of constructs for describing data and control behaviour, most programming languages focus only on one or the other aspect. Java is no exception: it offers (abstract) classes, interfaces, and packages; in contrast, only the low-level notion of threads is available. There are exceptions like Ada [23], whose design has clearly addressed abstract data and control behaviour (with packages and tasks), but even so there are several limitations; for example, a package is not a first-class value.

The design of specification languages has followed a similar trend, with state-based and property-oriented formalisms concentrating on high-level data constructs [5], and process algebras exploring control mechanisms. A current and active research topic is the integration of notations to achieve the benefits of both abstract data and control behaviour [20,44]. Circus is one of these integrated notations, whose focus is refinement (to code).

In this section, we present a combination of Z [49] and CSP [41], traditional languages for data modelling and a process algebra. Their combination in a language called Circus supports the specification of both data and behavioural aspects of concurrent systems, and a development technique. Such a combination has obvious advantages: Z is good at describing rich information structures using a predicative style (based on invariants, and pre and postconditions), and CSP is good at describing behavioural patterns of communication and synchronisation.

In *Circus*, Z constructs can be combined with executable commands, like assignments, conditionals, and loops. Reactive behaviour, including communication, parallelism, and choice, is defined with the use of CSP constructs.

In this section, we give an overview of *Circus*: we describe the structure of the *Circus* models, and explain how Z and CSP are combined. Beforehand, we say a bit more about Z (Sect. 3.1) and CSP themselves (Sect. 3.2). As an example, we provide a model of the leadership-election protocol (Sect. 3.3).

3.1   Z

A system specification in Z consists basically of a definition for a state and a collection of operations. The state is composed by variables representing information used and recorded in the system. The operations take inputs and produce outputs, and possibly update the state. Both the state and the operations are defined by schemas, which group variable declarations and a predicate.

Example 1. As a very simple example, we consider a system presented in [35] that calculates the mean of a sequence of numbers. The state of this system has only one component: the sequence *seq* of integers input so far.

$$\begin{array}{|l}
\hline
\_Calculator_____ \\
\quad seq : \text{seq}\,\mathbb{Z} \\
\hline
\end{array}$$

The state definition gives it a name, *Calculator*, and declares its component.

This system has three operations. The first, *Init*, initialises the state.

$$\begin{array}{|l}
\hline
\_Init_____ \\
\quad Calculator' \\
\hline
\quad seq' = \langle\rangle \\
\hline
\end{array}$$

The reference to *Calculator* indicates that this is an operation over that state. In an operation definition, we can refer to *seq* and to *seq'*. The former refers to the value of the state component before the operation, and the latter, to the value after the operation. The dash decoration on *Calculator*, however, indicates that *Init*, as an initialisation, can refer to *seq'* only. The predicate of *Init* specifies that, after the initialisation, the value of *seq* is the empty sequence.

The second operation, *Enter*, records an input value in the sequence.

$$\begin{array}{|l}
\hline
\_Enter_____ \\
\quad \Delta Calculator \\
\quad n? : \mathbb{Z} \\
\hline
\quad seq' = seq ^\frown \langle n?\rangle \\
\hline
\end{array}$$

The Δ in front of *Calculator* indicates that *Enter* changes the state. The variable $n?$ represents an input of *Enter*: the number to be inserted. The predicate defines that the new sequence of numbers can be obtained by inserting the input at the end of the existing sequence; $^\frown$ is the concatenation operator.

The last operation, *Mean*, calculates the mean of the numbers input so far.

```
┌─ Mean ─────────────────────────────────────────────────
│ Ξ Calculator
│ m! : ℤ
├────────────────────────────────────────────────────────
│ seq ≠ ⟨⟩
│ m! = (Σ seq) div (# seq)
└────────────────────────────────────────────────────────
```

The Ξ indicates that *Mean* does not change the state. The output is represented by the variable $m!$. The specification requires that the sequence *seq* is non-empty. This is a precondition for this operation: even though *Mean* can be executed when this condition is not satisfied, its result is not predictable in such a situation. If, however, the precondition is satisfied, the specification requires the output to be the sum of the elements in the sequence divided by its size. The Σ operator is not directly available in Z, but can be easily specified. □

3.2   CSP

In CSP, a system and its components are modelled by processes that interact with their environment not via inputs and outputs, like in Z, but via synchronisations that characterise events. These events, however, can model exchange of data, as well as simple interactions of interest. In the description of a CSP process, a first element of interest is the set of events in which it can participate; the definition of an event simply gives it a name.

Example 2. A process that controls a revolving door can be characterised in terms of the events *step-in*, *revolve*, *step-out*, and *stop*; the first denotes the arrival of someone in the area around the door, the second represents the start of the revolving movement, *step-out* is the event that captures the exit of a person from the door area, and, finally, *stop* occurs when the door stops moving.

In the specification of the door, inputs and outputs are not a concern; the relevant issue is the form in which the door interacts with the environment: the people that use the door. Below, we present the definition of processes $Door(i)$, where i is the number of people already using the door.

If there are no people using the door, the only possible event is for someone to arrive; afterwards, the door starts revolving, and proceeds to behave as a door that is being used by one person. In the specification of $Door(0)$, we use the prefix operator $a \rightarrow P$, which gives the unique event a in which the process is prepared to engage, and a process P that characterises its behaviour afterwards.

$$Door(0) = step\text{-}in \rightarrow revolve \rightarrow Door(1)$$

We use prefixing twice: first, the door is prepared to record the event *step-in*, then the only possible event is *revolve*, before the door behaves as $Door(1)$.

If there is one person using the door, then either someone else arrives or that person leaves. We use the choice operator $P \sqcup Q$ to specify this behaviour: this process is prepared to behave as P or Q; the choice is made by the environment.

$$Door(1) = step\text{-}in \rightarrow Door(2) \sqcup step\text{-}out \rightarrow stop \rightarrow Door(0)$$

If the event $step\text{-}in$ takes place, then the door behaves as a door used by two people. If $step\text{-}out$ takes place, the only possible event is $stop$, and then we have the behaviour of $Door(0)$ again. The definitions of $Door(0)$ and $Door(1)$ are mutually recursive; the use of recursion is very common in CSP.

Doors with two or more people are similar; for $n > 1$, $Door(n)$ is below.

$$Door(n) = step\text{-}in \rightarrow Door(n+1) \sqcup step\text{-}out \rightarrow Door(n-1)$$

If someone steps in an door with n people, for n greater than 1, then we have the behaviour of a door with $n+1$ people. If someone steps out, then the behaviour is that of a door with $n-1$ people.

In a big building, we usually have a number of these doors. They work in parallel, but independently. We define a process entrance with m doors as follows.

$Entrance = ||| \, i : 1 \, . \, . \, m \, \bullet$
$\quad Door(0)[step\text{-}in.i, revolve.i, step\text{-}out.i, stop.i / step\text{-}in, revolve, step\text{-}out, stop]$

In this process we have m copies of $Door(0)$ recording events $step\text{-}in.i$, $revolve.i$, $step\text{-}out.i$, $stop.i$, for i between 1 and m. The set of events of $Entrance$ comprise all of the $m \times 4$ events: 4 for each of the m doors. The parallel operator $|||$ is for an interleaving composition, where the parallel processes do not interact with each other. Above we use the iterated form $(||||)$ of this operator.

A polite door contains an additional component: a process that detects that someone has arrived and welcomes this person with a greeting message. This *Polite* process can be specified as follows.

$$Polite = step\text{-}in \rightarrow welcome \rightarrow Polite$$

The extra event $welcome$ signals the play of the greeting. The polite door can be characterised by the parallel execution of the standard $Door(0)$ and *Polite*.

$$PDoor = Door(0) [\![\{step\text{-}in\}]\!] \; Polite$$

In this parallel process $([\![\ldots]\!])$, there is interaction between the two components; they are not independent as in the previous example. Since $step\text{-}in$ is an event of both $Door$ and $Polite$, they synchronise on this event. Every time someone steps in, $Door(0)$ and $Polite$ act jointly; from the point of view of $PDoor$, just one event occurs. $\square$

As already explained, *Circus* includes both Z and CSP constructs. We present *Circus* next via our running example: the leadership-election protocol.

3.3   Leadership Election in *Circus*

A *Circus* model is formed by a sequence of paragraphs that specify types, constants, functions, and, crucially, processes. Like in CSP, processes define systems and their components. Their definitions use the types, constants and functions defined globally, as well Z and CSP constructs.

In our example, we first define two types: *DEVICEID* and *STATUS*.

$$DEVICEID == \mathbb{N}$$
$$STATUS :: = leader \mid follower \mid undecided \mid off$$

These types are sets that contain the valid identifiers for devices, and constants *leader*, *follower*, *undecided*, and *off* that represent the status of a device. For simplicity, we define the identifiers of the devices to be natural numbers. We need to use an ordered set, because the election conditions use the order of the devices to resolve ties. We could make this more abstract by requiring only a set of identifiers with a total order, but it is simpler to use the natural numbers.

We also have some global constants. *UP_LMT* is the maximum value for the petition of a device. *P* is the period of the protocol. *TIMEOUT* is how long a device waits for information from a neighbour before giving up, and marking it as offline. *ID* and *OD* are the input and output deadlines. The set *devices* contains all the identifiers of the devices in the network: a subset of *DEVICEID*.

$$\begin{array}{|l}
UP\_LMT : \mathbb{N} \\
P, TIMEOUT, ID, OD : \mathbb{N} \\
devices : \mathbb{P}\, DEVICEID \\
\hline
TIMEOUT \leq P \wedge ID \leq P \wedge OD \leq P \wedge \# \, devices > 0
\end{array}$$

A constraint ensures that the timeout, input and output deadlines are all less than or equal to the period *P*. Moreover, there must be at least one device.

The process that defines the functional requirements of the protocol is called *ABReqsLE*. It is introduced below.

process *ABReqsLE* $\widehat{=}$ **begin**

In its body, the first few paragraphs define the state space.

The state of a device includes its identifier *id*, *status*, and *petition*.

$$\begin{array}{|l}
\_\,DeviceState \_\! \\
id : DEVICEID \\
status : STATUS \\
petition : \mathbb{N} \\
\hline
id \in devices \\
petition \leq UP\_LMT
\end{array}$$

Constraints on the type ensure that *id* is for a device in the network, and the *petition* is valid, that is, below the limit defined by *UP_LMT*.

To execute the election protocol, a device needs additional information, captured in records of the type *ElectionState*. In addition to the state components in *DeviceState* described above, *ElectionState* records the highest petition of a device claiming to be a leader as well as its identifier: *highest* and *highestid* in the schema, that is, record type, *Highest* below.

$$Highest == [highest : \mathbb{N};\ highestid : DEVICEID]$$

The schema *ElectionState* includes all the components of *DeviceState* and *Highest*. It also records the number *nLeaders* of leaders in the network, the index i of the device currently communicating (lines 7–8 in Fig. 7) in a sequence *nodes* that records information about individual devices, and a function *next* that gives the index (in *nodes*) of the device considered in the next cycle.

ElectionState
DeviceState
Highest
$nLeaders : \mathbb{N}$
$i : \mathbb{N};\ nodes : \text{seq}\, DeviceState;\ next : \mathbb{N} \rightarrow \mathbb{N}^+$

$i \in \text{dom}\, nodes$
$\forall n : \mathbb{N}^+ \bullet next\ n = ((n - 1)\ \text{mod}\ (\#\, nodes)) + 1$
$devices = \{d : \text{ran}\, nodes \bullet d.id\}$
$\#\, nodes = \#\, devices$
$\theta\, DeviceState \in \text{ran}\, nodes$

The invariant states that the index i is an index for *nodes*. Moreover, the function *next* identifies indices of *nodes* in a way that iterates through this sequence, circling back to the beginning at the end.

The set *devices* includes the identifiers in the range of *nodes*. By requiring that the size of this set and the size of *nodes* are equal, we ensure that the range of *nodes* does not include two records for the same device identifier. Finally, the invariant establishes that the current device, identified by a record $\theta\, DeviceState$, containing the fields of *DeviceState* in *ElectionState*, is also in the range of *nodes*.

Unlike CSP processes, a Circus process has a state defined by a schema. It *ElectionState* that defines the state of the process *ABREqsLE* being specified.

state $st == ElectionState$

The next few paragraphs define data operations. Initially, there is no leader, the highest petition is 0 and the index i is that for the device itself.

InitElectionState
ElectionState'

$nLeaders' = 0 \wedge highest' = 0 \wedge (nodes'\ i').id = id$

This means that when all devices are in a network, in the first step of the protocol, they all broadcast their status to the others.

When a status *valC?* and petition *valP?* is received from a device whose identifier is *idDev?*, we can update the fields of *Highest* if the device claims to be a *leader* and the petition *valP?* is higher than previously recorded, or if it is the same and the identifier *idDev?* is greater than the previous identifier.

$$
\begin{array}{l}
\rule[0.5ex]{0.3em}{0.4pt}\ UpdateHighest \underline{\hspace{20em}} \\
\Delta Highest \\
idDev? : ID;\ valC? : STATUS;\ valP? : \mathbb{N} \\
\hline
valC? = leader \\
valP? > highest \lor (valP? = highest \land idDev? > highestid) \\
valP? > highest \Rightarrow highest' = valP? \land highestid' = idDev? \\
valP? = highest \Rightarrow highest' = valP? \land highestid' = idDev?
\end{array}
$$

This operation is partial; it should only be used when an update to *highest* or *highestid* is needed as indicated. This is ensured by its use in *UpdateDevice*, shown below, which also modifies the remaining components of *ElectionState*.

$$
\begin{array}{l}
\rule[0.5ex]{0.3em}{0.4pt}\ UpdateDevice \underline{\hspace{20em}} \\
\Delta ElectionState \\
idDev? : ID;\ valC? : STATUS;\ valP? : \mathbb{N} \\
\hline
\textbf{let } d == (\mu\ x : \operatorname{ran} nodes \mid x.id = idDev? \bullet x)\ \bullet \\
\left(
\begin{array}{l}
d.status = leader \land valC? \neq leader \land nLeaders' = nLeaders - 1 \\
\lor \\
d.status \neq leader \land valC? = leader \land nLeaders' = nLeaders + 1 \\
\lor \\
d.status = leader \land valC? = leader \land nLeaders' = nLeaders \\
\lor \\
d.status \neq leader \land valC? \neq leader \land nLeaders' = nLeaders
\end{array}
\right) \\
nodes' = nodes \oplus \{(nodes^{\sim} d)) \mapsto \\
\qquad \langle\!| id == idDev?, status == valC?, petition == valP? |\!\rangle\} \\
\theta DeviceState = \theta DeviceState' \land next' = next \land i' = i \\
UpdateHighest \lor [\Xi Highest \mid \neg\ (\textbf{pre } UpdateHighest)]
\end{array}
$$

UpdateDevice takes the information *d* on *idDev?* in *nodes* using the definite description operator μ and updates the number of leaders *nLeaders* depending on the previous *d.status* and current value *valC?* of its status. It also overrides ($\oplus$) *nodes* with the newly received information; with $nodes^{\sim} d$, we get the index of *d*. *UpdateDevice* also leaves the components of *DeviceState*, the function *next* and index *i* unchanged, and updates the components of *Highest* using *UpdateHighest*, if necessary, as captured by the precondition **pre** *UpdateHighest* of this operation.

In a *Circus* process, the Z data operations can be combined to define actions. In the definition of actions, we can also use CSP constructs.

The action *BReq1* specifies the communications the protocol. It identifies which device $((nodes\ i).id)$ is to be considered (recorded by *i*). If it is *id* itself, it broadcasts its state using the action *Broacast*.

$BReq1 \mathrel{\widehat{=}}$
  if $(nodes\ i).id = id \longrightarrow Broadcast(id, status, petition)$
  $[\!] (nodes\ i).id \neq id \longrightarrow$
$$\left(\begin{array}{l} receive.(nodes\ i).id?valC?valP \longrightarrow \\ \quad UpdateDevice((nodes\ i).id, valC, valP) \\ \square \\ timeout \longrightarrow UpdateOff((nodes\ i).id) \end{array} \right) ;$$
    if $status = undecided \longrightarrow$
$$\left(\begin{array}{l} \mathbf{if}\ nLeader > 0 \longrightarrow status := follower \\ [\!] nLeader \leq 0 \longrightarrow \\ \left(\begin{array}{l} \mathbf{if}\ id = next\ i \longrightarrow \\ \left(\begin{array}{l} \mathbf{if} \left(\begin{array}{l} (highest = petition \wedge highestid < id)\ \vee \\ highest < petition \end{array} \right) \longrightarrow \\ \quad status := leader \\ [\!]\neg \left(\begin{array}{l} (highest = petition \wedge highestid < id)\ \vee \\ highest < petition \end{array} \right) \longrightarrow \\ \quad status := follower \\ \mathbf{fi} \end{array} \right) \\ [\!] id \neq next\ i \longrightarrow status := undecided \\ \mathbf{fi} \end{array} \right) \\ \mathbf{fi} \end{array} \right)$$
    $[\!] status = leader \longrightarrow$
$$\left(\begin{array}{l} \mathbf{if}\ nLeader > 0 \longrightarrow status := undecided \\ [\!] nLeader \leq 0 \longrightarrow \\ \left(\begin{array}{l} \mathbf{if}\ id = next\ i \longrightarrow \\ \quad petition := min(UP\_LMT, petition + 1)\ ;\ \ status := leader \\ [\!] id \neq next\ i \longrightarrow status := leader \\ \mathbf{fi} \end{array} \right) \\ \mathbf{fi} \end{array} \right)$$
    $[\!] status = follower \longrightarrow$
$$\left(\begin{array}{l} \mathbf{if}\ nLeader = 0 \longrightarrow status := undecided \\ [\!] nLeader \neq 0 \longrightarrow status := follower \\ \mathbf{fi} \end{array} \right)$$
    fi
  fi

If the device under consideration $((nodes\ i))$ is not id itself, the protocol waits for information about the device on the channel $receive$ and updates the state using the operation $UpdateDevice$ shown above, or for a timeout on the channel $timeout$, in which case it udpates the state using the action $UpdateOff$. The CSP operator $\square$ offers an external choice between these actions. The next section gives a concise overview of basic features of the CSP notation. After updating the state with the received information, the device decides its own status based on its previous status (**if** $status = undecided \longrightarrow \ldots$ **fi**). We notice that the operation $UpdateDevice$ does not change the device's own state.

If the device is undecided, its new status depends on the number of leaders. If there are leaders, it becomes a follower (assignment *status := follower*), otherwise, the protocols considers the device *next i*. If it is *id* itself, then it compares its petition to the highest petition and becomes a leader or follower depending on whether or not its petition (or identifier) is greater than the highest petition (or identifier) recorded. If the next device is not *id*, the status remains undecided.

If *id*'s status is *leader*, and there are other leaders (besides itself as *nLeaders* only refer to leaders among the neighbours), then it becomes undecided. Otherwise, it remains a leader and increments its own petition (up to the maximum *UP_LMT*) if it is the next device to be considered. Finally, if *id* is a follower and there are no leaders, it becomes undecided. Otherwise, it stays a follower.

The actions used in *BReq1* above are defined next.

$$Broadcast \cong \textbf{val}\ id : DEVICEID;\ status : STATUS;\ petition : \mathbb{N} \bullet$$
$$||| \ i : devices \setminus \{id\} \bullet send.id.i.status.petition \longrightarrow \textbf{skip}$$

Broadcast sends in interleaving ($|||$) the *status* and *petition* of the device to each of the neighbouring devices using the channel *send*. These are the devices *d* in nodes whose identifier is not *id* itself. The parameters of *send* are the identifiers of the source and target devices, the status and petition values. The protocol assumes an asynchronous bus, so this communication does not deadlock even if the target device is unavailable. Since communications in *Circus* are synchronous, the model requires the definition of the bus (omitted here).

$$UpdateOff \cong \textbf{val}\ idDev : DEVICEID \bullet \textbf{var}\ valC : STATUS;\ valP : \mathbb{N} \bullet$$
$$valC, valP := off, 0\ ;\ UpdateDevice$$

UpdateOff uses the schema operation *UpdateDevice* to update the state of the process. It sets the *status* and *petition* to *off* and 0, before updating the state.

As already said, the process *ABReqsLE* describes the behavioural requirements for the protocol on a single device. Its behaviour is defined below by the main action. It initialises the state using the schema operation *InitElectionState* and starts a recursive action ($\mu X \bullet ...X$), which at each step executes the action *BReq1* and updates the index *i* using the function *next*.

$$\bullet InitElectionState\ ;\ (\mu X \bullet BReq1\ ;\ i := next\ i\ ;\ X)$$
end

The timing requirements are specified in a separate process *ATReqsLE* shown below. Its main behaviour is also defined by a recursion, but at each iteration it offers a choice between receiving information on *receive*, indicating a timeout using the channel *timeout*, or sending information to all neighbours in interleaving through the channel *send*. The particular values communicated through these channels are irrelevant here; they are defined in *ABReqsLE* specified above. Here, on the other hand, the time in which these events occur is important.

Communications on *send* and *receive* must start within *OD* and *ID* time units as defined by the deadline operator ◄. *OD* and *ID* are global constants previously defined. All communications lead to an action that potentially lets time pass until the end of a period P. The *Circus* statement **wait** $0 . . (P - t)$ is a nondeterministic choice of a delay of 0 up to $P - t$ time units. In the example, t is the time between the communication being offered and actually taking place. In each case, that is recorded via the @ operator, like in *timeout@t*.

> **process** $ATReqsLE \cong$ **begin**
> $TReq1 \cong (TReqCycle \blacktriangleright P \;|||\; \textbf{wait}\; P)\; ;\; TReq1$
> $TReqCycle \cong$
> $(|||\; i : 1 . . \# devices - 1 \bullet (send?x?y?z?w@t \longrightarrow \textbf{wait}\, 0 . . (P - t)) \blacktriangleleft OD)$
> $\square$
> $(receive?x?y?z?w@t \longrightarrow \textbf{wait}\, 0 . . (P - t)) \blacktriangleleft ID$
> $\square$
> $(timeout@t \longrightarrow \textbf{wait}\, 0 . . (P - t)) \blacktriangleleft P$
> $\bullet\, TReq1$
> **end**

Finally, the overall specification is given by the process *LeaderElection*.

> **process** $LeaderElection \cong$
> $(ABReqsLE [\![\{\!|\, send, receive, timeout \,|\!\}]\!] ATReqsLE) \setminus \{\!|\, timeout \,|\!\}$

It is the parallel composition $([\![. . .]\!])$ of the behavioural and timing processes, synchronising on the external channels *send* and *receive*, and on *timeout*, which is hidden $(\setminus)$ and, therefore, internal to *LeaderElection*. We note that parallelism is used not to define a parallel architecture for a design, but to define a conjunction of requirements: the behavioural requirements of *ABReqsLE* and the timing requirements of *ATReqsLE*. Synchronisation ensures that the communications transmit values as defined in *ABReqsLE* within the times defined by *ATReqsLE*.

In Sect. 5, we explain how we can refine this abstract specification of the leadership-election protocol to obtain a model of an SCJ program. Beforehand, in the next section, we say more about refinement and the *Circus* approach.

4 Algebraic Refinement

Circus distinguishes itself in that it is aimed at the (calculational) refinement of specifications. Besides Z and CSP, *Circus* also includes specification constructs usually found in refinement calculi [2,34,36] and Dijkstra's language of guarded commands [16], a simple imperative language with nondeterminism. The extra constructs that we use here are familiar: assignments, conditionals, and so on.

As a refinement language, *Circus* is a unified programming language, in which we can write specifications (in a combination of Z, Morgan's specification statements, and CSP), designs (using choice and concurrency constructs of CSP, for instance), and programs, and can relate all these kinds of artefacts to each other via refinement. Data refinement, failures-divergences refinement, and refinement to code (as a special case of data refinement) can all be carried out using *Circus*.

The notion of refinement captures the essence of the daily tasks of software engineers, who design systems based on their specifications, and programmers, who implement these designs. In both cases, the main objective is the construction of systems and programs in accordance with their specifications. The final product, above all, should be, or has to be, correct.

Refinement is the relationship that holds between a specification and its correct designs and implementations. Formal methods of program development are based on this notion, as are all other methods in some way. A formal technique, however, goes further since refinement of an initial specification to obtain an acceptable implementation is the primary aim. Acceptability may be judged, for instance, in terms of performance, but the guarantee provided is that the specification and the implementation are related by refinement.

In this section, at first we present the classical notions of refinement. Initially, refinement was extensively studied in the context of sequential programs [4, 26, 27], where the concern is the relation between inputs and outputs. It was identified that there are basically two ways of refining a specification. The first is the introduction and transformation of programming and control structures, like assignments, conditions, and loops. This is called algorithmic refinement.

The second form of refinement is related to the data structures used in the program. Systems may be specified in terms of data types that are appropriate to describe properties of the application domain, without, for example, any considerations related to efficiency. During design, however, ingenious decisions usually involve the introduction of data structures that are available in the programming language and make the computation tasks easier or faster. The change of data representation involved in this task is called data refinement [21, 24, 25].

For an object-oriented language like Java, there are new concerns related to the presence of classes and their use as data types [28]. Refining a class is very much like refining a data structure in a traditional imperative setting. Nevertheless, due to the presence of, for instance, type tests, type casts, and dynamic binding, new techniques are needed. Type tests and casts may be used to distinguish objects of different classes. Even if we have two classes with the same fields and methods, but different names, type tests (and casts) can be used to distinguish objects of these classes. Dynamic binding means that a method call may lead to the execution of several different pieces of code. To ensure correctness, we need to consider all possibilities. Pointers are also a challenge.

For concurrent reactive systems like those that we can specify in *Circus* and program in SCJ, the main concern is their interactions with other systems and the environment [40]. Like we have discussed in the previous section, functionality is not characterised by a relation between inputs and outputs, but by the ways in which communications and synchronisations can take place; inputs and outputs are particular forms of communications. Termination is not a strong requirement as systems that run indefinitely, but continuously interact with their environments in a useful way, are very much of interest. Refinement, in this context, has to consider the behaviour of the systems in each of their interactions.

Refinement of imperative programs, including data and algorithmic refinement is the subject of Sect. 4.1; there we use Z as a concrete notation. Refinement of concurrent reactive systems is addressed in Sect. 4.2.

4.1 Basic Concepts

A formal specification is the starting point of any formal development method. Correctness is a relative notion: a program is correct or wrong depending on whether it implements its specification or not; the specification is the basis for the evaluation. To guarantee correctness, we need a formal specification.

Specifying a system is the first step to get its implementation right. A formal development method takes such a specification as a basis to produce a correct implementation: one that refines the specification.

Refinement is based on the idea that a specification is a contract between the client and the developer. The client cannot complain if, when executed in situations that satisfy their preconditions, the operations of the implementation produce outputs that satisfy the properties stated in the specification. In this case we have a correct implementation.

Data Refinement. Our first opportunity for refinement typically comes in the change of representation of state components. As said before, a Z specification describes the relation between inputs and outputs when the system is initialised and a sequence of operations is executed. The values of the state components, however, are not visible. Similarly, in *Circus*, the state of a process, which is defined in Z, is not visible. We can only observe the behaviour of a process via its interactions with its environment, which use the channels that are in scope.

In Example 1, for instance, we use a sequence to record the numbers input; this is a natural way of describing the system. It is less space-consuming, however, to record just the sum and the number of integers input. If the operations are updated accordingly, it is perfectly valid to change the representation of the state in this way. This sort of change is known as data refinement; the original specification is regarded as abstract and the new specification, as concrete.

The other opportunity for refinement is the development of implementations for the operations; this is the subject of the next section, where we discuss algorithmic refinement. Since these implementations are affected by changes in the state, we consider data refinement first. At this stage, we change the operations only to adapt them to the new data types. In Z, we write the concrete specification in the same style as that used for the abstract specification.

Example 3. The concrete state suggested above can be defined as follows.

```
┌─ CalculatorC ──────────────────────────────
│  size, sum : ℤ
│
└─────────────────────────────────────────────
```

There are two components: the *size* of the sequence input and its *sum*.

The new definition for the operations is as follows. The initialisation, *InitC*, records that no numbers have been input.

```
┌─ InitC ──────────────────────────────────────────────
│ CalculatorC′
├──────────────────────────────────────────────────────
│ size′ = 0 ∧ sum′ = 0
└──────────────────────────────────────────────────────
```

The operation *EnterC*, which inputs a number, increments *size* and updates *sum* by adding the input to it.

```
┌─ EnterC ─────────────────────────────────────────────
│ ΔCalculatorC′
│ n? : ℤ
├──────────────────────────────────────────────────────
│ size′ = size + 1 ∧ sum′ = sum + n?
└──────────────────────────────────────────────────────
```

The operation that calculates the mean has a much simpler specification.

```
┌─ MeanC ──────────────────────────────────────────────
│ ΞCalculatorC′
│ m! : ℤ
├──────────────────────────────────────────────────────
│ size ≠ 0
│ m! = sum div size
└──────────────────────────────────────────────────────
```

The needed values are readily available in *sum* and *size*. □

After providing the concrete specification, we have to prove that it satisfies the refinement property mentioned above: clients that agreed on the abstract specification cannot complain if they get an implementation of the concrete specification [17,38,49]. The most widely used technique to carry out such a proof is known as simulation. It involves the definition of a relation between the abstract and concrete states that specifies how the information in the abstract state is represented in the concrete state. In the context of Z, this relation is known as a retrieve relation and is specified using a schema.

There are, actually, two simulation techniques that can be applied: forwards (or downwards) simulation and backwards (or upwards) simulation. Here, we concentrate on the forwards simulation technique, as it is often enough in practice. Upwards simulation is a similar technique. (The difference lies in the way it handles nondeterminism in data operations.)

For our example, the appropriate retrieve relation can be specified as follows.

```
┌─ Retrieve ───────────────────────────────────────────
│ Calculator
│ CalculatorC
├──────────────────────────────────────────────────────
│ size = #seq ∧ sum = Σseq
└──────────────────────────────────────────────────────
```

The inclusion of the abstract and of the concrete state definitions *Calculator* and *CalculatorC* reflects the fact that we are specifying a relation between them.

Basically, a concrete state is related to an abstract state when the value of *size* is indeed the size of *seq* and *sum* is the sum of the numbers in this sequence.

Given the retrieve relation, we need to check first that the initialisation is adequate: given an initial concrete state, there is a corresponding abstract initial state. In general, if A and C are the schemas that specify the abstract and concrete states, AI and CI are the corresponding initialisation operations, and R is the retrieve relation, then we have to prove the following.

$$\forall\, C' \bullet CI \Rightarrow \exists\, A' \bullet AI \wedge R' \qquad \text{(initialisation)}$$

The use of schemas in predicates is common in Z. We are required to prove that, for all values that the components of the concrete state may assume, if these values are those of an initial state, then there are initial values that can be assigned to the abstract state components that are related to those of the concrete initial state. The use of C', A', and R' is necessary because the predicates of CI and AI are written in terms of the dashed version of the state components.

For our data refinement, we are required to prove the following property.

$$\forall\, size', sum' : \mathbb{Z} \bullet size' = 0 \wedge sum' = 0 \Rightarrow$$
$$\exists\, seq' : \text{seq}\mathbb{Z} \bullet seq' = \langle\rangle \wedge size' = \# seq' \wedge sum' = \Sigma\, seq'$$

With two applications of a one-point rule we get $0 = \#\langle\rangle \wedge 0 = \Sigma\langle\rangle$, which is true as the size of and the sum of the elements of the empty sequence are 0. This reflects the fact that the initialisation of *CalculatorC* chooses values to *size* and *sum* that are in accordance with the initial value of *seq*. This is, of course, relative to the way in which we represent *seq* using *size* and *sum*.

We also need to prove that each of the operations CO of the concrete specification is in accordance with the specification of the corresponding operation AO of the abstract specification. We have to prove the following, where **pre** AO and **pre** CO refer to the precondition of the operations.

$$\forall\, A;\ C \bullet \textbf{pre}\, AO \wedge R \Rightarrow \textbf{pre}\, CO \qquad \text{(applicability)}$$
$$\forall\, A;\ C \bullet \textbf{pre}\, AO \wedge R \Rightarrow (\forall\, C' \bullet CO \Rightarrow \exists\, A' \bullet AO \wedge R') \qquad \text{(correctness)}$$

When refining an operation, there are usually two separate concerns: its precondition and its effect, also known as postcondition. The precondition of an operation characterises the situations in which it behaves properly. The first proof obligation above, applicability, requires that, whenever the precondition of the abstract operation holds, the related concrete states satisfy the precondition of the concrete operation. So, this proof obligation requires that whenever the abstract operation behaves properly, so does the concrete operation.

In our example, the preconditions of *Enter* and *EnterC* are both true, therefore applicability is not interesting. For *Mean*, the precondition is $seq \neq \langle\rangle$. For *MeanC*, the precondition is $size \neq 0$. Applicability is as follows.

$$\forall\, seq : \text{seq}\mathbb{Z};\ size, sum : \mathbb{Z} \bullet$$
$$seq \neq \langle\rangle \wedge size = \# seq \wedge sum = \Sigma\, seq \Rightarrow size \neq 0$$

This is also a simple proof-obligation: if *seq* is not empty, and *size* is its length, then *size* is certainly different from 0.

The second proof-obligation, correctness, is related to the effect of the operations. First of all, we are only interested in the situations in which the precondition of the abstract operation holds; if it does not, then there are no requirements on the concrete operation. If it does, for all states resulting from the execution of the concrete operation in a related state, exists a related abstract state that could be obtained with the execution of the abstract operation.

For *Mean* and *MeanC*, correctness is as follows.

$$\forall\ Calculator;\ \ CalculatorC\ \bullet\ seq \neq \langle\rangle \wedge Retrieve \Rightarrow$$
$$(\forall\ CalculatorC'\ \bullet\ MeanC \Rightarrow \exists\ Calculator'\ \bullet\ Mean \wedge Retrieve')$$

Three applications of the one-point rule (and basic predicate calculus properties) reduces this predicate to true.

A special case of simulation that involves simpler proof obligations is that in which the retrieve relation is a total function from the concrete to the abstract state. Most proof-obligations generated in a refinement, however, are long, but simple, and a lot of help is provided by tools [31]. Data refinement can also be applied to variable blocks and to modules. As long as we have a structure for information hiding, this kind of change of representation is always possible.

Algorithmic Refinement. Once we have decided on the data types to be used in the program, we can proceed to work on the implementation of the operations. There are basically two approaches to refinement in general: verification and calculation. For data refinement, we have proposed a new specification and then proved that it is satisfactory: we verified the proposed refinement to be correct.

For algorithmic refinement, we can use a calculational approach [2,34,36]. In such techniques, the initial specification is the starting point for a sequence of transformations, each captured by a refinement law, to gradually transform the specification into a program. Because refinement is a transitive relation, this establishes that the initial specification is refined by the final program.

Each law captures a model transformation, which is the essence of the very popular model-based approach to design and programming. Distinctively, however, laws of refinement, guarantee that the transformations that they specify preserve the behaviour of the original program. For Z, such a refinement calculus has been presented in [7,9,13], and it is called ZRC. Its laws can also be used to transform Z operations defined in a *Circus* process.

The language of ZRC, as of all refinement calculi, can be used to write specifications, designs, which involve programming and specification constructs, and programs. Besides Z, this language includes assignments, conditionals, iterations, and procedures, among other constructs, like in *Circus*. In a design, we may have, for instance, a loop whose body is a schema. Specifications, designs, and programs are all regarded as programs; refinement is a relation between programs in this more general sense. The refinement relation is usually denoted by $\sqsubseteq$.

For a calculation, the differentiated roles of preconditions and postconditions are very relevant. Since schemas do not distinguish them, it can be convenient to transform a schema into a so called specification statement. This is a construct that takes the form $w : [pre, post]$, where w is a list of variables, and pre and $post$ are predicates: the precondition and the postcondition. The list of variables is the frame, which determines the variables that can be changed.

For instance, $EnterC$ can be specified by the specification statement $size, sum : [true, size' = size + 1 \wedge sum' = sum + n?]$, where the state components are explicitly listed as part of the frame. Similarly, $MeanC$ can be specified as $m! : [size \neq 0, m! = sum \ div \ size]$. A refinement law in [13] explains how the conversion can take place. That work also includes laws that refine elaborate schema expressions to more refined programs; we have, for instance, a law to translate schema disjunctions into conditionals.

Refinement laws can be applied to transform a specification statement into a design or program; they embody common intuition about programming. We present $assigI$, a law that transforms a specification statement to an assignment.

Law $assigI$ Assignment introduction
$$w, v : [pre, post] \sqsubseteq v := e \ \textbf{provided} \ \ pre \Rightarrow post[e/v'][\_/']$$

Since the assignment $v := e$ potentially modifies the variable v, it must be in the frame of the specification statement. The proviso ensures that, when the precondition of the specification statement holds, its postcondition is satisfied if v' assumes the value e established by $v := e$. To put it more simply, it certifies that this assignment really implements the specification statement. The predicate $post[e/v'][\_/']$ is that obtained by substituting the expression e for v' and removing the dashes from the free variables of $post$.

With an application of $assigI$, we can transform the second specification statement presented above to $m! := sum \ div \ size$. The proviso generates the proof-obligation $size \neq 0 \Rightarrow sum \ div \ size = sum \ div \ size$, which follows by reflexivity of equality. The precondition is ignored; if it does not hold, the result of the assignment is not predictable. This is in accordance with the specification.

More interesting developments give rise to a sequence of law applications. Substantial examples can be found later on in Sect. 5. To give a flavour of the approach, we consider the law below, which splits a specification statement into another specification statement and an assignment.

Law $fassigI$ Following assignment introduction
$$w, v : [pre, post] \sqsubseteq w, v : [pre, post[e'/v']] \ ; \ v := e$$

This law introduces an assignment, which does not implement the specification statement by itself. We are still left with a specification before the assignment, which has the same precondition as the original one, but a modified postcondition. A substitution of e, with its free variables dashed, for v' records the fact that the assignment that follows makes the value of v to become e. With the substitution, the original postcondition is required to be established when v takes value e. This should be an easier task as illustrated next.

To refine $size, sum : [true, size' = size + 1 \wedge sum' = sum + n?]$, we can apply *fassigI* to introduce the assignment to sum. We are left with the program below.

$size, sum : [true, size' = size + 1 \wedge sum' + n? = sum + n?];$
$sum := sum + n?$

Since, the assignment already updates the sum, the new postcondition actually requires only that its value is not changed: $sum' + n? = sum + n?$ is equivalent to $sum' = sum$. This is an easier task. With an application of law *assigI* we can refine the remaining specification statement to $size := size + 1$.

Due to space restrictions, we cannot discuss ZRC or refinement calculi in more detail. Many interesting issues are involved in the development of code from specification using these techniques. An important point is that the sequence of laws applied defines the structure of the obtained program. In the simple examples above, we have just an assignment, or a sequence whose last component is an assignment. Conversely, if we have a program of a particular structure in mind, to a large extent, that defines the sequence of laws that need to be applied. So, we can use the calculational approach also to verify an existing program, by reconstructing the sequence of laws that can be used to generate it.

The refinement strategy presented in the next section can be applied in this spirit, to verify an existing SCJ program. As we discuss there, the constrained architecture of an SCJ program determines to some extent a particular sequence of *Circus* refinement laws that are useful to establish refinement. It is, therefore, possible to define a procedure (or strategy) to apply such laws.

We note, however, that the applications of the laws require additional information. For instance, if our target program has a sequence of statements ending in an assignment, we may decide to use the Law *fassigI* above to derive it. We, however, still need to define the particular variable that is to be assigned last, and the expression that is to be assigned to it. Specifically, in the application of *fassigI*, we need to define v and e; these are parameters of this law. If the target program is known in advance, it determines the right arguments for v and e. In this case, the application of the refinement law is fully determined.

Before presenting the refinement strategy for SCJ, we discuss refinement of processes, considering both CSP and *Circus* processes as examples.

4.2   Process Refinement

Further challenges are present when we consider the development of concurrent programs: processes that interact with each other and an external environment. When developing a process, we are not only interested in the inputs and outputs, but also in each of the interactions in which the process may engage. As previously explained, inputs and outputs are forms of interaction in this context.

Specification, design, and implementation of processes has been carefully studied in the context of CSP [22,40]. Like the languages of the refinement calculi discussed in Sect. 4.1, this is a unified language with an associated notion of refinement that can support the development of programs.

Refinement is based on the possible interactions of the processes. Basically, the interactions of the implementation process have to be interactions that could be performed by the specification process. For our example, we observe that it is not realistic to assume that an arbitrary number of people can use a door at the same time. A possible implementation of $Door(0)$ can be obtained if we consider that there is a limit max to this number of people and define $Door(max)$ as follows, where we assume $max > 2$.

$$Door(max) = step\text{-}out \rightarrow Door(max - 1)$$

When the maximum number of people is reached, the door is not prepared to accept the arrival of any further people. The only event enabled is *step-out*.

We observe that the number of people using a door is part of the state of *Door* and is not visible to the environment. In *Circus* and CSP, each process encapsulates its state information; interaction between the processes is achieved through events. Refinement, as said above, is concerned with these events.

On the other hand, since the state is hidden, we can consider data refinement. In the case of *Circus*, since the state and its data operations are defined using Z, the simulation technique adopted in Z can be used to data refine *Circus* processes. In CSP, the state is defined by parameters and the data model uses a functional language, so we have a simpler set up. For instance, we could use the negative integers to represent the number of people using a door, as shown below.

$$DoorN(0) = step\text{-}in \rightarrow revolve \rightarrow DoorN(-1)$$
$$DoorN(-1) = step\text{-}in \rightarrow DoorN(-2) \square step\text{-}out \rightarrow stop \rightarrow DoorN(0)$$
$$DoorN(-n) = step\text{-}in \rightarrow DoorN(-n - 1)$$
$$\square$$
$$step\text{-}out \rightarrow stop \rightarrow DoorN(-n + 1) \qquad \text{if} - n < -1$$

The processes $Door(0)$ and $DoorN(0)$ are equivalent. This sort of refinement, however, has not been the interest of the CSP community as the data language of CSP is very simple. The main concern is really interaction.

A further concern involved in the refinement of concurrent processes is related to the events in which a process may refuse to engage, and to the sequence of events that may lead to a divergent process. For instance, the specification of the door is a process that does not refuse the arrival of people in any circumstance; the implementation, on the other hand, may refuse this event if the door is full. From this point of view, it is not really a proper implementation.

Due to space restrictions, we do not discuss this any further. We note, however, that refinement in CSP and *Circus* ensures that safety and liveness properties are preserved. Safety requires that the sequences of interactions (traces) of the program are possible for the specification. Liveness requires that deadlock or divergence in the program can occur only if allowed in the specification.

Finally, we note that we use *Circus Time* in our work for SCJ. Refinement in *Circus Time* also ensures preservation of time properties. This requires that the deadlines and budgets defined in the specification are enforced by the deadlines and budgets defined for the components of the program.

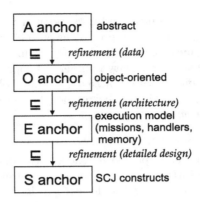

Fig. 8. Our approach to development and verification

5   Refining from *Circus* to SCJ

In this section, we describe the steps of our refinement approach.

In our strategy, refinement is carried out in three main steps, each characterised by an anchor: a *Circus* model written in a particular subset of *Circus* and following a particular pattern. Besides defining a target for a model transformation, an anchor captures a significant aspect of an SCJ program development: abstract specification, object-oriented design, missions, and SCJ infrastructure. Figure 8 shows the four Anchors: A, O, E, and S. The objective is to guarantee that the anchors are related by refinement.

The first refinement step produces the O anchor, and tackles the object-oriented data model of the program. The second step introduces the E anchor, and tackles the correctness of the mission and handler decomposition and of the use of memory areas. Finally, the third step, produces the S anchor, and tackles the correctness of the algorithms implemented. It also describes the sequence of missions and parallelism of handlers in the E anchor in terms of SCJ constructs.

Each of these refinement steps is divided into phases, which tackle individual aspects of the design of the target anchor. Typically, a refinement phase is realised in a series of stages, captured by the application of refinement laws. For some phases, specific refinement laws are always applicable. In other cases, there is a choice of laws depending on the design of the target anchor.

For the leadership-election protocol, for example, the *Circus* model described in Sect. 3 is the A anchor. Below, Sects. 5.1 to 5.3 describe the phases of each of the three refinement steps, and their stages.

5.1   Anchor O: Concrete State with Objects

The first step of our refinement strategy is a data refinement: it introduces concrete data to represent the abstract data types of the A anchor, and the shared data. The target is an O anchor, which introduces the use of classes and objects. The object-oriented constructs employed are those of *OhCircus*, which basically includes the possibility to define types via classes. The design of *OhCircus* is inspired by the Java approach to inheritance.

Due to the nature of data refinement (in *Circus*), the structure of the O anchor, in terms of processes and actions, is the same as that of the corresponding A anchor. As explained in Sect. 4, data refinement only replaces or adds state components to the model. The types of the concrete components may be specified by *OhCircus* classes, but creation and allocation of objects are not considered yet. The structure of the actions is not changed.

Although in a data refinement particular algorithms are not considered, it is unrealistic to assume that the developer makes no consideration of how the concrete data types proposed can be efficiently used to realise the functionality of the program. In the case of our strategy, in this step we do not consider explicitly the structure of missions and handlers of the target program. On the other hand, it is only to be expected that a developer is aware of the need to provide the program functionality via missions and handlers, and of the sharing of data that might be required between them.

Figure 9 describes our proposed strategy for this step. We take inspiration from Morgan's auxiliary variables technique [33] to facilitate the specification of the concrete components. So, in the first two phases of this step, CS and SD, we introduce components of the concrete model, but eliminate those of the abstract model only in the third and final phase, EL.

Fig. 9. Overview of the strategy for the Anchor O Step

Automation is restricted here, since data refinement embeds design decisions related to the way in which data is to be efficiently represented and shared in the program. On the other hand, once that creative design is carried out, as discussed, it may be possible to calculate the specification of the concrete model, if there is a functional relation between the concrete and the abstract states.

The phases address the following concerns: (a) refinement of abstract (model) variables by concrete variables used by the program (in Phase CS); and (b) introduction of state components for data shared between handlers and missions (in Phase SD). In all phases, including EL, we carry out a data refinement using simulation. If any of the new components have a class type, it needs to be declared. Introduction of a new class definition is a trivial refinement; the only complexity comes from the specification of the class itself.

For the leadership-election protocol, this step is not needed. In the case of a protocol, even the A anchor provides a data model that is already very concrete. So, in this case, the A and O anchors are the same. For an example of a refinement to an SCJ program that involves a substantial data refinement, we refer to [14].

process *SCJsystem* $\widehat{=}$ **begin**
  state *SCJstate* $==[x, y, z : \ldots \mid \ldots]$
  Init $\widehat{=}\ldots$
  Handler1 $\widehat{=}\ldots$ **var** $a, b, c \bullet \ldots$
  Handler2 $\widehat{=}\ldots$
  $\ldots$
  InitM1 $\widehat{=}\ldots$
  HandlersM1 $\widehat{=}$ (*Handler1* $\parallel$ *Handler2* $\parallel \ldots$) $\setminus$ *swevts*
  MArea1 $\widehat{=}$ **var** $l, m, n \ldots$
  Mission1 $=$ *InitM1*; (*HandlersM1* $[\![\,ns \mid mcs \mid \{\}\,]\!]$ *MArea1*) $\setminus$ *mcs*
  $\ldots$
  System $\widehat{=}$ *Mission1*; *Mission2*; $\ldots$
  $\bullet$ *Init*; *System*
end

Fig. 10. Anchor E: sketch of its structure

5.2 Anchor E: Execution Model

The second step of the refinement strategy introduces the architectural design of the program in accordance with the SCJ paradigm. The target E anchor embeds the structure of the missions and handlers. It is defined by a single process (and associated type and class definitions), still written using standard *Circus*, *OhCircus*, and *Circus Time* constructs.

The E anchor process for a non-terminating program takes the shape sketched in Fig. 10, where we consider a process named *SCJsystem*. Other patterns are considered in [32]. The state components of the E anchor, in Fig. 10, x, y, and z, are the variables that should be allocated in immortal memory (since they can be referenced by all missions). In the SCJ program, they can become, for instance, static fields of the `Safelet` subclass.

In the main action of the E anchor process, we call the local actions *Init* and *System* in sequence. *Init* is the specification of the program initialisation (which can be implemented in the `initialize` method of the `Safelet` subclass). *System* is a sequence of *Mission* actions; in Fig. 10, we have *Mission1*, *Mission2*, and so on. For applications in which the sequence of missions to be executed is defined dynamically (on the basis of values of variables in the immortal memory), the specification of *System* needs to be more elaborate.

For each mission, the E anchor process has a group of actions; in Fig. 10 we show those for *Mission1*. The variables to be allocated in mission memory are defined as local variables of an action *MArea*. These are the variables that are shared between two or more handlers. In Fig. 10, we show *MArea1* with variables l, m, and n. Internal channels represent calls to data operations that use or change these variables. Typically, these are methods of the objects held in these variables. An initialisation action, *InitM1* in Fig. 10, specifies how the values of these variables are to be initialised.

The handler actions, which in Fig. 10 are *Handler1*, *Handler2*, and so on, define the behaviour of the releases of the handlers. Their local variables are allocated in per-release memory. More elaborate algorithms may use temporary private memory areas to control allocation and deallocation of objects.

The *Handlers* action specifies the behaviour of the handler releases during the mission; in Fig. 10, we show *HandlersM1*. In the parallelisms between the handler actions, the synchronisation sets (omitted in Fig. 10) contain channels that represent the releases, if any, of aperiodic handlers by other handlers.

Access of handlers to objects in immortal memory is determined by the name sets in these parallelisms. Due to the restrictions on parallelism in *Circus*, we cannot have a race condition arising from handlers accessing the same state component (here, variable in immortal memory) at the same time.

As already said, the behaviour of the mission itself is given by a mission action; in Fig. 10, we sketch *Mission1*. What we have is a parallelism between the *Handlers* and the *MArea* actions. The synchronisation set *mcs* in this parallelism contains all channels representing calls to methods of the objects in the mission memory (which are defined in the *MArea* action). The name set associated with the *Handlers* action (that is, *ns* in Fig. 10) identifies the objects in immortal memory used by the handlers. The name set associated with the *MArea* action is always empty, since this action already encapsulates the data that it uses: the object variables to be allocated in mission memory.

The E anchor for the optimised leadership-election protocol in Fig. 7 is sketched in Fig. 11. In this case, we have a single mission, which we model using the action *ElectionMission*. All variables are allocated in the mission memory, and so are all local to *MArea*. As indicated in Fig. 7, we also have one periodic handler *CommunicatorH* and am aperiodic handler *ElectorH*.

It is the objective of the second step of our strategy to transform the O anchor to obtain a process in the shape of the E anchor identified in Fig. 10. Five phases define the refinement strategy in this step as depicted in Fig. 12. The first phase, CP, removes any parallelism used in the A anchor (and preserved in the O anchor) to specify requirements, since these parallelisms are typically not related to the concurrent design of the program.

As already mentioned, for the leadership-election protocol, for instance, we use parallelism in the A anchor to separate the behavioural and timing requirements. In *Circus* models automatically generated from domain-specific languages, typically, we have a parallelism between the components of the high-level model. It is the objective of our refinement strategy to change that architecture to that adopted by the mission paradigm of SCJ, without introducing errors.

The second phase, MS, introduces the sequences that reflect the architecture of the missions. The next two phases, HS and SH are repeated for each of the missions. In HS, we introduce the parallelism that reflects the behaviour of the handlers releases, and the control mechanisms that orchestrate their execution. In SH, we define how variables are shared between handlers. The final phase AR uses algorithmic refinement to derive the implementation of the methods.

process *ElectionE* $\widehat{=}$ **begin**

  CommunicatorH $\widehat{=} \mu X \bullet geti?i \longrightarrow$

$$
\left(
\begin{array}{l}
\left(
\begin{array}{l}
\textbf{if}(nodes\ i).id = id \longrightarrow Broadcast(id, status, petition); \\
\quad seti!(next\ i) \longrightarrow \textbf{skip} \\
[]\,(nodes\ i).id \neq id \longrightarrow \\
\quad \left(
\begin{array}{l}
\left(
\begin{array}{l}
receive.(nodes\ i).id?\,valC?\,valP \longrightarrow \\
\quad UpdateDevice((nodes\ i).id, valC, valP)) \blacktriangleleft ID \\
\Box \\
\textbf{wait}(ID + 1);\ UpdateOff((nodes\ i).id)
\end{array}
\right); \\
electorHrelease \longrightarrow \textbf{skip}
\end{array}
\right) \\
\textbf{fi} \\
[\!|\!|\ \textbf{wait}\ P
\end{array}
\right)\ ;\ X
\end{array}
\right.
$$

  ElectorH $\widehat{=} \mu X \bullet electorHrelease \longrightarrow$ $\left(\begin{array}{l} \textbf{if } status = undecided \longrightarrow \dots \\ []\ status = leader \longrightarrow \dots \\ []\ status = follower \longrightarrow \dots \\ \textbf{fi} \end{array} \right)$;

  $geti?x \longrightarrow seti!(next\ x) \longrightarrow X$

  . . .

  MArea $\widehat{=}$ **var** *id* : *DEVICEID*; *status* : *STATUS*; *petition* : $\mathbb{Z}$; . . . $\bullet \mu X \bullet$
  $setid?x \longrightarrow id := x;\ X \Box getid!id \longrightarrow X$
  $\Box$
  $setstatus?x \longrightarrow status := x;\ X \Box getstatus!status \longrightarrow X$
  . . .

  ElectionMission $\widehat{=}$
   (*MArea* $\|$ *CommunicatorH* $\|$ *ElectorH*) $\setminus \{\!| \dots |\!\}$

  ElectionMissionSequencer $\widehat{=}$ *ElectionMission*

  ElectionSafelet $\widehat{=}$ *ElectionMissionSequencer*

  $\bullet$ *ElectionSafelet*

end

Fig. 11. E anchor for the leadership-election protocol

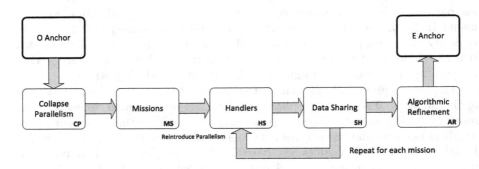

Fig. 12. Overview of the strategy for the Anchor E Step

5.3   Anchor S: Safety-Critical Java

The S anchor is written using *SCJ-Circus*. As explained in Sect. 3, a *Circus* model is composed of a sequence of paragraphs: syntactic units that introduce types, constants, processes, and so on. *SCJ-Circus* is based on *Circus*, *OhCircus*, and *Circus Time*, but includes several new paragraphs [32]. We have paragraphs for the declaration of safelets, mission sequencers, missions, and handlers. Their semantics is defined by standard *Circus* processes and actions.

In the last step of our refinement strategy, the process that defines the E anchor is split to yield the definition of these special SCJ paragraphs that compose the S anchor. For example, the state components of the E anchor, if any, become state components of the **safelet** paragraph. The *Init* action gives rise to the definition of the safelet **initialize** paragraph. For statically defined sequences of missions, a simple **sequencer** paragraph is always adequate. Each *Mission* action gives rise to a **mission** paragraph, and so on.

The introduction of the new SCJ paragraphs in this last step is justified by a refinement strategy detailed in [32]. The missions and handlers are already identified in the E anchor. What the transformations in this final step of the refinement strategy check is whether the design suggested in the structure of the E anchor indeed matches the concurrency model of SCJ.

As an example, we present, the S anchor for the leadership-election protocol. The paragraph **safelet** defines the `initialize` and `cleanUp` methods. In our example, they are empty (**skip**), and so this paragraph is omitted.

The paragraph for our mission sequencer is shown below. We note that, since we are considering just the election mission, the **getNextMission** paragraph only ever returns the identifier *ElectionMission* of a single mission.

> **sequencer** *MainMissionSequencer* $\widehat{=}$ **begin**
>
> **state** *MainMissionSequencerState* $==$ [*mission_done* : *bool*]
>
> **initial** $\widehat{=}$ *mission_done* := *false*
>
> **getNextMission** $\widehat{=}$
> **if** *mission_done* = *false* $\longrightarrow$
>   *mission_done* := *true*; **ret** := *ElectionMission*
> [] *mission_done* = *true* $\longrightarrow$ **ret** := *null*
> **fi**
>
> **end**

The **state** paragraph of an *SCJ-Circus* component defines the fields of the corresponding SCJ class, and the **initial** paragraph defines its constructor. The other paragraphs of these specialised components define methods of the SCJ class. Special paragraphs correspond to API methods. For instance, above we have **getNextMission** corresponding to the SCJ `getNextMission` method.

We use identifiers to refer to specific components: missions and handlers. For example, above, we use *ElectionMission* as an identifier for a mission. It is defined by the next *SCJ-Circus* paragraph.

The fields and constructor of the mission *Election* are defined by the schemas *ElectionState* and *InitElectionState* previously presented. In its API **initialize** method, it simply instantiates and registers the handlers *CommunicatorH* and *ElectionH*. As previously shown, the first is a periodic handler and the second, aperiodic. Creation of a handler *H*, specified by an *SCJ-Circus* paragraph **periodic** *H* or **aperiodic** *H*, is defined by the special expression **newHdlr** *H*.

> **mission** *ElectionMission* $\cong$ **begin**
>   **state** *st* $==$ *ElectionState*
>   **initial** $\cong$ *InitElectionState*
>   **initialize** $\cong$ **var** *ch, eh* : *ID* •
>   *eh* = **newHdlr** *ElectorH*;
>   *ch* = **newHdlr** *CommunicatorH*(*eh*);
>   *eh.register*() ; *ch.register*()
> **end**

Like in SCJ, corresponding to handlers, we have objects, instances of an *OhCircus* class. Such objects, like *eh* and *ch* in the example above, respond to a *register* method. It identifies the handler as part of the mission.

We note how close the definition of *ElectionMission* above is to an SCJ class that implements a mission. On the other hand, *ElectionMission* defines a *Circus* process, as do *CommunicatorH* and *ElectorH* used there, although these processes use classes that model the data of the handlers and mission. The meaning of the special method calls, like the calls to *register*, for instance, is given by a (hidden) event. In the case of *register*, it triggers a data operation that enriches the (encapsulated) state of the mission process to record an instance of the relevant handler. So, what we have is a *Circus* semantics for the SCJ paradigm, (very much as explained in [50] for SCJ itself).

The periodic handler *CommunicatorH* is introduced as shown below.

> **periodic** *CommunicatorH* $\cong$ **begin start** 0 **period** *P*

This paragraph also defines the start time and the period of the protocol as *P* (as required in the timing specification given by *ATReqsLE* in the A anchor). It starts right at the beginning of the mission.

The state of *CommunicatorH* records the instance of *ElectionH* used in the mission. Its value is defined by the constructor.

> **state** *st* $==$ [*electorH* : *ID*]
> **initial** $\cong$ **val** *eh* : *ID* • *electorH* := *eh*

At each cycle, the release of *ElectionH* checks which device is being considered. If the current device is itself, then it broadcasts its information just like in *ABReqsLE* and increments the index *i* to point to the next device. Otherwise it waits for either a communication on *receive* that must happen within *ID* time units and updates the state accordingly. If *ID* + 1 time units pass without *receive* occurring, it updates the current device's information to indicate it is inactive. It then initiates an election by releasing the aperiodic handler *electorH*.

$$
\begin{aligned}
&\textbf{handleAsyncEvent} \; \widehat{=} \\
&\quad \textbf{if}\,(nodes\;i).id = id \longrightarrow Broadcast(id, status, petition)\;;\;\; i := next\;i \\
&\quad [\!]\,(nodes\;i).id \neq id \longrightarrow \\
&\qquad \left(\begin{array}{l} receive.(nodes\;i).id?\,valC?\,valP \longrightarrow \\ \quad UpdateDevice((nodes\;i).id, valC, valP)) \blacktriangleleft ID \\ \square \\ \textbf{wait}(ID+1)\;;\;\; UpdateOff((nodes\;i).id) \end{array}\right)\;; \\
&\qquad electorH.release() \\
&\quad \textbf{fi} \\
&\textbf{end}
\end{aligned}
$$

The actions used in **handleAsyncEvent** are also defined inside *ElectionH*. Their definitions are as presented previously.

The variables in the state of the mission *ElectionMission* are those to be allocated in mission memory. Accordingly, they are directly accessible in the handlers, like *nodes*, *id*, *status*, *petition*, and *next* above.

The *ElectorH* handler implements the conditional over *status* in *ABReqsLE*.

$$
\begin{aligned}
&\textbf{aperiodic}\; ElectorH \; \widehat{=} \; \textbf{begin} \\
&\textbf{handleAsyncEvent} \; \widehat{=} \\
&\quad \left(\begin{array}{l} \textbf{if}\; status = undecided \longrightarrow \ldots \\ [\!]\, status = leader \longrightarrow \ldots \\ [\!]\, status = follower \longrightarrow \ldots \\ \textbf{fi} \end{array}\right)\;; \\
&\quad i := next\;i \\
&\textbf{end}
\end{aligned}
$$

It is not difficult to see that thee *SCJ-Circus* model can be automatically translated to SCJ code, actual Java code that can be compiled and executed.

6 Conclusions

In this tutorial, besides a didactic account of SCJ, we have given a brief introduction to *Circus*. In both cases, we have used the practical examples of a leadership-election protocol to illustrate the notations and concepts. Furthermore, we have reviewed the notion of refinement and formal techniques of program development in the context of both a traditional modelling language, like Z, and process algebra, namely, CSP and *Circus*.

To the best of our knowledge, all existing combinations of Z with a process algebra [19, 30, 44] model concurrent programs as communicating abstract data types, where events are identified with operations that change the state. This is not the *Circus* approach. Events are just atomic instantaneous interactions like in CSP, and data operations have to be explicitly called, if needed. This is in keeping with the approach used in programming languages, and facilitates the use *Circus* to verify correctness of programs. Besides the general *Circus* refinement calculus [10], there are results for Ada [8].

We did not, of course, aim at a comprehensive view of all the issues and techniques available. We hope, however, to have given general pointers to the subject to support further reading. Most of all, we hope to have made it clear that refinement is about organised and clear justification of the intuition that millions of programmers use everyday to reassure themselves and others of the correctness of their designs and programs. The lack of such a framework has lead to poorly documented, intricated, and many times mistaken developments.

An understanding of refinement as the underpinning notion of all development methods can help good engineers or programmers to achieve their goal more successfully. Knowledge of the properties of the refinement relation, in the form, for example, of refinement laws, can lead to improved programming skills, even if a formal refinement technique is not really applied.

Other tasks involved in the construction of programs, like testing [1], refactoring [15], and compilation [18,43,48] have already been characterised as related to refinement. A lot has already been achieved by the formal methods community in the last two or three decades; there is a lot yet to be done.

Acknowledgments. This work is funded by EPSRC grant EP/H017461/1. No primary data arises from the work reported here. We have benefitted from discussions with Frank Zeyda in the development of our case study.

References

1. Aichernig, B., Contract-based Mutation Testing in the Refinement Calculus. In: REFINE 2002. Electronic Notes in Theoretical Computer Science, Invited paper (2002)
2. Back, R.J.R., Wright, J.: Refinement Calculus: A Systematic Introduction. Graduate Texts in Computer Science. Springer, New York (1998)
3. Barnes, J.: High Integrity Software: The SPARK Approach to Safety and Security. Addison-Wesley, Boston (2003)
4. Bjorner, D., Jones, C.B.: Formal Specifications and Software Development. Prentice-Hall, Upper Saddle River (1982)
5. Bolognesi, T.: On state-oriented versus object-oriented thinking in formal behavioural specifications. Technical report -TR-20, ISTI-Istituto di Scienza e Tecnologie della Informazione Alessandro Faedo (2003)
6. Burns, A.: The Ravenscar profile. Ada Lett. **XIX**, 49–52 (1999)
7. Cavalcanti, A.L.C.: A refinement calculus for Z. Ph.D. thesis, Oxford University Computing Laboratory, Oxford, UK (1997). Technical Monograph TM-PRG-123, ISBN 00902928-97-X
8. Cavalcanti, A.L.C., Clayton, P., O'Halloran, C.: From control law diagrams to Ada via *Circus*. Form. Asp. Comput. **23**(4), 465–512 (2011)
9. Cavalcanti, A.L.C., Sampaio, A.C.A., Woodcock, J.C.P.: An inconsistency in procedures, parameters, and substitution the refinement calculus. Sci. Comput. Program. **33**(1), 87–96 (1999)

10. Cavalcanti, A.L.C., Sampaio, A.C.A., Woodcock, J.C.P.: A refinement strategy for Circus. Form. Asp. Comput. **15**(2–3), 146–181 (2003)
11. Cavalcanti, A.L.C., Sampaio, A.C.A., Woodcock, J.C.P.: Unifying classes and processes. Softw. Syst. Model. **4**(3), 277–296 (2005)
12. Cavalcanti, A.L.C., Wellings, A., Woodcock, J.C.P., Wei, K., Zeyda, F.: Safety-critical Java in Circus. In: Ravn, A.P. (ed.) 9th Workshop on Java Technologies for Real-Time and Embedded System. ACM Digital Library. ACM (2011)
13. Cavalcanti, A.L.C., Woodcock, J.C.P.: ZRC—a refinement calculus for Z. Form. Asp. Comput. **10**(3), 267–289 (1999)
14. Cavalcanti, A.L.C., Zeyda, F., Wellings, A., Woodcock, J.C.P., Wei, K.: Safety-critical Java programs from Circus models. Real-Time Syst. **49**(5), 614–667 (2013)
15. Cornélio, M.L., Cavalcanti, A.L.C., Sampaio, A.C.A.: Refactoring by transformation. In: Derrick, J., Boiten, E., Woodcock, J.C.P., Wright, J. (eds.) REFINE 2002. Electronic Notes in Theoretical Computer Science, Invited paper, vol. 70. Elsevier (2002)
16. Dijkstra, E.W.: Guarded commands, nondeterminacy and the formal derivation of programs. Commun. ACM **18**, 453–457 (1975)
17. Diller, A.Z.: An Introduction to Formal Methods, 2nd edn. Wiley, Hoboken (1994)
18. Duran, A.A., Cavalcanti, A.C.A., Sampaio, A.L.C.: Refinement algebra for formal bytecode generation. In: George, C., Miao, H. (eds.) ICFEM 2002. LNCS, vol. 2495, pp. 347–358. Springer, Heidelberg (2002). doi:10.1007/3-540-36103-0_36
19. Fischer, C.: CSP-OZ: a combination of object-Z and CSP. In: Bowman, H., Derrick, J. (eds.) Formal Methods for Open Object-Based Distributed Systems, vol. 2, pp. 423–438. Chapman & Hall, Boca Raton (1997)
20. Fischer, C.: How to combine Z with a process algebra. In: Bowen, J.P., Fett, A., Hinchey, M.G. (eds.) ZUM 1998. LNCS, vol. 1493, pp. 5–23. Springer, Heidelberg (1998). doi:10.1007/978-3-540-49676-2_2
21. Hoare, C.A.R.: Proof of correctness of data representations. Acta Informatica **1**, 271–281 (1972)
22. Hoare, C.A.R.: Communicating Sequential Processes. Prentice-Hall International, Upper Saddle River (1985)
23. Ichbiah, J.: Rationale for the design of the Ada programming language. ACM SIGPLAN Not. **14**(6B (special issue)), 1–261 (1979)
24. He, J., Hoare, C.A.R., Sanders, J.W.: Data refinement refined resume. In: Robinet, B., Wilhelm, R. (eds.) ESOP 1986. LNCS, vol. 213, pp. 187–196. Springer, Heidelberg (1986). doi:10.1007/3-540-16442-1_14
25. He, J., Hoare, C.A.R., Sanders, J.W.: Prespecification in data refinement. Inf. Process. Lett. **25**(1), 71–76 (1987)
26. Jones, C.B.: Software Development: A Rigorous Approach. Prentice-Hall, Upper Saddle River (1980)
27. Jones, C.B.: Systematic Software Development Using VDM. Prentice-Hall International, Upper Saddle River (1986)
28. Liskov, B.H., Wing, J.M.: A behavioural notion of subtyping. ACM Trans. Program. Lang. Syst. **16**(6), 1811–1841 (1994)
29. Locke, D., Andersen, B.S., Brosgol, B., Fulton, M., Henties, T., Hunt, J.J., Nielsen, J.O., Nilsen, K., Schoeberl, M., Tokar, J., Vitek, J., Wellings, A.: Safety Critical Java Specification, First Release 0.76. The Open Group, UK (2010). jcp.org/aboutJava/communityprocess/edr/jsr302/index.html
30. Mahony, B.P., Dong, J.S.: Blending object-Z and timed CSP: an introduction to TCOZ. In: 20th International Conference on Software Engineering (ICSE 1998), pp. 95–104. IEEE Computer Society Press (1998)

31. Meisels, I.: Software Manual for Windows Z/EVES Version 2.1. ORA Canada, TR-97-5505-04g (2000)
32. Miyazawa, A., Cavalcanti, A.L.C.: Refinement strategies for safety-critical Java. In: Cornélio, M.L., Roscoe, B. (eds.) SBMF 2015. LNCS, vol. 9526, pp. 93–109. Springer, Cham (2016). doi:10.1007/978-3-319-29473-5_6
33. Morgan, C.C.: Auxiliary variables in data refinement. Inf. Process. Lett. **29**(6), 293–296 (1988)
34. Morgan, C.C.: Programming from Specifications, 2nd edn. Prentice-Hall, Upper Saddle River (1994)
35. Morgan, C.C., Gardiner, P.H.B.: Data refinement by calculation. Acta Informatica **27**(6), 481–503 (1990)
36. Morris, J.M.: A theoretical basis for stepwise refinement and the programming calculus. Sci. Comput. Program. **9**(3), 287–306 (1987)
37. Motor Industry Software Reliability Association Guidelines. Guidelines for Use of the C Language in Critical Systems (2012)
38. Potter, B.F., Sinclair, J.E., Till, D.: An Introduction to Formal Specification and Z, 2nd edn. Prentice-Hall, Upper Saddle River (1996)
39. Reed, G.M., Roscoe, A.W.: A timed model for communicating sequential processes. Theoret. Comput. Sci. **58**, 249–261 (1988)
40. Roscoe, A.W.: The Theory and Practice of Concurrency. Prentice-Hall Series in Computer Science. Prentice-Hall, Upper Saddle River (1998)
41. Roscoe, A.W.: Understanding Concurrent Systems. Texts in Computer Science. Springer, London (2011)
42. RTCA/DO-178C/ED-12C: Software Considerations in Airborne Systems and Equipment Certification (2011)
43. Sampaio, A.C.A.: An Algebraic Approach to Compiler Design. AMAST Series in Computing, vol. 4. World Scientific, Singapore (1997)
44. Schneider, S., Treharne, H.: Communicating B machines. In: Bert, D., Bowen, J.P., Henson, M.C., Robinson, K. (eds.) ZB 2002. LNCS, vol. 2272, pp. 416–435. Springer, Heidelberg (2002). doi:10.1007/3-540-45648-1_22
45. Sherif, A., Cavalcanti, A.L.C., He, J., Sampaio, A.C.A.: A process algebraic framework for specification and validation of real-time systems. Form. Asp. Comput. **22**(2), 153–191 (2010)
46. Tofte, M., Talpin, J.-P.: Region-based memory management. Inf. Comput. **132**(2), 109–176 (1997)
47. Wellings, A.: Concurrent and Real-Time Programming in Java. Wiley, Hoboken (2004)
48. Wildman, L.: A formal basis for a program compilation proof tool. In: Eriksson, L.-H., Lindsay, P.A. (eds.) FME 2002. LNCS, vol. 2391, pp. 491–510. Springer, Heidelberg (2002). doi:10.1007/3-540-45614-7_28
49. Woodcock, J.C.P., Davies, J.: Using Z-Specification, Refinement, and Proof. Prentice-Hall, Upper Saddle River (1996)
50. Zeyda, F., Lalkhumsanga, L., Cavalcanti, A.L.C., Wellings, A.: Circus models for safety-critical Java programs. Comput. J. **57**(7), 1046–1091 (2014)

Runtime Verification for Linear-Time Temporal Logic

Martin Leucker[✉]

Institut für Softwaretechnik und Programmiersprachen, Universtität zu Lübeck,
Lübeck, Germany
leucker@isp.uni-luebeck.de

Abstract. In this paper and its accompanying tutorial, we discuss the topic of runtime verification for linear-time temporal logic specifications. We recall the idea of runtime verification, give ideas about specification languages for runtime verification and develop a solid theory for linear-time temporal logic. Concepts like monitors, impartiality, and anticipation are explained based on this logic.

1 Introduction

Software and software systems are increasingly ubiquitous in everyday life. Besides traditional applications such as word processors or spreadsheets running on workstations, software is an important part of consumer devices such as mobile phones or digital cameras, and functions as embedded control devices in cars or in power plants. Especially in such embedded application domains, it is essential to guarantee that the deployed software works in a correct, secure, and reliable manner, as life may depend on it.

For example, the software within a car's anti-skid system must speed with exactly the right velocity to stabilize the car. Moreover, for a power plant it is important that no intruder gets control over the plant and that it works also in case of a partial break-down of some of its parts.

Software engineering has been driven as a field by the struggle for guaranteed quality properties ever since, but nowadays and especially in the embedded domain, legislation and certification authorities are requiring proof of the most critical software properties in terms of a documented verification process.

Traditionally, one considers three main verification techniques: *theorem proving* [BC04], *model checking* [CGP01], and *testing* [Mye04, BJK+05]. Theorem proving, which is mostly applied manually, allows to show correctness of programs similarly as a proof in mathematics shows correctness of a theorem. Model checking, which is an automatic verification technique, is mainly applicable to finite-state systems. Testing covers a wide field of diverse, often ad-hoc, and incomplete methods for showing correctness, or, more precisely, for finding bugs.

These techniques are subject to a number of forces imposed by the software to build and the development process followed, and provide different trade-offs between them. For example, some require a formal model, like model checking,

© Springer International Publishing AG 2017
J.P. Bowen et al. (Eds.): SETSS 2016, LNCS 10215, pp. 151–194, 2017.
DOI: 10.1007/978-3-319-56841-6_5

give stronger or weaker confidence, like theorem proving over testing, or are graceful in case of error handling.

Runtime verification is being pursued as a *lightweight* verification technique complementing verification techniques such as model checking and testing and establishes another trade-off point between these forces. One of the main distinguishing features of runtime verification is due to its nature of being performed at runtime, which opens up the possibility to *act* whenever incorrect behavior of a software system is detected.

The aim of this course is to give a comprehensive introduction into runtime verification based on linear-time temporal logic. Rather than completeness, we aim for a solid formal underpinning of the concepts.

The paper is organized as follows: In the next section, we provide an informal introduction to the field of runtime verification. We sketch main ideas intuitively and describe several application areas. At the heart of runtime verification, we identify the specification of correctness properties and the synthesis of corresponding monitors, which may then be used for verification but also for steering a system. In Sects. 3–5, we develop formal semantics for one specification language viz. linear-time temporal logic together with corresponding monitoring procedures. In Sect. 3, we assume the execution be terminated, while in Sects. 4 and 5, we consider online monitoring with continuously expanding executions. In Sect. 4, we discuss the concept of impartiality in detail while Sect. 5 focusses on anticipation.

2   Fundamental Ideas of Runtime Verification

Let us start with recalling the fundamental concepts of verification and let us describe, from an abstract point of view, the concept of runtime verification.

First, let us clarify the terms *verification* and, to contrast its idea, also *validation*. Validation and verification can be distinguished by checking which of the following two questions gets answered: [Boe81]

Validation. Are we building the right product? – (Does the system meet the client's expectations?)

Verification. "Are we building the product right?" – (Does the system meet its specification?)

Definition 1 (Verification). *Verification is comparing code with its specification.*

A verification technique should therefore always be of a formal nature, while validation, necessarily, cannot fully rely on formal concepts as the customer's expectations are not formalized. As we will see, *runtime verification is a verification technique*, despite it only verifies partially the system under scrutiny.

We follow [DGR04] and define a *software failure* as a deviation between the *observed* behavior and the *required* behavior of the software system. A *fault* is defined as the deviation between the current behavior and the expected behavior, which is typically identified by a deviation of the current and the expected state of the system. A fault might lead to a failure, but not necessarily. An error, on the other hand, is a mistake made by a human that results in a fault and possibly in a failure.

As we have just learned, verification comprises all techniques suitable for showing that a system satisfies its specification.

Traditional verification techniques comprise theorem proving [BC04], model checking [CGP01], and testing [Mye04, BJK+05]. *Runtime verification,*[1] is a relatively new verification technique, which manifested itself within the previous years as a *lightweight* verification technique:

Definition 2 (Runtime Verification). Runtime verification *(RV) is the discipline of computer science that deals with the study, development and application of those verification techniques that allow for checking whether a* run *of a system under scrutiny* satisfies or violates *a given correctness property.*

Definition 3 (Run). *A* run *of a system is a possibly infinite sequence of the system's states. Formally, a run may be considered as a possibly infinite* word *or* trace.

Runs are formed by current variable assignments, or as the sequence of actions a system is emitting or performing.

Definition 4 (Execution). *An* execution *of a system is a finite prefix of a run and, formally, it is a finite trace. When running a program, we can only observe executions, which, however, restrict the corresponding evolving run as being their prefix.*

In runtime verification, we check whether a run of a system adhere to given correctness properties. RV is primarily used on executions. A monitor checks whether an execution meets a correctness property.

Definition 5 (Monitor). *A* monitor *is a device that reads a finite trace and yields a certain verdict.*

Figure 1 shows a monitor M which tests an execution of the system consisting of the components C_i against a formal correctness property. These components can be hardware components, procedures or any other structuring element of the system. The lines can be the wiring of hardware components, the call stack of procedures or any other connection of the components.

A monitor may use more than one input stream as opposed to what is shown in Fig. 1. Likewise, a monitor can check the relations of multiple values. In *distributed runtime verification*, a set of monitors operating at different locations may combine their monitoring power to deduce the suitable verdict [SVAR04, MB15, SS14, BLS06a].

Here, a verdict is typically a truth value from some truth domain. A truth domain is a lattice with a unique top element *true* and a unique bottom

---

[1] http://www.runtime-verification.org.

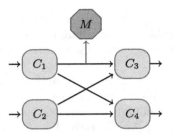

Fig. 1. Monitor M checks correctness of components C_i.

element *false*. This definition covers the standard two-valued truth domain $\mathbb{B} = \{true, false\}$ but also fits for monitors yielding a probability in $[0, 1]$ with which a given correctness property is satisfied. Sometimes, one might be even more liberal and consider also verdicts that are not elements of a truth domain, though we do not follow this view in this paper.

A monitor may on one hand be used to check the *current* execution of a system. In this setting, which is termed *online monitoring*, the monitor should be designed to consider executions in an *incremental fashion* and in an *efficient manner*. On the other hand, a monitor may work on a (finite set of) *recorded* execution(s), in which case we speak of *offline monitoring*.

RV and the Word Problem. In its simplest form, a monitor decides whether the current execution satisfies a given correctness property by outputting either *yes/true* or *no/false*. Formally, when $\llbracket \varphi \rrbracket$ denotes the set of valid executions given by property φ, runtime verification boils down to checking whether the execution w is an element of $\llbracket \varphi \rrbracket$. Thus, in its mathematical essence, runtime verification answers the *word problem*, i.e. the problem whether a given word is included in some language. Note that often, the word problem can be decided with lower complexity compared to, for example, the subset problem: Language containment for non-deterministic finite-automata is PSPACE-complete [SC85], while deciding whether a given word is accepted by a non-deterministic automaton is NLOGSPACE-complete [HU79].

2.1 Some Requirements on Monitors

Definition 6 (Impartiality). Impartiality *requires that a finite trace is not evaluated to true or, respectively false, if there still exists a (possibly infinite) continuation leading to another verdict.*

Definition 7 (Anticipation). Anticipation *requires that once every (possibly infinite) continuation of a finite trace leads to the same verdict, then the finite trace evaluates to this very same verdict.*

Intuitively, the first maxim postulates that a monitor only decides for *false*—meaning that a misbehavior has been observed—or *true*—meaning that the

current behavior fulfills the correctness property, regardless of how it continues—
only if this is indeed the case. Clearly, this maxim requires to have at least three
different truth values: *true, false,* and *inconclusive,* but of course more than
three truth values might give a more precise assessment of correctness. The second maxim requires a monitor to indeed report *true* or *false,* if the correctness
property is indeed violated or satisfied. In simple words, *impartiality* and *anticipation,* guarantee that the semantics is neither premature nor overcautious in
its evaluations.

See the forthcoming sections for a more elaborate discussion of these issues
in the context of linear temporal logic.

In runtime verification, monitors are typically generated automatically from
some high-level specification. As runtime verification has its roots in model checking, often some variant of linear temporal logic, such as LTL [Pnu77], is employed.
But also formalisms inspired by the linear μ-calculus have been introduced, for
example in [DSS+05], which explains an accompanying monitoring framework.

Actually, one of the key problems addressed in runtime verification is the
generation of monitors from high-level specifications, and we discuss this issue
in much more detail in this course.

2.2   Runtime Verification in the Plethora of Verification Techniques

RV Versus Testing. As runtime verification does not consider each possible execution of a system, but just a single or a finite subset, it shares similarities with
testing, which terms a variety of usually incomplete verification techniques.

Typically, in testing one considers a finite set of finite input-output sequences
forming a *test suite* [PL04]. Test-case execution is then checking whether the
output of a system agrees with the predicted one, when giving the input sequence
to the system under test.

A different form of testing, however, is closer to runtime verification, which
is sometimes termed *oracle-based testing.* Here, a test-suite is only formed by
input-sequences. To make sure that the output of the system is as anticipated,
a so-called *test oracle* has to be designed and "attached" to the system under
test. Thus, in essence, runtime verification can be understood as this form of
testing. There are, however, differences in the foci of runtime verification and
oracle-based testing:

- In testing, an oracle is typically defined directly, rather than generated from
  some high-level specification.
- On the other hand, providing a suitable set of input sequences to "exhaustively" test a system, is rarely considered in the domain of runtime verification.

Thus, runtime verification can also considered as a form of *passive testing.*

When monitors are equipped in the final software system, one may also understand runtime verification as "testing forever", which makes it, in a certain sense,
complete.

RV Versus Model Checking. In essence, model checking describes the problem of determining whether, given a model $\mathcal{M}$ and a correctness property φ, all computations of $\mathcal{M}$ satisfy φ. Model checking [CGP01], which is an automatic verification technique, is mainly applicable to finite-state systems, for which all computations can exhaustively be enumerated, though model checking techniques for certain pushdown systems or counter machines exist as well.

In the automata theoretic approach to model checking [VW86], a correctness property φ is transformed to an automaton $\mathcal{M}_{\neg\varphi}$ accepting all runs violating φ. This automaton is put in parallel to a model $\mathcal{M}$ to check whether $\mathcal{M}$ has a run violating φ.

Runtime verification has its origins in model checking, and, to a certain extend, the key problem of generating monitors is similar to the generation of automata in model checking. However, there are also important differences to model checking:

- While in model checking, *all executions* of a given system are examined to answer whether they satisfy a given correctness property φ, which corresponds to the language inclusion problem, runtime verification deals with the word problem.
- While model checking typically considers *infinite* traces, runtime verification deals with *finite* executions—as executions have necessarily to be finite.
- While in model checking a complete model is given allowing to consider arbitrary positions of a trace, runtime verification, especially when dealing with online monitoring, considers finite executions of increasing size. For this, a monitor should be designed to consider executions in an *incremental fashion.*

These differences make it necessary to adapt the concepts developed in model checking to be applicable in runtime verification. For example, while checking a property in model checking using a kind of backwards search in the model is sometimes a good choice, it should be avoided in online monitoring as this would require, in the worst case, the whole execution trace to be stored for evaluation.

From an application point of view, there are also important differences between model checking and runtime verification.

Runtime verification deals only with observed executions as they are generated by the real system. Thus runtime verification is applicable to *black box systems* for which no system model is at hand. In model checking, however, a suitable model of the system to be checked must be constructed as—before actually running the system—all possible executions must be checked.

If such a precise model of the underlying system is given, and, if moreover a bound on the size of its state space is known, powerful, so-called *bounded model-checking techniques* can be applied [BCC+03] for analyzing the system. The crucial idea, which is equally used in conformance testing [Vas73, Cho78], is that for every finite-state system, an infinite trace must reach at least one state twice. Thus, if a finite trace reaches a state a second time, the trace can be extended to an infinite trace by taking the corresponding loop infinitely often. Likewise, considering all finite traces of length up-to the state-place plus one, one has information on all possible loops of the underlying system, without actually working on the system's state space directly.

Clearly, similar correspondences would be helpful in runtime verification as well. However, in runtime verification, an upper bound on the system's state space is typically not known. More importantly, the states of an observed execution usually do not reflect the system's state completely but do only contain the value of certain variables of interest. Thus, seeing a state twice in an observed execution does not allow to infer that the observed loop can be taken ad infinitum.

That said, current research also focusses on the combination of runtime verification and model checking respectively formal verification techniques. See [Leu12, CAPS15] for details.

Furthermore, model checking suffers from the so-called *state explosion problem*, which terms the fact that analyzing all executions of a system is typically been carried out by generating the whole state space of the underlying system, which is often huge. Considering a single run, on the other hand, does usually not yield any memory problems, provided that when monitoring online only a finite *history* of the execution has to be stored.

Last but not least, in online monitoring, the complexity for *generating* the monitor is typically negligible, as the monitor is often only generated once. However, the *complexity of the monitor*, i. e. its memory and computation time requirements for checking an execution are of important interest, as the monitor is part of the running system and should influence the system as less as possible.

2.3   Applications

Runtime Reflection. Runtime verification itself deals (only) with the *detection* of violations (or satisfactions) of correctness properties. Thus, whenever a violation has been observed, it typically does not influence or change the program's execution, say for trying to repair the observed violation. However, runtime verification is the basis for concepts also dealing with observed problems, as we discuss in this section.

The idea of monitoring a system and reacting are to a certain extent covered by the popular notion of *FDIR*, which stands for *Fault Detection, Identification, and Recovery* or sometimes for *Fault Diagnosis, Isolation, and Recovery* or various combinations thereof [CR94]. The general idea of FDIR is that a failure within a system shows up by a fault. A fault, however, does typically not *identify* the failure: for example, there might be different *reasons* why a monitored client does not follow a certain protocol, one of them, e.g., that it uses an old version of a protocol. If this is identified as the failure, reconfiguration may switch the server to work with the old version of the protocol.

Crow and Rushby instantiated the scheme FDIR using Reiter's theory of diagnosis from first principles in [CR94]. Especially, the detection of errors is carried out using diagnosis techniques. In *runtime reflection* [BLS06b], runtime verification is proposed as a tool for fault detection, while a simplified version of Reiter's diagnosis is suggested for identification.

Runtime reflection (RR) is an architecture pattern for the development of reliable systems.

- A *monitoring layer* is enriched with
- a *diagnosis layer* and a subsequent
- *mitigation layer*.

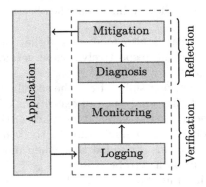

Fig. 2. An application and the layers of the runtime reflection framework.

The architecture consists of four layers as shown in Fig. 2, whose role will be sketched in the subsequent paragraphs.

The role of the *logging layer* is to observe system events and to provide them in a suitable format for the monitoring layer. Typically, the logging layer is realized by adding code annotations within the system to build. However, separated stand-alone loggers, logging for example network traffic, can realize this layer as well. While the goal of a logger is to provide information on the current run to a monitor, it may not assume (much) on the properties to be monitored.

The *monitoring layer* consists of a number of monitors (complying to the logger interface of the logging layer) which observe the stream of system events provided by the logging layer. Its task is to detect the presence of faults in the system without actually affecting its behavior. In runtime reflection, it is assumed to be implemented using runtime verification techniques. If a violation of a correctness property is detected in some part of the system, the generated monitors will respond with an alarm signal for subsequent diagnosis.

Following FDIR, we separate the detections of faults from the identification of failures. The *diagnosis layer* collects the verdicts of the distributed monitors and deduces an explanation for the current system state. For this purpose, the diagnosis layer may infer a (minimal) set of system components, which must be assumed faulty in order to explain the currently observed system state. The procedure is solely based upon the results of the monitors and general information on the system. Thus, the diagnostic layer is not directly communicating with the application.

The results of the system's diagnosis are then used in order to *reconfigure* the system to mitigate the failure, if possible. However, depending on the diagnosis and the occurred failure, it may not always be possible to re-establish a determined system behavior. Hence, in some situations, e. g., occurrence of fatal errors, a recovery system may merely be able to store detailed diagnosis information for off-line treatment.

Monitor-Oriented Programming. Monitoring-Oriented Programming (MOP) [CR07], proposed by Feng and Rosu, is a software development methodology, in which the developer specifies desired properties using a variety of (freely definable) specification formalisms, along with code to execute when properties are violated or validated. The MOP framework automatically generates monitors from the specified properties and then integrates them together with the user-defined code into the original system. Thus, it extends ideas from runtime verification by means for *reacting* on detected violations (or validations) of properties to check. This allows the development of *reflective* software systems: A software system can monitor its own execution such that the subsequent execution is influenced by the code a monitor is executing in reaction to its observations—again influencing the observed behavior and consequently the behavior of the monitor itself.

RR differs from monitor-oriented programming in two dimensions. First, MOP aims at a programming methodology, while RR should be understood as an architecture pattern. This implies that MOP support has to be tight to a programming language, for example Java resulting in jMOP, while in RR, a program's structure should highlight that it follows the RR pattern. The second difference of RR in comparison to MOP is that RR introduces a diagnosis layer not found in MOP.[2]

When to Use RV?. Let us conclude the description of runtime verification by listing certain application domains, highlighting the distinguishing features of runtime verification:

- The verification verdict, as obtained by model checking or theorem proving, is often referring to a *model of the real system* under analysis, since applying these techniques directly to the real implementation would be intractable. The model typically reflects most important aspects of the corresponding implementation, and checking the model for correctness gives useful insights to the implementation. Nevertheless, the implementation might behave slightly different than predicted by the model. Runtime verification may then be used to easily *check the actual execution* of the system, to make sure that the implementation really meets its correctness properties. Thus, runtime verification may act as a *partner to theorem proving and model checking*.

---

[2] Clearly, in the MOP framework, a diagnosis can be carried out in the code triggered by a monitor. This yields a program using the MOP methodology and following the RR pattern.

– Often, some information is available *only at runtime* or is conveniently checked at runtime. For example, whenever library code with no accompanying source code is part of the system to build, only a vague description of the behavior of the code might be available. In such cases, runtime verification is an *alternative to theorem proving and model checking.*
– The behavior of an application may *depend heavily on the environment* of the target system, but a precise description of this environment might not exist. Then it is not possible to obtain the information necessary to test the system in an adequate manner. Moreover, formal correctness proofs by model checking or theorem proving may only be achievable by taking certain assumptions on the behavior of the environment—which should be checked at runtime. In this scenario, runtime verification outperforms classical testing and *adds on formal correctness proofs* by model checking and theorem proving.
– In the case of systems where *security is important* or in the case of safety-critical systems, it is useful also to monitor behavior or properties that have been statically proved or tested, mainly to have a double check that everything goes well: Here, runtime verification acts as a partner of theorem proving, model checking, and testing.

The above mentioned items can be found in a combined manner especially in highly dynamic systems such as *adaptive, self-organizing,* or *self-healing* systems (see [HS06] for an overview on such approaches towards self-management).

The behavior of such systems depends heavily on the environment and changes over time, which makes their behavior hard to predict—and hard to analyze prior to execution. To assure certain correctness properties of especially such systems, we expect runtime verification to become a major verification technique.

Let us conclude this subsection with a general taxonomy of runtime verification aspects shown in Fig. 3.

2.4   Gathering Information About Executions

In this course, we mainly focus on specification means for correctness properties and corresponding monitor synthesis procedures. However, one of the fundamental question in runtime verification is also how to obtain the underlying atomic system events or observations that build the basis for correctness specifications. We leave details on this to other works but only list fundamental concepts.

A typical approach is instrument the code to provide logging information, say be means of code manipulations. These may be applied directly on the source code, the byte code or binary code level. The programmer of the underlying software may have also used dedicated logging frameworks and these are the sequence of log events is to be analyzed. Operating system typically also provide tools for providing trace information of running processes. A relatively new direction is to use debug capabilities of the processors of underlying execution platform and to monitor the system using dedicated hardware. Especially the latter approach caters for analyzing timing properties as the system does not get influenced itself by the monitoring process. Figure 4 summarizes the options.

Fig. 3. Taxonomy for RV

2.5   RV Frameworks

The popularity of runtime verification can also be witnessed by the large number of corresponding runtime verification frameworks. An (incomplete) list of current runtime verification frameworks as shown in Fig. 5.

We will now study several high-level specification languages and discuss adaptions of their semantics suitable for runtime verification. Mostly, we consider the linear-time temporal logic LTL, first considered for specifications of computations by Amir Pnueli [Pnu77].

2.6   A Primer on Linear-Time Temporal Logic

Runs are Words. The system to monitor is typically driven by some program that consists of several commands and hereby interacts with its environment.

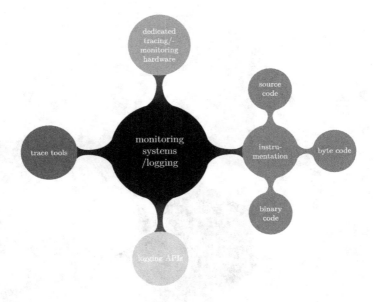

Fig. 4. Observing the System

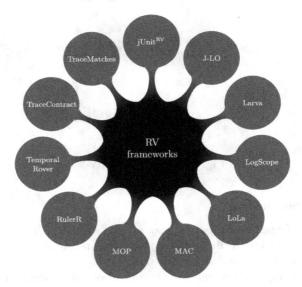

Fig. 5. An (imcomplete) list of runtime verification framworks

The idea of monitoring is now to observe and analyze partially such an execution which is built-up by artefacts. These artifacts may vary depending on the application of runtime verification. For example, we may observe *events* that occur within the system's execution, or, we may have access to the system's variables in each execution step, giving a comprehensive picture of the system's state. Often, we can monitor the system's input-/output behavior. These settings have in common that an execution can easily be described by a linear sequence of the artifacts to be observed.

In runtime verification, we therefore aim at specifying the shape of linear sequences. In a second step, the goal is to synthesize monitors that check whether a single or a set of linear sequences adheres to the specification.

Formally, executions and runs can be understood as (finite or infinite, respectively) *words* over the corresponding alphabet, i.e., the power set of the atomic propositions.

Let Σ be an alphabet and $n \in \mathbb{N}$.

We then use the following notation shown in Table 1.

Table 1. Notation for words.

Notation	Meaning
Σ^*	Set of all *finite* words over Σ
Σ^n	All words in Σ^* of length n
$\Sigma^{\leq n}$	All words in Σ^* of length at most n
$\Sigma^{\geq n}$	All words in Σ^* of length at least n
Σ^+	$= \Sigma^{\geq 1}$
Σ^ω	Set of all *infinite* words over Σ
Σ^∞	$= \Sigma^* \cup \Sigma^\omega$

A state can be seen as an element $a \in \Sigma$. Now a run is an infinite word $w \in \Sigma^\omega$ and an execution a finite prefix $w \in \Sigma^*$. Runtime verification is about checking if an execution is correct, so we need to specify the set of correct executions as a language $L \subseteq \Sigma^*$. Therefore a correctness property is a language L.

In general, logical calculi are a versatile tool and basis for deriving specification formalisms. Linear-time temporal logic (LTL) is especially useful for specifying properties of linear sequences. In the following we study different versions of LTL with a semantics adapted towards its application in runtime verification.

Linear temporal logic builds on propositional logic. As such, it allows the definition of *atomic propositions*, typically denoted by letters such as p or q, as well as the combination of formulas by *conjunction*, denoted by $\wedge$, *disjunction*, denoted by $\vee$, and *negation*, denoted by $\neg$. Clearly, only one of conjunction or disjunction is necessary in the presence of negation. However, for convenience, we typically use both operators in our logics.

Propositional logic can only talk about the current situation, let it be a certain time step, an event, a current memory assignment etc. It becomes a *temporal logic* by adding temporal quantifiers (sometimes also called operators).

Using propositional logic without temporal operators we describe only the first state.

Example 1. Consider AP $= \{p, q, r, s\}$ and an initial state s_0 of an execution w in which p and r holds. We then have

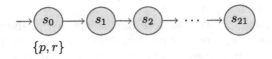

$\{p, r\}$

$w \models$ true	$w \not\models$ false
$w \models p$	$w \models p \wedge r \vee q$
$w \models \neg q \wedge \neg s$	$w \not\models q.$

In LTL, we usually have two operators *next*, denoted by X, and, *until*, denoted by U. *Next* is a unary operator and the meaning of a formula $X\varphi$ is that φ has to hold in the *next* situation, formally the next position of a linear sequence, or *word*. *Until* is a binary operator and the meaning of $\varphi \ U \ \psi$ is that ψ has to hold at some point and φ has to hold up-to this moment. With these two temporal operators, it is now possible to specify not only propositions of the current situation but also on future situations. However, for convenience, we work with further operators, as visualized in the following.

Formula: φ The formula φ holds for an execution if φ holds in the first state s_0 of that execution.

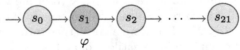

Next: $X\varphi$ The formula $X\varphi$ holds in state s_i if φ holds in state s_{i+1}.
If there is no state s_{i+1} then $X\varphi$ *never* holds.

Weak Next: $\overline{X}\varphi$ The formula $\overline{X}\varphi$ holds in state s_i if φ holds in state s_{i+1}.
If there is no state s_{i+1} then $\overline{X}\varphi$ *always* holds.

Globally: $G\varphi$ The formula $G\varphi$ holds in state s_i if φ holds in all states s_j for $j \geq i$.

Finally: $F\varphi$ The formula $F\varphi$ holds in state s_i if there is a state s_j for $j \geq i$ in which φ holds.

Until: $\varphi \, U \, \psi$ The formula $\varphi U \psi$ holds in state s_i if there is a state s_j for $j \geq i$ in which ψ holds and φ holds in all states s_k for $i \leq k < j$.

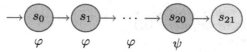

Notice that a state in which φ holds is not required in all cases!

Release: $\varphi \, R \, \psi$ The formula $\varphi R \psi$ holds in state s_i if there is a state s_j for $j \geq i$ in which φ holds and ψ holds in all states s_k for $i \leq k \leq j$.

If there is no such state s_j then the $\varphi R \psi$ holds if ψ holds in all states s_k for $k \geq i$.

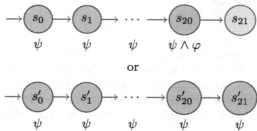

LTL Syntax. Let us give a precisedefinition of LTL's syntax.

Definition 8 (Syntax of LTL Formulae). *Let $p \in \text{AP}$ be an atomic proposition from a finite set of atomic propositions* AP. *The set of LTL formulae is inductively defined by the following grammar:*

$$\varphi ::= \text{true} \mid p \quad \mid \varphi \vee \varphi \mid X\varphi \mid \varphi U\varphi \mid F\varphi \mid$$
$$\text{false} \mid \neg p \mid \varphi \wedge \varphi \mid \overline{X}\varphi \mid \varphi R\varphi \mid G\varphi \mid$$
$$\neg\varphi$$

Thus, in total LTL's syntax as considered here consists of the logical contants true and false, conjunction and disjunction, negation, and the temporal operators *next* X, *weak next* $\overline{X}$, *until* U, and *release* R and its special casses *finally* F and *globally* G.

The previous definition of LTL's syntax is not minimal in the sense that, as we will see when considering the semantics, some operators can be expressed by others. For example, negation is only added for convenience as for every operator true, $\vee$, X, U and F also its dual operator false, $\wedge$, $\overline{X}$, R and G, respectively is added, and each atomic proposition p may be used *positively* as p or *negatively* as $\neg p$.

The *operator precedence* is needed to determine an unambiguous derivation of an LTL formula if braces are left out in nested expressions. The higher the rank of an operator is the later it is derivated.

Braces only need to be added if an operator of lower or same rank should be derivated later than the current one.

Definition 9 (operator precedence of LTL).

1. *negation operator:* $\neg$
2. *unary temporal operators:* $X, \bar{X}, G, F$
3. *binary temporal logic operators:* U, R
4. *conjunction operator:* $\wedge$
5. *disjunction operator:* $\vee$

Example 2.
$$G \ \neg x \ \vee \quad \neg x \ U \ Gy \quad \wedge z$$
$$\equiv G \left(\neg x \right) \vee \left(\left(\left(\neg x \right) U \left(Gy \right) \right) \wedge z \right)$$

3   FLTL Semantics

3.1   Semantics

We will now give a formal sematics matching the informal ideas from the last section on how LTL works. We first assume that the execution under scrutiny has terminated. Thus, we are given a final complete word over the alphabet $\Sigma = 2^{\mathrm{AP}}$ and we are after a two-valued semantics for Finite Linear Temporal Logic (FLTL), which tells us wether the execution/run fulfills the correctness property or not.

Given a word $w \in \Sigma^+$, we define when the word satisfies a given property φ. If so, we write $w \models \varphi$, and, if not, we sometimes write $w \not\models \varphi$. In other words, the semantics of LTL formula with respect to words is typically given as a relation $\models$ but we write, to simplify readability, $w \models \varphi$ rather than $(w, \varphi) \in \models$.

In the formal definition of LTL semantics we denote parts of a word as follows: Let $w = a_1 a_2 \dots a_n \in \Sigma^n$ be a finite word over the alphabet $\Sigma = 2^{\mathrm{AP}}$ and let $i \in \mathbb{N}$ with $1 \leq i \leq n$ be a position in this word. Then

- $|w| := n$ is the length of the word,
- $w_i = a_i$ is the i-th letter of the word and
- $w^i = a_i a_{i+1} \dots a_n$ is the subword starting with letter i.

We now give the formal two-valued semantics for LTL on finite completed non-empty words. It uses the standard ideas of LTL derived in the previous section. Recall that X and $\bar{X}$ represent that idea that property at the end of the trace *is not* or respectively, *is* satisfied.

Definition 10 (FLTL Semantics). *Let φ, ψ be LTL formulae and let $w \in \Sigma^+$ be a finite word. Then the semantics of φ with respect to w is inductively defined as in Fig. 6.*

Let us consider several examples. More specifically, let us consider several *patterns*. The patterns are taken from [DAC99]. On the website http://patterns. projects.cis.ksu.edu/ many more real world pattern are described.

In the following examples we consider a property φ whose validity should be specified with respect to a *scope* expressed by a property ψ. We consider these scopes:

$w \models$ true

$w \models p$	iff $p \in w_1$
$w \models \neg p$	iff $p \notin w_1$
$w \models \neg \varphi$	iff $w \not\models \varphi$
$w \models \varphi \vee \psi$	iff $w \models \varphi$ or $w \models \psi$
$w \models \varphi \wedge \psi$	iff $w \models \varphi$ and $w \models \psi$
$w \models X\varphi$	iff $|w| > 1$ and, for $|w| > 1, w^2 \models \varphi$
$w \models \overline{X}\varphi$	iff $|w| = 1$ or, for $|w| > 1, w^2 \models \varphi$
$w \models \varphi U\psi$	iff $\exists i, 1 \le i \le |w| : (w^i \models \psi$ and $\forall k, 1 \le k < i : w^k \models \varphi)$
$w \models \varphi R\psi$	iff $\exists i, 1 \le i \le |w| : (w^i \models \varphi$ and $\forall k, 1 \le k \le i : w^k \models \psi)$
	or $\forall i, 1 \le i \le |w| : w^i \models \psi$
$w \models F\varphi$	iff $\exists i, 1 \le i \le |w| : w^i \models \varphi$
$w \models G\varphi$	iff $\forall i, 1 \le i \le |w| : w^i \models \varphi$

Fig. 6. Semantics of FLTL

everytime: all states
before ψ: all states before the first state in which ψ holds (if there is such a state)
after ψ: all states after and including the first state in which ψ holds (if there is such a state)

And we consider the patterns *Absence*, *Existence*, and *Universality*.

Example 3 (Absence). The formula φ does not hold

everytime: $G\neg\varphi$
before ψ: $(F\psi) \rightarrow (\neg\varphi U\psi)$
after ψ: $G(\psi \rightarrow (G\neg\varphi))$

Example 4 (Existence). The formula φ holds in the future

everytime: $F\varphi$
before ψ: $G\neg\psi \vee \neg\psi U(\varphi \wedge \neg\psi)$
after ψ: $G\neg\psi \vee F(\psi \wedge F\varphi)$

Example 5 (Universality). The formula φ holds

everytime: $G\varphi$
before ψ: $(F\psi) \rightarrow (\varphi U\psi)$
after ψ: $G(\psi \rightarrow G\varphi)$

Let us now recall the idea of equivalent formulas

Definition 11 (Equivalence of Formulae). *Let* $\Sigma = 2^{\mathrm{AP}}$ *and* φ *and* ψ *be LTL formulae over* AP. φ *and* ψ *are equivalent, denoted by* $\varphi \equiv \psi$, *iff*

$$\forall w \in \Sigma^+ : w \models \varphi \Leftrightarrow w \models \psi.$$

Globally and finally can easily be expressed using until and release:

$$\mathrm{F}\varphi \equiv \mathrm{true}\,\mathrm{U}\varphi \qquad \mathrm{G}\varphi \equiv \mathrm{false}\,\mathrm{R}\varphi$$

The negation can always be moved in front of the atomic propositions using the dual operators:

De Morgan Rules of Propositional Logic

$$\neg(\varphi \vee \psi) \equiv \neg\varphi \wedge \neg\psi$$
$$\neg(\varphi \wedge \psi) \equiv \neg\varphi \vee \neg\psi$$

De Morgan Rules of Temporal Logic

$$\neg(\varphi\mathrm{U}\psi) \equiv \neg\varphi\mathrm{R}\neg\psi$$
$$\neg(\varphi\mathrm{R}\psi) \equiv \neg\varphi\mathrm{U}\neg\psi$$
$$\neg(\mathrm{G}\varphi) \equiv \mathrm{F}\neg\varphi$$
$$\neg(\mathrm{F}\varphi) \equiv \mathrm{G}\neg\varphi$$
$$\neg(\mathrm{X}\varphi) \equiv \overline{\mathrm{X}}\neg\varphi$$
$$\neg(\overline{\mathrm{X}}\varphi) \equiv \mathrm{X}\neg\varphi$$

Fixed Point Equations. The following *fixed point equations* can be used to stepwise unwind until and release:

$$\varphi\mathrm{U}\psi \equiv \psi \vee (\varphi \wedge \mathrm{X}(\varphi\mathrm{U}\psi))$$
$$\varphi\mathrm{R}\psi \equiv \psi \wedge (\varphi \vee \overline{\mathrm{X}}(\varphi\mathrm{R}\psi))$$

Consequently such fix point equations for globally and finally are special cases of the above ones:

$$\mathrm{G}\varphi \equiv \varphi \wedge \overline{\mathrm{X}}(\mathrm{G}\varphi)$$
$$\mathrm{F}\varphi \equiv \varphi \vee \mathrm{X}(\mathrm{F}\varphi)$$

Using all these equivalences one may notice that only a small set of LTL operators is needed in a minimal syntax to provide the full expressiveness of LTL.

Definition 12 (Negation Normal Form (NNF)). *An LTL formula* φ *is in Negation Normal Form (NNF) iff* $\neg$ *only occurs in front of atomic propositions* $p \in \mathrm{AP}$.

Lemma 1. *For every LTL formula there exists an equivalent formula in NNF.*

Proof. Recursively apply De Morgan rules of propositional logic and De Morgan rules of temporal logic.

Given the semantics of FLTL, it is easy to create a monitoring device that reads a finite string and an LTL formula and outputs the semantics of the string as a monitoring verdict. We leave this as an excercise to the reader. In the next section, we will elaborate a semantics that is suitable for finite but continuesly expanding words and we provide a more sophisticated monitoring procedure that may be slightly adapted to serve also for FLTL.

4   Impartial Runtime Verification

For now we are able to decide if a finite terminated execution/word models an LTL formula. This approach is reasonable whenever a terminated run of system is analyzed. Often, especially in online monitoring, the execution is still running so that the word to analyze is continuously expanding. Thus, instead of considering a terminated word we will start thinking about what happens if the word gets extended with more letters step by step. Regarding the maxims impartiality and anticipation, we will address the impartiality in this section. To this end, our monitor will be able to answer the question if a word models an LTL formula with one of the following statements:

- Yes it does and it will always do.
- Yes it does, but this may change.
- No it does not, but this may change.
- No it does not and will never do.

We will introduce the concept of truth domains providing multiple logical values that can be used as results if an LTL formula gets evaluated. Here, we build on the theory of lattices. After presenting a first monitoring approach for such a four-valued LTL semantics we will introduce automata-based monitoring. This answers the question on how the recursive evaluation function can be implemented in an efficient way. It gets translated into a Mealy machine—one of the most basic and easy to implement machine models.

4.1   Truth Domains

Definition 13 (Lattice). *A* lattice *is a partially ordered set* $(\mathcal{L}, \sqsubseteq)$ *where for each* $x, y \in \mathcal{L}$*, there exists*

1. *a unique greatest lower bound (glb), which is called the* meet *of x and y, and is denoted with $x \sqcap y$, and*
2. *a unique least upper bound (lub), which is called the* join *of x and y, and is denoted with $x \sqcup y$.*

If the ordering relation $\sqsubseteq$ is obvious we denote the lattice with the set $\mathcal{L}$.

Definition 14 (Finite Lattice). *A lattice $(\mathcal{L}, \sqsubseteq)$ is called* finite *iff $\mathcal{L}$ is finite.*

Every non-empty finite lattice has two well-defined unique elements: A least element, called *bottom*, denoted with $\bot$ and a greatest element, called *top*, denoted with $\top$.

Hasse diagrams are used to represent a finite partially ordered set. Each element of the set is represented as a vertex in the plane. For all $x, y \in \mathcal{L}$ where $x \sqsubseteq y$ but no $z \in \mathcal{L}$ exists where $x \sqsubseteq z \sqsubseteq y$ a line that goes *upward* from x to y is drawn.

Example 6 (Hasse Diagram). Hasse diagram for $\mathbb{B}_2 = \{\bot, \top\}$ with $\bot \sqsubseteq \top$:

Example 7 (Lattices).

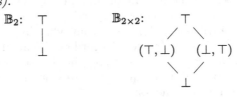

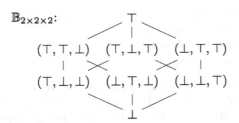

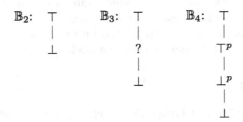

Definition 15 (Distributive Lattices). *A lattice $(\mathcal{L}, \sqsubseteq)$ is called a* distributive lattice *iff we have for all elements $x, y, z \in \mathcal{L}$*

$$x \sqcap (y \sqcup z) = (x \sqcap y) \sqcup (x \sqcap z) \; and$$
$$x \sqcup (y \sqcap z) = (x \sqcup y) \sqcap (x \sqcup z).$$

Definition 16 (De Morgan Lattice). *A distributive lattice* $(\mathcal{L}, \sqsubseteq)$ *is called a De Morgan lattice iff every element* $x \in \mathcal{L}$ *has a unique* dual *element* $\overline{x}$, *such that*

$$\overline{\overline{x}} = x \text{ and } x \sqsubseteq y \text{ implies } \overline{y} \sqsubseteq \overline{x}.$$

Definition 17 (Boolean Lattice). *A De Morgan lattice is called* Boolean *lattice iff for every element* x *and its dual element* $\overline{x}$ *we have*

$$x \sqcup \overline{x} = \top \text{ and } x \sqcap \overline{x} = \bot.$$

Every Boolean lattice has 2^n elements for some $n \in \mathbb{N}$.

Definition 18 (Truth Domain). *A* Truth Domain *is a finite De Morgan Lattice.*

Example 8 (Truth Domains). The following lattices are all Truth Domains:

- $\mathbb{B}_2 = \{\top, \bot\}$ with $\bot \sqsubseteq \top$ and
  $\overline{\top} = \bot$ and $\overline{\bot} = \top$.
- $\mathbb{B}_3 = \{\top, ?, \bot\}$ with $\bot \sqsubseteq ? \sqsubseteq \top$ and
  $\overline{\top} = \bot$, $\overline{?} = ?$ and $\overline{\bot} = \top$.
- $\mathbb{B}_4 = \{\top, \top^p, \bot^p, \bot\}$ with $\bot \sqsubseteq \bot^p \sqsubseteq \top^p \sqsubseteq \top$ and
  $\overline{\top} = \bot$, $\overline{\top^p} = \bot^p$, $\overline{\bot^p} = \top^p$ and $\overline{\bot} = \top$.

where we call ? also *inconclusive/don't know* and $\top^p$ and $\bot^p$ *presumably true* and *presumably false*, respectively.

4.2   Four-Valued Impartial LTL Semantics: FLTL$_4$

Let us now continue with the development of an impartial semantics of FLTL. Recall that the idea of impartiality is to for a go for a final verdict ($\top$ or $\bot$) only if you really know. In other words, *impartiality* requires that a finite trace is not evaluated to *true* or, respectively *false*, if there still exists an (possibly infinite) continuation leading to another verdict. Impartiality requires more than two truth values so that in general the semantics of a formula with respect to a trace is no longer a relation but a semantic function yielding a suitable truth value.

Definition 19 (Semantic Function). *The* semantic function

$$\text{sem}_k : \Sigma^+ \times \text{LTL} \to \mathbb{B}_k$$

maps a word $w \in \Sigma^+$ *and a an LTL formula* φ *to a logic value* $b \in \mathbb{B}_k$.
We use $[\![w \models \varphi]\!]_k = b$ *instead of* $\text{sem}_k(w, \varphi) = b$.

Clearly, this is a conservative extension and the semantics for (two-valued) FLTL can easily be given as a function:

We defined the FLTL semantics as *relation* $w \models \varphi$ between a word $w \in \Sigma^+$ and an LTL formula φ. This can be *interpreted as semantic function*

$$\text{sem}_2 : \Sigma^+ \times \text{LTL} \to \mathbb{B}_2,$$

$$\text{sem}_2(w, \varphi) = [\![w \models \varphi]\!]_2 := \begin{cases} \top & \text{if } w \models \varphi \\ \bot & \text{else.} \end{cases}$$

We can now define the notion of an impartial semantics formally:

Definition 20 (Impartial Semantics). *Let $\Sigma = 2^{\text{AP}}$ be an alphabet, $w \in \Sigma^+$ a word and φ an LTL formula. A semantic function is called* impartial *iff for all $u \in \Sigma^*$*

$$[\![w \models \varphi]\!] = \top \text{ implies } [\![wu \models \varphi]\!] = \top$$
$$[\![w \models \varphi]\!] = \bot \text{ implies } [\![wu \models \varphi]\!] = \bot.$$

We want to create impartial four-valued semantics for LTL on finite, non-completed words using the truth domain $(\mathbb{B}_4, \sqsubseteq)$. Let us look at examples our semantics should adhere to:

Example 9 ((FLTL vs. FLTL$_4$).

The indices 2 and 4 denote FLTL resp. FLTL$_4$.

$$[\![\emptyset \models Xa]\!]_2 = \bot \qquad\qquad [\![\emptyset \models Xa]\!]_4 = \bot^p$$
$$[\![\emptyset\emptyset \models Xa]\!]_2 = \bot \qquad\qquad [\![\emptyset\emptyset \models Xa]\!]_4 = \bot$$
$$[\![\emptyset\{a\} \models Xa]\!]_2 = \top \qquad\qquad [\![\emptyset\{a\} \models Xa]\!]_4 = \top$$
$$[\![\emptyset \models \overline{X}a]\!]_2 = \top \qquad\qquad [\![\emptyset \models \overline{X}a]\!]_4 = \top^p$$
$$[\![\emptyset\emptyset \models \overline{X}a]\!]_2 = \bot \qquad\qquad [\![\emptyset\emptyset \models \overline{X}a]\!]_4 = \bot$$
$$[\![\emptyset\{a\} \models \overline{X}a]\!]_2 = \top \qquad\qquad [\![\emptyset\{a\} \models \overline{X}a]\!]_4 = \top$$

At the end of the word X evaluates to $\bot^p$ instead of $\bot$ and $\overline{X}$ evaluates to $\top^p$ instead of $\top$. The idea of $\bullet^p$ is that it identifies the (two-valued) semantics if the word ends here but may change depending on the future. Fulfilling the introduced equivalences and fix point equations we get at the end of the word: U evaluates to $\bot^p$ instead of $\bot$, R evaluates to $\top^p$ instead of $\top$.

We now give the formal four-valued semantics for LTL on finite, non-completed and non-empty words:

Definition 21 (FLTL$_4$ Semantics). *Let φ, ψ be LTL formulae and let $w \in \Sigma^+$ be a finite word. Then the semantics of φ with respect to w is inductively defined as follows:*

$$[\![w \models \mathit{true}]\!]_4 = \top$$

$$[\![w \models \mathit{false}]\!]_4 = \bot$$

$$[\![w \models p]\!]_4 = \begin{cases} \top & \mathit{if}\ p \in w_1 \\ \bot & \mathit{if}\ p \notin w_1 \end{cases}$$

$$[\![w \models \neg p]\!]_4 = \begin{cases} \top & \mathit{if}\ p \notin w_1 \\ \bot & \mathit{if}\ p \in w_1 \end{cases}$$

$$[\![w \models \neg \varphi]\!]_4 = \overline{[\![w \models \varphi]\!]_4}$$

$$[\![w \models \varphi \vee \psi]\!]_4 = [\![w \models \varphi]\!]_4 \sqcup [\![w \models \psi]\!]_4$$

$$[\![w \models \varphi \wedge \psi]\!]_4 = [\![w \models \varphi]\!]_4 \sqcap [\![w \models \psi]\!]_4$$

$$[\![w \models X\varphi]\!]_4 = \begin{cases} [\![w^2 \models \varphi]\!]_4 & \mathit{if}\ |w| > 1 \\ \bot^p & \mathit{else} \end{cases}$$

$$[\![w \models \overline{X}\varphi]\!]_4 = \begin{cases} [\![w^2 \models \varphi]\!]_4 & \mathit{if}\ |w| > 1 \\ \top^p & \mathit{else} \end{cases}$$

$$[\![w \models \varphi U \psi]\!]_4$$

$$= \left(\bigsqcup_{1 \le i \le |w|} \left([\![w^i \models \psi]\!]_4 \sqcap \bigsqcap_{1 \le j < i} [\![w^j \models \varphi]\!]_4 \right) \right)$$

$$\sqcup \left(\bot^p \sqcap \bigsqcap_{1 \le i \le |w|} [\![w^i \models \varphi]\!]_4 \right)$$

$$[\![w \models \varphi R \psi]\!]_4$$

$$= \left(\bigsqcup_{1 \le i \le |w|} \left([\![w^i \models \varphi]\!]_4 \sqcap \bigsqcap_{1 \le j \le i} [\![w^j \models \psi]\!]_4 \right) \right)$$

$$\sqcup \left(\top^p \sqcap \bigsqcap_{1 \le i \le |w|} [\![w^i \models \psi]\!]_4 \right)$$

$$[\![w \models F\varphi]\!]_4 = \bot^p \sqcup \bigsqcup_{1 \le i \le |w|} [\![w^i \models \varphi]\!]_4$$

$$[\![w \models G\varphi]\!]_4 = \top^p \sqcap \bigsqcap_{1 \le i \le |w|} [\![w^i \models \varphi]\!]_4$$

Definition 22 (Equivalence of Formulae). *Let* $\Sigma = 2^{\mathrm{AP}}$ *and* φ *and* ψ *be LTL formulae over* AP. φ *and* ψ *are equivalent, denoted by* $\varphi \equiv \psi$, *iff*

$$\forall w \in \Sigma^+ : [\![w \models \varphi]\!] = [\![w \models \psi]\!].$$

Monitor Function. The idea of the monitoring function is to process a word while it is read, from-left-right. In other words, our goal is to build up a monitor function for evaluating each subsequent letter of non-completed words. Such a function takes an LTL formula φ in NNF and a letter $a \in \Sigma$, performs (not recursive) formula rewriting (progression) and returns $[\![a \models \varphi]\!]_4$ and a new LTL formula φ' that the next letter has to fulfill. To this end, we rewrite the LTL formula to keep track of what is done and what still needs to be checked.

For example, let $w \in \Sigma^+$ be a word and $p \in AP$ a letter. We can compute $[\![w \models Xp]\!]_4$ by doing nothing and letting someone else check $[\![w^2 \models p]\!]_4$. We can compute $[\![w \models a]\!]_4$ by checking $p \in w_1$.

Then the LTL formula is over. This is denoted by true or false as new formula.

It is straight forward to evaluate atomic propositions, positive operators of propositional logic ($\wedge, \vee$) and next-formulas. Thanks to De Morgan rules of propositional and temporal logic for negation ($\neg$) and fixed point equations for U and R those formulas do not have be treated explicitly.

Let $\Sigma = 2^{AP}$ be the finite alphabet, $p \in AP$ an atomic proposition, $a \in \Sigma$ a letter, and φ and ψ LTL formulae.

We then define the function $evlFLTL_4 : \Sigma \times LTL \to \mathbb{B}_4 \times LTL$ inductively as shown in Fig. 7.

Example 10 (Impartial Evaluation of Globally).
Consider $w = \{a\}\{a\}\emptyset$. First letter:

$$evlFLTL_4(\{a\}, Ga) = evlFLTL_4(\{a\}, a \wedge \overline{X}Ga)$$
$$= (v_1 \sqcap v_2, \varphi_1 \wedge \varphi_2)$$
$$= (\top \sqcap \top^p, true \wedge Ga)$$
$$= (\top^p, Ga)$$

$$\text{where } (v_1, \varphi_1) = evlFLTL_4(\{a\}, a) = (\top, true)$$
$$(v_2, \varphi_2) = evlFLTL_4(\{a\}, \overline{X}Ga) = (\top^p, Ga).$$

Next letters:

- $evlFLTL_4(\{a\}, Ga) = (\top^p, Ga)$
- $evlFLTL_4(\emptyset, Ga) = (\bot, false)$

4.3 Automata-Based Monitoring for FLTL$_4$

Within the automata-theoretic approach to monitoring, one creates an automaton, for example a deterministic one with output. Whenever a new observation on the underlying system is made, it is send to the automaton as input and the output yields the verdict for the trace observed so far.

The automaton synthesized for a property to check can typically be understood as a pre-computation of the respective monitoring function developed in the previous section. If, for example, the monitor is deterministic and realized as

$$\mathrm{evlFLTL_4}(a, \mathrm{true}) = (\top, \mathrm{true})$$

$$\mathrm{evlFLTL_4}(a, \mathrm{false}) = (\bot, \mathrm{false})$$

$$\mathrm{evlFLTL_4}(a, p) = \begin{cases} (\top, \mathrm{true}) & \text{if } p \in a \\ (\bot, \mathrm{false}) & \text{else} \end{cases}$$

$$\mathrm{evlFLTL_4}(a, \neg p) = \begin{cases} (\bot, \mathrm{false}) & \text{if } p \in a \\ (\top, \mathrm{true}) & \text{else} \end{cases}$$

$$\mathrm{evlFLTL_4}(a, \varphi \vee \psi) = (v_\varphi \sqcup v_\psi, \varphi' \vee \psi'), \text{ where}$$
$$(v_\varphi, \varphi') = \mathrm{evlFLTL_4}(a, \varphi) \text{ and}$$
$$(v_\psi, \psi') = \mathrm{evlFLTL_4}(a, \psi)$$

$$\mathrm{evlFLTL_4}(a, \varphi \wedge \psi) = (v_\varphi \sqcap v_\psi, \varphi' \wedge \psi'), \text{ where}$$
$$(v_\varphi, \varphi') = \mathrm{evlFLTL_4}(a, \varphi) \text{ and}$$
$$(v_\psi, \psi') = \mathrm{evlFLTL_4}(a, \psi)$$

$$\mathrm{evlFLTL_4}(a, \mathrm{X}\,\varphi) = (\bot^p, \varphi)$$

$$\mathrm{evlFLTL_4}(a, \overline{\mathrm{X}}\,\varphi) = (\top^p, \varphi)$$

$$\mathrm{evlFLTL_4}(a, \varphi \,\mathrm{U}\, \psi) = \mathrm{evlFLTL_4}(a, \psi \vee (\varphi \wedge \mathrm{X}(\varphi \,\mathrm{U}\, \psi)))$$

$$\mathrm{evlFLTL_4}(a, \varphi \,\mathrm{R}\, \psi) = \mathrm{evlFLTL_4}(a, \psi \wedge (\varphi \vee \overline{\mathrm{X}}(\varphi \,\mathrm{R}\, \psi)))$$

$$\mathrm{evlFLTL_4}(a, \mathrm{F}\,\varphi) = \mathrm{evlFLTL_4}(a, \varphi \vee \mathrm{X}\,\mathrm{F}\,\varphi)$$

$$\mathrm{evlFLTL_4}(a, \mathrm{G}\,\varphi) = \mathrm{evlFLTL_4}(a, \varphi \wedge \overline{\mathrm{X}}\,\mathrm{G}\,\varphi)$$

Fig. 7. Evaluation of LTL formulas with an impartial, four-valued semantics

a transition table, only a simple look-up in the table is necessary for processing the observation. Thus, the automata-theoretic approach to monitoring is considered to be efficient at runtime but of course, the precomputed transition table may be huge.

The goal of this subsection is to provide a synthesis procedure for $\mathrm{FLTL_4}$, based on the evaluation function given in the previous subsection.

The translation is guided by the following observation: $\mathrm{evlFLTL_4}$ gets a *letter* and a *formula* and outputs a *logic value* and a *new formula*. We use *formula* as *state* of the Mealy machine and *letter* as *input* and *logic value* as *output*. The *next state* (new formula) depends on the *state* (formula) and *input* (letter), while the *Output* depends on *state* (formula) and *input* (letter).

Definition 23 (Deterministic Mealy Machine). *A (deterministic) Mealy machine is a tupel* $\mathcal{M} = (\Sigma, Q, q_0, \Gamma, \delta)$ *where*

- *Σ is the* input alphabet,
- *Q is a finite set of* states,
- *$q_0 \in Q$ is the* initial state,
- *Γ is the* output alphabet *and*
- *$\delta : Q \times \Sigma \rightarrow \Gamma \times Q$ is the* transition function

Definition 24 (Run of a Deterministic Mealy Machine). *A run of a (deterministic) Mealy machine $\mathcal{M} = (\Sigma, Q, q_0, \Gamma, \delta)$ on a finite word $w \in \Sigma^n$ with outputs $o_i \in \Gamma$ is a sequence*

$$t_0 \overset{(w_1, o_1)}{\to} t_1 \overset{(w_2, o_2)}{\to} \ldots \overset{(w_{n-1}, o_{n-1})}{\to} t_{n-1} \overset{(w_n, o_n)}{\to} t_n$$

such that

- $t_0 = q_0$ *and*
- $(t_i, o_i) = \delta(t_{i-1}, w_i)$

The output of the run is o_n.

Our synthesis procedure will first generate *alternating* machines, which then may be translated into non-deterministic or deterministic machines. Intuitively, an alternating machine may proceed from a boolean combination of states to a subsequent boolean combination of states, following the transition function. Non-deterministic and deterministic machines are, respectively, intuitively in a set or a single state.

Alternating Mealy Machine

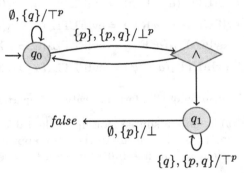

Input $\emptyset$ $\{p\}$ $\{q\}$ $\emptyset$ $\{q\}$
Output $\top^p$ $\bot^p$ $\top^p$ $\bot$ $\bot$

Definition 25 (Positive Boolean Combination (PBC)). *Given a set Q we define the set of all* positive *Boolean combinations (PBC) over Q, denoted by $B^+(Q)$, inductively as follows:*

- $\{\text{true}, \text{false}\} \subseteq B^+(Q)$,
- $Q \subseteq B^+(Q)$ *and*
- $\forall \alpha, \beta \in B^+(Q) : \alpha \vee \beta, \alpha \wedge \beta \in B^+(Q)$.

Example 11. Consider $\text{AP} = \{a, b, c\}$

- $a \in B^+(\text{AP}), \{a\} \notin B^+(\text{AP})$,
- $a \wedge b \vee a \wedge c \in B^+(\text{AP})$,

– true $\in B^+(\mathrm{AP})$ and false $\in B^+(\mathrm{AP})$.

Now, we are ready to define alternating Mealy machines, their extended transition function as well as their runs:

Definition 26 (Alternating Mealy Machine (AMM)). *A alternating Mealy machine (AMM) is a tupel* $\mathcal{M} = (\Sigma, Q, q_0, \Gamma, \delta)$ *where*

- Σ *is the* input alphabet,
- Q *is a finite set of* states,
- $q_0 \in Q$ *is the* initial state *and*
- Γ *is a finite, distributive lattice, the* output lattice,
- $\delta : Q \times \Sigma \to B^+(\Gamma \times Q)$ *is the* transition function

Sometimes, we understand $\delta : Q \times \Sigma \to B^+(\Gamma \times Q)$ as a function $\delta : Q \times \Sigma \to \Gamma \times B^+(Q)$, yielding a tuple with the first component having the value of the respective meets and joins of individual outputs and second component having the positive Boolean combination of the respective second components.

Definition 27 (Extended Transition Function). *Let* $\delta : Q \times \Sigma \to \Gamma \times B^+(Q)$ *be the transition function of an alternating mealy machine. Then the extended transition function* $\hat{\delta} : B^+(Q) \times \Sigma \to \Gamma \times B^+(Q)$ *is inductively defined as follows*

- $\hat{\delta}(q, a) = \delta(q, a)$,
- $\hat{\delta}(\text{true}, a) = (\top, \text{true})$, $\hat{\delta}(\text{false}, a) = (\bot, \text{false})$,
- $\hat{\delta}(q_1 \vee q_2, a) = (o_1 \sqcup o_2, q_1' \vee q_2')$ *and*
- $\hat{\delta}(q_1 \wedge q_2, a) = (o_1 \sqcap o_2, q_1' \wedge q_2')$,
  where $(o_1, q_1') = \hat{\delta}(q_1, a)$ *and* $(o_2, q_2') = \hat{\delta}(q_2, a)$.

Definition 28 (Run of an Alternating Mealy Machine). *A run of an alternating Mealy machine* $\mathcal{M} = (\Sigma, Q, q_0, \Gamma, \delta)$ *on a finite word* $w \in \Sigma^n$ *with outputs* $o_i \in \Gamma$ *is a sequence*

$$t_0 \overset{(w_1, o_1)}{\to} t_1 \overset{(w_2, o_2)}{\to} \ldots \overset{(w_{n-1}, o_{n-1})}{\to} t_{n-1} \overset{(w_n, o_n)}{\to} t_n$$

such that

$$t_0 = q_0 \text{ and } (t_i, o_i) = \hat{\delta}(t_{i-1}, w_i),$$

where $\hat{\delta}$ *is the extended transition function of* $\mathcal{M}$.
    The output *of the run is* o_n.

Let us now derive the necessary machinery for translation alternating machines to deterministic ones.

Definition 29 (Model Relation for PBCs). *Let* Q *be a set. A subset* $S \subseteq Q$ *is a* model *of a positive Boolean combination* $\alpha \in B^+(Q)$, *denoted by* $S \models \alpha$, *iff* α *evaluates to true in propositional logic interpreting all* $p \in S$ *as true and all* $p \in Q \backslash S$ *as false.*

Definition 30 (Equivalence of PBCs). *Let Q be a set and $\alpha \in B^+(Q)$ and $\beta \in B^+(Q)$ be positive Boolean combinations over Q. α and β are* equivalent, *denoted by $\alpha \equiv \beta$, iff*

$$\forall S \subseteq Q : S \models \alpha \Leftrightarrow S \models \beta.$$

Definition 31 (Equivalence Classes of PBCs). *Let Q be a set. The* equivalence class $[\alpha]$ *of a positive Boolean combination $\alpha \in B^+(Q)$ over Q is defined as follows*

$$[\alpha] = \{\beta \in B^+(Q) \mid \alpha \equiv \beta\}.$$

The set of all equivalence classes of positive Boolean combinations over Q is denoted by the following quotient set

$$B^+(Q)/\equiv \, = \{[\alpha] \mid \alpha \in B^+(Q)\}.$$

Alternating Mealy machines can easily be translated into (deterministic) Mealy machines. The idea is to use $B^+(Q)/\equiv$ instead of $B^+(Q)$ as a state space and to extend the transition function correspondingly. This is well defined:

Lemma 2. *Let $\hat{\delta}$ be the extended transition function of an AMM $\mathcal{M} = (\Sigma, Q, q_0, \Gamma, \delta)$, $a \in \Sigma$, $o, p \in \Gamma$ and $\alpha, \beta, \alpha', \beta' \in B^+(Q)$ such that*

$$\alpha \equiv \beta,$$
$$(o, \alpha') = \hat{\delta}(\alpha, a) \ and$$
$$(p, \beta') = \hat{\delta}(\beta, a).$$

Then

$$o = p \ and \qquad (*)$$
$$\alpha' \equiv \beta'.$$

The proof of $(*)$ requires the output lattice to be distributive.

In other words, equivalent combinations of states yield the same output and an equivalent combination of successor states. Thus, whenever we perform a transition, we can normalize the resulting Boolean combination of states without changing the output for an input word. As for any fixed set of states, there are only finitely many non-equivalent formulae, we have the general result that we can transform an alternating machine to a deterministic one. However, let us be more specific.

We can use $B^+(Q)/\equiv$ instead of Q as states. We still need a well defined representative for $[\alpha]$ for $\alpha \in B^+(Q)$. In other words: Given $\alpha \in Q$, how to find $[\alpha]$? We use disjunctive normal form of α.

Definition 32 (Disjunctive Normal Form (DNF)). *A positive Boolean combination $\alpha \in B^+(Q)$ over a set Q is in* disjunctive normal form *(DNF) iff*

$$\alpha = \bigvee_{i=1}^{n} \bigwedge_{j=1}^{m} q_{i,j}$$

for $q_{i,j} \in Q$. A disjunctive normal form $\alpha \in B^+(Q)$ is called minimal if there is no disjunctive normal form $\beta \in B^+(Q)$ s. t. $\alpha \equiv \beta$ and β contains less operators.

Lemma 3. For every positive Boolean combination $\alpha \in B^+(Q)$ there exists a positive Boolean combination β such that $\alpha \equiv \beta$ and β is in minimal DNF.

Proof uses distributivity of propositional logic.

$B^+(Q)/\equiv$ is finite. Let Q be the set of states of an AMM. Then Q is finite. Then there are at most $2^{|Q|}$ many different α for

$$\alpha = \bigvee_{i=1}^{n} q_i \text{ and } n \text{ different } q_i \in Q.$$

Then there are at most $2^{2^{|Q|}}$ many different β for

$$\beta = \bigvee_{i=1}^{n} \bigwedge_{j=1}^{m} q_{i,j} \text{ minimal and } q_{i,j} \in Q.$$

Then there are at most $2^{2^{|Q|}}$ many different $[\beta]$ for $\beta \in B^+(Q)$.

Example 12 (Alternating Mealy Machine).

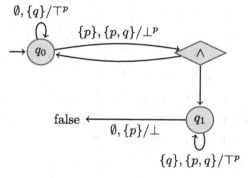

Example 13 (Translated Mealy Machine).

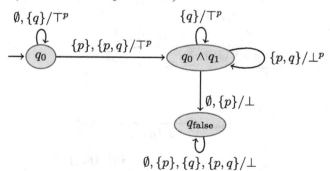

Using similar ideas, we can translate an AMM to Non-Deterministic or Universal MM.

Automata Based RV. We monitor an LTL formula φ by evaluating its current subformula ψ w.r.t. the current letter a.

The monitor function evlFLTL$_4$, which takes an LTL formula ψ in NNF and a letter $a \in \Sigma$ and returns $[\![a \models \psi]\!]_4$ and a new LTL formula ψ', can be interpreted as transition function of an AMM where the states are subformulae of φ, the initial state is φ, the current state is ψ, we read the letter a, we output $[\![a \models \psi]\!]_4$ and the next state is the new formula ψ'.

Let $\Sigma = 2^{AP}$ be the finite alphabet, $p \in AP$ an atomic proposition, $a \in \Sigma$ a letter, φ, ψ_1, ψ_2 LTL formulae in NNF and Q the set of all subformulae of φ.

We then define the transition function $\delta_4^a : Q \times \Sigma \to B^+(\mathbb{B}_4 \times Q)$ of the monitor AMM $\mathcal{M}_\varphi = (\Sigma, Q, \varphi, \mathbb{B}_4, \delta_4^a)$ inductively as follows:

$$\delta_4^a(\text{true}, a) = (\top, \text{true})$$
$$\delta_4^a(\text{false}, a) = (\bot, \text{false})$$
$$\delta_4^a(p, a) = \begin{cases} (\top, \text{true}) & \text{if } p \in a \\ (\bot, \text{false}) & \text{else} \end{cases}$$
$$\delta_4^a(\neg p, a) = \begin{cases} (\top, \text{true}) & \text{if } p \notin a \\ (\bot, \text{false}) & \text{else} \end{cases}$$
$$\delta_4^a(\psi_1 \vee \psi_2, a) = \delta_4^a(\psi_1, a) \vee \delta_4^a(\psi_2, a)$$
$$\delta_4^a(\psi_1 \wedge \psi_2, a) = \delta_4^a(\psi_1, a) \wedge \delta_4^a(\psi_2, a)$$
$$\delta_4^a(X\psi_1, a) = (\bot^p, \psi_1)$$
$$\delta_4^a(\overline{X}\psi_1, a) = (\top^p, \psi_1)$$

$$\delta_4^a(\psi_1 U \psi_2, a) = \delta_4^a(\psi_2 \vee (\psi_1 \wedge X(\psi_1 U \psi_2)), a)$$
$$\delta_4^a(\psi_1 R \psi_2, a) = \delta_4^a(\psi_2 \wedge (\psi_1 \vee \overline{X}(\psi_1 R \psi_2)), a)$$
$$\delta_4^a(F\psi_1, a) = \delta_4^a(\psi_1 \vee (X(F\psi_1)), a)$$
$$\delta_4^a(G\psi_1, a) = \delta_4^a(\psi_1 \wedge (\overline{X}(G\psi_1)), a)$$

Example 14. Graph of the monitor $\mathcal{M}_\varphi$ of the formula $\varphi = G(p \to XGq)$:

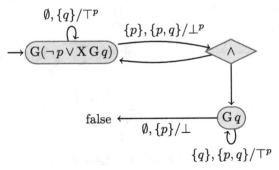

In practical implementations one may omit the AMM and generate the MM directly out of the LTL formula. Define a function smplfy : LTL $\to$ LTL that transforms LTL formulae into a unique normal form. Use all simplified positive Boolean combinations of subformulae of φ as states for $\mathcal{M}_\varphi$. Define $\delta_4 : Q \times \Sigma \to \mathbb{B}_4 \times Q$ inductively as follows:

$$\delta_4(\psi_1 \vee \psi_2, a) = (v_{\psi_1} \sqcup v_{\psi_2}, \mathrm{smplfy}(\psi_1' \vee \psi_2')), \text{ where}$$
$$(v_{\psi_1}, \psi_1') = \delta_4(\psi_1, a) \text{ and}$$
$$(v_{\psi_2}, \psi_2') = \delta_4(\psi_2, a)$$
$$\delta_4(\psi_1 \wedge \psi_2, a) = (v_{\psi_1} \sqcap v_{\psi_2}, \mathrm{smplfy}(\psi_1' \wedge \psi_2')), \text{ where}$$
$$(v_{\psi_1}, \psi_1') = \delta_4(\psi_1, a) \text{ and}$$
$$(v_{\psi_2}, \psi_2') = \delta_4(\psi_2, a)$$
$$\delta_4(\psi_1, a) = \delta_4^a(\psi_1, a) \text{ for any other formula } \psi_1.$$

5   Anticipatory LTL Semantics

Using the monitor construction for FLTL$_4$ we are able to build an automata based impartial LTL monitor. Our monitor can tell us if a property is fulfilled or violated by a run and if this may change or will last forever. In this section we will go for anticipation. Recall that, in simple words, *impartiality* means to say $\top$ or $\bot$ only if you are sure while *anticipation* means to say $\top$ or $\bot$ once you can be sure.

In the next sections we will follow the same steps as for creating the impartial monitor:

– Define an anticipatory LTL semantics.
– Recall a suitable automaton type and its translation towards a deterministic one.
– Define a monitor construction based on the new semantics.

In the next subsections we will introduce the necessary machinery to finally be able to present a monitor construction for LTL$_3$.

LTL on Infinite Words. The idea of the anticipatory semantics is to say $\top$ once every infinite continuation evaluates to $\top$, to say $\bot$ once every infinite continuation evaluates to $\bot$, and to otherwise say ?, as the verdict may depend on the future of the underlying execution.

As our anticipatory semantics depends on infinite continuations, we recall the LTL semantics on infinite words.

An infinite word w is an infinite sequence over the alphabet $\Sigma = 2^{\mathrm{AP}}$. w can be interpreted as function $w : \mathbb{N} \setminus \{0\} \to \Sigma$. w can be interpreted as concatenation of many finite and one infinite words.

Example 15 (Infinite Words).
Consider the alphabet $\Sigma = 2^{\mathrm{AP}}$ with $\mathrm{AP} = \{p, q\}$.

– $\{p\}^\omega$ denotes the infinite word where every letter is $\{p\}$ and can be interpreted as $w(i) = \{p\}$ for all $i \geq 1$.

– $\emptyset(\{q\}\{p\})^\omega$ can be interpreted as

$$w(i) = \begin{cases} \emptyset & \text{if } i = 1 \\ \{q\} & \text{if } i \equiv 0 \mod 2 \\ \{p\} & \text{else} \end{cases}$$

Semantics. We have introduced LTL first for finite words, as this was needed for runtime verification on finite, terminated executions. However LTL on infnite words is currently the traditional way to define LTL semantics due to its typical use in model checking, where most often infinite runs are considered. Moreover, the semantics is slightly simpler to define for the next-operators. Actually the semantics of $X\varphi$ and $\overline{X}\varphi$ do not differ—on infinite traces. This is due to the fact that for an infinite trace, there always exists a subsequent positon in which φ can be evaluated.

In the formal definition of LTL semantics we denote parts of a word as follows: Let $w = a_1 a_2 a_3 \ldots \in \Sigma^\omega$ be an infinite word over the alphabet $\Sigma = 2^{AP}$ and let $i \in \mathbb{N}$ with $i \geq 1$ be a position in this word. Then

– $w_i = a_i$ is the i-th letter of the word,
– $w^{(i)} = a_1 a_2 \ldots a_i$ is the prefix of w of length i and
– w^i is the subword of w s.t. $w = w^{(i-1)} w^i$.

We now give the formal two-valued semantics for LTL on infinite words:

Definition 33 (LTL Semantics on Infinite Words). *Let φ, ψ be LTL formulae and let $w \in \Sigma^\omega$ be an infinite word. Then the semantics of φ with respect to w is inductively defined as follows:*

$$
\begin{array}{lll}
w \models \text{true} & & \\
w \models p & \textit{iff } p \in w_1 & \\
w \models \neg p & \textit{iff } p \notin w_1 & \\
w \models \neg \varphi & \textit{iff } w \not\models \varphi & \\
w \models \varphi \vee \psi & \textit{iff } w \models \varphi \textit{ or } w \models \psi & \\
w \models \varphi \wedge \psi & \textit{iff } w \models \varphi \textit{ and } w \models \psi & \\
w \models X\varphi & \textit{iff } w^2 \models \varphi & \\
w \models \overline{X}\varphi & \textit{iff } w^2 \models \varphi & \\
w \models \varphi U\psi & \textit{iff } \exists i \geq 1 : (w^i \models \psi \textit{ and } \forall k, 1 \leq k < i : w^k \models \varphi) & \\
w \models \varphi R\psi & \textit{iff } \exists i \geq 1 : (w^i \models \varphi \textit{ and } \forall k, 1 \leq k \leq i : w^k \models \psi) & \\
& \quad \textit{or } \forall i \geq 1 : w^i \models \psi & \\
w \models F\varphi & \textit{iff } \exists i \geq 1 : w^i \models \varphi & \\
w \models G\varphi & \textit{iff } \forall i \geq 1 : w^i \models \varphi &
\end{array}
$$

We defined the LTL semantics on infinite words as *relation* $w \models \varphi$ between a word $w \in \Sigma^\omega$ and a LTL formula φ. This can be *interpreted as semantic function*

$$\mathrm{sem}_\omega : \Sigma^\omega \times \mathrm{LTL} \to \mathbb{B}_2,$$

$$\mathrm{sem}_\omega(w, \varphi) = [\![w \models \varphi]\!]_\omega := \begin{cases} \top & \text{if } w \models \varphi \\ \bot & \text{else.} \end{cases}$$

The set of models of an LTL formula φ defines a language $\mathcal{L}(\varphi) \subseteq \Sigma^\omega$ of infinite words over $\Sigma = 2^{\mathrm{AP}}$ as follows:

$$\mathcal{L}(\varphi) = \{w \in \Sigma^\omega \mid [\![w \models \varphi]\!]_\omega = \top\}.$$

Note that the De Morgan rules, equivalences for G and F and the fixed point equations for U and R are still valid.

5.1   Anticipatory LTL Semantics: LTL$_3$

Recall that *anticipation* requires that once every (possibly infinite) continuation of a finite trace leads to the same verdict, then the finite trace evaluates to this very same verdict.

FLTL$_4$ is not anticipatory: $[\![\{p\} \models \mathrm{XXfalse}]\!]_4 = \bot^p$ but it should yield $\bot$ as any finite extension will eventually reveal that the formula is falsified.

Definition 34 LTL$_3$ (Semantics). *Let φ be an LTL formula and let $u \in \Sigma^*$ be a finite word. Then the semantics of φ with respect to u is defined as follows:*

$$[\![u \models \varphi]\!]_3 = \begin{cases} \top & \text{if } \forall w \in \Sigma^\omega : [\![uw \models \varphi]\!]_\omega = \top \\ \bot & \text{if } \forall w \in \Sigma^\omega : [\![uw \models \varphi]\!]_\omega = \bot \\ ? & \text{else.} \end{cases}$$

Example 16. Consider $\varphi = \mathrm{G}(p \to \mathrm{F}\mathit{false})$ and $\emptyset\{q\}\{p\}\emptyset \in \Sigma^*$ for $\Sigma = 2^{\mathrm{AP}}$ and $\mathrm{AP} = \{p, q\}$. We then have

- $[\![\emptyset \models \varphi]\!]_3 =?$
- $[\![\emptyset\{q\} \models \varphi]\!]_3 =?$
- $[\![\emptyset\{q\}\{p\} \models \varphi]\!]_3 = \bot$
- $[\![\emptyset\{q\}\{p\}\emptyset \models \varphi]\!]_3 = \bot$
- $[\![\emptyset\{q\}\{p\}u \models \varphi]\!]_3 = \bot$ for all $u \in \Sigma^*$

Possible Verdicts of LTL Formulae. Consider a word $w \in \Sigma^*$ for $\Sigma = 2^{\mathrm{AP}}$ and propositions $p, q \in \mathrm{AP}$. We then have

- $[\![w \models p\mathrm{U}q]\!]_3 \in \{\top, ?, \bot\}$
- $[\![w \models p\mathrm{R}q]\!]_3 \in \{\top, ?, \bot\}$
- $[\![w \models \mathrm{F}p]\!]_3 \in \{\top, ?\}$

- $\llbracket w \models Gp \rrbracket_3 \in \{?, \bot\}$
- $\llbracket w \models GFp \rrbracket_3 = ?$
- $\llbracket w \models FGp \rrbracket_3 = ?$

5.2   Monitorable Properties

In this subsection, we study the notion of monitorable properties. In essence, a property is called *monitorable* if there is no finite point in time from we may conclude that we stay with the verdict? for ever. For comparison, we also recall the notion of safety and co-safety properties, which we do first.

Definition 35 (Good, Bad and Ugly Prefixes). *Given a language $L \subseteq \Sigma^\omega$ of infinite words over Σ we call a finite word $u \in \Sigma^*$*

- *a good prefix for L if $\forall w \in \Sigma^\omega : uw \in L$,*
- *a bad prefix for L if $\forall w \in \Sigma^\omega : uw \notin L$ and*
- *an ugly prefix for L if $\forall v \in \Sigma^* : uv$ is neither a good prefix nor a bad prefix.*

Example 17 (The Good, The Bad and The Ugly).

- $\{p\}\{q\}$ is a good prefix for $\mathcal{L}(Fq)$.
- $\{p\}\{q\}\{p\}$ is a good prefix for $\mathcal{L}(Fq)$.
- $\{p\}\{q\}$ is a bad prefix for $\mathcal{L}(Gp)$.
- every $w \in \Sigma^*$ is an ugly prefix for $\mathcal{L}(GFp)$.
- $\{p\}$ is an ugly prefix for $\mathcal{L}(p \rightarrow GFp)$.

LTL_3 *indentifies good/bad prefixes* Given an LTL formula φ and a finite word $u \in \Sigma^*$, then

$$\llbracket u \models \varphi \rrbracket_3 = \begin{cases} \top & \text{if } u \text{ is a good prefix for } \mathcal{L}(\varphi) \\ \bot & \text{if } u \text{ is a bad prefix for } \mathcal{L}(\varphi) \\ ? & \text{otherwise} \end{cases}$$

Safety Properties assert that nothing bad happens. Such a property is *violated* iff something *bad* happens after *finitely many steps*. ($\rightarrow$ A bad prefix exists.)

Co-Safety Properties assert that something good happens. Such a property is *fulfilled* iff something *good* happens after *finitely many steps*. ($\rightarrow$ A good prefix exists.)

Definition 36 ((Co-)Safety Languages). *A language $L \subseteq \Sigma^\omega$ is called*

- *a safety language if for all $w \notin L$ there is a prefix $u \in \Sigma^*$ of w which is a bad prefix for L.*
- *a co-safety language if for all $w \in L$ there is a prefix $u \in \Sigma^*$ of w which is a good prefix for L.*

Definition 37 ((Co-)Safety Properties). *An LTL formula* φ *is called*

- a safety property *if its set of models* $\mathcal{L}(\varphi)$ *is a safety language.*
- a co-safety property *if its set of models* $\mathcal{L}(\varphi)$ *is a co-safety language.*

Example 18 Consider propositions $p, q \in \mathrm{AP}$.

Formula	Safety	Co-Safety
$\mathrm{G}\,p$	✔	✘
$\mathrm{F}\,p$	✘	✔
$\mathrm{X}\,p$	✔	✔
$\mathrm{G}\,\mathrm{F}\,p$	✘	✘
$\mathrm{F}\,\mathrm{G}\,p$	✘	✘
$\mathrm{X}\,p \vee \mathrm{G}\,\mathrm{F}\,p$	✘	✘
$p\,\mathrm{U}\,q$	✘	✔
$p\,\mathrm{R}\,q$	✔	✘

- $p\mathrm{U}q$ is not a safety property, because $\{p\}^\omega \not\models p\mathrm{U}q$, but there is no bad prefix.
- $p\mathrm{U}q$ is a co-safety property, because every infinite word $w \in \Sigma^\omega$ with $w \models p\mathrm{U}q$ must contain the releasing q in a finite prefix.
- $p\mathrm{R}q$ is not a co-safety property, because $\{q\}^\omega \models p\mathrm{R}q$, but there is no good prefix.
- $p\mathrm{R}q$ is a safety property, because every infinite word $w \in \Sigma^\omega$ with $w \not\models p\mathrm{R}q$ must contain the violating absence of q in a finite prefix.

Let us now turn our attention to the notion of monitorabilty, which intuitively characterizes a property as monitorable, if eventually, we might get a definite verdict when monitoring it.

Definition 38 (Monitorable Languages). *A language* $L \subseteq \Sigma^\omega$ *is called* monitorable *iff* L *has no ugly prefix.*

Definition 39 (Monitorable Properties). *An LTL formula* φ *is called* monitorable *iff its set of models* $\mathcal{L}(\varphi)$ *is monitorable.*

Safety Properties

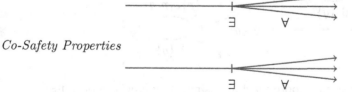

Co-Safety Properties

Remark 1. Safety and Co-Safety Properties are monitorable.

Theorem 1. *The class of* monitorable properties

- *comprises safety- and co-safety properties, but*

– is strictly larger than their union.

Proof. Consider AP $= \{p, q, r\}$ and $\varphi = ((p \vee q)\mathrm{U}r) \vee \mathrm{G}p$. $\{p\}^{\omega} \models \varphi$ without good prefix, therefore φ is not a co-safety property. $\{q\}^{\omega} \not\models \varphi$ without bad prefix, therefore φ is not a safety property. Every finite word $u \in \Sigma^*$ that is not a bad prefix can become a good prefix by appending $\{r\}$. Every finite word $u \in \Sigma^*$ that is not a good prefix can become a bad prefix by appending $\emptyset$. No ugly prefix exists as every prefix is either good, bad or can become good or bad by appending $\{r\}$ or $\emptyset$.

5.3   Monitor Construction for Anticipatory Runtime Verification

In this section we will recall the idea of translating LTL (with its two-valued semantics on infinite words) into Büchi automata and then use this to present a monitor construction for anticipatory and impartial runtime verification.

Our goal is to construct a Moore machine $\mathcal{M}^{\varphi}$ for an LTL formula φ that reads a word letter by letter and outputs in every state the value of $\llbracket w \models \varphi \rrbracket_3$ where w is the word read so far.

A first idea would be to reuse the evlFLTL$_4$ function and to perform an additional check on the resulting formula. More precisely, one could return $\top$ or $\bot$ if the formula is a tautology or unsatisfiable, respectively, and to return? in any other case. However, a satisfiability check is a complex task so that we are after a different approach.

Instead, we follow the idea to construct a Büchi automaton (BA) accepting precisely the models of the LTL formula and analyse it. More precisely, we identify good states $\top$ in which the BA will accept on every continuation, bad states $\bot$, in which the BA will reject on every continuation, yielding other states ?, in which no conclusion is possible yet.

For example consider AP $= \{p, q\}$ and $\Sigma = 2^{\mathrm{AP}}$ and the following automaton:

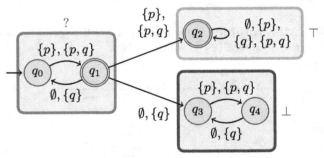

Our goal is to create a Moore machine using these labels as outputs.

While it is algorithmically easy to identify the $\bot$-states in a non-deterministic machine, the $\top$-states are difficult to estimate as they require universality check. Therefore, we take a slighltly different approach. We only identify bad states ($\bot$) and label everything else as not bad ($\neq \bot$). Perform this for the LTL formulae φ and $\neg\varphi$. Good states for φ are bad states for $\neg\varphi$.

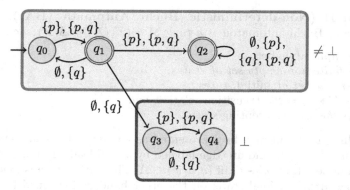

Note that an LTL formula can be complemented by adding ¬. And that complementing a BA potentially needs *exponential time*.

Büchi Automata (BA).

Definition 40 (ω-regular Languages). *A language $L \subseteq \Sigma^\omega$ over an alphabet Σ is called ω-regular iff there are regular languages $U_i, V_i \subseteq \Sigma^*$ for $i \in \{1, \ldots, m\}$ such that*

$$L = \bigcup_{i=1}^{m} U_i \circ V_i^\omega.$$

Example 19 (ω-regular Languages). Consider an alphabet $\Sigma = 2^{AP}$ for AP = $\{p, q\}$.

$$\mathcal{L}(Gp) = \{\{p\}, \{p, q\}\}^\omega$$
$$\mathcal{L}(Fp) = \Sigma^* \circ \{\{p\}, \{p, q\}\} \circ \Sigma^\omega$$

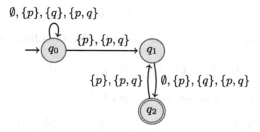

Fig. 8. A examplifying Büchi automaton

Büchi automata were first introduced by Büchi in [Buc62] for obtaining a decision procedure for the monadic second-order theory of structures with one successor. Let us establish the key concepts of this kind of automata to the extent needed in our thesis. For a thorough introduction to Büchi automata we refer to [Tho90]. We start directly with their definition:

Definition 41 (Non-deterministic Büchi Automata (BA)). *A (non-deterministic)* Büchi automaton *is a tuple* $\mathcal{A} = (\Sigma, Q, Q_0, \Delta, F)$ *such that*

- Σ *is the* input alphabet,
- Q *is the finite non-empty set of* states,
- $Q_0 \subseteq Q$ *is the set of* initial states,
- $\Delta \subseteq Q \times \Sigma \times Q$ *is the* transition relation *and*
- $F \subseteq Q$ *is the set of* accepting states.

A Büchi automaton may be represented as an edge-labeled directed graph. Its nodes are the states and an edge labeled by $a \in \Sigma$ leads from a node (state) $q \in Q$ to a node (state) $q' \in Q$ iff $(q, a, q') \in \Delta$. The initial state is marked with an incoming arrow. A final state, on the other hand, is identified by a second circle around the node. Figure 8 shows an exemplifying Büchi automaton over the alphabet $\Sigma = 2^{\text{AP}}$ for AP $= \{p, q\}$.

The automaton operates on infinite input words. The idea of its behavior is that it chooses (non-deterministically) a possible successor state q' such that $(q, a, q') \in \Delta$, provided it is in the state q and reads an action a. Of course, the automaton starts in its initial state.

Definition 42 (Run of a BA). *A run of a BA* $\mathcal{A} = (\Sigma, Q, Q_0, \Delta, F)$ *on an infinite word* $w \in \Sigma^\omega$ *is a function* $\rho : \mathbb{N} \to Q$ *such that*

- $\rho(0) \in Q_0$ *and*
- $\forall i \in \mathbb{N} \backslash \{0\} : (\rho(i-1), w_i, \rho(i)) \in \Delta$.

Sometimes, we represent a run ρ only by its sequence of images. For example, a run of the automaton shown in Fig. 8 on the word $\{p\}\{p,q\}(\{q\}\{p\})^\omega$ is given by the sequence $q_0 q_0 q_1 (q_2 q_1)^\omega$.

Definition 43 (Accepting Runs of a BA). *A run* ρ *of a BA* $\mathcal{A} = (\Sigma, Q, Q_0, \Delta, F)$ *is called* accepting *iff*

$$\text{Inf}(\rho) \cap F \neq \emptyset,$$

where $\text{Inf}(\rho)$ *denotes the* set of states visited infinitely often *given by*

$$\text{Inf}(\rho) = \left\{ q \in Q \; \middle| \; |\{k \in \mathbb{N} \mid \rho(k) = q\}| = \infty \right\}.$$

$\mathcal{A}$ accepts w *if there is an accepting run* ρ *of* $\mathcal{A}$ *on* w.

Again the language $\mathcal{L}(\mathcal{A}) \subseteq \Sigma^\omega$ of an automata $\mathcal{A}$ with the alphabet Σ is defined as follows:

$$\mathcal{L}(\mathcal{A}) = \{w \in \Sigma^\omega \mid \mathcal{A} \text{ accepts } w\}.$$

We make use of the fundamental result by Vardi and Wolper:

Theorem 2 (From LTL to BA [VW86]**).** *For a given LTL formula* φ *over an alphabet* Σ *we can construct a BA* $\mathcal{A}^\varphi$ *that accepts precisely the models of* φ. *Moreover, the size of the automaton is exponential in the lenght of the formula.*

5.4   Emptiness per State

For a given LTL formula φ over an alphabet Σ we will construct a Moore machine $\mathcal{M}^\varphi$ that reads finite words $w \in \Sigma^*$ and outputs $[\![w \models \varphi]\!]_3 \in \mathcal{B}_3$.

For the next steps let

$$\mathcal{A}^\varphi = (\Sigma, Q^\varphi, Q_0^\varphi, \delta^\varphi, F^\varphi)$$

denote the BA accepting all models of φ and

$$\mathcal{A}^{\neg\varphi} = (\Sigma, Q^{\neg\varphi}, Q_0^{\neg\varphi}, \delta^{\neg\varphi}, F^{\neg\varphi})$$

denote the BA accepting all words falsifying φ.

Definition 44 (BA With Adjusted Initial State). *For an BA $\mathcal{A}$, we denote by $\mathcal{A}(q)$ the BA that coincides with $\mathcal{A}$ except for the set of initial states Q_0, which is redefined in $\mathcal{A}(q)$ as $Q_0 = \{q\}$.*

Definition 45 (Emptiness per State). *We then define a function $\mathcal{F}^\varphi : Q^\varphi \to \mathbb{B}_2$ (with $\mathbb{B}_2 = \{\top, \bot\}$) where we set $\mathcal{F}^\varphi(q) = \top$ iff $\mathcal{L}(\mathcal{A}^\varphi(q)) \neq \emptyset$.*

Using $\mathcal{F}^\varphi$, we define the NFA $\hat{\mathcal{A}}^\varphi = (\Sigma, Q^\varphi, Q_0^\varphi, \delta^\varphi, \hat{F}^\varphi)$ with $\hat{F}^\varphi = \{q \in Q^\varphi \mid \mathcal{F}^\varphi(q) = \top\}$. Analogously, we set $\hat{\mathcal{A}}^{\neg\varphi} = (\Sigma, Q^{\neg\varphi}, Q_0^{\neg\varphi}, \delta^{\neg\varphi}, \hat{F}^{\neg\varphi})$ with $\hat{F}^{\neg\varphi} = \{q \in Q^{\neg\varphi} \mid \mathcal{F}^{\neg\varphi}(q) = \top\}$.

To determine $F^\varphi(q)$, we identify in linear time the strongly connected components in A^φ, which can be done using Tarjan's algorithm [Tar72] or nested depth-first algorithms as examined in [SE05].

Lemma 4 (LTL$_3$ Evaluation). *With the notation as before, we have*

$$[\![w \models \varphi]\!]_3 = \begin{cases} \top & \text{if } w \notin \mathcal{L}(\hat{\mathcal{A}}^{\neg\varphi}) \\ \bot & \text{if } w \notin \mathcal{L}(\hat{\mathcal{A}}^\varphi) \\ ? & \text{if } w \in \mathcal{L}(\hat{\mathcal{A}}^\varphi \cap \mathcal{L}(\hat{\mathcal{A}}^{\neg\varphi})) \end{cases}$$

Proof. $[\![w \models \varphi]\!]_3 = \top$ if $w \notin \mathcal{L}(\hat{\mathcal{A}}^{\neg\varphi})$

- Feeding a finite prefix $w \in \Sigma^*$ to the BA $\mathcal{A}^{\neg\varphi}$, we reach the set $\delta^{\neg\varphi}(Q_0^{\neg\varphi}, w) \subseteq Q^{\neg\varphi}$ of states.
- If $\exists q \in \delta^{\neg\varphi}(Q_0^{\neg\varphi}, w) : \mathcal{L}(\mathcal{A}^{\neg\varphi}(q)) \neq \emptyset$ then we can choose $\sigma \in \mathcal{L}(\mathcal{A}^{\neg\varphi}(q))$ such that $w\sigma \in \mathcal{L}(\mathcal{A}^{\neg\varphi})$.
- Such a state q exists by definition iff $w \in \mathcal{L}(\hat{\mathcal{A}}^{\neg\varphi})$.
- If $w \notin \mathcal{L}(\hat{\mathcal{A}}^{\neg\varphi})$ then every possible continuation $w\sigma$ of w will be rejected by $\mathcal{A}^{\neg\varphi}$, i.e. $[\![w\sigma \models \varphi]\!]_\omega = \top$ for all $\sigma \in \Sigma^\omega$. Therefore we have $[\![w \models \varphi]\!]_3 = \top$. $[\![w \models \varphi]\!]_3 = \bot$ if $w \notin \mathcal{L}(\hat{\mathcal{A}}^\varphi)$
- can be seen by substituting φ for $\neg\varphi$. $[\![w \models \varphi]\!]_3 = ?$ if $w \in \mathcal{L}(\hat{\mathcal{A}}^{\neg\varphi}) \cap \mathcal{L}(\hat{\mathcal{A}}^\varphi)$
- If $\exists q \in \delta^{\neg\varphi}(Q_0^{\neg\varphi}, w) : \mathcal{L}(\mathcal{A}^{\neg\varphi}(q)) \neq \emptyset$ and $\exists q' \in \delta^\varphi(Q_0^\varphi, w) : \mathcal{L}(\mathcal{A}^\varphi(q')) \neq \emptyset$ then we can choose $\sigma \in \mathcal{L}(\mathcal{A}^{\neg\varphi}(q))$ and $\sigma' \in \mathcal{L}(\mathcal{A}^\varphi(q'))$ such that $[\![w\sigma \models \varphi]\!]_2 = \bot$ and $[\![w\sigma' \models \varphi]\!]_2 = \top$.
- Hence we have $[\![w \models \varphi]\!]_3 = ?$.

Deterministic Moore Machine (FSM). Our goal is now to derive a deterministic Moore machine. As an example, let us consider the Moore machine that we will obtain for pUq

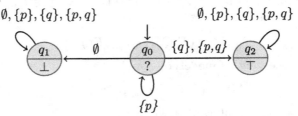

Definition 46 (Deterministic Moore Machine (FSM)). *A (deterministic) Moore machine is a tupel* $\mathcal{M} = (\Sigma, Q, q_0, \Gamma, \delta, \lambda)$ *where*

- Σ *is the* input alphabet,
- Q *is a finite set of* states,
- $q_0 \in Q$ *is the* initial state,
- Γ *is the* output alphabet,
- $\delta : Q \times \Sigma \to Q$ *is the* transition function *and*
- $\lambda : Q \to \Gamma$ *is the* output function.

Definition 47 (Run of a Deterministic Moore Machine). *A run of a (deterministic) Moore machine* $\mathcal{M} = (\Sigma, Q, q_0, \Gamma, \delta, \lambda)$ *on a finite word* $w \in \Sigma^n$ *with outputs* $o_i \in \Gamma$ *is a sequence*

$$t_0 \overset{w_1}{\to} t_1 \overset{w_2}{\to} \ldots \overset{w_{n-1}}{\to} t_{n-1} \overset{w_n}{\to} t_n$$

such that

- $t_0 = q_0$,
- $t_i = \delta(t_{i-1}, w_i)$ *and*
- $o_i = \lambda(t_i)$.

The output of the run is $o_n = \lambda(t_n)$.

Let $\tilde{\mathcal{A}}^\varphi = (\Sigma, \tilde{Q}^\varphi, q_0^\varphi, \tilde{\delta}^\varphi, \tilde{F}^\varphi)$ and $\tilde{\mathcal{A}}^{\neg\varphi} = (\Sigma, \tilde{Q}^{\neg\varphi}, q_0^{\neg\varphi}, \tilde{\delta}^{\neg\varphi}, \tilde{F}^{\neg\varphi})$ be the equivalent DFAs of the NFAs $\hat{\mathcal{A}}^\varphi$ and $\hat{\mathcal{A}}^{\neg\varphi}$.

Definition 48 (Monitor $\mathcal{M}^\varphi$ for an LTL formula φ). *We define the product automaton* $\overline{\mathcal{A}}^\varphi = \tilde{\mathcal{A}}^\varphi \times \tilde{\mathcal{A}}^{\neg\varphi}$ *as the Moore machine* $(\Sigma, \overline{Q}, \overline{q}_0, \mathbb{B}_3, \overline{\delta}, \overline{\lambda})$, *where*

- $\overline{Q} = \tilde{Q}^\varphi \times \tilde{Q}^{\neg\varphi}$,
- $\overline{q}_0 = (\tilde{q}_0^\varphi, \tilde{q}_0^{\neg\varphi})$,
- $\overline{\delta}((q, q'), a) = (\tilde{\delta}^\varphi(q, a), \tilde{\delta}^{\neg\varphi}(q', a))$ *and*
- $\overline{\lambda} : \overline{Q} \to \mathbb{B}_3$ *with*

$$\overline{\lambda}((q, q')) = \begin{cases} \top & \text{if } q' \notin \tilde{F}^{\neg\varphi} \\ \bot & \text{if } q \notin \tilde{F}^\varphi \\ ? & \text{if } q \in \tilde{F}^\varphi \text{ and } q' \in \tilde{F}^{\neg\varphi}. \end{cases}$$

The monitor $\mathcal{M}^\varphi$ of φ is obtained by minimizing $\overline{\mathcal{A}}^\varphi$.

The overall construction is summarized in Fig. 9.

Figure 10 shows an example construction for the formula pUq.

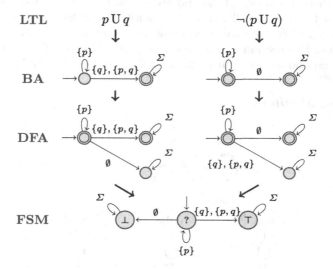

Fig. 9. The overall construction for LTL3 monitors.

Fig. 10. The monitor construction for $p\mathbin{U}q$ in LTL_3

5.5 Analysis

Let us first look at the complexity of the monitor construction. To this, recall the construction as depicted in Fig. 11.

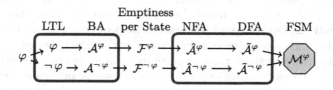

Fig. 11. The complexity of the LTL_3 monitor construction

Thus, $|M| \in 2^{2^{O(|\varphi|)}}$ and the complexity is dominated by the translation of the underlying formulas into the Büchi automaton and the determinisation of the respective NFA. As the resulting monitor is unique, the whole construction is optimal. That said, the latter steps of the translation can also by done "on-the-fly" allowing to trade space for runtime.

Practical examples show that resulting monitors for typical properties are of small sizes. See [BLS11] for details.

Let us briefly look at the general shape of a monitor. Due to minimization, there are at most two sinks outputting $\bot$ or $\top$. In all other states, the output is ?. However, there might be (single) sink outputting ?, while other states outputting ? may reach the $\top$ or $\bot$-states. A simple analysis reveals that a sink labelled ? is there if and only if the underlying property is monitorable. The previous constructions yield a 2EXPTIME algorithm for deciding monitorability. However, the exact complexity of deciding monitorability is so-far unknown.

Let us close this section by sketching the general shape of an LTL$_3$ monitor and the corresponding types of prefixes leading to respectively bad, ugly, and good states.

Structure of Monitors

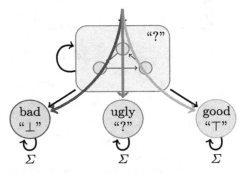

Classification of Prefixes of Words

Bad prefixes Ugly prefixes Good prefixes

6   Conclusion

In this paper, we provided an introduction to the field of runtime verification and a detailed overview of the approach based on monitoring linear-time temporal logic specifications. On this road, we learned about the difference of monitoring completed runs and monitoring ongoing executions. In the latter case, we realized that multiple verdicts rather than two are more appropriate. We provided two approaches for the monitoring expanding executions incorporating the ideas of impartiality and anticipation. Impartiality means to stay with the verdicts $\top$ and $\bot$ once decided for them while anticipation requires to go for $\top$ and $\bot$ (and stay there) as soon as possible (in the sense made precise in the previous sections). Moreover, we discussed that automata-based approaches can be understood as pre-computations of rewriting-based approaches and hereby, we were able to bridge these two worlds.

We have explored only a very limited area of the rapidly expanding field of runtime verification. We have not covered applications where further entities come into play such as data or concurrency. Moreover, we only touched monitoring but did not discuss steering of a system or enforcing properties at runtime. Nevertheless, we have given a first detailed introduction into one main part of the field.

Acknowledgement. Many thanks goes to the team at ISP for fruitful discussions about the content of this chapter, especially to Malte Schmitz.

References

[BC04]   Bertot, Y., Castéran, P.: Interactive Theorem Proving and Program Development Coq'Art: The Calculus of Inductive Constructions. Texts in Theoretical Computer Science. Springer, Heidelberg (2004)

[BCC+03] Biere, A., Cimatti, A., Clarke, E.M., Strichman, O., Zhu, Y.: Bounded model checking. Adv. Comput. **58**, 117–148 (2003)

[BJK+05] Broy, M., Jonsson, B., Katoen, J.-P., Leucker, M., Pretschner, A. (eds.): Model-Based Testing of Reactive Systems, Advanced Lectures. LNCS, vol. 3472. Springer, Heidelberg (2005). The volume is the outcome of a research seminar that was held in Schloss Dagstuhl in January 2004

[BLS06a] Bauer, A., Leucker, M., Schallhart, C.: Model-based runtime analysis of distributed reactive systems. In: Proceedings of the Australian Software Engineering Conference (ASWEC 2006), pp. 243–252. IEEE (2006)

[BLS06b] Bauer, A., Leucker, M., Schallhart, C.: Model-based runtime analysis of distributed reactive systems. In: ASWEC, pp. 243–252 (2006)

[BLS11]   Bauer, A., Leucker, M., Schallhart, C.: Runtime verification for LTL and TLTL. ACM Trans. Softw. Eng. Methodol. (TOSEM), **20**(4) (2011, in press)

[Boe81]   Boehm, B.W.: Software Engineering Economics. Prentice Hall, Englewood Cliffs (1981)

[Buc62]   Büchi, J.R.: On a decision method in restricted second order arithmetic. In: Proceedings of the International Congress on Logic, Method, and Philosophy of Science, pp. 1–12. Stanford University Press, Stanford (1962)

[CAPS15] Chimento, J.M., Ahrendt, W., Pace, G.J., Schneider, G.: STARVOORS: a tool for combined static and runtime verification of Java. In: Bartocci, E., Majumdar, R. (eds.) RV 2015. LNCS, vol. 9333, pp. 297–305. Springer, Heidelberg (2015). doi:10.1007/978-3-319-23820-3_21

[CGP01]   Clarke, E.M., Grumberg, O., Peled, D.: Model Checking. MIT Press, Cambridge (2001)

[Cho78]   Chow, T.S.: Testing software design modeled by finite-state machines. IEEE Trans. Softw. Eng. **4**(3), 178–187 (1978)

[CR94]   Crow, J., Rushby, J.: Model-based reconfiguration: diagnosis and recovery. NASA Contractor report 4596, NASA Langley Research Center (1994)

[CR07]   Chen, F., Rosu, G.: Mop: an efficient and generic runtime verification framework. In: OOPSLA, pp. 569–588 (2007)

[DAC99]   Dwyer, M.B., Avrunin, G.S., Corbett, J.C.: Patterns in property specifications for finite-state verification. In: ICSE, pp. 411–420 (1999)

[DGR04]   Delgado, N., Gates, A.Q., Roach, S.: A taxonomy and catalog of runtime software-fault monitoring tools. IEEE Trans. Softw. Eng. **30**(12), 859–872 (2004)

[DSS+05] D'Angelo, B., Sankaranarayanan, S., Sánchez, C., Robinson, W., Finkbeiner, B., Sipma, H.B., Mehrotra, S., Manna, Z.: LOLA: Runtime monitoring of synchronous systems. In: TIME (2005)

[HS06] Hinchey, M.G., Sterritt, R.: Self-managing software. IEEE. Comput. **39**(2), 107–109 (2006)

[HU79] Hopcroft, J.E., Ullman, J.D.: Introduction to Automata Theory, Languages and Computation. Addison-Wesley, Boston (1979)

[Leu12] Leucker, M.: Sliding between model checking and runtime verification. In: Qadeer, S., Tasiran, S. (eds.) RV 2012. LNCS, vol. 7687, pp. 82–87. Springer, Heidelberg (2013). doi:10.1007/978-3-642-35632-2_10

[MB15] Mostafa, M., Bonakdarpour, B.: Decentralized runtime verification of LTL specifications in distributed systems. In: IEEE International Parallel and Distributed Processing Symposium, IPDPS 2015, Hyderabad, India, 25–29 May 2015, pp. 494–503. IEEE Computer Society (2015)

[Mye04] Myers, G.J.: The Art of Software Testing, 2nd edn. Wiley, Hoboken (2004)

[PL04] Pretschner, A., Leucker, M.: Model-based testing – a glossary. In: Broy, M., Jonsson, B., Katoen, J.-P., Leucker, M., Pretschner, A. (eds.) Model-Based Testing of Reactive Systems. LNCS, vol. 3472, pp. 607–609. Springer, Heidelberg (2005). doi:10.1007/11498490_27

[Pnu77] Pnueli, A.: The temporal logic of programs. In: FOCS, pp. 46–57 (1977)

[SC85] Sistla, A.P., Clarke, E.M.: The complexity of propositional linear temporal logics. J. ACM **32**(3), 733–749 (1985)

[SE05] Schwoon, S., Esparza, J.: A note on on-the-fly verification algorithms. In: Halbwachs, N., Zuck, L.D. (eds.) TACAS 2005. LNCS, vol. 3440, pp. 174–190. Springer, Heidelberg (2005). doi:10.1007/978-3-540-31980-1_12

[SS14] Scheffel, T., Schmitz, M.: Three-valued asynchronous distributed runtime verification. In: Twelfth ACM/IEEE International Conference on Formal Methods and Models for Codesign, MEMOCODE 2014, Lausanne, Switzerland, 19–21 October 2014, pp. 52–61. IEEE (2014)

[SVAR04] Sen, K., Vardhan, A., Agha, G., Rosu, G.: Efficient decentralized monitoring of safety in distributed systems. In: Finkelstein, A., Estublier, J., Rosenblum, D.S. (eds.) 26th International Conference on Software Engineering (ICSE 2004), 23–28 May 2004, Edinburgh, UK, pp. 418–427. IEEE Computer Society (2004)

[Tar72] Tarjan, R.E.: Depth-first search and linear graph algorithms. SIAM J. Comput. **1**(2), 146–160 (1972)

[Tho90] Thomas, W.: Automata on infinite objects (Chap. 4). In: van Leeuwen, J. (ed.) Handbook of Theoretical Computer Science, Volume B, pp. 133–191. Elsevier Science Publishers B. V., Amsterdam (1990)

[Vas73] Vasilevski, M.P.: Failure diagnosis of automata. Cybernetic **9**(4), 653–665 (1973)

[VW86] Vardi, M.Y., Wolper, P.: An automata-theoretic approach to automatic program verification (preliminary report). In: LICS, pp. 332–344 (1986)

Formal Reasoning on Infinite Data Values: An Ongoing Quest

Taolue Chen[1], Fu Song[2], and Zhilin Wu[3(✉)]

[1] Department of Computer Science, Middlesex University London, London, UK
[2] School of Information Science and Technology,
ShanghaiTech University, Shanghai, China
[3] State Key Laboratory of Computer Science, Institute of Software,
Chinese Academy of Sciences, Beijing, China
wuzl@ios.ac.cn

Abstract. With motivations from formal verification and databases, formal models to reason about software systems that contain data values from an infinite domain became a research focus in theoretical computer science community during the last decade. In this chapter, we present a tutorial to summarise the state of the art of these formal models. We focus on automata models and logics. We organise the models according to the different approaches to deal with the data values from an infinite domain. Specifically, we present the following models, register automata (and related logics), data automata (and related logics), pebble automata, and symbolic automata and transducers. In addition, we also incorporate two application-oriented sections, respectively on formal models to reason about programs manipulating dynamic data structures, and on formal models for the static analysis of data-parallel programs. For these two sections, we choose to present separation logic with data constraints, logic of graph reachability and stratified sets, streaming transducers, and streaming numerical transducers. For each model, we introduce the basic definitions, use some examples to illustrate the model, and state the main theoretical properties of the model. We hope that this tutorial will be useful if one wants to have a bird's eye of view on this field and know the basic concepts underlying those models.

1 Introduction

In computer science, formal models usually refer to mathematical models to specify, recognise, generate, and transform a specific class of structures (e.g., words and trees). They typically include logic, automata, formal grammars, and rewriting systems. Formal models, as the basis of many branches of computer science, are subject to extensive investigations through the history of computer science [vL90]. Turing machines, together with λ-calculus, recursive functions, etc., are one of the first formal models of computation, which have a profound impact on almost every area of computer science. Another example is context-free grammars, which are the foundations of syntax analysis of programming languages, and hence all modern compliers.

© Springer International Publishing AG 2017
J.P. Bowen et al. (Eds.): SETSS 2016, LNCS 10215, pp. 195–257, 2017.
DOI: 10.1007/978-3-319-56841-6_6

Logic and automata are two classes of the most well-known formal models. They have found numerous applications in algorithms and complexity, programming languages, verification, databases, artificial intelligence, etc. For instance, most automated verification techniques, in particular model checking, are based on logics and automata over infinite words and trees. In the database community, the query languages on semi-structured data (e.g. XML documents) are based on logics and automata over unranked trees. In addition, path query languages for graph databases are typically based on finite automata and regular expressions. Logic and automata are closely related: logics are usually succinct, declarative, and abstract, whilst automata are specific, imperative, and of low-level. It is quite common that logics are used as specification languages, and automata, accounting for the combinatorial aspect of the logics somehow, provide algorithmic means to reason about the specifications. A classical example is the satisfiability problem and model checking problem of *linear temporal logics* (LTL), which can be reduced to the nonemptiness and language inclusion problem of Büchi automata respectively [WVS83, VW86], yielding an efficient and elegant solution.

To some extent, it is fair to say that classical formal models deal with objects from a finite domain, which can be formalized by a finite alphabet. Intuitively, finite alphabets can be used to represent the events in concurrent systems and tags in XML documents. Formal models (logics and automata) over the finite alphabets have been investigated extensively and intensively. The Chomsky hierarchy classified the language (and the associated automata models) over finite alphabets into four levels: linear grammars and finite-state automata, context-free grammars and pushdown automata, context-sensitive grammars and linear-bounded automata, and phrase structure grammars and Turing machines. The theoretical properties of each level of the hierarchy, as well as their relationships, have been thoroughly investigated [HU79]. Over finite words and trees, finite-state automata have been shown to be expressively equivalent to the monadic second-order logic (MSO) [Büc60, Elg61, TW68]. On the other hand, over infinite words, Büchi automata and MSO have been proved to have the same expressibility [Büc62]. It is also worth mentioning that algebraic foundations of finite-state automata on finite words and trees have been established. One classical result in this field is that a regular language on finite words is expressible in first-order logic if and only if the syntactic monoid associated with the language is aperiodic [Sch65, MP71].

In the last decade, motivated by the formal analysis and verification of computer programs and query languages for XML documents and graph databases, formal models to reason about data values from an *infinite* domain have become a research focus of (theoretical) computer science [Seg06, D'A12, Kar16]. In these models, the alphabet is extended from a finite set Σ to $\Sigma \times \mathbb{D}$, where $\mathbb{D}$ is an infinite data domain (e.g., the set of integers). These infinite alphabets can be intuitively interpreted as follows:

- if Σ denotes the events, then $\mathbb{D}$ denotes the time of the events or the identifiers of the processes or threads where the event occurs,
- in XML documents and graph databases, if Σ denotes tags of elements in XML documents or labels of graph nodes, then $\mathbb{D}$ denotes the attributes of elements or nodes.

In many cases, adding infinite data to the formal models with finite alphabets leads to undecidability of even very basic algorithmic problems. However, researchers have managed to discover quite a few remarkable exceptions where decidability, or even efficiency, are preserved. It is usually an art to identify the trade-off between decidability and expressiveness, which makes the field versatile and intricate. Nevertheless, this field is of vital importance from both theoretical and practical viewpoints: on the one hand, formal models over infinite alphabets are natural extensions of their counterparts over finite alphabets, so are of particular theoretical interests; on the other hand, they are intimately related to various applications from, for example, formal verification and XML databases.

The current chapter aims to provide a tutorial and survey for the state-of-the-art research in automata and logics over infinite alphabets and, in particular, their applications in program verification. This is not the first attempt, because of the importance of the subject. Segoufin provided an extensive survey on automata and logics over infinite alphabets in 2006 [Seg06]. In addition, we are aware of at least two other related surveys:

- D'Antoni's survey [D'A12] covered the automata and logics on data words and trees up to 2012, including register automata, data automata, pebble automata, symbolic automata, and related logics.
- Chap. 4 of Kara's dissertation [Kar16] included an up-to-date survey on automata and logics on data words, for instance, register automata, data automata, first-order logic, and temporal logics on data words.

This chapter provides a broader and up-to-date survey which covers the latest developments in this field (for example, formalisms for reasoning about dynamic data structures and data-parallel programs).

However, the reader should bear in mind that our survey is by no means comprehensive, nor subsumes the other excellent surveys mentioned above. Indeed, our selection of material may be subjective with respect to our own research interests and is bounded by the volume of this chapter. In particular

- we restrict the discussions to finite words and trees and do not present the results of these models and logics on ω-words and trees,
- we are mostly driven by program verification, so do not include a huge body of work on atoms (also known as nominal sets or Fraenkel-Mostowski sets) which are used to define properties on data words and data trees in an abstract manner (see, e.g., [Boj13, BKLT13]),
- we do not include the work of extending Petri nets with data [HLL+16],
- finally, we do not cover the work on the automatic verification of database-driven systems [Via09].

Plan of the Chapter. Section 2 describes some notations used throughout this chapter. Section 3 presents register automata and related logics. Section 4 discusses data automata and first-order logic on data words. Section 5 introduces pebble automata, including their various sub-models. Section 6 discusses variable automata and temporal logics with data variable quantifications. Section 7 is devoted to symbolic automata and transducers. Sections 8 and 9 describe the formalisms for reasoning about programs manipulating dynamic data structures and data-parallel programs respectively.

2   Preliminaries

We use $\mathbb{N}, \mathbb{Z}, \mathbb{Q}$ to denote the set of natural numbers, the set of integers, and the set of rational numbers respectively. For any $n \in \mathbb{N}$, we write $[n]$ for $\{1, \cdots, n\}$.

We make use of a finite alphabet Σ and an infinite set $\mathbb{D}$ of data values.

Words and Data Words. A *word* w is a finite sequence over Σ. A *data word* w is a finite sequence over $\Sigma \times \mathbb{D}$. In particular, ε is used to denote the empty word or data word. A *language* is a set of words and a *data language* is a set of data words. Let $w = (\sigma_1, d_1) \ldots (\sigma_n, d_n)$ be a data word and $i \in [n]$. Then the *type* of i in w, denoted by $\mathsf{type}_w(i)$, is $\rhd$ if $i < n$ and $\overline{\rhd}$ otherwise. Intuitively, $\rhd$ means that the current position is not the rightmost position of the data word and $\overline{\rhd}$ denotes the negation of this condition. In addition, the Σ-projection of w, denoted by $\mathsf{prj}_\Sigma(w)$, is $\sigma_1 \ldots \sigma_n$. When Σ is obvious from the context, we also write $\mathsf{prj}_\Sigma(w)$ as $\mathsf{prj}(w)$ for brevity. For a data word $w = (\sigma_1, d_1) \ldots (\sigma_n, d_n)$, let $|w|$ denote the *length* of w, that is, n.

Trees and Data Trees. A *tree domain* T is a nonempty finite subset of $\mathbb{N}^*$ such that (1) for every $xi \in T$ with $i \in \mathbb{N}$, we have $x \in T$, and (2) for every $xi \in T$ with $i \in \mathbb{N}$ and every $j : 0 \leq j < i$, we have $xj \in T$. In particular, we have $\varepsilon \in T$ for every tree domain T. Let $t, t' \in T$. We use $t \preceq_a t'$ to denote the fact that t is an *ancestor* of t', that is, $t' = tt''$ for some $t'' \in \mathbb{N}^*$. In addition, we use $t \preceq_s t'$ to denote the fact that t a *left-sibling* of t', that is, $t = t''i$ and $t' = t''j$ for some $t'' \in \mathbb{N}^*$ such that $i \leq j$. A Σ-*labeled tree* $\mathcal{T}$ is pair (T, L), where T is a tree domain and $L : T \to \Sigma$ is a labeling function. A Σ-*labeled data tree* $\mathcal{T}$ is a pair (T, L, D), where (T, L) is a Σ-labeled tree, and $D : T \to \mathbb{D}$ assigns each node a data value. A *tree language* is a set of Σ-labeled trees and a *data tree language* is a set of Σ-labeled data trees. Let $\mathcal{T}$ be a Σ-labeled tree (T, L) or a Σ-labeled data tree (T, L, D), and $t \in T$. Then the type of t in $\mathcal{T}$, denoted by $\mathsf{type}_{\mathcal{T}}(t)$, is defined as a subset of $\{\triangledown, \overline{\triangledown}, \rhd, \overline{\rhd}\}$ such that

- if $ti \in T$ for some $i \in \mathbb{N}$, then $\triangledown \in \mathsf{type}_{\mathcal{T}}(t)$, otherwise, $\overline{\triangledown} \in \mathsf{type}_{\mathcal{T}}(t)$,
- if $t = t'i$ and $t'j \in T$ for some $j \in \mathbb{N}$ such that $j > i$, then $\rhd \in \mathsf{type}_{\mathcal{T}}(t)$, otherwise, $\overline{\rhd} \in \mathsf{type}_{\mathcal{T}}(t)$.

Intuitively, $\triangledown$ means that the current node is not a leaf and $\overline{\triangledown}$ denotes the negation of this condition. Similarly, $\rhd$ means that the current node is not the rightmost sibling of its parent and $\overline{\triangleright}$ denotes the negation of this condition. We use TreeTypes to denote the set of all possible types of nodes in trees or data trees. More specifically, TreeTypes $= \{\{type_1, type_2\} \mid type_1 \in \{\triangledown, \overline{\triangledown}\}, type_2 \in \{\triangleright, \overline{\triangleright}\}\}$. When Σ is obvious from the context, we usually use data trees to denote Σ-labeled data trees.

Nondeterministic Finite-State Automata (NFA). An NFA $\mathcal{A}$ is a tuple $(Q, \Sigma, q_0, \delta, F)$ such that Q is a finite set of states, Σ is a finite alphabet, $q_0 \in Q$ is the initial state, $\delta \subseteq Q \times \Sigma \times Q$ is a finite set of transitions, and $F \subseteq Q$ is a finite set of final states. A *deterministic* NFA (DFA) is an NFA $\mathcal{A} = (Q, \Sigma, q_0, \delta, F)$ such that for each $(q, \sigma) \in Q \times \Sigma$, there is at most one $q' \in Q$ satisfying that $(q, \sigma, q') \in \delta$. A NFA or DFA $\mathcal{A} = (Q, \Sigma, q_0, \delta, F)$ is *complete* if for each $q \in Q$ and $\sigma \in \Sigma$, there is $q' \in Q$ such that $(q, \sigma, q') \in \delta$.

The semantics of NFAs is defined as follows: We use δ^* to denote the reflexive and transitive closure of δ, that is, $(q, \varepsilon, q) \in \delta^*$ and $(q, w_1w_2, q') \in \delta^*$ iff there is $q'' \in Q$ such that $(q, w_1, q'') \in \delta^*$ and $(q'', w_2, q') \in \delta^*$. A word w is accepted by an NFA $\mathcal{A} = (Q, \Sigma, q_0, \delta, F)$ if $(q_0, w, q') \in \delta^*$ for some $q' \in F$. Let $\mathcal{L}(\mathcal{A})$ denote the language defined by $\mathcal{A}$, that is, the set of words accepted by $\mathcal{A}$.

The following decision problems are considered for NFAs:

- Nonemptiness problem: Given an NFA $\mathcal{A}$, decide whether $\mathcal{L}(\mathcal{A}) \neq \varnothing$.
- Universality problem: Given an NFA $\mathcal{A}$, decide whether $\mathcal{L}(\mathcal{A}) = \Sigma^*$.
- Language inclusion problem: Given two NFAs $\mathcal{A}_1$ and $\mathcal{A}_2$, decide whether $\mathcal{L}(\mathcal{A}_1) \subseteq \mathcal{L}(\mathcal{A}_2)$.
- Equivalence problem: Given two NFAs $\mathcal{A}_1$ and $\mathcal{A}_2$, decide whether $\mathcal{L}(\mathcal{A}_1) = \mathcal{L}(\mathcal{A}_2)$.

A language $L \subseteq \Sigma^*$ is *regular* if there is an NFA $\mathcal{A}$ defining L, that is, $L = \mathcal{L}(\mathcal{A})$. Given a regular language L, the *complement* language of L is $\Sigma^* \setminus L$. We say that NFAs are *closed under intersection (resp. union)* if for every pair of NFAs $\mathcal{A}_1$ and $\mathcal{A}_2$, there is an NFA $\mathcal{A}$ such that $\mathcal{L}(\mathcal{A}) = \mathcal{L}(\mathcal{A}_1) \cap \mathcal{L}(\mathcal{A}_2)$ (resp. $\mathcal{L}(\mathcal{A}) = \mathcal{L}(\mathcal{A}_1) \cup \mathcal{L}(\mathcal{A}_2)$). On the other hand, NFAs are closed under *complementation* if for each NFA $\mathcal{A}$, there is an NFA $\mathcal{A}'$ such that $\mathcal{L}(\mathcal{A}') = \Sigma^* \setminus \mathcal{L}(\mathcal{A})$. A complete DFA $\mathcal{A} = (Q, \Sigma, q_0, \delta, F)$ is *minimal* if for each complete DFA $\mathcal{A}' = (Q', \Sigma, q_0', \delta', F')$ such that $\mathcal{L}(\mathcal{A}) = \mathcal{L}(\mathcal{A}')$, it holds that $|Q| \leq |Q'|$.

Theorem 1 ([HU79]). *The following results hold for NFAs:*

- *NFAs are closed under all Boolean operations (i.e. intersection, union and complementation).*
- *For each NFA, an equivalent DFA can be constructed in exponential time.*
- *For each regular language L, there is an unique minimal complete DFA (up to isomorphism) defining L.*
- *The nonemptiness problem of NFAs is in NLOGSPACE and the universality problem (as well as language inclusion problem and equivalence problem) of NFAs is PSPACE-complete.*

Many-Sorted First-Order Logic. We assume a signature $\Omega = (\mathfrak{S}, \mathfrak{F}, \mathfrak{P})$, where $\mathfrak{S}$ is a countable set of *sorts*, $\mathfrak{F}$ is a countable set of *function symbols*, and $\mathfrak{P}$ is a countable set of *predicate symbols*. Each function and predicate symbol has an associated *arity*, which is a tuple of sorts in $\mathfrak{S}$. A function symbol with a single sort is called a *constant*. A predicate symbol with a single sort is called a *set*, which intuitively denotes a set of elements of that sort.

An Ω-term is built as usual from the function symbols in $\mathfrak{F}$ and variables taken from a set $\mathcal{X}$ that is disjoint from $\mathfrak{S}$, $\mathfrak{F}$, and $\mathfrak{P}$. Each variable $x \in \mathcal{X}$ has an associated sort in $\mathfrak{S}$. In addition, we assume that the variables in $\mathcal{X}$ are linearly ordered $\preceq_\mathcal{X}$. When writing $t(\boldsymbol{x})$ for a vector of distinct variables $\boldsymbol{x}$ such that $\boldsymbol{x} = (x_1, \ldots, x_n)$ follows the ascending order of the linear order $\preceq_\mathcal{X}$, we assume that the variables occurring in the term t are from $\boldsymbol{x}$. For a term $t(\boldsymbol{x})$ of sort s such that $\boldsymbol{x} = (x_1, \ldots, x_n)$ and each x_i for $i \in [n]$ is of sort $s_i \in \mathfrak{S}$, the term t is said to be *of arity* $(s_1 \times \cdots \times s_n) \to s$. In addition, for a vector of terms $(t_1, \ldots, t_m)$ such that all the variables of $t_1, \ldots, t_m$ are from $\boldsymbol{x} = (x_1, \ldots, x_n)$, if $x_1 \preceq_\mathcal{X} x_2 \preceq_\mathcal{X} \cdots \preceq_\mathcal{X} x_n$, each x_i for $i \in [n]$ is of sort s_i, and each t_j for $j \in [m]$ is of sort s'_j, then $(t_1, \ldots, t_m)$ is said to be a term of arity $(s_1, \ldots, s_n) \to (s'_1, \ldots, s'_m)$. For readability, a term of arity $(s_1, \ldots, s_n) \to (s'_1, \ldots, s'_m)$ is also called a $(s_1, \ldots, s_n)/(s'_1, \ldots, s'_m)$-term. We use $(t_1, \ldots, t_m)(\boldsymbol{x})$ to denote a vector of terms whose variables are from $\boldsymbol{x}$. For convenience, we also write $t(\boldsymbol{x})$ as $\lambda \boldsymbol{x}.\, t$ and $(t_1, \ldots, t_m)(\boldsymbol{x})$ as $\lambda \boldsymbol{x}.\, (t_1, \ldots, t_m)$.

We assume the standard notions of Ω-atoms, Ω-literals, and Ω-formulae, whose definitions can be found in some textbooks on mathematical logic (see e.g. [Gal85]). The set of free variables of a Ω-formula ψ is denoted by $\mathsf{free}(\psi)$. When writing $\psi(\boldsymbol{x})$, we assume that the free variables of ψ are from $\boldsymbol{x}$. For a formula $\psi(\boldsymbol{x})$ such that $\boldsymbol{x} = (x_1, \ldots, x_n)$ and each x_i for $i \in [n]$ is of sort $s_i \in \mathfrak{S}$, the formula ψ is said to be *of arity* $s_1 \times \cdots \times s_n$. A formula ψ that contains exactly one free variable (resp. two, $n \geq 3$ free variables) is called a *unary* (resp. *binary*, *n*-ary) Ω-formula. A formula ψ contains no free variables is called a 0-ary formula, aka a sentence. For $i, j \in \mathbb{N} \backslash \{0\}$, a formula $\psi(\boldsymbol{x})$ of arity s^j (where $\boldsymbol{x} = (x_1, \ldots, x_j)$), and an s^i/s^j-term $\boldsymbol{f} = (f_1, \ldots, f_j)$, we use $\psi[\boldsymbol{f}/\boldsymbol{x}]$ to denote the formula obtained from ψ by simultaneously replacing x_1 with f_1, $\cdots$, and x_j with f_j.

An Ω-interpretation I maps: (i) each sort $s \in \mathfrak{S}$ to a set s^I, (ii) each function symbol $f \in \mathfrak{F}$ of arity $s_1 \times \cdots \times s_n \to s$ to a total function $f^I : s_1^I \times \cdots \times s_n^I \to s^I$ if $n > 0$, and to an element of s^I if $n = 0$, and (iii) each predicate symbol $p \in \mathfrak{P}$ of sort $s_1 \times \cdots \times s_n$ to a subset of $p^I \subseteq s_1^I \times \cdots s_n^I$. An Ω-assignment η maps each variable $x \in \mathcal{X}$ of sort $s \in \mathfrak{S}$ to an element of s^I.

- For a term t, the interpretation of t under (I, η) for an Ω-interpretation I and Ω-assignment η, denoted by $t^{(I, \eta)}$, can be defined inductively on the syntax of terms.
- The satisfiability relation between pairs of an Ω-interpretation and an Ω-assignment, and Ω-formulae, written $I \models_\eta \psi$, is defined inductively, as usual.

We say that (I, η) is a model of ψ if $I \models_\eta \psi$. For an Ω-sentence ψ, we also write $I \models \psi$ if there is an Ω-assignment η such that $I \models_\eta \psi$.

Let Ω be a signature and $\mathcal{I}$ be a set of Ω-interpretations. Then $\mathsf{Th}(\mathcal{I})$, *the Ω-theory associated with $\mathcal{I}$*, is the set of Ω-sentences ψ such that for each $I \in \mathcal{I}$, $I \models \psi$.

Linear Temporal Logic. Let Σ be an alphabet. Then linear temporal logic (LTL) over Σ is defined by the following rules,

$$\varphi \stackrel{\text{def}}{=} \sigma \mid \neg\varphi \mid \varphi \vee \varphi \mid \mathsf{X}\,\varphi \mid \varphi \,\mathsf{U}\,\varphi,$$

where $\sigma \in \Sigma$.

Some additional temporal operators, F and G, can be derived from U, $\mathsf{F}\varphi_1 \equiv$ true $\mathsf{U}\,\varphi_1$ and $\mathsf{G}\varphi_1 \equiv \neg\mathsf{F}\neg\varphi_1$.

LTL formulae φ are interpreted on pairs (w, i), where w is a word over Σ and i is a position of w. The semantics is formalised as a relation $(w, i) \models \varphi$ defined as follows. Let φ be an LTL formula, $w = \sigma_1 \ldots \sigma_n$ be a word, and $i \in [n]$.

- $(w, i) \models \sigma$ iff $\sigma_i = \sigma$,
- $(w, i) \models \neg\varphi_1$ iff not $(w, i) \models \varphi_1$,
- $(w, i) \models \varphi_1 \vee \varphi_2$ iff $(w, i) \models \varphi_1$ or $(w, i) \models \varphi_2$,
- $(w, i) \models \mathsf{X}\,\varphi_1$ iff $i < n$ and $(w, i + 1) \models \varphi_1$,
- $(w, i) \models \varphi_1 \,\mathsf{U}\,\varphi_2$ iff there is $k : i \le k \le n$ such that $(w, k) \models \varphi_2$ and for each $j : i \le j < k$, $(w, j) \models \varphi_1$.

In addition, LTL formulae can be turned into *positive normal forms*, where the negation symbols are only before atomic formulae, by introducing the dual operators $\overline{\mathsf{X}}$ and R for X and U, that is, $\overline{\mathsf{X}}\varphi_1 \equiv \neg\mathsf{X}\neg\varphi_1$ and $\varphi_1 \,\mathsf{R}\,\varphi_2 \equiv \neg((\neg\varphi_1)\,\mathsf{U}\,(\neg\varphi_2))$. To help understand the semantics of R, we present its semantics explicitly here: $(w, i) \models \varphi_1 \,\mathsf{R}\,\varphi_2$ iff either for all $k : i \le k \le n$, we have $(w, k) \models \varphi_2$, or there is $k : i \le k \le n$ such that $(w, k) \models \varphi_1$, and for each $j : i \le j \le k$, $(w, j) \models \varphi_2$. For instance, $\neg\mathsf{F}(a \wedge \mathsf{X}\mathsf{G}b)$ can be turned into the positive normal form $\mathsf{G}(a \vee \overline{\mathsf{X}}\mathsf{F}\neg b)$.

More specifically, the positive normal forms of LTL formulae are defined by the following rules,

$$\varphi \stackrel{\text{def}}{=} \sigma \mid \neg\sigma \mid \varphi \vee \varphi \mid \varphi \wedge \varphi \mid \mathsf{X}\,\varphi \mid \overline{\mathsf{X}}\varphi \mid \varphi\,\mathsf{U}\,\varphi \mid \varphi\,\mathsf{R}\,\varphi,$$

where $\sigma \in \Sigma$.

3   Register Automata, LTL with Freeze Quantifiers, and XPath

Kaminski and Francez initialised the research of automata models over infinite alphabets. They introduced nondeterministic register automata ([KF94]), an extension of finite state automata with a set of registers which can store a symbol from an infinite alphabet.

Let R be a finite set of registers. In addition, we assume that cur $\notin R$ is a distinguished register which stores the data value in the current position of data words. We use $R^\odot$ to denote $R \cup \{\mathsf{cur}\}$. A *guard* formula over R is defined by the rules $g \overset{\text{def}}{=} \mathsf{true} \mid \mathsf{false} \mid r_1 = r_2 \mid r_1 \neq r_2 \mid g \wedge g \mid g \vee g$, where $r_1, r_2 \in R^\odot$. Let G_R denote the set of all guard formulae over R. An *assignment* η over R is a partial function from R to $R^\odot$. Let A_R denote the set of assignments over R. A *valuation* ρ over R is a function from $R^\odot$ to $\mathbb{D}$. For a valuation η, $r \in R^\odot$, and $d \in \mathbb{D}$, we use $\eta[d/r]$ to denote the valuation which is the same as η, except that d is assigned to the register r.

Definition 1 (Nondeterministic register automata). *A nondeterministic register automaton (NRA) $\mathcal{A}$ is a tuple $(Q, \Sigma, R, q_0, \tau_0, \delta, F)$ where:*

- *Q is a finite set of states,*
- *Σ is the finite alphabet,*
- *R is a finite set of registers,*
- *$q_0 \in Q$ is the initial state,*
- *$\tau_0 : R \to \mathbb{D}$ assigns initial values to the registers;*
- *$\delta \subseteq Q \times \Sigma \times \mathsf{G}_R \times \mathsf{A}_R \times Q$ is a finite set of transition rules (for readability, we also write a transition (q, σ, g, η, q') as $q \xrightarrow{(\sigma, g, \eta)} q'$),*
- *$F \subseteq Q$ is the set of final states.*

Semantics of NRAs. Given an NRA $\mathcal{A} = (Q, R, q_0, \tau_0, \delta, F)$, a *configuration* of $\mathcal{A}$ is a pair (q, ρ), where $q \in Q$ and ρ is a valuation. A configuration (q, ρ) is said to be *initial* if $q = q_0$ and $\rho(r) = \tau_0(r)$ for each $r \in R$. A *run* of $\mathcal{A}$ over a data word $w = (\sigma_1, d_1) \ldots (\sigma_n, d_n)$ is a sequence of configurations $(q_0, \rho_0) \ldots (q_n, \rho_n)$ such that (q_0, ρ_0) is the initial configuration, and for each $i \in [n]$, there is a transition $q_{i-1} \xrightarrow{(\sigma_i, g_i, \eta_i)} q_i$ in δ such that $\rho_{i-1}[d_i/\mathsf{cur}] \models g_i$ and ρ_i is obtained from ρ_{i-1} and η_i as follows: for each $r \in R$, if $r \in \mathsf{dom}(\eta_i)$, then $\rho_i(r) = (\rho_{i-1}[d_i/\mathsf{cur}])(\eta_i(r))$, otherwise, $\rho_i(r) = \rho_{i-1}(r)$. A run is said to be *accepting* if $q_n \in F$. A data word w is said to be *accepted* by $\mathcal{A}$ if there is an accepting run of $\mathcal{A}$ on w. Let $\mathcal{L}(\mathcal{A})$ denote the set of data words accepted by $\mathcal{A}$. We say that a data language L is defined by an NRA $\mathcal{A}$ if $\mathcal{L}(\mathcal{A}) = L$.

Example 1. Let $\Sigma = \{a\}$. The NRA illustrated in Fig. 1 defines the data language L "in the data word, a data value occurs twice", where q_0 is the initial state, q_2 is an accepting state, and $\varnothing$ denotes the assignment with the empty domain.

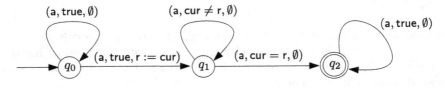

Fig. 1. An example of NRAs: "a data value occurs twice"

A *deterministic* NRA (DRA) is an NRA $\mathcal{A} = (Q, R, q_0, \tau_0, \delta, F)$ such that for each pair of distinct transitions $(q, \sigma, g_1, \eta_1, q_1')$ and $(q, \sigma, g_2, \eta_2, q_2')$ in $\mathcal{A}$, it holds that $g_1 \wedge g_2$ is unsatisfiable.

Theorem 2 ([KF94, NSV01, DL09]). *The following results hold for NRAs:*

- *NRAs are closed under union and intersection, but not closed under complementation.*
- *The nonemptiness problem of NRAs is PSPACE-complete, the universality problem of NRAs (as well as the language inclusion and equivalence problems) is undecidable.*
- *The nonemptiness, language inclusion, and equivalence problems of DRAs are PSPACE-complete.*

For instance, the complement of the data language L in Example 1, that is, the data language comprising the data words where each data value occurs at most once, cannot be defined by NRAs. Intuitively, to guarantee that each data value occurs at most once, one needs unbounded many registers to store the data values that have been met so far when reading a data word from left to right.

Researchers also considered two extensions of nondeterministic register automata, alternating register automata and two-way nondeterministic register automata.

We next define alternating register automata over data words. We follow the notations in [Fig12].

Definition 2 (Alternating register automata). *An* alternating register automaton with k registers *(ARA$_k$) over data words is a tuple* $\mathcal{A} = (\Sigma, R, Q, q_0, \tau_0, \delta)$, *where* $R = \{r_1, \ldots, r_k\}$ *is a set of k registers*, Σ, Q, q_0, τ_0 *are the same as those in NRAs, and* $\delta : Q \to \Phi$ *is the transition function, where* Φ *is defined by the following grammar,*

$$\Phi \stackrel{\text{def}}{=} \text{true} \mid \text{false} \mid \sigma \mid \overline{\sigma} \mid \triangleright? \mid \overline{\triangleright}? \mid \text{eq}_r \mid \overline{\text{eq}_r} \mid q \vee q' \mid q \wedge q' \mid \text{store}_r(q) \mid \triangleright q,$$

where $r \in R$ *and* $q, q' \in Q$.

Intuitively, $\sigma, \overline{\sigma}$ are used to detect the occurrences of letters from Σ. $\triangleright?$ and $\overline{\triangleright}?$ are used to describe the types of positions in data words, eq_r and $\overline{\text{eq}_r}$ are used to check whether the data value in the register r is equal to the current one, $q \vee q'$ makes a nondeterministic choice, $q \wedge q'$ creates two threads with the state q and q' respectively, $\text{store}_r(q)$ stores the current data value to the register r and transfers to the state q, $\triangleright q$ moves the reading head of the current thread one position to the right and transfers to the state q.

Semantics of ARAs. For defining semantics of ARAs, we introduce the concept of configurations.

Let $\mathcal{A}$ be an ARA$_k$. A *configuration* c of $\mathcal{A}$ is a tuple $(i, \alpha, \sigma, d, \Lambda)$, where $i \in \mathbb{N} \setminus \{0\}$ denotes a position of a data word, $\alpha \in \{\triangleright, \overline{\triangleright}\}$ denotes the type of position i in the data word, $(\sigma, d) \in \Sigma \times \mathbb{D}$ is the letter-data pair in position

i, $\Lambda \subseteq Q \times \mathbb{D}^R$ is a finite set of active threads in position i where each thread $(q, \rho) \in \Lambda$ denotes that the state of the thread is q and the valuation of the registers of the thread is ρ. Let $\mathcal{C}_\mathcal{A}$ denote the set of configurations of $\mathcal{A}$.

To define runs of $\mathcal{A}$ on data words, we introduce two types of transition relations on configurations, the *non-moving* relation $\longrightarrow_\epsilon \subseteq P_\mathcal{A} \times P_\mathcal{A}$ and the *moving* relation $\longrightarrow_\triangleright \subseteq \mathcal{C}_\mathcal{A} \times \mathcal{C}_\mathcal{A}$. For a given configuration $c = (i, \alpha, \sigma, d, \{(q, \rho)\} \cup \Lambda)$, the non-moving relation updates a thread (q, ρ) of c according to the transition function $\delta(q)$, and does not move the reading head. Formally, $\longrightarrow_\epsilon \subseteq \mathcal{C}_\mathcal{A} \times \mathcal{C}_\mathcal{A}$ is defined as follows,

- $(i, \alpha, \sigma, d, \{(q, \rho)\} \cup \Lambda) \longrightarrow_\epsilon (i, \alpha, \sigma, d, \Lambda)$, if $\delta(q) = \text{true}$;
- $(i, \alpha, \sigma, d, \{(q, \rho)\} \cup \Lambda) \longrightarrow_\epsilon (i, \alpha, \sigma, d, \Lambda)$, if $\delta(q) = \sigma$;
- $(i, \alpha, \sigma, d, \{(q, \rho)\} \cup \Lambda) \longrightarrow_\epsilon (i, \alpha, \sigma, d, \Lambda)$, if $\delta(q) = \overline{\sigma'}$ and $\sigma \neq \sigma'$;
- $(i, \alpha, \sigma, d, \{(q, \rho)\} \cup \Lambda) \longrightarrow_\epsilon (i, \alpha, \sigma, d, \Lambda)$, if $\delta(q) = \triangleright?$ and $\alpha = \triangleright$;
- $(i, \alpha, \sigma, d, \{(q, \rho)\} \cup \Lambda) \longrightarrow_\epsilon (i, \alpha, \sigma, d, \Lambda)$, if $\delta(q) = \overline{\triangleright}?$ and $\alpha = \overline{\triangleright}$;
- $(i, \alpha, \sigma, d, \{(q, \rho)\} \cup \Lambda) \longrightarrow_\epsilon (i, \alpha, \sigma, d, \Lambda)$, if $\delta(q) = eq_r$ and $\rho(r) = d$;
- $(i, \alpha, \sigma, d, \{(q, \rho)\} \cup \Lambda) \longrightarrow_\epsilon (i, \alpha, \sigma, d, \Lambda)$, if $\delta(q) = \overline{eq_r}$ and $\rho(r) \neq d$;
- for $j = 1, 2$, $(i, \alpha, \sigma, d, \{(q, \rho)\} \cup \Lambda) \longrightarrow_\epsilon (i, \alpha, \sigma, d, \{(q_j, \rho)\} \cup \Lambda)$, if $\delta(q) = q_1 \vee q_2$;
- $(i, \alpha, \sigma, d, \{(q, \rho)\} \cup \Lambda) \longrightarrow_\epsilon (i, \alpha, \sigma, d, \{(q_1, \rho), (q_2, \rho)\} \cup \Lambda)$, if $\delta(q) = q_1 \wedge q_2$;
- $(i, \alpha, \sigma, d, \{(q, \rho)\} \cup \Lambda) \longrightarrow_\epsilon (i, \alpha, \sigma, d, \{(q', \rho')\} \cup \Lambda)$, if $\delta(q) = \text{store}_r(q')$ and $\rho' = \rho[d_i/r]$.

A configuration $(i, \alpha, \sigma, d, \Lambda)$ is *moving* if $\alpha = \triangleright$, $\Lambda \neq \varnothing$, and for every $(q, \rho) \in \Lambda$, we have $\delta(q) = \triangleright q'$. The moving relation $\longrightarrow_\triangleright$ advances some threads of a moving configuration to the right. More precisely,

$$(i, \alpha, \sigma, d, \Lambda) \longrightarrow_\triangleright (i+1, \alpha', \sigma', d', \Lambda'),$$

if $(i, \alpha, \sigma, d, \Lambda)$ is a moving configuration, $\alpha' \in \{\triangleright, \overline{\triangleright}\}$, $\sigma' \in \Sigma$, $d' \in \mathbb{D}$, and $\Lambda' = \{(q', \rho) \mid (q, \rho) \in \Lambda, \delta(q) = \triangleright q'\}$.

Finally, we define the transition relation $\rightarrowtail \ = \ \longrightarrow_\epsilon \cup \longrightarrow_\triangleright$.

A *run* of $\mathcal{A}$ over a data word $w = (\sigma_1, d_1) \ldots (\sigma_n, d_n)$ is a sequence of configurations $C_0 \ldots C_m$ such that

- $C_0 = (1, \text{type}_w(1), \sigma_1, d_1, \{(q_0, \tau_0)\})$,
- for each $j \in [m]$, there is $i \in [n]$ such that $C_j = (i, \text{type}_w(i), \sigma_i, d_i, \Lambda)$,
- for each $j \in [m]$, $C_{j-1} \rightarrowtail C_j$.

A run $C_0 \ldots C_m$ is *accepting* if $C_m = (i, \text{type}_w(i), \sigma_i, d_i, \varnothing)$ for some $i \in [n]$. A data word w is *accepted* by $\mathcal{A}$ if there is an accepting run of $\mathcal{A}$ over w. Let $\mathcal{L}(\mathcal{A})$ denote the set of data words accepted by $\mathcal{A}$.

Example 2. Let $\Sigma = \{a\}$. Then the ARA$_1$ $\mathcal{A} = (\{q_0, q_1, \ldots, q_7, q_a, q_{\overline{eq_r}}\}, \Sigma, R = \{r\}, q_0, \tau_0, \delta)$ defines the data language "in the data word, no data values occur twice", that is, the complement language of L in Example 1. Here $\tau_0(r) = c$ for some arbitrary $c \in \mathbb{D}$, $\delta(q_0) = q_a \wedge q_1$, $\delta(q_a) = a$, $\delta(q_1) = \text{store}_r(q_2)$, $\delta(q_2) = \triangleright q_3$, $\delta(q_3) = q_a \wedge q_4$, $\delta(q_4) = q_{\overline{eq_r}} \wedge q_5$, $\delta(q_{\overline{eq_r}}) = \overline{eq_r}$, $\delta(q_5) = q_6 \wedge q_7$, $\delta(q_6) = \triangleright q_3$, $\delta(q_7) = \text{store}_r(q_3)$. Intuitively, in each position, the data value in the position is stored into the register r and a new thread is created, moreover, this data value (stored in r) will be checked to be different from each data value in the right of the position.

Theorem 3 ([DL09, Fig12]). *The following facts hold for ARA_k's:*

- *For each $k \geq 1$, ARA_k's are closed under all Boolean operations.*
- *The nonemptiness problem of ARA_2's is undecidable.*
- *The nonemptiness problem of ARA_1's is decidable and non-primitive recursive.*

The nonemptiness of ARA_1 was proved by defining a well-quasi-order over the set of configurations and utilising the framework of well-structured transition systems to achieve the decidability.

In [DL09], alternating register automata were introduced to solve the satisfiability problem of LTL with freezing quantifiers. Therefore, in the following, we define LTL with freezing quantifiers and illustrate how the satisfiability of LTL with freeze quantifiers can be reduced to the nonemptiness of alternating register automata.

Definition 3 (LTL with freeze quantifiers). *Let $R = \{r_1, \ldots, r_k\}$. The syntax of Linear Temporal Logic with freeze quantifiers over Σ and R (denoted by $LTL_k^{\downarrow}$) is defined by the following rules,*

$$\varphi \stackrel{def}{=} \sigma \mid \downarrow_{r_i} \varphi \mid \uparrow_{r_i} \mid \varphi \vee \varphi \mid \neg \varphi \mid \mathsf{X}\varphi \mid \varphi \, \mathsf{U} \, \varphi,$$

where $\sigma \in \Sigma, r_i \in R$.

Semantics of $LTL_k^{\downarrow}$. $LTL_k^{\downarrow}$ formulae are interpreted over a tuple (w, j, ρ), where $w = (\sigma_1, d_1) \ldots (\sigma_n, d_n)$ is a data word, $j \in [n]$ is a position of w, and ρ is an assignment over R. The semantics of $LTL_k^{\downarrow}$ is classical for Boolean and temporal operators. For the modalities σ, $\downarrow_{r_i}$ and $\uparrow_{r_i}$,

- $(w, j, \rho) \models \sigma$, if $\sigma_j = \sigma$,
- $(w, j, \rho) \models \downarrow_{r_i} \varphi$, if $(w, j, \rho[d_j/r_i]) \models \varphi$,
- $(w, j, \rho) \models \uparrow_{r_i}$ if $\rho(r_i) = d_j$.

An $LTL_k^{\downarrow}$ formula φ is said to be *closed* if each occurrence of $\uparrow_{r_i}$ is in the scope of an occurrence of $\downarrow_{r_i}$. For a closed $LTL_k^{\downarrow}$ formula φ, if $(w, 1, \rho) \models \varphi$, then $(w, 1, \rho') \models \varphi$ for any assignment ρ'. We define $\mathcal{L}(\varphi)$ as the set of data words w such that $(w, 1, \rho) \models \varphi$ for some ρ. A data language L is said to be defined by a closed $LTL_k^{\downarrow}$ formula φ if $\mathcal{L}(\varphi) = L$. An $LTL_k^{\downarrow}$ formula φ is said to be *satisfiable* if $\mathcal{L}(\varphi) \neq \varnothing$.

Similarly to LTL, $LTL_k^{\downarrow}$ formulae can be turned into *positive normal form*, that is, the formulae where the negation symbols are only before atomic formulae σ and $\uparrow_{r_i}$.

Example 3. The LTL$_1^\downarrow$ formula $\mathsf{G}(\downarrow_{r_1} \neg\mathsf{XF} \uparrow_{r_1})$ defines the data language in Example 2. In addition, the LTL$_1^\downarrow$ formula $\mathsf{G}(a \to \downarrow_{r_1} \mathsf{F}(b\wedge \uparrow_{r_1}))$, or $\mathsf{G}(\neg a\vee \downarrow_{r_1} \mathsf{F}(b\wedge \uparrow_{r_1}))$ in positive normal form, defines the data language "for each occurrence of a, there is an occurrence of b on the right with the same data value".

Theorem 4 ([DL09]). *The following facts hold for LTL$_k^\downarrow$:*

- *The satisfiability problem of LTL$_2^\downarrow$ is undecidable.*
- *The satisfiability problem of LTL$_1^\downarrow$ is decidable.*

From each LTL$_1^\downarrow$ formula, an equivalent ARA$_1$ can be constructed by an easy induction on the syntax of the positive normal form of LTL$_1^\downarrow$ formulae. Then the decidability of LTL$_1^\downarrow$ follows from Theorem 3. We use the following example to illustrate the construction of ARA$_1$ from LTL$_1^\downarrow$ formulae.

Example 4. Consider the LTL$_1^\downarrow$ formula $\varphi = \mathsf{G}(\neg a \vee \downarrow_{r_1} \mathsf{F}(b\wedge \uparrow_{r_1}))$. From φ, we construct an ARA$_1$ $\mathcal{A}_\varphi$ as follows:

- The set of states are q_ψ, where ψ is a subformula of φ or $\psi = \mathsf{X}\psi_1$ where ψ_1 is a subformula of φ.
- The initial state is q_φ.
- The transition function δ is defined as follows.
  - $\delta(q_\varphi) = q_{\neg a\vee \downarrow_{r_1}\mathsf{F}(b\wedge\uparrow_{r_1})} \wedge q_{\mathsf{X}\varphi}$, $\delta(q_{\mathsf{X}\varphi}) = \triangleright q_\varphi$,
  - $\delta(q_{\neg a\vee \downarrow_{r_1}\mathsf{F}(b\wedge\uparrow_{r_1})}) = q_{\neg a} \vee q_{\downarrow_{r_1}\mathsf{F}(b\wedge\uparrow_{r_1})}$, $\delta(q_{\neg a}) = \overline{a}$, $\delta(q_{\downarrow_{r_1}\mathsf{F}(b\wedge\uparrow_{r_1})}) =$ store$_{r_1}(q_{\mathsf{F}(b\wedge\uparrow_{r_1})})$,
  - $\delta(q_{\mathsf{F}(b\wedge\uparrow_{r_1})}) = q_{b\wedge\uparrow_{r_1}} \vee q_{\mathsf{XF}(b\wedge\uparrow_{r_1})}$,
  - $\delta(q_{b\wedge\uparrow_{r_1}}) = q_b \wedge q_{\uparrow_{r_1}}$, $\delta(q_b) = b$, $\delta(q_{\uparrow_{r_1}}) = \mathsf{eq}_{r_1}$, $\delta(q_{\mathsf{XF}(b\wedge\uparrow_{r_1})}) = \triangleright q_{\mathsf{F}(b\wedge\uparrow_{r_1})}$.

Two-way nondeterministic register automata can be defined as an extension of nondeterministic register automata in the same way as the two-way extension of finite-state automata. It turns out that the nonemptiness of two-way deterministic register automata is already undecidable.

Theorem 5 ([DL09]). *The nonemptiness problem of two-way deterministic register automata is undecidable.*

Alternating register automata on unranked trees have also been considered, mainly motivated to solve the satisfiability problem of fragments of Data-XPath (XPath with data value comparisons). In the following, we introduce a model of alternating one-register tree automata with guess and spread mechanism, denoted by ATRA$_1$(guess, spread), then illustrate how the satisfiability of forward Data-XPath, a fragment of Data-XPath containing only forward navigation modalities, can be reduced to the nonemptiness of ATRA$_1$(guess, spread).

Definition 4 (Alternating one-register tree automata with guess and spread mechanism). *An alternating one-register tree automaton with the guess and spread mechanism (denoted by ATRA$_1$(guess, spread)) $\mathcal{A}$ is defined as a tuple $(\Sigma, Q, q_0, \tau_0, \delta)$, such that Σ, Q, q_0 are as in ARA$_1$, $\tau_0 \in \mathbb{D}$ denotes the* *initial value of the (unique) register, and* $\delta : Q \to \Phi$ *is the transition function, where* Φ *is defined by the following grammar,*

$$\Phi \overset{def}{=} \text{true} \mid \text{false} \mid \sigma \mid \overline{\sigma} \mid \odot? \mid \overline{\odot}? \mid \text{eq} \mid \overline{\text{eq}} \mid q \vee q' \mid q \wedge q' \mid$$
$$\text{store}(q) \mid \rhd q \mid \triangledown q \mid \text{guess}(q) \mid \text{spread}(q, q'),$$

where $q, q' \in Q$, *and* $\odot \in \{\rhd, \triangledown\}$. *An* $ATRA_1$ *is an* $ATRA_1(\text{guess, spread})$ *without guess and spread mechanisms.*

Semantics of $ATRA_1(\text{guess, spread})$. Let $\mathcal{A}$ be an $ATRA_1(\text{guess, spread})$. We introduce the concepts of node configurations and tree configurations as follows.

A *node configuration* c of $\mathcal{A}$ is a tuple $(t, \alpha, \sigma, d, \Lambda)$, where $t \in \mathbb{N}^*$, $\alpha \in$ TreeTypes, $\sigma \in \Sigma$, $d \in \mathbb{D}$, and $\Lambda \subseteq Q \times \mathbb{D}$ is a finite set of active threads where each thread $(q, d) \in \Lambda$ denotes that the state of the thread is q and the register holds the data value d.

A *tree configuration* C of $\mathcal{A}$ is a finite set of node configurations. Let $N_{\mathcal{A}}$ denote the set of node configurations of $\mathcal{A}$, and $T_{\mathcal{A}} \subseteq 2^{N_{\mathcal{A}}}$ be the set of tree configurations. In addition, to define a run of $\mathcal{A}$, we introduce two types of transition relations, the *non-moving* relation $\longrightarrow_\epsilon \subseteq N_{\mathcal{A}} \times N_{\mathcal{A}}$ and the *moving* relation $\longrightarrow_\rhd \subseteq N_{\mathcal{A}} \times N_{\mathcal{A}}$. For a given node configuration $c = (t, \alpha, \sigma, d, \{(q, d')\} \cup \Lambda)$, the non-moving relation updates a thread (q, d') of c according to the transition function $\delta(q)$, and does not move the reading head. Formally, $\longrightarrow_\epsilon \subseteq N_{\mathcal{A}} \times N_{\mathcal{A}}$ is defined as follows:

- $(t, \alpha, \sigma, d, \{(q, d')\} \cup \Lambda) \longrightarrow_\epsilon (t, \alpha, \sigma, d, \Lambda)$, if $\delta(q) = \text{true}$;
- $(t, \alpha, \sigma, d, \{(q, d')\} \cup \Lambda) \longrightarrow_\epsilon (t, \alpha, \sigma, d, \Lambda)$, if $\delta(q) = \sigma$;
- $(t, \alpha, \sigma, d, \{(q, d')\} \cup \Lambda) \longrightarrow_\epsilon (t, \alpha, \sigma, d, \Lambda)$, if $\delta(q) = \overline{\sigma'}$ and $\sigma \neq \sigma'$;
- $(t, \alpha, \sigma, d, \{(q, d')\} \cup \Lambda) \longrightarrow_\epsilon (t, \alpha, \sigma, d, \Lambda)$, if $\delta(q) = \odot?$ and $\odot \in \alpha$, where $\odot = \triangledown$ or $\rhd$;
- $(t, \alpha, \sigma, d, \{(q, d')\} \cup \Lambda) \longrightarrow_\epsilon (t, \alpha, \sigma, d, \Lambda)$, if $\delta(q) = \overline{\odot}?$ and $\overline{\odot} \in \alpha$, where $\odot = \triangledown$ or $\rhd$;
- $(t, \alpha, \sigma, d, \{(q, d')\} \cup \Lambda) \longrightarrow_\epsilon (t, \alpha, \sigma, d, \Lambda)$, if $\delta(q) = \text{eq}$ and $d' = d$;
- $(t, \alpha, \sigma, d, \{(q, d')\} \cup \Lambda) \longrightarrow_\epsilon (t, \alpha, \sigma, d, \Lambda)$, if $\delta(q) = \overline{\text{eq}}$ and $d' \neq d$;
- for $j = 1, 2$, $(t, \alpha, \sigma, d, \{(q, d')\} \cup \Lambda) \longrightarrow_\epsilon (t, \alpha, \sigma, d, \{(q_j, d')\} \cup \Lambda)$, if $\delta(q) = q_1 \vee q_2$;
- $(t, \alpha, \sigma, d, \{(q, d')\} \cup \Lambda) \longrightarrow_\epsilon (t, \alpha, \sigma, d, \{(q_1, d'), (q_2, d')\} \cup \Lambda)$, if $\delta(q) = q_1 \wedge q_2$;
- $(t, \alpha, \sigma, d, \{(q, d')\} \cup \Lambda) \longrightarrow_\epsilon (t, \alpha, \sigma, d, \{(q', d)\} \cup \Lambda)$, if $\delta(q) = \text{store}(q')$.
- $(t, \alpha, \sigma, d, \{(q, d')\} \cup \Lambda) \longrightarrow_\epsilon (t, \alpha, \sigma, d, \{(q', d'')\} \cup \Lambda)$ for each $d'' \in \mathbb{D}$, if $\delta(q) = \text{guess}(q')$.
- $(t, \alpha, \sigma, d, \Lambda) \longrightarrow_\epsilon (t, \alpha, \sigma, d, \{(q', d') \mid (q, d') \in \Lambda\} \cup \Lambda)$, if $\delta(q) = \text{spread}(q, q')$.

A node configuration $(t, \alpha, \sigma, d, \Lambda)$ is *moving* if

- $\Lambda \neq \varnothing$, and for every $(q, d) \in \Lambda$, we have $\delta(q) = \triangledown q'$ or $\rhd q'$,
- if there is $(q, d) \in \Lambda$ such that $\delta(q) = \odot q'$, then $\odot \in \alpha$, where $\odot = \triangledown$ or $\rhd$.

The moving relation $\longrightarrow_{\triangledown}$ (resp. $\longrightarrow_{\triangleright}$) advances some threads of a moving node configuration to its leftmost child (resp. to its right sibling). Suppose $(t, \alpha, \sigma, d, \Lambda)$ is a moving node configuration.

- If $\triangledown \in \alpha$, then

$$(t, \alpha, \sigma, d, \Lambda) \longrightarrow_{\triangleright} (t0, \alpha', \sigma', d', \Lambda'),$$

where $\alpha' \in \mathsf{TreeTypes}$, $\sigma' \in \Sigma$, $d' \in \mathbb{D}$, and $\Lambda' = \{(q', d) \mid (q, d) \in \Lambda, \delta(q) = \triangledown q'\}$.
- If $\triangleright \in \alpha$ and $t = t'i$, then

$$(t, \alpha, \sigma, d, \Lambda) \longrightarrow_{\triangleright} (t'(i+1), \alpha', \sigma', d', \Lambda'),$$

where $\alpha' \in \mathsf{TreeTypes}$, $\sigma' \in \Sigma$, $d' \in \mathbb{D}$, and $\Lambda' = \{(q', d) \mid (q, d) \in \Lambda, \delta(q) = \triangleright q'\}$.

The transition relation $\rightarrowtail$ of tree configurations is defined as follows. Let C_1, C_2 be two tree configurations. Then $C_1 \rightarrowtail C_2$ if one of the following conditions hold:

- $C_1 = \{c\} \cup C'$ and $C_2 = \{c'\} \cup C'$ such that $c \longrightarrow_{\varepsilon} c'$.
- $C_1 = \{c\} \cup C'$, $c = (t, \alpha, \sigma, d, \Lambda)$, $\alpha = \{\triangleright, \overline{\triangledown}\}$, $C_2 = \{c'\} \cup C'$ such that $c \longrightarrow_{\triangleright} c'$.
- $C_1 = \{c\} \cup C'$, $c = (t, \alpha, \sigma, d, \Lambda)$, $\alpha = \{\overline{\triangleright}, \triangledown\}$, $C_2 = \{c'\} \cup C'$ such that $c \longrightarrow_{\triangledown} c'$.
- $C_1 = \{c\} \cup C'$, $c = (t, \alpha, \sigma, d, \Lambda)$, $\alpha = \{\triangleright, \triangledown\}$, $C_2 = \{c'_1, c'_2\} \cup C'$ such that $c \longrightarrow_{\triangleright} c'_1$ and $c \longrightarrow_{\triangledown} c'_2$.

A *run* of $\mathcal{A}$ over a data tree $\mathcal{T} = (T, L, D)$ is a sequence of tree configurations $C_0 \ldots C_n$ such that

- $C_0 = \{(\varepsilon, \mathsf{type}_{\mathcal{T}}(\varepsilon), L(\varepsilon), D(\varepsilon), \{(q_0, \tau_0)\})\}$,
- for each $i \in [n]$ and each $(t, \alpha, \sigma, d, \Lambda) \in C_i$, we have $t \in T$, $\alpha = \mathsf{type}_{\mathcal{T}}(t)$, $\sigma = L(t)$, and $d = D(t)$,
- for each $i \in [n]$, $C_{i-1} \rightarrowtail C_i$.

A run $C_0 \ldots C_n$ is *accepting* if $C_n \subseteq \{(t, \mathsf{type}_{\mathcal{T}}(t), L(t), D(t), \varnothing) \mid t \in T\}$. A data tree $\mathcal{T}$ is *accepted* by $\mathcal{A}$ if there is an accepting run of $\mathcal{A}$ over $\mathcal{T}$. Let $\mathcal{L}(\mathcal{A})$ denote the set of data trees accepted by $\mathcal{A}$.

Theorem 6 ([Fig12]). *The following results hold for $ATRA_1$'s and $ATRA_1(guess, spread)$'s:*

- *$ATRA_1$'s are closed under all Boolean operations. On the other hand, $ATRA_1(guess, spread)$'s are closed under union and intersection, but not closed under complementation.*
- *The nonemptiness problem of $ATRA_1(guess, spread)$'s is decidable and non-primitive recursive.*

It was shown in [Fig12] that the data tree language L in Example 5 is not definable in $\text{ATRA}_1(\text{guess, spread})$'s. On the other hand, the complement of L is definable in $\text{ATRA}_1(\text{guess, spread})$'s. This demonstrates that $\text{ATRA}_1(\text{guess, spread})$'s are not closed under complementation. Similarly to ARA_1's, the decidability of the nonemptiness problem of $\text{ATRA}_1(\text{guess, spread})$'s is also proved by utilising well-structured transition systems.

Data trees can also be seen as an abstraction of XML documents. XPath is a widely used query and navigation language for XML documents.

Definition 5 (Data-aware XPath). *Let* $\mathcal{O} \subseteq \{\downarrow, \uparrow, \rightarrow, \leftarrow, \downarrow^*, \uparrow^*, \rightarrow^*, \leftarrow^*\}$. *Data-aware XPath with set of axes from* $\mathcal{O}$, *denoted by* $XPath(\mathcal{O}, =)$, *comprises two types of formulae, path expressions* α *and node expressions* φ, *defined as follows:*

$$\alpha \overset{def}{=} o \mid [\varphi] \mid \alpha \cdot \alpha, \text{ where } o \in \mathcal{O},$$

$$\varphi \overset{def}{=} \sigma \mid \neg\varphi \mid \varphi \vee \varphi \mid \varphi \wedge \varphi \mid \langle \alpha \rangle \mid \langle \alpha = \alpha \rangle \mid \langle \alpha \neq \alpha \rangle, \text{ where } \sigma \in \Sigma.$$

Suppose $\mathcal{F} = \{\downarrow, \rightarrow, \downarrow^*, \rightarrow^*\}$. *Then we call* $XPath(\mathcal{F}, =)$ *as the* forward fragment *of* $XPath(\mathcal{O}, =)$.

Semantics of $XPath(\mathcal{O}, =)$. $XPath(\mathcal{O}, =)$ formulae are interpreted on data trees $\mathcal{T} = (T, L, D)$. The semantics of path expressions and node expressions are specified by $[\![\alpha]\!]^{\mathcal{T}} \subseteq T \times T$ and $[\![\varphi]\!]^{\mathcal{T}} \subseteq T$ as follows:

- $[\![\downarrow]\!]^{\mathcal{T}} = \{(t, ti) \mid ti \in T\}$, $[\![\uparrow]\!]^{\mathcal{T}} = \{(ti, t) \mid ti \in T\}$,
- $[\![\rightarrow]\!]^{\mathcal{T}} = \{(ti, t(i+1)) \mid t(i+1) \in T\}$, $[\![\leftarrow]\!]^{\mathcal{T}} = \{(t(i+1), ti) \mid t(i+1) \in T\}$,
- $[\![\downarrow^*]\!]^{\mathcal{T}} = \{(t, t') \mid t, t' \in T, t \preceq_a t'\}$, $[\![\uparrow^*]\!]^{\mathcal{T}} = \{(t', t) \mid t, t' \in T, t \preceq_a t'\}$,
- $[\![\rightarrow^*]\!]^{\mathcal{T}} = \{(t, t') \mid t, t' \in T, t \preceq_s t'\}$, $[\![\leftarrow^*]\!]^{\mathcal{T}} = \{(t', t) \mid t, t' \in T, t \preceq_s t'\}$,
- $[\![[\varphi]]\!]^{\mathcal{T}} = \{(t, t) \mid t \in [\![\varphi]\!]^{\mathcal{T}}\}$,
- $[\![\alpha_1 \cdot \alpha_2]\!]^{\mathcal{T}} = \{(t, t') \in T \times T \mid \exists t'' \in T.\ (t, t'') \in [\![\alpha_1]\!]^{\mathcal{T}}, (t'', t') \in [\![\alpha_2]\!]^{\mathcal{T}}\}$,
- $[\![\sigma]\!]^{\mathcal{T}} = \{t \in T \mid L(t) = \sigma\}$, $[\![\neg\varphi]\!]^{\mathcal{T}} = T \setminus [\![\varphi]\!]^{\mathcal{T}}$,
- $[\![\varphi_1 \vee \varphi_2]\!]^{\mathcal{T}} = [\![\varphi_1]\!]^{\mathcal{T}} \cup [\![\varphi_2]\!]^{\mathcal{T}}$, $[\![\varphi_1 \wedge \varphi_2]\!]^{\mathcal{T}} = [\![\varphi_1]\!]^{\mathcal{T}} \cap [\![\varphi_2]\!]^{\mathcal{T}}$,
- $[\![\langle \alpha \rangle]\!]^{\mathcal{T}} = \{t \in T \mid \exists t'.\ (t, t') \in [\![\alpha]\!]^{\mathcal{T}}\}$,
- $[\![\langle \alpha_1 = \alpha_2 \rangle]\!]^{\mathcal{T}} = \{t \in T \mid \exists t', t''.\ (t, t') \in [\![\alpha_1]\!]^{\mathcal{T}}, (t, t'') \in [\![\alpha_2]\!]^{\mathcal{T}}, D(t') = D(t'')\}$,
- $[\![\langle \alpha_1 \neq \alpha_2 \rangle]\!]^{\mathcal{T}} = \{t \in T \mid \exists t', t''.\ (t, t') \in [\![\alpha_1]\!]^{\mathcal{T}}, (t, t'') \in [\![\alpha_2]\!]^{\mathcal{T}}, D(t') \neq D(t'')\}$.

Let φ be a node expression in $XPath(\mathcal{O}, =)$ and $\mathcal{T}$ be a data tree. Then $\mathcal{T}$ satisfies φ, denoted by $\mathcal{T} \models \varphi$, if $\varepsilon \in [\![\varphi]\!]^{\mathcal{T}}$. We use $\mathcal{L}(\varphi)$ denote the set of data trees satisfying φ. The satisfiability problem of $XPath(\mathcal{O}, =)$ is defined as follows: Given a node expression φ, decide whether $\mathcal{L}(\varphi) \neq \varnothing$. The query containment problem of $XPath(\mathcal{O}, =)$ is defined as follows: Given two node expressions φ_1, φ_2, decide whether $\mathcal{L}(\varphi_1) \subseteq \mathcal{L}(\varphi_2)$. Since the node expressions of $XPath(\mathcal{O}, =)$ are closed under complementation, it follows that the query containment problem of $XPath(\mathcal{O}, =)$ can be reduced to the satisfiability problem.

Example 5. Let L be the data tree language comprising the data trees such that "no data values in two distinct positions are the same". Then L can be defined by the XPath$(\mathcal{F}, =)$ formula φ,

$$\varphi \stackrel{\text{def}}{=} \neg\langle\downarrow^* [\langle\alpha_\varepsilon =\downarrow^+\rangle \vee \langle\downarrow^*=\to^+\downarrow^*\rangle]\rangle,$$

where $\alpha_\varepsilon \stackrel{\text{def}}{=} [\bigvee_{\sigma\in\Sigma}\sigma]$, $\downarrow^+=\downarrow\cdot\downarrow^*$ and $\to^+=\to\cdot\to^*$.

Theorem 7 ([Fig12]). *The satisfiability problem (hence the query containment problem) of XPath$(\mathcal{F}, =)$ is decidable.*

Theorem 7 is proved by a reduction to the nonemptiness of ATRA_1(guess, spread), that is, for each XPath$(\mathcal{F}, =)$ node expression φ, an ATRA_1(guess, spread) $\mathcal{A}_\varphi$ can be constructed such that φ is satisfiable iff $\mathcal{A}_\varphi$ is nonempty. Nevertheless, although the satisfiability of XPath$(\mathcal{F}, =)$ can be reduced to the nonemptiness of ATRA_1(guess, spread), ATRA_1(guess, spread)'s are still unable to capture XPath$(\mathcal{F}, =)$. For instance, the XPath$(\mathcal{F}, =)$ formula φ in Example 5 is not definable in ATRA_1(guess, spread)'s [Fig12].

Further Reading. Kaminski and Tan initialised the investigation on regular expressions over infinite alphabets in [KT06]. Later on, with the motivations from path query processing in graph databases, Libkin et al. revisited this topic, proposed regular expressions with memories, and showed they are expressively equivalent to NRAs [LTV15]. Cheng and Kaminski investigated context free languages over infinite alphabets and showed that context free grammars over infinite alphabets and pushdown register automata are expressively equivalent [CK98]. Murawski et al. showed that the emptiness problem of pushdown register automata is EXPTIME-complete [MRT14].

4   Data Automata and First-Order Logic on Data Words

In the following, we will introduce data automata and its variants, as well as first-order logic on data words. Data automata were introduced by Bojanczyk et al. in [BMS+06,BDM+11], aiming at solving the satisfiability problem of first-order logic with two variables on data words.

We introduce some additional notations for data words first.

Let $w = (\sigma_1, d_1)\ldots(\sigma_n, d_n)$ be a data word and $i \in [n]$. The *profile* of w, denoted by $\mathsf{prof}(w)$, is $\sigma_1'\ldots\sigma_n'$ such that $\sigma_1' = (\sigma, \bot)$, and for each $i : 2 \le i \le n$, $\sigma_i' = (\sigma, \top)$ if $d_i = d_{i-1}$, and $\sigma_i' = (\sigma, \bot)$ otherwise. A *class of w* is a maximal nonempty set of positions $X \subseteq [n]$ with the same data value. Let $X \subseteq [n]$. Then $w|_X$ denotes the restriction of w to the set of positions in X. For instance, let $w = (a, 1)(b, 2)(a, 2)(b, 1)$, then $\mathsf{prof}(w) = (a, \bot)(b, \bot)(a, \top)(b, \bot)$, the class of w corresponding to the data value 1 is $X = \{1, 4\}$, and $w|_X = (a, 1)(b, 1)$.

The concept of class strings is used in the definition of data automata and its variants.

Definition 6 (Class strings). *Suppose the alphabet Σ satisfies that $0, 1 \notin \Sigma$. For a data word $w = (\sigma_1, d_1) \ldots (\sigma_n, d_n)$ and a class X of w:*

- *the X-class string of w, denoted by $\mathsf{cstr}_X(w)$, is defined as $w|_X$,*
- *the position-preserving X-class string of w, denoted by $\mathsf{pcstr}_X(w)$, is defined as the word $\sigma_1' \ldots \sigma_n'$ such that for each $i \in [n]$, if $i \in X$, then $\sigma_i' = \sigma_i'$, otherwise, $\sigma_i' = 0$,*
- *the letter-preserving X-class string of w, denoted by $\mathsf{lcstr}_X(w)$, is defined as the word $(\sigma_1, b_1) \ldots (\sigma_n, d_n)$ such that for each $i \in [n]$, if $i \in X$, then $b_i = 1$, otherwise, $b_i = 0$.*

Example 6. Suppose $w = (a, 1)(b, 2)(a, 2)(b, 1)$ and $X = \{1, 4\}$. Then $\mathsf{cstr}_X(w) = w|_X = ab$, $\mathsf{pcstr}_X(w) = a00b$, and $\mathsf{lcstr}_X(w) = (a, 1)(b, 0)(a, 0)(b, 1)$.

Definition 7 (Data automata). *A data automaton (DA) $\mathcal{D}$ is a tuple $(\mathcal{A}, \mathcal{B})$ s.t. $\mathcal{A} = (Q_1, \Sigma \times \{\bot, \top\}, \Gamma, q_{1,0}, \delta_1, F_1)$ is a nondeterministic letter-to-letter transducer over finite words from the alphabet $\Sigma \times \{\bot, \top\}$ to some output alphabet Γ, and $\mathcal{B} = (Q_2, \Gamma, q_{2,0}, \delta_2, F_2)$, called the class condition, is a finite-state automaton over Γ.*

Semantics of DAs. We first introduce the concept of class strings. Let $\mathcal{D} = (\mathcal{A}, \mathcal{B})$ be a DA and $w = (\sigma_1, d_1) \ldots (\sigma_n, d_n)$ be a data word. Then w is accepted by $\mathcal{D}$ if over $\mathsf{prof}(w)$, the transducer $\mathcal{A}$ produces a word $\gamma_1 \ldots \gamma_n$ over the alphabet Γ, such that for each class X of $w' = (\gamma_1, d_1) \ldots (\gamma_n, d_n)$, $\mathsf{cstr}_X(w')$, the X-class string of w', is accepted by $\mathcal{B}$. Let $\mathcal{L}(\mathcal{D})$ denote the set of data words accepted by $\mathcal{D}$.

Example 7. Let $\Sigma = \{a\}$. Then the data language comprising the "data words where at least one data value occurs twice" is accepted by the data automaton $\mathcal{D} = (\mathcal{A}, \mathcal{B})$ (see Fig. 2, where $(a, \bot)/\#$ denotes the input and output letter are $(a, \bot)$ and $\#$, similarly for $(a, \top)/\#$, and so on), where

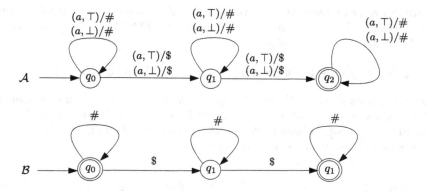

Fig. 2. An example of data automata

- $\mathcal{A}$, upon reading $\mathsf{prof}(w)$ for a data word w, guesses two positions, relabels the two positions by \$, and relabels all the other positions by #,
- and $\mathcal{B}$ accepts the language $\#^*\$\#^*\$\#^* \cup \#^*$.

Let $w = (a,1)(a,2)(a,3)(a,1)$. Then $\mathcal{A}$ produces a word $\$\#\#\$$ on $\mathsf{prof}(w)$. Since the three class strings of $w' = (\$,1)(\#,2)(\#,3)(\$,1)$, that is, $\$\$$, #, and #, are accepted by $\mathcal{B}$, it follows that w is accepted by $\mathcal{D}$.

On the other hand, let $\Sigma = \{a,b\}$, then the data language comprising the data words w such that "for each occurrence of a, there is an occurrence of b in the right with the same data value" can be accepted by the data automaton $\mathcal{D}' = (\mathcal{A}', \mathcal{B}')$, where

- $\mathcal{A}'$ is the transducer that outputs a (resp. b) when reading $(a,\bot)$ or $(a,\top)$ (resp. $(b,\bot)$ or $(b,\top)$),
- and $\mathcal{B}'$ is the finite-state automaton accepting a^*b.

Let $w = (a,1)(a,2)(b,2)(a,1)(b,1)$. Then $\mathcal{A}'$ outputs $w' = aabab$ on $\mathsf{prof}(w)$. Let X_1 and X_2 be two classes of $w'' = w$ corresponding to the data value 1 and 2 respectively. Then the X_1-class string and X_2-class string of w'', that is, $\mathsf{prj}(w''|X_1) = aab$ and $\mathsf{prj}(w''|X_2) = ab$, are accepted by $\mathcal{B}'$, it follows that w is accepted by $\mathcal{D}'$.

Theorem 8 ([BMS+06,BDM+11,BS10]). *The following facts hold for DAs:*

- *DAs are closed under intersection and union, but not under complementation.*
- *DAs are strictly more expressive than NRAs.*
- *The nonemptiness problem of DAs is decidable and has the same complexity as the reachability problem of Petri nets.*

By using data automata, it was shown in [BDM+11] that the satisfiability problem of first-order logic with two variables on data words is decidable, whereas, the satisfiability problem of first-order logic with three variables on data words is undecidable.

Definition 8 (FO over data words). *Let* Vars *denote a countably infinite set of variables. First-order logic over data words (FO[+1, <, ∼]) comprises the formulae φ defined by the rules,*

$$\varphi \stackrel{def}{=} x = y \mid x + 1 = y \mid x < y \mid P_\sigma(x) \mid x \sim y \mid \neg\varphi \mid \varphi \vee \varphi \mid \exists x.\ \varphi,$$

where $x, y \in$ Vars and $\sigma \in \Sigma$. Intuitively, $x \sim y$ is used to denote the equivalence of data values in two positions represented by x, y. In addition, FO2[+1, <, ∼] (resp. FO3[+1, <, ∼]) is used to denote the fragment of FO[+1, <, ∼] where only two variables (resp. three variables) can be used.

Semantics of FO[+1, <, ∼]. An FO[+1, <, ∼] formula φ is interpreted on a tuple (w, θ), where $w = (\sigma_1, d_1) \ldots (\sigma_n, d_n)$ is a data word, and $\theta : \mathsf{free}(\varphi) \to [n]$ assigns each free variable of φ a position of w:

- $(w, \theta) \models x = y$ iff $\theta(x) = \theta(y)$,
- $(w, \theta) \models x + 1 = y$ iff $\theta(x) + 1 = \theta(y)$,
- $(w, \theta) \models x < y$ iff $\theta(x) < \theta(y)$,
- $(w, \theta) \models P_\sigma(x)$ iff $\sigma_{\theta(x)} = \sigma$,
- $(w, \theta) \models x \sim y$ iff $d_{\theta(x)} = d_{\theta(y)}$,
- $(w, \theta) \models \neg\varphi$ iff not $(w, \theta) \models \varphi$,
- $(w, \theta) \models \varphi_1 \vee \varphi_2$ iff $(w, \theta) \models \varphi_1$ or $(w, \theta) \models \varphi_2$,
- $(w, \theta) \models \exists x. \; \varphi_1$ iff there is $i' \in [n]$ such that $(w, \theta[i'/x]) \models \varphi_1$, where $\theta[i'/x]$ is the same as θ, except assigning i' to x.

Let φ be a FO$[+1, <, \sim]$ sentence. Then a data word w satisfies φ, denoted by $w \models \varphi$, if $(w, \theta) \models \varphi$ for some θ. Let $\mathcal{L}(\varphi)$ denote the set of data words satisfying φ. The satisfiability problem of FO$[+1, <, \sim]$ is to decide whether $\mathcal{L}(\varphi) \neq \varnothing$, for a given FO$[+1, <, \sim]$ sentence φ.

Example 8. The data language "each data value occurs at most once" can be expressed by the FO2$[+1, <, \sim]$ formula $\varphi = \forall x. \forall y. \; (x < y \rightarrow \neg \; x \sim y)$.

Theorem 9 ([BMS+06,BDM+11]). *The following facts hold for FO$[+1, <, \sim]$:*

- *The satisfiability problem of FO3$[+1, <, \sim]$ is undecidable.*
- *The satisfiability problem of FO2$[+1, <, \sim]$ is decidable.*

The decidability of FO2$[+1, <, \sim]$ is proved by a reduction to the nonemptiness problem of data automata, that is, for each FO2$[+1, <, \sim]$ formula φ, a data automaton $\mathcal{D}_\varphi$ can be constructed such that $\mathcal{L}(\varphi) = \mathcal{L}(\mathcal{D}_\varphi)$.

In [ACW12], Alur et al. considered a variant of data automata, called extended data automata, defined as follows.

Definition 9 (Extended data automata). *An extended data automaton (EDA) $\mathcal{D}$ is a tuple $(\mathcal{A}, \mathcal{B})$ s.t. $\mathcal{A} = (Q_1, \Sigma \times \{\bot, \top\}, \Gamma, q_{1,0}, \delta_1, F_1)$ is a nondeterministic letter-to-letter transducer over finite words from the alphabet Σ to some output alphabet Γ, and $\mathcal{B} = (Q_2, \Gamma \cup \{0\}, q_{2,0}, \delta_2, F_2)$ is a finite-state automaton over $\Gamma \cup \{0\}$ such that $0 \notin \Gamma$.*

Semantics of EDAs. The semantics of EDAs is defined similarly as that of DAs, with $\mathsf{cstr}_X(w')$ replaced by $\mathsf{pcstr}_X(w')$.

It turns out that the expressibility of EDAs is the same as that of DAs.

Theorem 10 ([ACW12]). *EDAs are expressively equivalent to DAs.*

Since it is a famous open problem whether the reachability of Petri nets can be decided with elementary complexity, it is also open whether the nonemptiness of data automata can be decided in elementary time. In order to lower the complexity, weaker versions of data automata were introduced. Kara et al. introduced weak data automata (WDA) in [KST12] and showed that the nonemptiness problem of WDAs can be decided in 2NEXPTIME (nondeterministic double exponential time). Later on, Wu introduced commutative data automata (CDA), which are strictly more expressive than WDAs, showed that the nonemptiness problem of CDAs can be solved in 3NEXPTIME (nondeterministic triple exponential time) [Wu12].

Definition 10 (Weak data automata). *A* weak data automaton *(WDA) is a tuple* $(\mathcal{A}, \mathcal{C})$ *such that* $\mathcal{A} = (Q, \Sigma \times \{\bot, \top\}, \Gamma, \delta, q_0, F)$ *is a letter-to-letter transducer and* $\mathcal{C}$ *is a class condition specified by a collection of*

- *key constraints of the form* $\mathsf{Key}(\gamma)$ *(where* $\gamma \in \Gamma$*), interpreted as "every two* γ*-positions have different data values",*
- *inclusion constraints of the form* $D(\gamma) \subseteq \bigcup_{\gamma' \in R} D(\gamma')$ *(where* $\gamma \in \Gamma, R \subseteq \Gamma$*), interpreted as "for every data value occurring in a* γ*-position, there is* $\gamma' \in R$ *such that the data value also occurs in a* γ'*-position",*
- *and denial constraints of the form* $D(\gamma) \cap D(\gamma') = \varnothing$ *(where* $\gamma, \gamma' \in \Gamma$*), interpreted as "no data value occurs in both a* γ*-position and a* γ'*-position".*

Semantics of WDAs. A data word $w = (\sigma_1, d_1) \ldots (\sigma_n, d_n)$ *is accepted* by a WDA $\mathcal{D} = (\mathcal{A}, \mathcal{C})$ iff there is an accepting run of $\mathcal{A}$ over $\mathsf{prof}(w)$ which produces a word $\gamma_1 \ldots \gamma_n$ such that the data word $w' = (\gamma_1, d_1) \ldots (\gamma_n, d_n)$ satisfies all the constraints in $\mathcal{C}$, where the satisfaction of the constraints on w' is defined as follows:

- w' satisfies $\mathsf{Key}(\gamma)$ iff for every pair of positions $i, j \in [n]$ such that $i \neq j$ and $\gamma_i = \gamma_j = \gamma$, it holds that $d_i \neq d_j$,
- w' satisfies $D(\gamma) \subseteq \bigcup_{\gamma' \in R} D(\gamma')$ iff for each $i \in [n]$ such that $\gamma_i = \gamma$, there is $j \in [n]$ such that $\gamma_j \in R$ and $d_i = d_j$.
- w' satisfies $D(\gamma) \cap D(\gamma') = \varnothing$ iff for every pair of positions $i, j \in [n]$ such that $\gamma_i = \gamma$ and $\gamma_j = \gamma'$, it holds that $d_i \neq d_j$.

Let L be a language over the alphabet Σ. Then L is *commutative* iff for every $\sigma_1, \sigma_2 \in \Sigma$ and $u, v \in \Sigma^*$, $u\sigma_1\sigma_2 v \in L$ iff $u\sigma_2\sigma_1 v \in L$. Commutative regular languages have a characterisation in quantifier-free simple Presburger formulae defined in the following: *Quantifier-free simple Presburger formulae* (QFSP formulae) over a variable set X are Boolean combinations of atomic formulae of the form $x_1 + \cdots + x_m \leq c$, or $x_1 + \cdots + x_m \geq c$, or $x_1 + \cdots + x_m = c$, or $x_1 + \cdots + x_m \equiv r \bmod p$, where $x_1, \ldots, x_m \in X$, $c, r, p \in \mathbb{N}$, $p \geq 2$, and $0 \leq r < p$.

Suppose $\Sigma = \{\sigma_1, \ldots, \sigma_k\}$ and $v \in \Sigma^*$. The *Parikh image* of v, denoted by $\mathsf{Parikh}(v)$, is a k-tuple $(\#_{\sigma_1}(v), \ldots, \#_{\sigma_k}(v))$, where for each $i : 1 \leq i \leq k$, $\#_{\sigma_i}(v)$ is the number of occurrences of σ_i in v. Let $V_\Sigma = \{x_{\sigma_1}, \ldots, x_{\sigma_k}\}$ and φ be an QFSP formula over V_Σ. The word v is said to satisfy φ, denoted by $v \models \varphi$, iff $\varphi[\mathsf{Parikh}(v)/V_\Sigma]$ holds, where $\varphi[\mathsf{Parikh}(v)/V_\Sigma]$ denotes the formula obtained from φ by replacing each x_{σ_i} with $\#_{\sigma_i}(v)$. The *language defined by* φ, denoted by $\mathcal{L}(\varphi)$, is the set of words $v \in \Sigma^*$ such that $v \models \varphi$.

Definition 11 (Commutative data automata). *A* commutative data automaton *(CDA)* $\mathcal{D}$ *is a tuple* $(\mathcal{A}, \varphi)$ *such that* $\mathcal{A} = (Q, \Sigma \times \{\bot, \top\}, \Gamma, \delta, q_0, F)$ *is a letter-to-letter transducer and* φ *is a QFSP formula over the variable set* V_Γ*, where* $V_\Gamma = \{x_\gamma \mid \gamma \in \Gamma\}$.

Semantics of CDAs. A data word $w = (\sigma_1, d_1) \ldots (\sigma_n, d_n)$ is *accepted* by a CDA $\mathcal{D} = (\mathcal{A}, \varphi)$ iff there is an accepting run of $\mathcal{A}$ over $\mathsf{prof}(w)$ which produces a word $\gamma_1 \ldots \gamma_n$ such that the data word $w' = (\gamma_1, d_1) \ldots (\gamma_n, d_n)$ satisfies that for each class X of w', $\mathsf{cstr}_X(w') \models \varphi$.

Theorem 11 ([KST12, Wu12]). *The following results hold for WDAs and CDAs:*

- *DAs are strictly more expressive than CDAs, which is in turn strictly more expressive than WDAs.*
- *WDAs and CDAs are closed under union and intersection, but not under complementation.*
- *The nonemptiness problem of WDAs and CDAs can be decided in 2NEXP-TIME and 3NEXPTIME respectively.*

An extension of data automata, called class automata, were introduced, in order to capture the expressiveness of XPath with data comparison modalities ([BL12]). Class automata in [BL12] were defined on data trees, here for simplicity, we restrict our attention to class automata on data words.

Definition 12 (Class automata). *A class automaton (CA) $\mathcal{C}$ is a tuple $(\mathcal{A}, \mathcal{B})$ such that $\mathcal{A} = (Q, \Sigma \times \{\bot, \top\}, \Gamma, \delta, q_0, F)$ is a letter-to-letter transducer and $\mathcal{B} = (Q_2, \Gamma \times \{0,1\}, q_{2,0}, \delta_2, F_2)$ is a finite-state automaton over $\Gamma \times \{0,1\}$.*

Semantics of CAs. The semantics of CAs is defined similarly as that of DAs, with $\mathsf{cstr}_X(w')$ replaced by $\mathsf{lcstr}_X(w')$.

It turns out class automata are expressive enough to simulate two-counter machines and its nonemptiness problem is undecidable.

Theorem 12 ([BL12]). *The nonemptiness problem of CAs is undecidable.*

In [Wu11], Wu proposed a restriction of class automata, called class automata with *priority class condition* (PCA), and showed that PCAs strictly extend data automata, and at the same time have a decidable nonemptiness problem.

Further Reading. Manuel and Ramanujam proposed class counting automata, which includes a counter for each data value occurring in a data word, and showed that the nonemptiness problem of class counting automata is EXPSPACE-complete [MR11a]. The model is in a style similar to class memory automata. In addition, Tan studied data trees over a linearly ordered infinite data domain and proposed ordered-data tree automata, which is in the same flavour as data automata, and showed their nonemptiness problem can be solved in 3NEXPTIME [Tan14]. To solve the satisfiability problem of an extension of LTL over multi-attributed data words (i.e. data words where a tuple of data values, instead of a single one, occur in each position), Decker et al. introduced nested data automata (NDA) and showed that although the nonemptiness of NDAs is undecidable in general, the nonemptiness problems of two natural sub-models are decidable [DHLT14].

5   Pebble Automata

Pebble automata were introduced by Neven et al. in [NSV01,NSV04]. In contrast to register automata which are finite state machines equipped with *registers*, pebble automata are finite state machines equipped with a finite number of *pebbles*. These pebbles are placed on, or lifted from, the input data word in a *stack* discipline, i.e., first in last out, with the purpose of marking positions of the data word. One pebble can only mark one position and the most recently placed pebble serves as the head of the automaton.

As we are dealing with two-way automata here, as a convention, we delimit the input data word by two special symbols $\{\lhd, \rhd\} \notin \mathbb{D}$ for the left and the right hand of the data word. Hence, automata always work on the extended data word of the form $\rhd w \lhd$. The positions of $\rhd$ and $\lhd$ are 0 and $|w|+1$, respectively. (Recall that $|w|$ denotes the length of the data word w.)

Definition 13 (Pebble automata, [NSV04]). *A nondeterministic two-way k-pebble automaton (2N-kPA)* $\mathcal{A}$ *is a tuple* $(Q, \Sigma, q_0, \delta, F)$ *where:*

- *Q is a finite set of* states,
- *Σ is a finite* alphabet,
- *$q_0 \in Q$ is the* initial *state*,
- *$F \subseteq Q$ is the set of* final *states, and*
- *δ is a finite set of* transitions *of the form* $\alpha \to \beta$ *where:*
  - *α is of the form* (i, σ, V, q), *where* $i \in [k]$, $\sigma \in \Sigma$, $V \subseteq [i-1]$; *and*
  - *β is of the form* (q, act) *with* $q \in Q$ *and*

$$\mathsf{act} \in \{\mathsf{stay}, \mathsf{left}, \mathsf{right}, \mathsf{place\text{-}new\text{-}pebble}, \mathsf{lift\text{-}current\text{-}pebble}\}.$$

Semantics of 2N-kPAs. Given a data word $w = (\sigma_1, d_1) \ldots (\sigma_n, d_n)$, a *configuration* of $\mathcal{A}$ on w is a triple $[i, q, \theta]$ where $i \in [k]$, $q \in Q$, and $\theta : [i] \to [n] \cup \{0, n+1\}$. The function θ is the *pebble assignment* which defines the positions of the pebbles. (Recall that, as mentioned earlier, we assume an extended data word where position 0 is $\rhd$ and position $(n+1)$ is $\lhd$.) The initial configuration is $\gamma_0 = [1, q_0, \theta_0]$ where $\theta_0(1) = 0$ is the initial pebble assignment. A configuration (i, q, θ) is *accepting* if $q \in F$.

A transition $(i, \sigma, V, p) \to \beta$ applies to a configuration $[j, q, \theta]$ if the following three conditions hold:

1. $i = j$ and $p = q$;
2. $V = \{l < i \mid d_{\theta(l)} = d_{\theta(i)}\}$;
3. $\sigma_{\theta(i)} = \sigma$

Intuitively, in a configuration $[i, q, \theta]$, pebble i is in control, serving as the head pebble. $(i, \sigma, V, p) \to \beta$ applies to the configuration if pebble i is the current head, p is the current state, V is the set of pebbles that see the same data value as the head pebble, and the current symbol seen by the head pebble is σ.

We then define the transition relation $\vdash$ as follows: $[i, q, \theta] \vdash [i', q', \theta']$ iff there is a transition $\alpha \to (p, \mathsf{act})$ that applies to $[i, q, \theta]$ such that $q' = p$, $\theta'(j) = \theta(j)$ for all $j < i$, and

- if act = stay, then $i' = i$ and $\theta'(i) = \theta(i)$,
- if act = left, then $i' = i$ and $\theta'(i) = \theta(i) - 1$,
- if act = right, then $i' = i$ and $\theta'(i) = \theta(i) + 1$,
- if act = place-new-pebble, then $i' = i + 1$ and $\theta'(i+1) = \theta'(i) = \theta(i)$,
- if act = lift-current-pebble, then $i' = i - 1$.

Strong vs Weak PAs. In the above definition, new pebbles are placed at the position of the most recent pebble. (Formally, in the definition of act = place-new-pebble, one has $\theta'(i+1) = \theta'(i) = \theta(i)$.) An alternative would be to place new pebbles at the beginning of the data word. Formally, in the place-new-pebble case, one has $\theta'(i+1) = 1$, and $\theta'(i) = \theta(i)$. In literature, the former is often referred to as *weak* PAs, and the latter is referred to as *strong* (a.k.a., ordinary) PAs. While the choice makes no difference in the two-way case (as defined here), it is significant in the *one-way* case (i.e., when act = left is not allowed). For instance, it is known that one-way non-deterministic weak PAs are weaker than one-way strong PAs, see [NSV04, Theorem 4.5].

Alternating PAs. As in Sect. 3, we can define the *alternating* version of PAs. Alternating automata additionally have a set $U \subseteq Q$ of *universal* states. The sets from $Q \setminus U$ are called *existential*. (Clearly, if $U = \varnothing$, then we have a nondeterministic PA as in Definition 13.)

Acceptance. The acceptance criteria are based on the notion of *leads to acceptance* as follows. For every configuration $\gamma = [i, q, \theta]$,

- if $q \in F$, then γ leads to acceptance;
- if $q \in U$, then γ leads to acceptance if and only if for *all* configurations γ' such that $\gamma \vdash \gamma'$, γ' leads to acceptance;
- if $q \notin F \cup U$, then γ leads to acceptance if and only if there is at least one configuration γ' such that $\gamma \vdash \gamma'$ and γ' leads to acceptance.

A data word w is said to be *accepted* by $\mathcal{A}$ if γ_0 leads to acceptance. Let $\mathcal{L}(\mathcal{A})$ denote the set of data words accepted by $\mathcal{A}$. We say that a data language L is defined by a PA $\mathcal{A}$ if $\mathcal{L}(\mathcal{A}) = L$.

Remark 1. In Definition 13, we adopt the pebble numbering from [NSV04], in which the pebbles placed on the input word are numbered from 1 to i. However, in some literature, for instance, in [Tan10, BSSS06], the pebble numbering is used differently—it is from k to i. The reason for this reverse numbering is that it allows to view the computation between placing and lifting pebble i as a computation of an $(i-1)$-pebble automaton.

Example 9. To show how a PA works, we consider the data language L comprising the data words where at least one data value occurs twice. The reader should be easily convinced that L is accepted by the 1N-2PA $\mathcal{A} = (Q, q_1, F, \delta)$, where

- $Q = \{q_1, q_2, q_\rightarrow, q_{acc}\}$;
- $F = \{q_{acc}\}$;
- δ consists of the following transitions:
  1. $(1, \sigma, \varnothing, q_1) \rightarrow (q_1, \text{right})$
  2. $(1, \sigma, \varnothing, q_1) \rightarrow (q_\rightarrow, \text{place-new-pebble})$
  3. $(2, \sigma, \{1\}, q_\rightarrow) \rightarrow (q_2, \text{right})$
  4. $(2, \sigma, \varnothing, q_2) \rightarrow (q_2, \text{right})$
  5. $(2, \sigma, \{1\}, q_2) \rightarrow (q_{acc}, \text{stay})$

Some sub-classes of PAs can be defined in a standard way. A PA is *deterministic*, if in each configuration at most one transition rule applies. And, as mentioned before, if there are no left-transitions, then the PA is one-way. For the automata models we consider "control" as deterministic (D), non-deterministic (N), or alternating (A), as well as the one-way and two-way variants. We denote these automata models by dC-kPA where $d \in \{1, 2\}$, C = {D, N, A}, and $k \in \mathbb{N} \setminus \{0\}$. Here, 1 and 2 stand for one- and two-way, respectively, D, N, and A stand for deterministic, non-deterministic, and alternating, and k stands for the number of pebbles. In addition, when necessary we also write S for Strong and W for Weak, which are specific to one-way PAs.

Expressiveness of PA Models. As we have introduced a variety of pebble automata, it is natural to ask their expressiveness. A class C_1 of PAs is strictly stronger than the class C_2 of PAs is for all data languages L accepted by a PA in C_2, L can be accepted by a PA in C_1 and there exists at least one language which can be accepted by a PA in C_1, but not by any PA in C_1. Figure 3 summarises the known results, where, all classes of PAs in the same box are equivalent in expressiveness, while $\rightarrow$ means the source class is at least as expressive as the target, and the arrow decorated by $\neq$ means it is strictly more expressive. The only class which was not addressed in Fig. 3 is strong 1A-PAs, whose relation with other classes does not appear in literature and is to be studied.

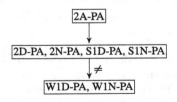

Fig. 3. Expressiveness of PAs

5.1   (Un)Decidability of Emptiness of PAs

As usual, one of the fundamental problems regarding PAs is the *emptiness problem*, which is to determine, given a PA $\mathcal{A}$, whether $L(\mathcal{A}) = \varnothing$. It was shown in [NSV04] that this problem is generally undecidable, even for weak 1D-PAs. The intuition is, when a PA lifts pebble i, the control is transferred to pebble $(i - 1)$. Therefore, even weak 1D-PAs can make several left-to-right sweeps of the input data word. This result is very strong in the sense that it implies that almost all standard decision problems are undecidable for virtually all classes of pebble automata (cf. Fig. 3).

More technically, [NSV04] gave a reduction from the PCP to the emptiness of weak 1D-5PAs. Tan observed that the proof can be adapted to weak 1D-3PAs, yielding an even stronger result. In [Tan10, KT10], a tighter boundary between decidability and undecidability was drawn in terms of the number of pebbles. In summary,

Theorem 13 ([NSV04, Tan10, KT10]). *The following facts hold for pebble automata:*

- *The nonemptiness problem for strong 2N-2PAs is undecidable.*
- *The nonemptiness problem for weak 1D-3PAs is undecidable.*
- *The nonemptiness problem for weak 1D-2PAs is decidable, but is not primitive recursive.*

Top View Weak PAs. Theorem 13 suggests that PAs are in general highly undecidable. To mitigate this, Tan [Tan10] proposed a subclass of pebble automata, the *top view weak* pebble automata. Roughly speaking, top view weak PAs are weak one-way PAs where the equality test is performed only between the data values seen by the *two most recently placed pebbles*. That is, if pebble i is the head pebble, then it can only compare the data value it reads with the data value read by pebble $(i - 1)$. It is not allowed to compare its data value with those read by pebble $1, \ldots, (i - 2)$. Formally,

Definition 14 (Top view weak PA, [Tan10]). *A top view (weak) k-PA is a tuple $\mathcal{A} = (Q, \Sigma, q_0, \delta, F)$ where Q, q_0, F are defined as before, and δ consists of transitions of the form $(i, \sigma, V, q) \to (q', \mathsf{act})$, where V is either $\varnothing$ or $\{i - 1\}$ and $\mathsf{act} \neq \mathsf{left}$.*

A transition $(i, \sigma, V, q) \to (q', \mathsf{act})$ applies to a configuration $[j, q, \theta]$ if

1. $i = j$ and $p = q$;
2. $V = \begin{cases} \varnothing & \text{if } d_{\theta(i-1)} \neq d_{\theta(i)} \\ \{i - 1\} & \text{if } d_{\theta(i-1)} = d_{\theta(i)} \end{cases}$
3. $\sigma_{\theta(i)} = \sigma$

Note that evidently top view weak 2-PAs and weak 2-PAs are the same.

Theorem 14 ([Tan10]). *For every top view weak k-PA $\mathcal{A}$, there is a (one-way) ARA_1 $\mathcal{A}'$ such that they accept the same language. Moreover, the construction of $\mathcal{A}'$ is effective.*

The following result follows from Theorem 14 and Theorem 3.

Corollary 1. *The emptiness problem for* top view weak k-PAs *is decidable.*

It turns out that top view weak PAs admits many nice properties [Tan13]:

- Expressiveness: it is shown that for every $\text{LTL}_1^\downarrow$ formula ψ, there exists a weak k-PA $\mathcal{A}_\psi$, such that $\mathcal{L}(\mathcal{A}_\psi) = \mathcal{L}(\psi)$. It turns out that the automaton $\mathcal{A}_\psi$ is a top view weak k-PA. Thus, the class of languages accepted by top view weak k-PAs contains the languages definable by LTL with one freeze quantifier.
- Decidability: The emptiness problem is decidable.
- Efficiency: The membership problem, that is, testing whether a given data word of length n is accepted by a deterministic top view weak k-PA can be solved in $\mathcal{O}(n^k)$ time.
- Closure properties: Top view weak k-PAs are closed under all boolean operations.
- Robustness: Alternation and non-determinism do *not* add expressive power to top view weak k-PAs.

Tan [Tan10] observed that the finiteness of the number of pebbles for top view weak PAs is not necessary. He defined top view weak PAs with unbounded number of pebbles, i.e., top view weak unbounded PAs. It is straightforward to show that 1-way deterministic 1-RAs can be simulated by top view weak unbounded PAs. (Each time the register automaton changes the content of the register, the top view weak unbounded PAs places a new pebble.) Furthermore, top view weak unbounded PAs can be simulated by ARA_1's (1-way alternating one-register automata), similar to Theorem 14. Thus, the emptiness problem for top view unbounded weak PAs is still decidable.

Further Reading. Tan [Tan13] used graph reachability problem to investigate the strict hierarchy of pebble automata based on the number of pebbles and the comparison of the expressiveness of pebble automata with the other formalisms over infinite alphabets. [BSSS06] studied pebble tree-walking automata on trees.

6   Variable Automata and LTL with Data Variable Quantifications

Another idea to deal with data values from an infinite data domain is to use *logical variables* to represent data values. The differences between logical variables and registers are as follows: While logical variables and registers are both used to represent the data values from an infinite data domain, logical variables are *declarative* in the sense that they cannot be updated, but can be existentially or universally quantified, on the other hand, registers are *imperative* in the sense that they can be updated, but cannot be quantified.

In this section, we introduce variable automata, LTL with data variable quantifications, and its variant, indexed temporal logics, where the data values are interpreted as process identifiers.

Variable automata were proposed by Grumberg et al. as a natural extension of NFAs to infinite alphabets [GKS10].

Definition 15 (Variable automata). *Let Σ be a finite alphabet and $X \cup \{y\}$ be a finite set of variables, where X is a set of bound variables, and $y \notin X$ is a free variable. A variable automaton (VA) $\mathcal{A}$ is an NFA $(Q, \Sigma \times (X \cup \{y\}), q_0, \delta, F)$.*

Semantics of VAs. Suppose $\mathcal{A} = (Q, \Sigma \times (X \cup \{y\}), q_0, \delta, F)$ is a VA and $w = (\sigma_1, d_1) \ldots (\sigma_n, d_n)$ is a data word. A *run* of $\mathcal{A}$ on w is a sequence of transitions $q_0 \xrightarrow{(\sigma_1, z_1)} q_1 \cdots q_{n-1} \xrightarrow{(\sigma_n, z_n)} q_n$ such that

- for each $i \in [n]$, $(q_{i-1}, (\sigma_i, z_i), q_i) \in \delta$,
- for every $i, j \in [n]$ such that $z_i, z_j \in X$, it holds that $z_i = z_j$ iff $d_i = d_j$,
- for each $i, j \in [n]$ such that $z_i \in X$ and $z_j = y$, it holds that $d_i \neq d_j$.

A run of $\mathcal{A}$ on w is accepting if $q_n \in F$. Let $\mathcal{L}(\mathcal{A})$ denote the set of data words accepted by $\mathcal{A}$.

Example 10. Let $\Sigma = \{a, b\}$ and L be the data language comprising the data words $w = (a, d_1)(b, d_2) \ldots (b, d_{n-1})(a, d_n)$ such that $d_1 = d_n$ and for each i : $1 < i < n$, $d_i \neq d_1$. Then L can be defined the VA $\mathcal{A}$ illustrated in Fig. 4.

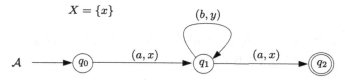

Fig. 4. An example of VA

Theorem 15 ([GKS10]). *The following results hold for variable automata:*

- *VAs are closed under union, but not closed under intersection or complementation.*
- *VAs and NRAs are incomparable with respect to the expressive power.*
- *The nonemptiness problem of VAs is NL-complete, the universality and language inclusion problems of VAs are undecidable.*

Mens and Rahonis consisdered variable tree automata (VTA) in [MR11b]. They showed VTAs have similar theoretical properties as VAs.

LTL with data variable quantifications (VLTL) is obtained by extending LTL with existential and universal quantifications on data variables. VLTL was first considered by Grumberg et al. in [GKS12, GKS13, GKS14]. Later on, Song and Wu did an extensive investigation on the decision problems of different fragments of VLTL in [SW14, SW16].

Definition 16 (LTL with data variable quantifications). *Let $\mathcal{X}$ be a countable set of variables. Then LTL with data variable quantifications (denoted by VLTL) is defined by the following rules:*

$$\varphi \stackrel{def}{=} \sigma \mid \mathsf{val}(x) \mid \neg\varphi \mid \varphi \vee \varphi \mid \mathsf{X}\varphi \mid \varphi \; \mathsf{U} \; \varphi \mid \exists x. \; \varphi,$$

where $\sigma \in \Sigma$ and $x \in \mathcal{X}$.

The set of free variables of VLTL formula φ, denoted by $\mathsf{free}(\varphi)$, can be defined in a standard way as first-order logics. A VLTL formula φ is *closed* if $\mathsf{free}(\varphi) = \varnothing$.

Semantics of VLTL. VLTL formulae φ are interpreted on a tuple (w, i, θ), where $w = (\sigma_1, d_1) \ldots (\sigma_n, d_n)$ is a data word, i is a position of the data word, and $\theta : \mathsf{free}(\varphi) \to \mathbb{D}$ assigns each variable from $\mathsf{free}(\varphi)$ a data value:

- $(w, i, \theta) \models \sigma$ iff $\sigma_i = \sigma$,
- $(w, i, \theta) \models \mathsf{val}(x)$ iff $d_i = \theta(x)$,
- $(w, i, \theta) \models \neg\varphi$ iff not $(w, i, \theta) \models \varphi$,
- $(w, i, \theta) \models \varphi_1 \vee \varphi_2$ iff $(w, i, \theta) \models \varphi_1$ or $(w, i, \theta) \models \varphi_2$,
- $(w, i, \theta) \models \mathsf{X}\varphi$ iff $i < n$ and $(w, i+1, \theta) \models \varphi$,
- $(w, i, \theta) \models \varphi_1 \mathsf{U} \varphi_2$ iff there exists $k : i \leq k \leq n$ such that $(w, k, \theta) \models \varphi_2$ and for each $j : i \leq j < k$, $(w, j, \theta) \models \varphi_1$,
- $(w, i, \theta) \models \exists x. \varphi$ iff there exists $d \in \mathbb{D}$ such that $(w, i, \theta[d/x]) \models \varphi$, where $\theta[d/x]$ denotes the assignment function that is the same as θ, except that x is assigned with the data value d.

Similarly to LTL, we can also define the positive normal form of VLTL. Specifically, VLTL formulae in positive normal form are defined by the following rules,

$$\varphi \stackrel{\text{def}}{=} \sigma \mid \neg\sigma \mid \mathsf{val}(x) \mid \neg\mathsf{val}(x) \mid \varphi \vee \varphi \mid \varphi \wedge \varphi \mid \mathsf{X}\varphi \mid \overline{\mathsf{X}}\varphi \mid$$
$$\varphi \mathsf{U} \varphi \mid \varphi \mathsf{R} \varphi \mid \exists x. \varphi \mid \forall x. \varphi.$$

In the following, we assume that all VLTL formulae are in positive normal form.

We consider the following fragments of VLTL:

- Let $\exists^*$-VLTL denote the fragment of VLTL where no universal quantifiers appear.
- Let NN-$\exists^*$-VLTL denote the fragment of $\exists^*$-VLTL where the existential quantifiers are non-nested, more precisely, the formulae φ in $\exists^*$-VLTL such that for each subformula $\exists x. \varphi'$ and each subformula of $\exists y. \varphi''$ of φ', there are no free occurrences of x in φ''.
- Let VLTL$_{pnf}$ denote the fragment of VLTL where the formulae in prenex normal form, that is, VLTL formulae of the form $\mathcal{Q}_1 x_1. \ldots \mathcal{Q}_n x_n. \varphi$, where $\mathcal{Q}_1, \ldots, \mathcal{Q}_n \in \{\exists, \forall\}$ and φ is a quantifier-free VLTL formula. Moreover, for a quantifier prefix $\Theta = \mathcal{Q}_1 \ldots \mathcal{Q}_k \in \{\exists, \forall\}^+$, let Θ-VLTL$_{pnf}$ denote the fragment of VLTL$_{pnf}$ where all the formulae are of the form $\mathcal{Q}_1 x_1. \ldots \mathcal{Q}_k x_k. \varphi$, where φ is a quantifier-free VLTL formula.
- Let $\forall$-VLTL$_{pnf}^{gdlt}$ denote the set of $\forall$-VLTL$_{pnf}$ formulae $\forall x. \psi$ such that all the occurrences of σ and $\neg\sigma$ in ψ are *guarded* by the positive occurrences of $\mathsf{val}(x)$. More precisely, ψ is a quantifier-free VLTL formula defined by the following rules,

$$\psi := \sigma \wedge \mathsf{val}(x) \mid \neg(\sigma \wedge \mathsf{val}(x)) \mid \neg\sigma \wedge \mathsf{val}(x) \mid \neg(\neg\sigma \wedge \mathsf{val}(x))$$
$$\mathsf{val}(x) \mid \neg\mathsf{val}(x) \mid \psi \vee \psi \mid \psi \wedge \psi \mid \mathsf{X}\psi \mid \overline{\mathsf{X}}\psi \mid \psi \mathsf{U} \psi \mid \psi \mathsf{R} \psi,$$

where $\sigma \in \Sigma$, $x \in X$, and the superscript "*gdlt*" means "guarded letters". For instance, the formula $\forall x.\ \mathsf{G}[(openFile \wedge \mathsf{val}(x)) \rightarrow \mathsf{XF}(closeFile \wedge \mathsf{val}(x))]$ is in $\forall\text{-VLTL}_{pnf}^{gdlt}$, while the formula

$$\forall x.\ \mathsf{G}[(openFile \wedge \mathsf{val}(x)) \rightarrow (write \wedge \neg\mathsf{val}(x))\ U\ (closeFile \wedge \mathsf{val}(x))]$$

is not, since the occurrence of *write* is not guarded by a positive occurrence of $\mathsf{val}(x)$.

Theorem 16 ([SW14,SW16]). *The following results hold for VLTL:*

- *The satisfiability problem of $\exists^*$-VLTL is undecidable.*
- *The satisfiability problem of $\forall$-VLTL$_{pnf}$ is undecidable.*
- *The satisfiability problem of NN-$\exists^*$-VLTL is decidable and non-primitive recursive.*
- *The satisfiability problem of $\forall$-VLTL$_{pnf}^{gdlt}$ is decidable.*

As mentioned before, since process identifiers are a concrete type of data values, indexed linear temporal logic (ILTL) used to specify and reason about parameterized concurrent systems can be seen as variants of VLTL. ILTL was first proposed by German and Sistla in ([SG87,GS92]). They showed that the validity (resp. model checking) problem of the indexed LTL is decidable (resp. undecidable). The differences between ILTL and VLTL are as follows:

- VLTL interpreted over data words where each position carries only one data value or a fixed number of data values, whereas ILTL is interpreted over computation traces in parameterised systems (cf. the semantics of ILTL formulae below).
- While computation traces can also be seen as data words by treating process identifiers as data values, these data words are significantly different than the traditional ones studied before. Namely, each position of these data words carries an *unbounded* number of data values, and all the data values occur in every position.

Definition 17 (Indexed Linear Temporal Logics). *Let AP and AP' be the set of global and local atomic propositions. The formulae of indexed linear temporal logic (ILTL) are defined by the following rules,*

$$\varphi \stackrel{def}{=} \mathsf{true} \mid \mathsf{false} \mid p \mid \neg p \mid p'(x) \mid \neg p'(x) \mid \varphi \vee \varphi \mid \varphi \wedge \varphi \mid$$
$$\mathsf{X}\varphi \mid \varphi\ \mathsf{U}\ \varphi \mid \varphi\ \mathsf{R}\ \varphi \mid \exists x.\ \varphi \mid \forall x.\ \varphi,$$

where $p \in AP$, $p' \in AP'$, and $x \in X$.

Let $\mathsf{free}(\varphi)$ denote the set of free variables occurring in φ. An ILTL formula containing no free variables is called a *closed* ILTL formula. For an ILTL formula φ, let $\neg\varphi$ denote its complement (negation), and let $\overline{\varphi}$ denote the *positive normal form* of $\neg\varphi$, that is obtained by pushing the negation inside of operators. For instance, if $\varphi = \exists x.\ \mathsf{F}p'(x)$, then $\overline{\varphi} = \forall x.\ \mathsf{G}\neg p'(x)$.

Semantics of ILTL. ILTL formulae are interpreted over computation traces of parameterised systems. Let $\mathcal{I}$ be an infinite set of process identifiers. A *computation trace* over $AP \cup AP'$ is a tuple $trc = (\alpha, I, (\beta_i)_{i \in I})$, where $\alpha \in (2^{AP})^\omega$ is an ω-sequence of valuations over the global atomic propositions from AP, $I \subseteq \mathcal{I}$ is a *finite* set of process identifiers, and for each $i \in I$, $\beta_i \in (2^{AP'})^\omega$ is a local computation trace, i.e. an ω-sequence of valuations over the local atomic propositions from AP'.

Let φ be an ILTL formula, $trc = (\alpha, I, (\beta_i)_{i \in I})$ be a computation trace, $\theta : \mathsf{free}(\varphi) \to I$ be an assignment of the process identifiers (from I) to the free variables in φ, and $n \in \mathbb{N}$. Then (trc, θ, n) satisfies φ, denoted by $(trc, \theta, n) \models \varphi$, is defined as follows:

- $(trc, \theta, n) \models p$ (resp. $\neg p$) if $p \in \alpha[n]$ (resp. $p \notin \alpha[n]$),
- $(trc, \theta, n) \models p'(x)$ (resp. $\neg p'(x)$) if $p' \in \beta_{\theta(x)}[n]$ (resp. $p' \notin \beta_{\theta(x)}[n]$),
- $(trc, \theta, n) \models \exists x. \varphi_1$ if there is $i \in I$ such that $(trc, \theta[i/x], n) \models \varphi_1$, where $\theta[i/x]$ is the same as θ, except for assigning i to x,
- $(trc, \theta, n) \models \forall x. \varphi_1$ if for each $i \in I$, $(trc, \theta[i/x], n) \models \varphi_1$,
- $(trc, \theta, n) \models \varphi_1 \vee \varphi_2$ if $(trc, \theta, n) \models \varphi_1$ or $(trc, \theta, n) \models \varphi_2$,
- $(trc, \theta, n) \models \varphi_1 \wedge \varphi_2$ if $(trc, \theta, n) \models \varphi_1$ and $(trc, \theta, n) \models \varphi_2$,
- $(trc, \theta, n) \models \mathsf{X}\varphi$ if $(trc, \theta, n+1) \models \varphi$,
- $(trc, \theta, n) \models \varphi_1 \mathsf{U} \varphi_2$ if there is $m \geq n$ s.t. $(trc, \theta, m) \models \varphi_2$, and for all $l : n \leq l < m$, $(trc, \theta, l) \models \varphi_1$,
- $(trc, \theta, n) \models \varphi_1 \mathsf{R} \varphi_2$ if either for all $m \geq n$, $(trc, \theta, m) \models \varphi_2$, or there is $m \geq n$ s.t. $(trc, \theta, m) \models \varphi_1$, and for all $l : n \leq l \leq m$, $(trc, \theta, l) \models \varphi_2$.

Note that if φ is a closed ILTL formula, then θ has an empty domain and thus is omitted. Namely we simply write $(trc, n) \models \varphi$. In addition, for a closed ILTL formula φ, we use $trc \models \varphi$ to abbreviate $(trc, 0) \models \varphi$. For a closed ILTL formula φ, let $\mathcal{L}(\varphi)$ denote the set of computation traces trc such that $trc \models \varphi$. The *satisfiability* problem of ILTL is defined as follows: Given a closed ILTL formula φ, decide whether $\mathcal{L}(\varphi)$ is empty.

We shall consider the following fragments of ILTL with abbreviations:

- ILTL_{pnf} denotes the fragment of ILTL where formulae are in *prenex normal form*, that is $\{\forall, \exists\}$ quantifications appear only at the beginning of the formula. In particular, let $\Theta \subseteq \{\exists, \forall\}^*$. Then $\Theta\text{-ILTL}_{pnf}$ denotes the fragment of ILTL_{pnf} where the quantifier prefixes belong to Θ.
- NN-ILTL denotes the fragment of ILTL where the quantifiers are *not* nested, that is, for each formula $\mathcal{Q}_1 x.\varphi_1$ such that $\mathcal{Q}_2 y.\varphi_2$ is a subformula of φ_1, it holds that x is not a free variable of φ_2, where $\mathcal{Q}_1, \mathcal{Q}_2 \in \{\forall, \exists\}$.
- $\text{ILTL}(\mathcal{O})$ for $\mathcal{O} \subseteq \{\mathsf{X}, \mathsf{F}, \mathsf{G}, \mathsf{U}, \mathsf{R}\}$ denotes the fragment of ILTL where only temporal operators from $\mathcal{O}$ are used. Moreover, we use $\text{ILTL}\backslash\mathsf{X}$ as an abbreviation of $\text{ILTL}(\mathsf{U}, \mathsf{R})$, where the X operator is forbidden.
- ILTL^{locap} denotes the fragment of ILTL where there are no global atomic propositions, that is, $AP = \varnothing$.

These notations might be combined to define more (refined) fragments, e.g. the logic $(\text{ILTL}(\mathsf{F}, \mathsf{G}))_{pnf}$ denotes the fragment of ILTL_{pnf} where only temporal operators F and G are used.

Theorem 17. *The following results hold for ILTL:*

- *The satisfiability problems of* $\forall\exists\text{-}ILTL_{pnf}$ *and* $\exists\forall\exists\text{-}ILTL_{pnf}^{locap}$ *are undecidable.*
- *The satisfiability problems of* $\exists^*\forall^*\text{-}ILTL_{pnf}$ *and* $\exists^*\forall^*\text{-}(ILTL \setminus X)_{pnf}$ *are EXPSPACE-complete, and the satisfiability problem of* $\exists^*\forall^*\text{-}(ILTL(F, G))_{pnf}$ *is NEXPTIME-complete.*
- *The satisfiability problems of* $NN\text{-}ILTL$, $NN\text{-}ILTL(X, F, G)$, $NN\text{-}ILTL \setminus X$, *and* $NN\text{-}ILTL(F, G)$ *are EXPSPACE-complete.*

7   Symbolic Automata and Transducers

In this section, we introduce symbolic automata and transducers, another line of work to reason about data values from an infinite domain. Unlike the data domain $\mathbb{D}$ discussed in previous sections, where only the equality and inequality relation between data values are available, the data domain $\mathbb{D}$ in this section has a richer structure where more complex predicates, e.g. the predicate defining the set of even natural numbers, can be used. Over an infinite data domain, where complex predicates can be used, symbolic automata and transducers are natural extensions of finite automata and transducers over finite alphabets, by replacing the letters from a finite alphabet with the predicates over the infinite data domain. The concept of symbolic finite-state automata/transducers was initially introduced by Watson in [Wat96], then investigated by van Noord and Gerdemann in [vNG01], with motivation from natural language processing. The recent development of this topic by Veanes, Bjørner, et al., was mainly driven by regular expression analysis and advanced web security analysis [VB11a, VHL+12, Vea13].

In the following, we first present symbolic automata and then symbolic transducers. In the literature on symbolic automata and transducers, a data word is normally defined as an element of $\mathbb{D}^*$, instead of an element of $(\Sigma \times \mathbb{D})^*$ as in the previous sections. In this section, we follow this convention and define data words as elements of $\mathbb{D}^*$.

7.1   Symbolic Automata

The data domain $\mathbb{D}$ equipped with predicates used in symbolic automata is formalised by effective Boolean algebra, which is defined as follows.

Definition 18 (Effective Boolean algebra). *An effective Boolean algebra* Υ *is a tuple* $(\Omega, \| \circ \|, \Psi)$ *satisfying the following constraints:*

- $\Omega = (\mathfrak{S}, \mathfrak{F}, \mathfrak{P})$ *is a signature such that* $\mathfrak{S}$ *is a singleton set* $\{s\}$, $\mathfrak{F}$, *and* $\mathfrak{P}$ *are recursively enumerable sets.*
- $\| \circ \|$ *is an* Ω-interpretation such that $\|s\|$ *is a recursively enumerable set, called the universe (denoted by* $\mathbb{D}$).

- $\Psi = \bigcup_{i \in \mathbb{N} \backslash \{0\}} \Psi^{(i)}$ such that for each $i \in \mathbb{N} \backslash \{0\}$, $\Psi^{(i)}$ is a recursively enumerable set of i-ary Ω-formulae closed under Boolean connectives $\vee, \wedge, \neg$. For each $\psi(\boldsymbol{x}) \in \Psi$, we use $\|\psi\|$ to denote the set $\{\eta(\boldsymbol{x}) \mid \eta \text{ is an } \Omega\text{-assignment, and } \|\circ\| \models_\eta \psi(\boldsymbol{x})\}$. Elements of $\|\psi\|$ are called the witnesses of ψ.

Let $\Upsilon = (\Omega, \|\circ\|, \Psi)$ be an effective Boolean algebra and $\psi \in \Psi$. Then ψ is satisfiable, denoted by isSat(ψ), if $\|\psi\| \neq \varnothing$. In addition, Υ is decidable iff it is decidable to check isSat(ψ) for $\psi \in \Psi$.

Definition 19 (Symbolic finite-state automata). A symbolic finite-state automaton (SFA) is a tuple $\mathcal{A} = (Q, \Upsilon, q_0, \delta, F)$, where:

- Q is a finite set of states,
- $\Upsilon = (\Omega, \|\circ\|, \Psi)$ is a decidable effective Boolean algebra,
- $q_0 \in Q$ is the initial state,
- $F \subseteq Q$ is the set of final states,
- $\delta \subseteq Q \times \Psi^{(1)} \times Q$ is a finite set of symbolic transitions.

An SFA $\mathcal{A} = (Q, \Upsilon, q_0, \delta, F)$ is deterministic if for every $(q_1, \psi, q_2), (q_1, \psi', q_2') \in \delta$, if isSat($\psi \wedge \psi'$) holds, then $q_2 = q_2'$.

Semantics of SFAs. Let $\mathcal{A} = (Q, \Upsilon, q_0, \delta, F)$ be an SFA. A symbolic transition $t = (q_1, \psi, q_2) \in \delta$ in the SFA $\mathcal{A}$ can be concretised into a set $\|t\|$ of concrete (standard) transitions $\rightarrow \subseteq Q \times \mathbb{D} \times Q$ defined as follows: For every $d \in \mathbb{D}$, $q_1 \xrightarrow{d} q_2 \in \|t\|$ iff $d \in \|\psi\|$. Intuitively, suppose that $\mathcal{A}$ is in the state q_1 and reading a data value d, if there is a transition $(q_1, \psi, q_2) \in \delta$ such that $d \in \|\psi\|$, then $\mathcal{A}$ moves from q_1 to q_2 after consuming the input data value d.

Given a data word $w = d_1 ... d_n \in \mathbb{D}^*$, $q_1 \xrightarrow{w} q_{n+1}$ if there exist states $q_2, ..., q_n \in Q$ such that for all $i \in [n]$, $q_i \xrightarrow{d_i} q_{i+1} \in \|t\|$ for some transition $t \in \delta$. A data word w is accepted at the state q of $\mathcal{A}$ iff there exists a state $q_f \in F$ such that $q \xrightarrow{w} q_f$. Let $\mathcal{L}_q(\mathcal{A})$ denote the set of data words accepted at the state q of $\mathcal{A}$. Then the data language defined by $\mathcal{A}$, denoted by $\mathcal{L}(\mathcal{A})$, is $\mathcal{L}_{q_0}(\mathcal{A})$.

Example 11. Let us consider the language $L_{2^{31}}$ over integers, in which either the second letter is less than -2^{31} and the last letter is greater than 2^{31}, or the second letter is greater than 2^{31} and the last letter is less than -2^{31}. $L_{2^{31}}$ cannot be defined by any finite state automaton. Let $\mathcal{A}_{2^{31}} = (\{q_0, q_1, q_2, q_3, q_4\}, \Upsilon, q_0, \delta, \{q_4\})$ be the SFA such that Υ is linear arithmetic over integers and δ is illustrated in Fig. 5 (where 2^{31} is an abbreviation the sequence of 32 bits 10^{31}). $\mathcal{A}_{2^{31}}$ defines the data language $L_{2^{31}}$.

An ϵ-SFA $\mathcal{A}$ is a tuple $\mathcal{A} = (Q, \Upsilon \cup \{\epsilon\}, q_0, \delta, F)$, where Q, Υ, q_0 and F are defined as for SFAs, and $\delta \subseteq Q \times (\Psi^{(1)} \cup \{\epsilon\}) \times Q$. An ϵ-transition (q_1, ϵ, q_2) in an ϵ-SFA $\mathcal{A}$ allows it to move from the state q_1 to the state q_2 without consuming any input data value. The semantics of ϵ-SFA can be defined as a natural extension of that of SFAs.

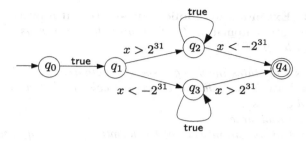

Fig. 5. The SFT $\mathcal{A}_{2^{31}}$

Let $\mathcal{A} = (Q, \Upsilon, q_0, \delta, F)$ be an SFA. A state $q \in Q$ is called *partial* if there is $d \in \mathbb{D}$ such that there are no $q' \in Q$ satisfying that $q \xrightarrow{d} q'$. Note that given a state $q \in Q$, we can decide whether q is partial by checking whether $\bigvee\limits_{(q,\psi,q')\in\delta} \psi$ is valid, that is, whether $\bigwedge\limits_{(q,\psi,q')\in\delta} \neg\psi$ is unsatisfiable. Then $\mathcal{A}$ is *minimal* if the following conditions hold:

- $\mathcal{A}$ is deterministic,
- $\mathcal{A}$ is complete, that is, $\mathcal{A}$ contains no partial states,
- $\mathcal{A}$ is clean, that is, for every $(q_1, \psi, q_2) \in \delta$, it holds that $\mathsf{isSat}(\psi)$ and there is $w \in \mathbb{D}^*$ such that $q_0 \xrightarrow{w} q_1$,
- $\mathcal{A}$ is normalized, that is, for each pair of states $q_1, q_2 \in Q$, there is at most one transition between them (otherwise, two transitions $(q_1, \psi_1, q_2), (q_1, \psi_2, q_2) \in \delta$ can be combined into one transition $(q_1, \psi_1 \vee \psi_2, q_2)$),
- for all $q_1, q_2 \in Q$, $q_1 = q_2$ iff $\mathcal{L}_{q_1}(\mathcal{A}) = \mathcal{L}_{q_2}(\mathcal{A})$.

Let $\mathcal{L} \subseteq \mathbb{D}^*$ be a data language. Then the *Kleene-closure* of $\mathcal{L}$, denoted by $\mathcal{L}^*$, is defined as $\{\varepsilon\} \cup \{w_1 \ldots w_n \mid n \geq 1, w_i \in \mathcal{L}\}$. The *reversal* of $\mathcal{L}$, denoted by $\mathcal{L}^{\mathsf{rev}}$, is defined as $\{d_1 \ldots d_n \mid d_n \ldots d_1 \in \mathcal{L}\}$.

It turns out SFAs preserve all the nice properties of finite-state automata.

Theorem 18 ([vNG01, VHL+12, DV14]). *The following results hold for SFAs:*

- *Each ϵ-SFA can be transformed into an equivalent SFA in linear time.*
- *SFAs are closed under determinization, all the Boolean operations, concatenation, Kleene-closure and reversal.*
- *The nonemptiness, the universality and the equivalence problems of SFAs are decidable.*

SFAs can only enforce constraints on the data value of a single position, and are incapable of comparing data values in different positions, which is the main reason why SFAs preserve all the nice properties of finite-state automata. In the following, we introduce an extension of SFAs that are capable of comparing data values in different positions, called extended symbolic finite-state automata (ESFA). ESFAs extend SFAs with lookahead, that is, by allowing to read several consecutive input data values in a single transition.

Definition 20 (Extended symbolic finite-state automata). *An extended symbolic finite-state automaton (ESFA) over the sort s is a tuple $\mathcal{A} = (Q, \Upsilon, q_0, \delta, F)$, where:*

- *Q is a finite set of states including a specific state q_f,*
- *$\Upsilon = (\Omega, \| \circ \|, \Psi)$ is a decidable effective Boolean algebra such that $\Omega = (\mathfrak{S}, \mathfrak{F}, \mathfrak{P})$ and $\mathfrak{S} = \{s\}$,*
- *$q_0 \in Q$ is the initial state,*
- *δ is a finite set of transition rules of the form $t = (q_1, \ell, \psi, q_2)$, where*
  - *$q_1 \in Q \setminus \{q_f\}$ and $q_2 \in Q$ are respectively the source and target states of t,*
  - *$\ell \in \mathbb{N} \setminus \{0\}$ is the lookahead of t,*
  - *$\psi \in \Psi^{(\ell)}$, that is, ψ is an ℓ-ary formula in Ψ,*
- *F is a set of final rules of the form $t = (q_1, \ell, \psi, q_f)$ such that if $\ell > 0$, then t satisfies the same constraints as for transition rules, otherwise (i.e. $\ell = 0$), then $\psi = $ true. Intuitively, a final rule (q_1, ℓ, ψ, q_f) is used when the rest of the input data word is of length ℓ, where $\ell = 0$ corresponds to the situation that $\mathcal{A}$ already reaches the right end of the data word. It is a generalisation of final states in finite-state automata.*

The lookahead of an ESFA $\mathcal{A}$ is the maximum of the lookaheads of the (transition or final) rules in $\mathcal{A}$.

Semantics of ESFAs. Let $\mathcal{A} = (Q, \Upsilon, q_0, \delta, F)$ be an ESFA. The semantics of the rules $t = (q_1, \ell, \psi, q_2) \in \delta$ of $\mathcal{A}$ is defined as follows: If $\ell = 0$, then $\psi = $ true and $q_2 = q_f$, therefore, $\|t\| = \{q_1 \xrightarrow{\varepsilon} q_f\}$. Otherwise,

$$\|t\| = \{q_1 \xrightarrow{w} q_2 \mid w = d_1 \ldots d_\ell \in (\mathbb{D}_s)^\ell, (d_1, \ldots, d_\ell) \in \|\psi\|\}.$$

Intuitively, using the transition $t = (q_1, \ell, \psi, q_2)$, $\mathcal{A}$ reads the next ℓ input data values w (including the one in the current position), if the corresponding tuple of data values satisfies ψ, then $\mathcal{A}$ consumes the word w and moves from the state q_1 to the state q_2.

Given a data word $w \in \mathbb{D}^*$, $q_1 \xrightarrow{w} q_{n+1}$ if there exist states $q_2, ..., q_n \in Q$ and data words $w_1, ..., w_n \in \mathbb{D}^*$ such that $w = w_1...w_n$ and for all $i \in [n]$, $q_i \xrightarrow{w_i} q_{i+1}$. A data word $w \in \mathbb{D}^*$ is *accepted* by $\mathcal{A}$ iff $q_0 \xrightarrow{w} q_f$. The data language defined by $\mathcal{A}$, denoted by $\mathcal{L}(\mathcal{A})$, is the set of data words accepted by $\mathcal{A}$.

An ESFA $\mathcal{A} = (Q, \Upsilon, q_0, \delta, F)$ is *deterministic* if for every pair of rules (q_1, ℓ, ψ, q_2) and $(q_1, \ell', \psi', q_2')$ in $\mathcal{A}$,

- if $q_2, q_2' \in Q \setminus \{q_f\}$ and $\mathsf{isSat}(\psi \wedge \psi')$, then $q_2 = q_2'$ and $\ell = \ell'$;
- if $q_2 = q_2' = q_f$ and $\mathsf{isSat}(\psi \wedge \psi')$, then $\ell = \ell'$;
- if $q_2 \in Q \setminus \{q_f\}$, $q_2' = q_f$ and $\mathsf{isSat}(\psi \wedge \psi')$, then $\ell > \ell'$.

Example 12. Let us consider the ESFA $\mathcal{A}_{script} = (\{q_0, q_1, q_f\}, \Upsilon, q_0, \delta, F)$ such that

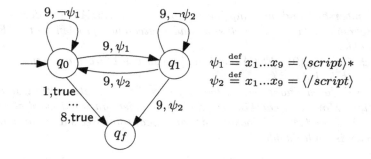

$$\psi_1 \stackrel{\text{def}}{=} x_1...x_9 = \langle script \rangle *$$
$$\psi_2 \stackrel{\text{def}}{=} x_1...x_9 = \langle /script \rangle$$

Fig. 6. The ESFA $\mathcal{A}_{script}$

- $\varUpsilon$ is the theory of UTF-8 characters where all the function symbols are constants and the set of predicate symbols is empty,
- δ and F are illustrated in Fig. 6, where ψ_1 is an abbreviation of the formula $x_1 = \langle \land x_2 = s \land x_3 = c \land \cdots \land x_8 =\rangle$ and ψ_2 is an abbreviation of the formula $x_1 = \langle \land x_2 = / \land x_3 = s \land \cdots \land x_9 =\rangle$.

Then the ESFA $\mathcal{A}_{script}$ defines the set of words w such that each occurrence of $\langle script \rangle$ is followed by an occurrence of $\langle /script \rangle$ in the future. Note that although $\mathcal{A}_{script}$ is over a finite alphabet, it is much more succinct than the corresponding finite-state automaton defining the same language, where an enumeration of all the possible subwords of length 9 satisfying $\neg\psi_1$ or $\neg\psi_2$ is necessary.

A formula $\psi \in \varPsi^{(\ell)}$ (where $\ell > 0$) is *Cartesian* if $\|\psi\|$ is equivalent to $D_1 \times \cdots \times D_\ell$ for some $D_1, \ldots, D_\ell \subseteq \mathbb{D}_s$. An ESFA $\mathcal{A}$ is *Cartesian* if for each rule (q_1, ℓ, ψ, q_2) in $\mathcal{A}$ such that $\ell > 0$, it holds that ψ is Cartesian. For a satisfiable formula $\psi(\boldsymbol{x}) \in \varPsi^{(\ell)}$ (where $\ell > 0$), to decide whether ψ is Cartesian is equivalent to check whether for some witness $(d_1, ..., d_\ell)$ of ψ,

$$\forall x_1, ...x_\ell(\psi(x_1, ..., x_\ell)) \iff \bigwedge_{1 \leq i \leq \ell} \psi(d_1, ..., d_{i-1}, x_i, d_{i+1}, ..., d_\ell).$$

A formula $\psi(\boldsymbol{x}) \in \varPsi^{(\ell)}$ (where $\ell > 0$) is *monadic* if it is equivalent to a Boolean combination of unary formulae. For instance, $\psi(x_1, x_2) \stackrel{\text{def}}{=} x_1 = x_2 \bmod 2$ is a monadic formula since it is equivalent to $(x_1 = 0 \bmod 2 \land x_2 = 0 \bmod 2) \lor (x_1 = 1 \bmod 2 \land x_2 = 1 \bmod 2)$, while $\psi(x_1, x_2) \stackrel{\text{def}}{=} x_1 < x_2$ is not. In [VBNB14], a semi-decision procedure was provided to compute an equivalent Boolean combination of unary formulae, from a given quantifier-free formula over a decidable background theory.

An ESFA $\mathcal{A}$ is *monadic* if for each rule (q_1, ℓ, ψ, q_2) of $\mathcal{A}$ such that $\ell > 0$, ψ is monadic.

Theorem 19 ([DV15]). *The following results hold for ESFAs:*

- *Cartesian ESFAs, monadic ESFAs and SFAs are expressively equivalent, moreover, this also holds for the deterministic case.*

- *The membership and nonemptiness problems of ESFAs are decidable, but the universality, language inclusion and equivalence problems of ESFAs are undecidable.*
- *For each $\ell \in \mathbb{N} \setminus \{0\}$, ESFAs with lookahead $\ell + 1$ are more expressive than ESFAs with lookahead ℓ.*
- *ESFAs are closed under union, but not closed under intersection or complementation. Moreover, checking whether there exists an input word accepted by two ESFAs $\mathcal{A}$ and $\mathcal{A}'$ with lookahead 2 over quantifier free successor arithmetic and tuples is undecidable.*

In [DV15], the last result in Theorem 19 was shown by reducing the reachability problem of Minsky machines to the problem checking whether there exists an input word accepted by two ESFAs $\mathcal{A}$ and $\mathcal{A}'$ with lookahead 2 over quantifier free successor arithmetic and tuples from $\mathbb{N}^3$.

Remark 2. In the definition of ESFAs, when the reading head is in the position i and a transition with $\ell \geq 2$ lookahead is used, then after the transition, the reading head will be moved to the position $i + \ell$, instead of the next position to the right of i, that is, $i + 1$. This special semantics of lookaheads in ESFAs is essential for the decidability of nonemptiness problem. (Otherwise, we are already be able to reduce the reachability problem of Minsky machines to the nonemptiness problem of ESFAs.)

7.2   Symbolic Transducers

Similar to symbolic automata, symbolic transducers are introduced as extensions of finite-state transducers, where the input letters are replaced by formulae over an infinite data domain and the output letters are replaced by terms.

For the definition of symbolic transducers, we introduce the concept of background theories and label theories. Intuitively, background theories are many-sorted Boolean algebra satisfying the additional constraint that the set of formulae is closed under substitutions. Label theories extend background theories further by adding inequalities of terms into the set of formulae.

Definition 21 (Background theories). *A background theory Υ is a tuple $(\Omega, \| \circ \|, \Psi)$ satisfying the following constraints:*

- $\Omega = (\mathfrak{S}, \mathfrak{F}, \mathfrak{P})$ *is a signature satisfying that each of $\mathfrak{S}, \mathfrak{F}, \mathfrak{P}$ is a recursively enumerable set.*
- $\| \circ \|$ *is an Ω-interpretation such that for each $s \in \mathfrak{S}$, $\|s\|$ is a recursively enumerable set (denoted by $\mathbb{D}_s$).*
- $\Psi = \bigcup_{s \in \mathfrak{S}^+} \Psi^{(s)}$ *such that for each $s = (s_1, \ldots, s_i) \in \mathfrak{S}^+$, $\Psi^{(s)}$ is a recursively enumerable set of Ω-formulae of arity $s_1 \times \cdots \times s_i$ closed under Boolean connectives $\vee, \wedge, \neg$. In addition, Ψ is closed under substitutions, that is, for each s/s'-term $\boldsymbol{f}$ and $\psi(\boldsymbol{x}) \in \Psi^{(s')}$, we have $\psi[\boldsymbol{f}/\boldsymbol{x}] \in \Psi^{(s)}$. For each $\psi(\boldsymbol{x}) \in \Psi$, we use $\|\psi\|$ to denote the set $\{\eta(\boldsymbol{x}) \mid \eta$ is an Ω-assignment, and $\| \circ \| \models_\eta \psi(\boldsymbol{x})\}$. Elements of $\|\psi\|$ are called the* witnesses *of ψ.*

The notion $\mathsf{isSat}(\psi)$ for $\psi \in \Psi$ and the decidability of Υ can be defined similarly as effective Boolean algebra.

Definition 22 (Label theories). *A label theory Υ with the input sort s_{in} and output sort s_{out} is a tuple $(\Omega, \| \circ \|, \Psi, \Psi')$ satisfying the following constraints:*

- $(\Omega, \| \circ \|, \Psi)$ *is a background theory such that* $\Omega = (\mathfrak{S}, \mathfrak{F}, \mathfrak{P})$ *and* $s_{\mathsf{in}}, s_{\mathsf{out}} \in \mathfrak{S}$,
- $\Psi' = \bigcup\limits_{i \in \mathbb{N}\setminus\{0\}} (\Psi')^{(s_{\mathsf{in}}^i)}$ *such that for each* $i \in \mathbb{N} \setminus \{0\}$, $(\Psi')^{(s_{\mathsf{in}}^i)}$ *comprises the formulae of the form* $\psi(\boldsymbol{x}) \wedge f(\boldsymbol{x}) \neq g(\boldsymbol{x})$, *where* $\psi(\boldsymbol{x}) \in \Psi^{(s_{\mathsf{in}}^i)}$ *and* f, g *are* $s_{\mathsf{in}}^i / s_{\mathsf{out}}$*-terms.*

A label theory is decidable if it is decidable to check $\mathsf{isSat}(\psi)$ *for* $\psi \in \Psi \cup \Psi'$.

Given a formula $\psi(\boldsymbol{x}) \in (\Psi)^{(s_{\mathsf{in}}^i)}$ and two $s_{\mathsf{in}}^i / s_{\mathsf{out}}$-terms $f(\boldsymbol{x}), g(\boldsymbol{x})$, f and g are *equivalent up to* ψ, denoted by $f \simeq_\psi g$, if $\mathsf{isSat}(\psi(\boldsymbol{x}) \wedge f(\boldsymbol{x}) \neq g(\boldsymbol{x}))$ does not hold. Two sequences of $s_{\mathsf{in}}^i / s_{\mathsf{out}}$-terms $\boldsymbol{f} = f_1...f_n$ and $\boldsymbol{g} = g_1...g_m$ are *equivalent up to* ψ, denoted by $\boldsymbol{f} \simeq_\psi \boldsymbol{g}$, iff $n = m$ and for every $j \in [n]$, $f_j \simeq_\psi g_j$.

Given a $s_{\mathsf{in}}^i / s_{\mathsf{out}}$-term $\boldsymbol{f} = f_1...f_n$ and a sequence of data values $\boldsymbol{d} = (d_1, \ldots, d_i) \in (\mathbb{D}_{s_{\mathsf{in}}})^i$, let $\|\boldsymbol{f}\|(\boldsymbol{d})$ denote the sequence $\|f_1\|(\boldsymbol{d})...\|f_n\|(\boldsymbol{d})$, that is, a data word of sort s_{out}.

Definition 23 (Symbolic finite-state transducers). *A symbolic finite-state transducer (SFT) is a tuple* $\mathcal{A} = (Q, \Upsilon, s_{\mathsf{in}}, s_{\mathsf{out}}, q_0, \delta, F)$, *where:*

- Q, q_0 *and* F *are defined as those for SFAs,*
- $\Upsilon = (\mathfrak{S}, \mathfrak{F}, \mathfrak{P})$ *is a decidable label theory with the input sort s_{in} and output sort s_{out},*
- δ *is a finite set of symbolic transitions* $(q, \psi, \boldsymbol{f}, q')$ *such that* $q, q' \in Q$, $\psi \in \Psi^{s_{\mathsf{in}}}$ *and* $\boldsymbol{f}$ *is a sequence of $s_{\mathsf{in}}/s_{\mathsf{out}}$-terms.*

Let $\mathcal{A} = (Q, \Upsilon, s_{\mathsf{in}}, s_{\mathsf{out}}, q_0, \delta, F)$ be an SFT. Then $\mathcal{A}$ is *deterministic* if for all $(q_1, \psi, \boldsymbol{f}, q_2), (q_1, \psi', \boldsymbol{f'}, q_2') \in \delta$, if $\mathsf{isSat}(\psi \wedge \psi')$, then $q_2 = q_2'$ and $\boldsymbol{f} \simeq_{\psi \wedge \psi'} \boldsymbol{f'}$.

Semantics of SFTs. Similar to SFAs, a symbolic transition $t = (q_1, \psi, \boldsymbol{f}, q_2) \in \delta$ in the SFT $\mathcal{A}$ can be concretised into a potentially infinite set $\|t\|$ of *concrete transitions* $\rightarrow \subseteq Q \times \mathbb{D}_{s_{\mathsf{in}}} \times (\mathbb{D}_{s_{\mathsf{out}}})^* \times Q$, where $q_1 \xrightarrow{d/w} q_2 \in \|t\|$ iff $d \in \|\psi\|$ and $w = \|\boldsymbol{f}\|(d)$. Intuitively, suppose $\mathcal{A}$ is at the state q_1 and reading the input data value $d \in \mathbb{D}_{s_{\mathsf{in}}}$, if there is a transition $(q_1, \psi, \boldsymbol{f}, q_2) \in \delta$ such that $d \in \|\psi\|$, then $\mathcal{A}$ can move from the state q_1 to the state q_2 after reading d, moreover it produces a data word $w \in (\mathbb{D}_{s_{\mathsf{out}}})^*$.

Given a data word $u = d_1...d_n \in (\mathbb{D}_{s_{\mathsf{in}}})^*$, $q_1 \xrightarrow{u/w} q_{n+1}$ if there exist states $q_2, ..., q_n \in Q$ and data words $w_1, ..., w_n \in (\mathbb{D}_{s_{\mathsf{out}}})^*$ such that $w = w_1...w_n$ and for each $i \in [n]$, $q_i \xrightarrow{d_i/w_i} q_{i+1}$. The *transduction* $\mathcal{T}_\mathcal{A}$ defined by the SFT $\mathcal{A}$ is a relation $\mathcal{T}_\mathcal{A} \subseteq (\mathbb{D}_{s_{\mathsf{in}}})^* \times (\mathbb{D}_{s_{\mathsf{out}}})^*$ defined as follows: For each $u \in (\mathbb{D}_{s_{\mathsf{in}}})^*$ and $w \in (\mathbb{D}_{s_{\mathsf{out}}})^*$, $(u, w) \in \mathcal{T}_\mathcal{A}$ iff there exists $q' \in F$ such that $q_0 \xrightarrow{u/w} q'$. For each

$u \in (\mathbb{D}_{s_{in}})^*$, define $\mathcal{T}_{\mathcal{A}}(u) = \{w \in (\mathbb{D}_{s_{out}})^* \mid (u, w) \in \mathcal{T}_{\mathcal{A}}\}$. The SFT $\mathcal{A}$ is *single-valued* if for all $u \in (\mathbb{D}_{s_{in}})^*$, $|\mathcal{T}_{\mathcal{A}}(u)| \leq 1$. The SFT $\mathcal{A}$ is *finite-valued* if there exists a bound $K \geq 0$ such that for all $u \in (\mathbb{D}_{s_{in}})^*$, $|\mathcal{T}_{\mathcal{A}}(u)| \leq K$.

Example 13. Let us consider the simple SFT

$$\mathcal{A}_{\mathbf{xor}} = (\{q_0\}, \Upsilon, BV^2, BV, q_0, \{(q_0, \mathsf{true}, f, q_0)\}, \{q_0\}),$$

where BV^2 and BV are respectively bit vectors with length 2 and 1, the function $f \stackrel{\text{def}}{=} \lambda b_0, b_1. \; b_0 \; \mathbf{xor} \; b_1$ (**xor** is the bitwise exclusive or operator). The SFT $\mathcal{A}_{\mathbf{xor}}$ transforms each sequence of bit pairs $(b_0^1, b_1^1)...(b_0^n, b_1^n)$ into a sequence of bits $b^1...b^n$ such that for all $i \in [n]$, $b^i = b_0^i \; \mathbf{xor} \; b_1^i$.

Let $\Upsilon_1 = (\Omega_1, \| \circ \|_1, \Psi_1, \Psi_1')$ be a label theory with input sort s_1 and output sort s_2, and $\Upsilon_2 = (\Omega_2, \| \circ \|_2, \Psi_2, \Psi_2')$ be a label theory with input sort s_2 and output sort s_3. Then Υ_1 and Υ_2 are said to be *composable* if the following constraints hold: Let $\Omega_1 = (\mathfrak{S}_1, \mathfrak{F}_1, \mathfrak{P}_1)$ and $\Omega_2 = (\mathfrak{S}_2, \mathfrak{F}_2, \mathfrak{P}_2)$, then

- $\mathfrak{S}_1 \cap \mathfrak{S}_2 = \{s_2\}$,
- for each $i, j \in \mathbb{N} \setminus \{0\}$, the set of functions from $\mathfrak{F}_1$ of arity $s_2^i \rightarrow s_2^j$ is the same as the set of functions from $\mathfrak{F}_2$ of arity $s_2^i \rightarrow s_2^j$, moreover, for each such function f, $\|f\|_1 = \|f\|_2$, finally, all these function symbols are the only ones shared by $\mathfrak{F}_1$ and $\mathfrak{F}_2$,
- for each $i \in \mathbb{N} \setminus \{0\}$, the set of predicates from $\mathfrak{P}_1$ of arity s_2^i is the same as the set of predicates from $\mathfrak{P}_2$ of arity s_2^i, moreover, for each such predicate p, $\|p\|_1 = \|p\|_2$, finally, all these predicate symbols are the only ones shared by $\mathfrak{P}_1$ and $\mathfrak{P}_2$.

From two composable label theories Υ_1 and Υ_2, a label theory $\Upsilon = (\Omega, \| \circ \|, \Psi, \Psi')$, called the *composition* of Υ_1 and Υ_2, can be defined as follows.

- the input sort and output sort of Υ are s_1 and s_3 respectively,
- $\Omega = (\mathfrak{S}_1 \cup \mathfrak{S}_2, \mathfrak{F}_1 \cup \mathfrak{F}_2, \mathfrak{P}_1 \cup \mathfrak{P}_2)$.
- The $\| \circ \|$-interpretations of sorts, function symbols, and predicate symbols from $\Omega_1 \cap \Omega_2$ are those of $\| \circ \|_1$. On the other hand, the $\| \circ \|$-interpretations of sorts, function symbols, and predicate symbols from $(\Omega_1 \setminus \Omega_2) \cup (\Omega_2 \setminus \Omega_1)$ inherit from $\| \circ \|_1$ or $\| \circ \|_2$.
- Ψ is closure of $\Psi_1 \cup \Psi_2$ under Boolean connectives and substitutions (i.e. the minimum set of formulae that subsumes $\Psi_1 \cup \Psi_2$ and is closed under Boolean connectives and substitutions).
- $\Psi' = \bigcup\limits_{i \in \mathbb{N} \setminus \{0\}} (\Psi')^{(s_1^i)}$ such that for each $i \in \mathbb{N} \setminus \{0\}$, $(\Psi')^{(s_1^i)}$ comprises the formulae of the form $\psi(\boldsymbol{x}) \wedge f(\boldsymbol{x}) \neq g(\boldsymbol{x})$, where $\psi(\boldsymbol{x}) \in \Psi^{(s_1^i)}$ and f, g are s_1^i/s_3-terms.

SFTs are said to be *closed under composition* if for each pair of SFTs $\mathcal{A}_1$ with the input/output sort s_1/s_2, and $\mathcal{A}_2$ with the input/output sort s_2/s_3, there is an SFT $\mathcal{A}$ such that for each data word $w \in (\mathbb{D}_{s_1})^*$, it holds that

$\mathcal{T}_{\mathcal{A}}(w) = \mathcal{T}_{\mathcal{A}_2}(\mathcal{T}_{\mathcal{A}_1}(w))$. Two SFTs $\mathcal{A}_1$ and $\mathcal{A}_2$ with the input/output sort s_1/s_2 are *equivalent* if for each $w \in (\mathbb{D}_{s_1})^*$, $\mathcal{T}_{\mathcal{A}_1}(w) = \mathcal{T}_{\mathcal{A}_2}(w)$. The equivalence problem of SFTs is to decide the equivalence of two given SFTs with the same input/output sorts.

Theorem 20 ([vNG01, VHL+12, VB16]). *The following results hold for SFTs:*

- *SFTs are closed under composition if their label theories are composable.*
- *The equivalence problem of finite-valued SFTs is decidable.*

We would like to mention that the equivalence problem of finite state transducers (hence for SFTs) is undecidable [FV98].

Similarly to the extension of SFAs into ESFAs, SFTs can be naturally generalised into extended symbolic finite-state transducers (ESFTs).

Definition 24 (Extended symbolic finite-state transducers). *An extended symbolic finite-state transducer (ESFT) $\mathcal{A}$ is a tuple $(Q, \Upsilon, s_{\text{in}}, s_{\text{out}}, q_0, \delta, F)$, where Q, Υ, $s_{\text{in}}, s_{\text{out}}$ and $q_0 \in Q$ are defined as those for SFTs, and δ is a finite set of transition rules of the form $t = (q_1, \ell, \psi, \boldsymbol{f}, q_2)$, where:*

- $q_1 \in Q \setminus \{q_f\}$ *and* $q_2 \in Q$ *are respectively the source and target states of t,*
- $\ell \in \mathbb{N} \setminus \{0\}$ *is the* lookahead *of t,*
- $\psi \in \Psi^{(s_{\text{in}}^{\ell})}$,
- $\boldsymbol{f}$ *is a sequence of $s_{\text{in}}^{\ell}/s_{\text{out}}$-terms, each of them representing a function from $(\mathbb{D}_{s_{\text{in}}})^i$ to $\mathbb{D}_{s_{\text{out}}}$,*

and F is a set of final rules $t = (q_1, \ell, \psi, \boldsymbol{f}, q_f)$ such that if $\ell > 0$, then t satisfies the same constraints as transition rules, otherwise (i.e. $\ell = 0$), $\psi = \text{true}$.

The lookahead of an ESFT is defined similarly as for ESFAs.

Semantics of ESFTs. Let $\mathcal{A} = (Q, \Upsilon, s_{\text{in}}, s_{\text{out}}, q_0, \delta, F)$ be an ESFT. The semantics of rules $t = (q_1, \ell, \psi, \boldsymbol{f}, q_2)$ of $\mathcal{A}$ is defined as follows:

$$\|t\| = \{q_1 \xrightarrow{u/w} q_2 \mid u \in \|\psi\|, w \in \|\boldsymbol{f}\|(u)\}.$$

Intuitively, the transition $t = (q_1, \ell, \psi, \boldsymbol{f}, q_2)$ reads ℓ adjacent input data values u that satisfies ψ, then produces a sequence of data values $w \in \|\boldsymbol{f}\|(u)$.

Given a data word $u \in (\mathbb{D}_{s_{\text{in}}})^*$, $q_1 \xrightarrow{u/w} q_{n+1}$ if there exist states $q_2, ..., q_n \in Q$, words $u_1, ..., u_n \in (\mathbb{D}_{s_{\text{in}}})^*$ and words $w_1, ..., w_n \in (\mathbb{D}_{s_{\text{out}}})^*$ such that $u = u_1...u_n$, $w = w_1...w_n$ and for each $i \in [n]$, $q_i \xrightarrow{u_i/w_i} q_{i+1}$. The *transduction* $\mathcal{T}_{\mathcal{A}}$ defined by $\mathcal{A}$ is a relation on $(\mathbb{D}_{s_{\text{in}}})^* \times (\mathbb{D}_{s_{\text{out}}})^*$ defined as follows: For each $u \in (\mathbb{D}_{s_{\text{in}}})^*$ and $w \in (\mathbb{D}_{s_{\text{out}}})^*$, $(u, w) \in \mathcal{T}_{\mathcal{A}}$ iff $q_0 \xrightarrow{u/w} q_f$. In addition, we use $\mathcal{T}_{\mathcal{A}}(u)$ to denote the set $\{w \in (\mathbb{D}_{s_{\text{out}}})^* \mid (u, w) \in \mathcal{T}_{\mathcal{A}}\}$.

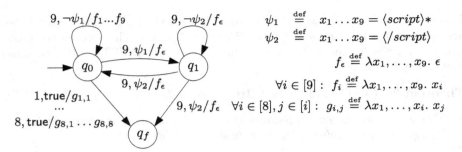

$$\psi_1 \overset{\text{def}}{=} x_1 \ldots x_9 = \langle script \rangle *$$
$$\psi_2 \overset{\text{def}}{=} x_1 \ldots x_9 = \langle /script \rangle$$

$$f_\epsilon \overset{\text{def}}{=} \lambda x_1, \ldots, x_9.\ \epsilon$$

$$\forall i \in [9] : f_i \overset{\text{def}}{=} \lambda x_1, \ldots, x_9.\ x_i$$

$$\forall i \in [8], j \in [i] : g_{i,j} \overset{\text{def}}{=} \lambda x_1, \ldots, x_i.\ x_j$$

Fig. 7. The ESFT $\mathcal{A}_{script}$

Example 14. Let us consider the ESFT $\mathcal{A}_{script} = (\{q_0, q_1, q_f\}, \Upsilon, s, s, q_0, \delta, \{q_0, q_1\})$, where Υ is the theory of UTF-8 characters where all the function symbols are constants and the set of predicate symbols is empty, s is the sort of UTF-8 characters, δ is shown in Fig. 7. $\mathcal{A}_{script}$ removes all the non-empty data subwords following each occurrence of $\langle script \rangle$ until $\langle /script \rangle$ occurs.

An ESFT $\mathcal{A} = (Q, \Upsilon, s_{in}, s_{out}, q_0, \delta, F)$ is *deterministic* if for all rules $(q_1, \ell, \psi, \boldsymbol{f}, q_2), (q_1, \ell', \psi', \boldsymbol{f}', q_2') \in \delta \cup F$:

- if $q_2, q_2' \in Q \setminus \{q_f\}$ and $\mathsf{isSat}(\psi \wedge \psi')$, then $q_2 = q_2'$, $\ell = \ell'$ and $\boldsymbol{f} \simeq_{\psi \wedge \psi'} \boldsymbol{f}'$,
- if $q_2 = q_2' = q_f$, $\mathsf{isSat}(\psi \wedge \psi')$ and $\ell = \ell'$, then $\boldsymbol{f} \simeq_{\psi \wedge \psi'} \boldsymbol{f}'$,
- if $q_2 \in Q \setminus \{q_f\}, q_2' = q_f$ and $\mathsf{isSat}(\psi \wedge \psi')$, then $\ell > \ell'$.

An ESFT $\mathcal{A}$ is *single-valued* if $|\mathcal{T}_\mathcal{A}(u)| \leq 1$ for all $u \in (\mathbb{D}_{s_{in}})^*$. An ESFT $\mathcal{A}$ is *finite-valued* if there exists $K \geq 0$ such that $|\mathcal{T}_\mathcal{A}(u)| \leq K$ for all $u \in (\mathbb{D}_{s_{in}})^*$. Cartesian and monadic ESFTs are defined similarly as for ESFAs.

Theorem 21 ([DV15]). *The following results hold for ESFTs:*

- *Cartesian ESFTs, monadic ESFTs, and SFTs are expressively equivalent, moreover, this fact holds in the deterministic case.*
- *ESFTs with lookahead $\ell + 1$ are more expressive than ESFTs with lookahead ℓ.*
- *ESFTs are not closed under composition (even if the label theories are composable).*
- *The equivalence problem of single-valued ESFTs over quantifier free successor arithmetic and tuples is undecidable, but is decidable for single-valued Cartesian ESFTs.*

It is open whether the equivalence problem of finite-valued Cartesian ESFTs is decidable or not.

Further Reading. Symbolic visibly pushdown automata (SVPA) were investigated in [DA14]. Another extension of SFAs, called symbolic finite-state automata with registers (SRA), was also investigated in [DV15]. It turns out that adding registers into SFAs entails undecidability, even for the nonemptiness problem, since Minsky machines can be easily simulated by SRAs. In addition, symbolic finite-state tree automata (SFTAs) were investigated in [VB11a, VB15, VD16]. It was shown that SVPAs and SFTAs preserve all the desirable properties of visibly pushdown automata and tree automata respectively. Symbolic tree transducers (STT) were also investigated. It was shown in [FV14] that symbolic tree transducers are not closed under compositions, which corrected an incorrect claim in [VB11b].

8   Formalisms with Data Constraints for the Verification of Programs Manipulating Dynamic Data Structures

Dynamic data structures, or heaps, are widely used in system software, e.g., operating systems and device drivers. Formal analysis and verification of programs manipulating dynamic data structures are notoriously difficult. For instance, the sizes of dynamic data structures are unbounded, their shapes may change during the execution of the program, and their nodes may contain data values from an infinite domain, or even worse, there may be pointer arithmetics applied to the pointer variables. Researchers have proposed various approaches to reason about dynamic data structures, e.g., shape analysis [SRW02], separation logic [Rey02], and forest automata [HHR+12]. Noteworthily most work focuses on the shape properties, e.g., whether the data structure is a list, or a binary tree, but disregards data and size constraints, e.g., whether the lists and trees are sorted or the trees are balanced.

8.1   Separation Logic with Inductive Definitions and Data Constraints

Separation logic (SL) is an extension of Hoare logic. Since its introduction, SL has become a widely used formalism for analysing and verifying heap-manipulating programs [BCO05, DOY06, CDOY11]. As an assertion language, SL can express how data structures are laid out in memory in a succinct way. In a nutshell, this language features: (i) a spatial conjunction operator that decomposes the heap into disjoint regions, each of which can be reasoned about independently, and (ii) inductive predicates that describe the shape of unbounded linked data structures such as lists, trees, etc. We shall present a version of separation logic with data constraints, which may include pure constraints on data values and capture desired properties of structural heaps such as the size, height, sortedness and even near-balanced tree properties.

As in Sect. 7, we consider a data domain $\mathbb{D}$, but this time we have an explicit logical language to specify (much) more involved properties over $\mathbb{D}$. As a general framework, we are a bit abstract here and assume a theory $(\mathbb{D}, \mathcal{L})$ where $\mathcal{L}$ is a suitable logical structure interpreted over $\mathbb{D}$. Typical cases include Presburger arithmetic (in which $(\mathbb{D}, \mathcal{L}) = (\mathbb{N}, +, \leq, 0, 1)$), logical theories supported by modern SMT solvers, or even logical theories on sets or multisets. As a convention, *data variables* are typically denoted by DVars, ranged over by lowercase letters $x, y, \cdots$.

To define a *separation logic with data constraints*, we further assume an infinite set $\mathbb{L}$ of locations. As a convention, $l, l', \cdots \in \mathbb{L}$ denote locations. Accordingly, we introduce a set of *location variables* LVars ranged over by uppercase letters $E, F, X, Y, \cdots$. We further consider two kinds of *fields*, i.e., location fields from $\mathcal{F}$ and data fields from $\mathcal{D}$. Each field $f \in \mathcal{F}$ (resp. $d \in \mathcal{D}$) is associated with $\mathbb{L}$ (resp. $\mathbb{D}$). A *term* is either a variable from DVars∪LVars, or the constant symbol nil. We usually use t and $\boldsymbol{t}$ to denote a term and a tuple of terms.

Logic formulae may contain a set of (user-defined) inductive predicates, which are collected in $\mathcal{P}$ and will defined momentarily. In the following, the logic is denoted by $\mathsf{SLID}[\mathcal{P}, \mathcal{L}]$.

Syntax. $\mathsf{SLID}[\mathcal{P}, \mathcal{L}]$ formulae comprise three types of formulae: *pure formulae* Π, *data formulae* Δ, and *spatial formulae* Σ, which are defined by the following rules:

$$\Pi \stackrel{\text{def}}{=} \quad E = F \mid E \neq F \mid \Pi \wedge \Pi \qquad \text{(pure formulae)}$$

$$\Sigma \stackrel{\text{def}}{=} \quad \mathsf{emp} \mid E \mapsto \rho \mid P(\boldsymbol{t}) \mid \Sigma * \Sigma \qquad \text{(spatial formulae)}$$

$$\rho \stackrel{\text{def}}{=} \quad (f, X) \mid (d, x) \mid \rho, \rho$$

$$\Delta \stackrel{\text{def}}{=} \quad \text{formulae from } \mathcal{L} \qquad \text{(data formulae)}$$

where $P \in \mathcal{P}$, $f \in \mathcal{F}$, and $d \in \mathcal{D}$. For spatial formulae Σ, formulae of the form emp, $E \mapsto \rho$, or $P(\boldsymbol{t})$ are called *spatial atoms*. In particular, formulae of the form $E \mapsto \rho$ and $P(\boldsymbol{t})$ are called *points-to atoms* and *predicate atoms* respectively. Each predicate $P \in \mathcal{P}$ has a fixed arity, and is of the form

$$P(\boldsymbol{t}) \stackrel{\text{def}}{=} \bigvee_{i=1}^{n} \exists \boldsymbol{w}_i.(\Pi_i \wedge \Delta_i \wedge \Sigma_i),$$

We call $\exists \boldsymbol{w}_i.(\Pi_i \wedge \Delta_i \wedge \Sigma_i)$ the *rule* of $P(\boldsymbol{t})$. In addition, if in a rule $\exists \boldsymbol{w}_i.(\Pi_i \wedge \Delta_i \wedge \Sigma_i)$, Σ_i contains predicate atoms, the rule is called an *inductive rule*; otherwise, it is called a *base rule*.

Remark 3. Separation logic, as an extension of first-order logic, usually encompasses two connectives: the separating conjunction ($*$) and its adjoin (the separating implication $-*$, aka the *magic wand*). It turns out that the magic wand is so powerful that, adding it to the logic would make the logic undecidable immediately (with only very few exceptions). Moreover, although very interesting from a theoretical perspective, its importance in program verification is debatable, since in many cases, the use of the magic wand can be avoided. In light of this, we exclude this connective in our logic.

Semantics. Formulae of $\mathsf{SLID}[\mathcal{P}, \mathcal{L}]$ are interpreted on the *(memory) states*. Formally, a *state* is a pair (s, h), where

- s is a *stack*, which is a partial function from LVars $\cup$ DVars to $\mathbb{L} \cup \mathbb{D}$ such that $dom(s)$ is finite and s respects the data type,

- h is a *heap*, which is a partial function from $\mathbb{L} \times (\mathcal{F} \cup \mathcal{D})$ to $\mathbb{L} \cup \mathbb{D}$ such that
    - h respects the data type of fields, that is, for each $l \in \mathbb{L}$ and $f \in \mathcal{F}$ (resp. $l \in \mathbb{L}$ and $d \in \mathcal{D}$), if $h(l,f)$ (resp. $h(l,d)$) is defined, then $h(l,f) \in \mathbb{L}$ (resp. $h(l,d) \in \mathbb{D}$); and
    - h is field-consistent, i.e. every location in h possess the same set of fields.

For a heap h, we use $\mathsf{ldom}(h)$ to denote the set of locations $l \in \mathbb{L}$ such that $h(l,f)$ or $h(l,d)$ is defined for some $f \in \mathcal{F}$ and $d \in \mathcal{D}$. Moreover, we use $\mathrm{Flds}(h)$ to denote the set of fields $f \in \mathcal{F}$ or $d \in \mathcal{D}$ such that $h(l,f)$ or $h(l,d)$ is defined for some $l \in \mathbb{L}$. Two heaps h_1 and h_2 are said to be *field-compatible* if $\mathrm{Flds}(h_1) = \mathrm{Flds}(h_2)$. We write $h_1 \# h_2$ if $\mathsf{ldom}(h_1) \cap \mathsf{ldom}(h_2) = \varnothing$. Moreover, we write $h_1 \uplus h_2$ for the disjoint union of two field-compatible fields h_1 and h_2 (this implies that $h_1 \# h_2$).

Let (s,h) be a state and φ be an $\mathsf{SLID}[\mathcal{P}, \mathcal{L}]$ formula. The semantics of $\mathsf{SLID}[\mathcal{P}, \mathcal{L}]$ formulae is defined as follows,

- $(s,h) \vDash E = F$ if $s(E) = s(F)$,
- $(s,h) \vDash E \neq F$ if $s(E) \neq s(F)$,
- $(s,h) \vDash \Pi_1 \wedge \Pi_2$ if $(s,h) \vDash \Pi_1$ and $(s,h) \vDash \Pi_2$,
- $(s,h) \vDash \mathsf{emp}$ if $\mathsf{ldom}(h) = \varnothing$,
- $(s,h) \vDash E \mapsto \rho$ if $\mathsf{ldom}(h) = s(E)$, and for each $(f, X) \in \rho$, $h(s(E), f) = s(X)$, and for each $(d, x) \in \rho$, $h(s(E), d) = s(x)$,
- $(s,h) \vDash P(t)$ if $(s,h) \in [\![P(t)]\!]$,
- $(s,h) \vDash \Sigma_1 * \Sigma_2$ if there are h_1, h_2 such that $h = h_1 \uplus h_2$, $(s, h_1) \vDash \Sigma_1$ and $(s, h_2) \vDash \Sigma_2$.

where the semantics of predicates $[\![P(t)]\!]$ is given by the least fixpoint of a monotone operator constructed from the body of rules for P in a standard way, as in [BFGP14].

Example 15. Linked list segments are defined by the inductive predicate $\mathsf{ls}(E, F)$,

$$\mathsf{ls}(E, F) \stackrel{\mathrm{def}}{=} (E = F \wedge \mathsf{emp}) \vee (\exists X.\ E \mapsto (\mathtt{next}, X) * \mathsf{ls}(X, F)).$$

In addition, acyclic list segments are defined by the inductive predicate $\mathsf{als}(E, F)$ whose definition is obtained from that of $\mathsf{ls}(E, F)$ by adding $E \neq F$ to the inductive rule. Sorted list segments are defined by the inductive predicate $\mathsf{sls}(E, F, x)$,

$$\mathsf{sls}(E, F, x) \stackrel{\mathrm{def}}{=} (E = F \wedge \mathsf{emp}) \vee (\exists X, x'.\ x \leq x' \wedge$$
$$E \mapsto ((\mathtt{next}, X), (\mathtt{data}, x)) * \mathsf{sls}(X, F, x')).$$

And sorted acyclic list segments are defined by the inductive predicate $\mathsf{asls}(E, F, x)$ whose definition is obtained from that of $\mathsf{sls}(E, F, x)$ by adding $E \neq F$ to the inductive rule. Linked list segments with consecutive data values are defined by

$$\mathsf{pls}(E, F, x) \stackrel{\mathrm{def}}{=} (E = F \wedge \mathsf{emp}) \vee (\exists X, x'.\ x' = x + 1 \wedge$$
$$E \mapsto ((\mathtt{next}, X), (\mathtt{data}, x)) * \mathsf{pls}(X, F, x')).$$

For the purpose of program verification, the following two decision problems play a vital role, which are the subjects of much of the current research in this area.

- Satisfiability: Given an $\mathsf{SLID}[\mathcal{P}, \mathcal{L}]$ formula φ, decide whether $\llbracket \varphi \rrbracket$ is empty.
- Entailment: Given two $\mathsf{SLID}[\mathcal{P}, \mathcal{L}]$ formulae φ, ψ such that $\mathsf{Vars}(\psi) \subseteq \mathsf{Vars}(\varphi)$, decide whether $\varphi \vDash \psi$ holds.

We comment that the former problem is fundamental in studying logics, and usually serves as the first task in developing (automated) tool support. The latter question enables automated verification of programs with SL assertions in a Hoare logic style.

Not surprisingly, these questions are challenging, since in general the entailment problem of separation logic with inductive predicates (even without data constraints) is already undecidable [AGH+14]. Over the past ten years, researchers have developed various techniques to tackle the challenges, by considering different fragments, or utilizing incomplete decision procedures (in particular, by considering heuristics).

Linearly Compositional Fragment. In [GCW16], Gu *et al.* defined a *linearly compositional* fragment, where the inductive predicates, as well as the data constraints, must obey certain restrictions. A predicate $P \in \mathcal{P}$ is *linearly compositional* if

- the parameters of P can be divided into three categories: source parameters $E, \boldsymbol{\alpha}$, destination parameters $F, \boldsymbol{\beta}$, and static parameters $\boldsymbol{\xi}$, such that $E, \boldsymbol{\alpha}$ and $F, \boldsymbol{\beta}$ are symmetric, in the sense that the two vectors of parameters are of the same length, and the two parameters in the same positions of the two vectors are of the same data type, in addition, E, F are location variables,
- the inductive definition of P is given by

$$P(E, \boldsymbol{\alpha}; F, \boldsymbol{\beta}; \boldsymbol{\xi}) \overset{\text{def}}{=} (E = F \wedge \boldsymbol{\alpha} = \boldsymbol{\beta} \wedge \mathsf{emp}) \qquad (R_0)$$
$$\vee (\exists \boldsymbol{X} \exists \boldsymbol{x}. \ \Delta \wedge E \mapsto \rho * P(Y, \boldsymbol{\gamma}; F, \boldsymbol{\beta}; \boldsymbol{\xi})) \ (R_1)$$

The term "linearly compositional" reflects that: (1) $P(E, \boldsymbol{\alpha}; F, \boldsymbol{\beta}; \boldsymbol{\xi})$ can only define linear data structures, for instance, singly or doubly linked lists, lists with tail pointers, (2) $P(E, \boldsymbol{\alpha}; F, \boldsymbol{\beta}; \boldsymbol{\xi})$ satisfies the so-called *composition lemma* $P(E_1, \boldsymbol{\alpha_1}; E_2, \boldsymbol{\alpha_2}; \boldsymbol{\xi}) * P(E_2, \boldsymbol{\alpha_2}; E_3, \boldsymbol{\alpha_3}; \boldsymbol{\xi}) \Rightarrow P(E_1, \boldsymbol{\alpha_1}; E_3, \boldsymbol{\alpha_3}; \boldsymbol{\xi})$, which is essential for deciding the entailment problem by extending the procedure based on graph homomorphism introduced in [CHO+11].

Furthermore, the data formulae are defined as:

$$\Delta \overset{\text{def}}{=} \mathsf{true} \mid x \circ c \mid x \circ y + c \mid \Delta \wedge \Delta$$

where $\circ \in \{=, \leq, \geq\}$ and c is an integer constant.

We have the following constraints on the inductive rule (R_1):

1. None of the variables from F, β occur elsewhere in R_1, that is, in Δ, or $E \mapsto \rho$.
2. Each conjunct of Δ is of the form $\alpha_i \, \mathbf{o} \, c$, $\alpha_i \, \mathbf{o} \, \xi_j$, or $\alpha_i \, \mathbf{o} \, \gamma_i + c$ for $\mathbf{o} \in \{=, \leq, \geq\}$, $1 \leq i \leq |\alpha| = |\gamma|$, $1 \leq j \leq |\xi|$, and $c \in \mathbb{Z}$.
3. For each $1 \leq i \leq |\alpha|$ such that α_i is a data variable, either α_i occurs in ρ, or Δ contains $\alpha_i = \gamma_i + c$ for some $c \in \mathbb{Z}$.
4. Each variable occurs in $P(Y, \gamma; F, \beta; \xi)$ (resp. ρ) at most once.
5. All location variables from $\alpha \cup \xi \cup X$ occur in ρ.
6. $Y \in X$ and $\gamma \subseteq \{E\} \cup X \cup x$.

The first constraint on (R_1) above is essential to guarantee that $P(E, \alpha; F, \beta; \xi)$ satisfies the composition lemma (cf. [ESW15]). We will use $\mathrm{Flds}(P)$ to denote the set of fields occurring in the inductive rule (R_1) of P and $\mathrm{PLFld}(P)$ to denote the unique location field f such that (f, Y) occurs in the inductive rule (R_1) of P (the uniqueness of f is due to the aforementioned 4-th constraint of (R_1)).

We write $\mathsf{SLID}_{\mathsf{LC}}[\mathcal{P}]$ for the collection of separation logic formulae $\varphi = \Pi \wedge \Delta \wedge \Sigma$ satisfying the following constraints,

- **linearly compositional predicates**: all predicates from $\mathcal{P}$ are linearly compositional,
- **domination of principal location field**: for each pair of predicates $P_1, P_2 \in \mathcal{P}$, if $\mathrm{Flds}(P_1) = \mathrm{Flds}(P_2)$, then $\mathrm{PLFld}(P_1) = \mathrm{PLFld}(P_2)$,
- **uniqueness of predicates**: there is $P \in \mathcal{P}$ such that each predicate atom of Σ is of the form $P(-)$, and for each points-to atom occurring in Σ, the set of fields of this atom is $\mathrm{Flds}(P)$.

Example 16. The inductive predicate $\mathsf{ls}(E, F)$ in Example 15 is linearly compositional, while all the others therein are not. For instance, als does not satisfy the constraint that the source parameter F occurs only once in the inductive rule, $\mathsf{sls}(E, F, x)$ does not satisfy that the source parameters and destination parameters are symmetric. Nevertheless, the predicates $\mathsf{sls}(E, F, x)$ and $\mathsf{pls}(E, F, x)$ can be adapted into linearly compositional predicates $\mathsf{sls}(F, x; F, x')$ and $\mathsf{pls}'(E, x; F, x')$ by adding one extra destination parameter x',

$$\mathsf{sls}'(E, x; F, x') \stackrel{\mathrm{def}}{=} (E = F \wedge x = x' \wedge \mathsf{emp}) \vee (\exists X, x_1. \, x \leq x_1 \wedge$$
$$E \mapsto ((\mathsf{next}, X), (\mathsf{data}, x)) * \mathsf{sls}'(X, x_1; F, x')),$$

$$\mathsf{pls}'(E, x; F, x') \stackrel{\mathrm{def}}{=} (E = F \wedge x = x' \wedge \mathsf{emp}) \vee (\exists X, x_1'. \, x_1 = x + 1 \wedge$$
$$E \mapsto ((\mathsf{next}, X), (\mathsf{data}, x)) * \mathsf{pls}'(X, x_1; F, x')).$$

Theorem 22. *The following facts hold for* $\mathsf{SLID}_{\mathsf{LC}}[\mathcal{P}]$.

- *The satisfiability problem of* $\mathsf{SLID}_{\mathsf{LC}}[\mathcal{P}]$ *is in NP.*
- *The entailment problem of* $\mathsf{SLID}_{\mathsf{LC}}[\mathcal{P}]$ *formulae is in* Π_3^{P}.

It is an interesting open problem to extend the results in Theorem 22 to compositional inductive predicates that are capable of defining non-linear data structures, e.g. trees.

Semi-decision Procedures for Separation Logic with Inductive Definitions and Data Constraints. Bouajjani et al. considered a fragment of separation logic with the ls predicate and data constraints, called SLD (Singly-linked list with Data Logic), where data constraints are specified by universal quantifiers over index variables [BDES12]. They showed that the entailment problem of SLD is undecidable in general, but provided a sound—but incomplete—decision procedure. In addition, they identified a decidable fragment of SLD. The logic SLD in [BDES12] focuses on singly linked lists, and it is unclear how to extend to other linear structures such as doubly linked lists. The decision procedure in [BDES12] is incomplete for fragments that can express list segments where the data values are consecutive. (Note that this can be expressed in the logic $\mathsf{SLID}_{\mathsf{LC}}[\mathcal{P}]$ aforementioned; see $\mathsf{pls}'(E, x; F, x')$ in Example 16.)

In [CDNQ12], Chin *et al.* proposed an entailment checking procedure that can handle *well-founded* predicates (that may be recursively defined) using unfold/fold reasoning. In [LSC16], the authors present a semi-decision procedure for a fragment of separation logic with inductive predicates and Presburger arithmetic. The authors present S2SAT, a decision procedure combining under-approximation and over-approximation for simultaneously checking SAT and UNSAT properties for a sound and complete theory augmented with inductive predicates. To check the *satisfiability* (but not entailment) of a formula, the procedure iteratively unfolds the formula and examines the derived disjuncts. In each iteration, it searches for a proof of either satisfiability or unsatisfiability. They also identify a syntactically restricted fragment of the logic for which the procedure is terminating and thus complete.

Other Work on Decision Procedures for First-Order Separation Logic with Data Constraints. Bansal et al. considered first-order separation logic on lists with ordered data and identified the decidability frontier of the satisfiability problem [BBL09]. Very recently, Reynolds et al. proposed a decision procedure for the quantifier-free fragment of first-order separation logic interpreted over heap graphs with data elements ranging over a parametric multi-sorted (possibly infinite) domain [RISK16].

8.2 GRASS: Logic of Graph Reachability and Stratified Sets

GRASS stands for logic of **G**raph **R**eachability **A**nd **S**tratified **S**ets, which was introduced by Piskac *et al.* [PWZ13, PWZ14]. The main motivation of these logics is to encode separation logic with inductive predicates into decidable fragments of many-sorted first-order logic, where inductive predicates (e.g. singly linked lists) are encoded by reachability predicates without relying on induction and separating conjunction is encoded by set constraints, and thus offering an SMT-based decision procedure and tool support for separation logic with inductive definitions. An appealing feature of this approach is that the translation into many-sorted first-order logic offers a convenient way to combine shape properties and data constraints, by utilising the Nelson-Oppen framework [NO79].

In the following, we first define the logic GRASS.

Definition 25 (GRASS logic, [PWZ14]). *The GRASS logic can be defined as many-sorted first-order logic with the signature* $\Omega_{GS} = (\mathfrak{S}_{GS}, \mathfrak{F}_{GS}, \mathfrak{P}_{GS})$, *where*

- $\mathfrak{S}_{GS} = \{\mathsf{node}, \mathsf{field}, \mathsf{set}\}$;
- $\mathfrak{F}_{GS}$ *consists of* null : node, read : $\mathsf{field} \times \mathsf{node} \to \mathsf{node}$, write : $\mathsf{field} \times \mathsf{node} \times \mathsf{node} \to \mathsf{node}$, *and a countable infinite set of constant symbols for each sort in* $\mathfrak{S}_{GS}$;
- $\mathfrak{P}_{GS}$ *consists of* B : $\mathsf{field} \times \mathsf{node} \times \mathsf{node} \times \mathsf{node}$ *and* $\in$: $\mathsf{node} \times \mathsf{set}$.

Semantics. The semantics of GRASS formulae is defined with respect to a theory $\mathsf{Th}(\mathcal{I}_{GS})$, where $\mathcal{I}_{GS}$ is a set of Ω_{GS}-interpretations such that an Ω_{GS}-interpretation I is in $\mathcal{I}_{GS}$ if I satisfies the following conditions.

- I interprets the sort node as a finite set node^I.
- The sort field is interpreted as the set of all functions $\mathsf{node}^I \to \mathsf{node}^I$.
- The sort set is interpreted as the set of all subsets of node^I.
- The function symbols read and write represent field look-up and field update. They must satisfy the following properties,
  - $\forall u \in \mathsf{node}^I$, $f \in \mathsf{field}^I$, $\mathsf{read}^I(f, u) = f(u)$,
  - $\forall u, v \in \mathsf{node}^I$, $f \in \mathsf{field}^I$, $\mathsf{write}^I(f, u, v)$ is the function $f' \in \mathsf{field}^I$ such that for each $w \in \mathsf{node}^I$, if $w = u$, then $f'(w) = u$, otherwise, $f'(w) = f(w)$.
- The between predicate $B(f, x, y, z)$ denotes that x reaches z via an f-path that must go though y. Formally, $B(f, x, y, z)$ satisfies that for each $(f, u, v, w) \in \mathsf{field}^I \times \mathsf{node}^I \times \mathsf{node}^I \times \mathsf{node}^I$, $B^I(f, u, v, w)$ holds iff $(u, w) \in f^* \wedge (u, v) \in (\{(u_1, f(u_1)) \mid u_1 \in \mathsf{node}^I \wedge u_1 \neq w\})^*$, where f^* is the reflexive and transitive closure of f, similarly for $(\{(u_1, f(u_1)) \mid u_1 \in \mathsf{node}^I \wedge u_1 \neq w\})^*$.
- Finally, $\in^I$, the interpretation of $\in$ in I, is the set membership relation, that is, for each $u \in \mathsf{node}^I$ and $S \in \mathsf{set}$, $u \in^I S$ holds iff u is an element of $\mathfrak{S}$.

We will use $R(f, x, y)$ as a short-hand for $B(f, x, y, y)$, which intuitively means that there is an f-path from x to y.

Although the satisfiability problem of GRASS is undecidable in general, decidable fragments have been considered in [PWZ13, PWZ14]. In the following, we will use the fragment of GRASS in [PWZ13] to illustrate the idea, where the specialisation of GRASS to lists was considered and it was shown how to translate separation logic formulae over lists into GRASS. The interested reader can refer to [PWZ14] for the fragment GRIT which is devoted to tree structures.

Let us call the fragment of GRASS in [PWZ13] as GRASS$_{list}$.

Definition 26 (GRASS$_{list}$, [PWZ13]). *We assume that $\mathcal{X}$ is a countably infinite set of variables of sorts node and set. We use the lower-case symbols $x, y \in \mathcal{X}$ for variables of sort node and upper-case symbols $X, Y \in \mathcal{X}$ for variables of sort set. In addition, we assume that $\mathsf{next} \in \mathsf{field}$ is used to denote the next-pointers between locations in lists. Then the syntax of GRASS$_{list}$ is defined by the following rules,*

$T_L \overset{def}{=} x \mid \text{next}(T_L), \ where \ x \in \mathcal{X},$

$A \overset{def}{=} T_L = T_L \mid T_L \xrightarrow{\text{next}\backslash T_L} T_L,$

$U \overset{def}{=} A \mid \neg U \mid U \wedge U \mid U \vee U,$

$T_S \overset{def}{=} X \mid \varnothing \mid T_S \backslash T_S \mid T_S \cup T_S \mid T_S \cap T_S \mid \{x.U\}, \ s.t. \ \text{next}(x) \ does \ not \ occur \ in \ U,$

$B \overset{def}{=} T_S = T_S \mid T_L \in T_S,$

$F \overset{def}{=} A \mid B \mid \neg F \mid F \wedge F \mid F \vee F.$

A GRASS formula is a propositional combination of atoms. There are two types of atoms.

- *Atoms of type A are either equalities between terms of type T_L and reachability predicates. The terms of type T_L represent nodes in the graph. They are associated with the sort* node *and are constructed from variables and application of* next. *Reachability predicates $t_1 \xrightarrow{\text{next}\backslash t_3} t_2$ intuitively means that there is a path in the graph that from t_1 to t_2 without going through t_3.*
- *Atoms of type B are equalities between terms of sort* set *and membership tests. Terms of type* set *represent stratified sets[1], i.e., their elements are interpreted as nodes in the graph. Terms of sort* set *include set comprehensions of the form $\{x.U\}$, where U is a Boolean combination of atoms of type A.*

We will use $t_1 \xrightarrow{\text{next}} t_2$ as an abbreviation of $t_1 \xrightarrow{\text{next}\backslash t_2} t_2$, which intuitively means that t_2 is reachable from t_1 by following the field next. In addition, we use $t_1 \neq t_2$ as an abbreviation of $\neg(t_1 = t_2)$. For a variable $x \in \mathcal{X}$, we use $\{x\}$ to denote the singleton set $\{y. \ y = x\}$. The side condition that $\text{next}(x)$ does not occur in U in the terms $\{x. \ U\}$ is important to ensure the decidability of the logic.

Note that GRASS$_{list}$ includes some syntactic sugar that is not in GRASS defined above. We will illustrate how this syntactic sugar can be casted into the original definition of GRASS.

- $\text{next}(t) \equiv \text{read}(\text{next}, t),$
- $t_1 \xrightarrow{\text{next}\backslash t_3} t_2 \equiv R(\text{next}, t_1, t_2) \wedge \forall x. \ (B(\text{next}, t_1, x, t_2) \wedge x \neq t_2) \rightarrow x \neq t_3,$
- Set operations can be reformulated into GRASS as well. For instance, $(X_1 \backslash X_2) \cup X_3 = Y \equiv \forall x. \ ((x \in X_1 \wedge \neg x \in X_2) \vee x \in X_3) \leftrightarrow x \in Y$, and $X = \{x\} \equiv x \in X \wedge \forall y. \ y \in X \leftrightarrow y = x.$

We use $X = Y \uplus Z$ as an abbreviation of the formula $X = Y \cup Z \wedge Y \cap Z = \varnothing$, which intuitively means that X is the disjoint union of Y and Z.

Example 17. Consider the formula $F \equiv Y = \{x. \ x \xrightarrow{\text{next}} y\} \wedge Z = \{x. \ x \xrightarrow{\text{next}} z\} \wedge X = Y \uplus Z$. This formula expresses that the subgraph of the heap graph induced by the set of nodes X comprises two disjoint connected components, one in which all nodes reach y, and one in which all nodes reach z.

---

[1] The notion of stratified sets comes from [Zar03].

Theorem 23 ([PWZ13]). *The satisfiability problem of GRASS$_{list}$ is NP-complete.*

In the following, we first illustrate how SLID[als], i.e. the logic SLID with only a single inductive predicate als(x, y) and no data constraints (cf. Example 15 for the definition of als, adapted slightly by replacing E, F with x, y), can be translated into GRASS$_{list}$. Specifically, SLID[als] formulae $\Pi \wedge \Sigma$ are defined by the following rules,

$$\Pi \stackrel{\text{def}}{=} x = y \mid x \neq y \mid \Pi \wedge \Pi, \qquad \Sigma \stackrel{\text{def}}{=} x \mapsto (\text{next}, y) \mid \text{als}(x, y) \mid \Sigma * \Sigma,$$

where Π and Σ are called the pure and spatial formulae respectively.

The translation is done by induction the syntax of SLID[als] formulae. Since the translation of pure formulae is trivial (the identity translation), we only describe the translation of spatial formulae, denoted by $tr_X(\Sigma)$ (where X denotes the set of locations), below.

- $tr_X(\text{emp}) \stackrel{\text{def}}{=} X = \varnothing$,
- $tr_X(x \mapsto (\text{next}, y)) \stackrel{\text{def}}{=} X = \{x\} \wedge \text{next}(x) = y$,
- $tr_X(\text{als}(x, y)) \stackrel{\text{def}}{=} x \xrightarrow{\text{next}} y \wedge X = \{z.\ x \xrightarrow{f \backslash y} z \wedge z \neq y\}$,
- $tr_X(\Sigma_1 * \Sigma_2) \stackrel{\text{def}}{=} X = X_1 \uplus X_2 \wedge tr_{X_1}(\Sigma_1) \wedge tr_{X_2}(\Sigma_2)$, where X_1 and X_2 are two fresh variables of sort set.

As a matter of fact, we can even translate the Boolean combination of SLID[ls] formulae into GRASS$_{list}$ since GRASS$_{list}$ is closed under negations.

Extension with Data Constraints. One notable feature of this translation of separation logic formulae into GRASS$_{list}$ is that it offers a convenient way to specify and reason about data constraints in dynamic data structures, by using the Nelson-Oppen combination framework. To support reasoning about data constraints, we extend the signature of GRASS$_{list}$ with an additional sort data for data values, data fields interpreted as the functions from node^I to data^I, and sets with data elements. The read and write functions are extended accordingly. In the following, we assume that there is a unique data field d and we use $d(x)$ to denote the value of a node x corresponding to field d.

We can combine GRASS$_{list}$ with any decidable quantifier-free first-order theory that is signature-disjoint from GRASS$_{list}$ and stably-infinite to interpret the data sort. The extensions that we discuss build on such quantifier-free combinations. [PWZ14] considers three categories of extensions with data: (1) monadic predicates on the data value of one node, (2) binary predicates between the data values of two distinct nodes, and (3) constraints on the content of data structures, that is, sets of data values occurring in data structures.

- Monadic predicates. These predicates are able to express properties such as upper and lower bounds on the values contained in a tree. Such formulae have the following form: $\forall x. x \in X \rightarrow Q(d(x))$ where Q is a monadic predicate over data and X a variable of sort set. This class of formulae also forms a so-called Ψ-**local theory extension** [IJS08]. Then we can slightly adapt the decision procedure for GRASS$_{list}$ to obtain a complete decision procedure for the extension of GRASS$_{list}$ with monadic-predicate data constraints.

– Binary predicates. These predicates are introduced to define, for instance, a sorted linked list, in which we need to relate data values in two distinct nodes. To ensure completeness of the decision procedure, the binary predicates must satisfy that the expressed binary relations are *transitive* as well as some other constraints. (They are too technical to be stated here clearly. Those who are interested can read Sect. 7 of [PWZ14] for these additional constraints) One typical transitive binary predicate is the order relation between data values. The transitivity requirement prevents us from expressing data constraints involving counting, e.g., length constraints or multiset constraints. With binary predicates, we can express the sortedness property as follows: $\forall x, y \in X.\ x \xrightarrow{\text{next}} y \to d(x) \le d(y)$.

– Set constraints. This class of extensions enables reasoning about functional correctness properties. Essentially a way of referring to the content of lists is needed. While one can define the content of a list whose footprint is X as $C(X) = \{z \mid \exists x \in X.\ z = x.d\}$. This definition goes beyond GRASS$_{list}$, due to the existential quantifier appearing inside the set comprehension. In [PWZ13], the authors proposed a solution by adding a witness function that maps a data value back to a node in the graph which stores the data value. They define the witness function in an axiomatic way, any show that the axioms still give a Ψ-local theory extension.

Limitations of This Approach. Unfortunately, there is no precise characterization of the limit of extensions that preserve the property of local theory extensions on which the decision procedure is built. However, not all extensions are local, in particular, the constraints involving counting, e.g. length constraints and multiset constraints.

Other Works on First-/Second-Order Logics Combining Shape Properties and Data Constraints. Bouajjani et al. proposed a fragment of many-sorted first-order logic with reachability predicates, called CSL (Composite Structure Logic [BDES09]), to reason about programs manipulating composite dynamic data structures. The formulae in CSL allow a limited form of alternation between existential and universal quantifiers and they can express constraints on reachability between positions in the heap following some pointer fields, linear constraints on the lengths of the lists, as well as constraints on the data values attached to these positions. For data constraints, the logic CSL is parameterized by a first-order logic over the associated data domain. They proved that the satisfiability problem of CSL is decidable whenever the underlying data logic is decidable. In addition, Madhusudan et al. defined a fragment of monadic second-order logic, called STRAND (STRucture ANd Data), to reason about both shape properties and data constraints, in tree structures [MPQ11]. While the satisfiability of STRAND logic is undecidable in general, several decidable fragments were identified in [MPQ11].

8.3   Streaming Transducers

In [AC11], Alur and Cerny proposed *streaming transducers* to show that for a class of single-pass list processing programs, the equivalence problem of the programs in this class is decidable. The intuition of streaming transducers is to model linked lists as data words, use a set of data word variables to store some intermediate information for the outputs, and at the same time use a set of registers ranging over an ordered data domain to guide the control flow of transducers. In the following, we present the definition of streaming transducers and some basic facts known for streaming transducers.

Let $\mathbb{D}$ be an infinite set of data values. We will use $<$ to denote the strict total order over $\mathbb{D}$. Examples of $(\mathbb{D}, <)$ include $(\mathbb{Z}, <)$, the set of integers with the order relation, and $(\mathbb{Q}, <)$, the set of rational numbers with the order relation. As for NRAs in Sect. 3, let R be a set of registers and $\mathsf{cur} \notin R$ be a distinguished register to denote the data value in the current position, in addition, let $R^{\circledcirc}$ denote $R \cup \{\mathsf{cur}\}$. A *guard* formula over R is defined by the rules $g \stackrel{\text{def}}{=} \mathsf{true}$ | false | $\mathsf{cur} \circ r$ | $g \wedge g \wedge g \vee g$, where $r \in R$ and $\circ \in \{=, \neq, <, >\}$. Let G_R denote the set of guards over R. Let ρ be a valuation that assigns each $r \in R$ a data value from $\mathbb{D}$, and $d \in \mathbb{D}$. Then $\rho[d/\mathsf{cur}]$ satisfies a guard g, denoted by $\rho[d/\mathsf{cur}] \models g$, is defined as follows:

- $\rho[d/\mathsf{cur}] \models \mathsf{cur} = r$ if $d = \rho(r)$, similarly for $\rho[d/\mathsf{cur}] \models \mathsf{cur} \neq r$, $\rho[d/\mathsf{cur}] \models \mathsf{cur} < r$, and $\rho[d/\mathsf{cur}] \models \mathsf{cur} > r$,
- $\rho[d/\mathsf{cur}] \models g \wedge g$ and $\rho[d/\mathsf{cur}] \models g \vee g$ are defined in a standard way.

Definition 27 (Streaming transducers). *A streaming transducer (ST) S is a tuple $(Q, \Sigma, \Gamma, R, X, q_0, \tau_0, \delta, O)$, where:*

- *Q is a finite set of states,*
- *R is a finite set of registers,*
- *X is a finite set of data word variables,*
- *$q_0 \in Q$ is the initial state,*
- *$\tau_0 : R \to \mathbb{D}$ assigns each register an initial data value,*
- *δ is a finite set of transitions comprising the tuples $(q, \sigma, g, q', \alpha)$, where $q, q' \in Q$, $\sigma \in \Sigma$, g is a guard on R, α is a **function** (instead of a partial function) which assigns each $r \in R$ a variable $r' \in R^{\circledcirc}$, and assigns each $x \in X$ a sequence from $((\Gamma \times R^{\circledcirc}) \cup X)^*$,*
- *O is a partial output function from Q to $((\Gamma \times R) \cup X)^*$.*

In addition, S satisfies the following constraints.

- **deterministic**: *for each pair of distinct transitions $(q, \sigma, g_1, q_1, \alpha_1), (q, \sigma, g_2, q_2, \alpha) \in \delta$, it holds that $g_1 \wedge g_2$ is unsatisfiable,*
- **copyless**: *for each $q \in Q$ and $x \in X$, there is at most one occurrence of x in $O(q)$, in addition, for each $x \in X$ and $(q, \sigma, g, q', \alpha) \in \delta$, there is at most one occurrence of x in the set of words $\{\alpha(y) \mid y \in X\}$.*

Semantics of STs. Given a data word $w = (\sigma_1, d_1) \ldots (\sigma_n, d_n)$ and an ST $\mathcal{S} = (Q, \Sigma, \Gamma, R, X, q_0, \delta, O)$, a *configuration* of $\mathcal{S}$ on w, is a pair (i, ρ), where ρ is a *valuation* ρ on $R \cup X$, that is, a function which assigns each $r \in R$ a data value from $\mathbb{D}$, and assigns each $x \in X \cap \mathrm{dom}(\rho)$ a data word over the alphabet Γ. The initial configuration is (q_0, ρ_0) where $\rho_0(r) = \tau_0(r)$ for each $r \in R$, and $\rho_0(x) = \varepsilon$ for each $x \in X$. A configuration (q', ρ') is said to be a successor of another configuration (q, ρ), denoted by $(q, \rho) \longrightarrow (q', \rho')$, if there are $d \in \mathbb{D}$ and a transition $(q, \sigma, g, q', \alpha) \in \delta$ such that $\rho[d/\mathsf{cur}] \models g$ and for each $r \in R$, $\rho'(r) = (\rho[d/\mathsf{cur}])(\alpha(r))$, and for each $x \in X$, $\rho'(x) = (\rho[d/\mathsf{cur}])(\alpha(x))$, where $(\rho[d/\mathsf{cur}])(\alpha(x))$ is obtained from $\alpha(x)$ by replacing each occurrence of $y \in R \cup X$ in $\alpha(x)$ with $(\rho[d/\mathsf{cur}])(y)$. A *run* of $\mathcal{S}$ on w is a sequence of configurations $(q_0, \rho_0)(q_1, \rho_1) \ldots (q_n, \rho_n)$ such that $(q, \rho_i) \longrightarrow (q, \rho_{i+1})$ for each $i : 0 \leq i < n$. Note that since $\mathcal{S}$ is deterministic, there is at most one run of $\mathcal{S}$ on w. The *output* of $\mathcal{S}$ on w, denoted by $\mathcal{S}(w)$, is defined as $\rho_n(O(q_n))$, if there is a run of $\mathcal{S}$ on w, say $(q_0, \rho_0)(q_1, \rho_1) \ldots (q_n, \rho_n)$, such that $O(q_n)$ is defined, otherwise, $\mathcal{S}(w)$ is undefined.

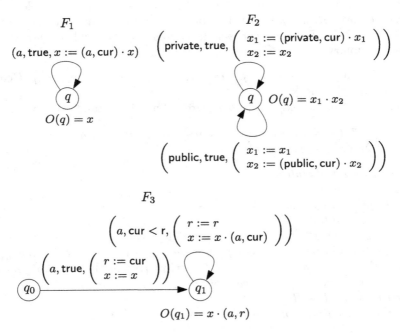

Fig. 8. Examples of streaming transducers

Example 18. Here are a few examples of streaming transducers (see Fig. 8).

- Let $\Sigma = \{a\}$. Let F_1 be the transduction that reverses a data word. Then F_1 is defined by an ST $\mathcal{S}_1 = (\{q\}, \Sigma, \Sigma, R = \varnothing, X = \{x\}, q, \delta, O)$, where
  - $\delta = \{(q, a, \mathsf{true}, q, \alpha)\}$ such that $\alpha(x) = (a, \mathsf{cur}) \cdot x$,
  - $O(q) = x$.

- Let $\Sigma = \{\mathsf{private}, \mathsf{public}\}$. Let F_2 be the transduction that outputs $w_1 \cdot w_2$ from w, where w_1 and w_2 are the subsequences of w that contain the private and public entries respectively. Then F_2 is defined by an ST $\mathcal{S}_2 = (\{q\}, \Sigma, \Sigma, R = \varnothing, X = \{x_1, x_2\}, q, \delta, O)$, where
    - $\delta = \{(q, \mathsf{private}, \mathsf{true}, q, \alpha_1), (q, \mathsf{public}, \mathsf{true}, q, \alpha_2)\}$ such that $\alpha_1(x_1) = x_1 \cdot$ (private, cur), $\alpha_1(x_2) = x_2$, $\alpha_2(x_1) = x_1$, and $\alpha_2(x_2) = x_2 \cdot$ (public, cur),
    - $O(q) = x_1 \cdot x_2$.
- Let $\Sigma = \{a\}$. Let F_3 be the transduction to move the data value in the first position to the last position, provided that the sequence of data values in the data word, except the data value in the first position, is sorted, in addition, all these data values are less than the data value in the first position. Then F_3 is defined by an ST $\mathcal{S}_3 = (\{q_0, q_1\}, \Sigma, \Sigma, R = \{r\}, X = \{x\}, q_0, \delta, O)$, where:
    - $\delta = \{(q_0, \mathsf{true}, q_1, \alpha_1), (q_1, \mathsf{cur} < r, q_1, \alpha_2)\}$ such that $\alpha_1(r) = \mathsf{cur}$, $\alpha_1(x) = x$, $\alpha_2(r) = r$, and $\alpha_2(x) = x \cdot (a, \mathsf{cur})$.
    - $O(q_1) = x \cdot (a, r)$.

It is easy to check that each of $\mathcal{S}_1, \mathcal{S}_2, \mathcal{S}_3$ defined above satisfies the copyless constraint.

STs are said to be closed under composition if for each pair of STs $\mathcal{S}_1$ with the input/output alphabet Σ/Γ, and $\mathcal{S}_2$ with the input/output alphabet Γ/Π, there is an ST $\mathcal{S}$ such that for each data word w over the alphabet Σ, it holds that $\mathcal{S}(w) = \mathcal{S}_2(\mathcal{S}_1(w))$.

The equivalence problem of SNTs: Given two STs $\mathcal{S}_1$ and $\mathcal{S}_2$, decide whether they are equivalent, in the sense that for each data word w, $\mathcal{S}_1(w) = \mathcal{S}_2(w)$.

Theorem 24 ([AC11]). *The following results hold for streaming transducers:*

- *STs are not closed under composition.*
- *The equivalence problem of STs is PSPACE-complete.*
- *The equivalence problem of the two-way extension of STs is undecidable.*

The PSPACE-hardness of the equivalence problem follows from the fact that the equivalence of DRAs is PSPACE-hard (cf. Theorem 2).

At last, we would like to remark that since its introduction, most of the work on streaming transducers focus on finite alphabets, see e.g. [AC10, AD12, ADGT13].

Other Automata Models to Reason About Dynamic Data Structures with Data Constraints. Forest automata were also extended with order constraints to reason about the behaviour of programs manipulating dynamic data structures, where a sound but incomplete procedure was proposed to decide the language inclusion problem of two forest automata [AHJ+13].

9   Formalisms for Analysing Programs in the MapReduce Framework

The MapReduce framework is a popular programming model proposed by Dean and Ghemawat from Google Inc. for data-parallel computations [DG04]. Since its introduction, various data-parallel computing platforms based on the MapReduce framework, e.g. Apache Hadoop[2], Apache SPARK[3], Microsoft SCOPE [CJL+08], Yahoo! Pig Latin [ORS+08], and Facebook Hive [TSJ+09], have appeared and a huge number of big-data processing jobs are executed on these platforms daily.

In the MapReduce framework, the *reducer* produces an output from a list of inputs. Due to the scheduling policy of the platform, the inputs may arrive at the reducers in different order. The *commutativity problem* of reducers asks if the output of a reducer is independent of the order of its inputs. A formal analysis of the commutativity problem of reducers in the MapReduce framework was first considered in [CHSW15], where it was shown that (1) the commutativity problem is undecidable in general, if multiplication operators are available, and (2) if the data domain is a finite set, then the commutativity problem is decidable and reduced to the equivalence problem of two-way finite-state automata.

Very recently, Chen et al. proposed a model of reducers, called streaming numerical transducers (SNTs), and extended the decidability result in [CHSW15] to the infinite data domain [CSW16]. The model of SNTs originates from the observation that in practice MapReduce programs are usually used for data analytics and thus require very simple control flow. By exploiting this simplicity, in SNTs, the control and data flow of programs are separated and arithmetic operations are disallowed in the control flow. The design of SNTs is inspired by streaming transducers [AC11] (see Sect. 8.3). Nevertheless, the two models are intrinsically different since the outputs of SNTs are integers while those of streaming transducers are data words.

In this section, as in symbolic automata, we assume data words are elements of $\mathbb{D}^*$. In addition, we assume this data domain is the integer domain $\mathbb{Z}$. An SNT scans a data word $w = d_1 \ldots d_n$ from left to right, records and aggregates information in variables, and outputs an integer when it finishes reading the data word.

Let Z be a set of variables. Then an *expression* over Z is defined recursively by the following rules: $e \in \mathsf{E}_Z \stackrel{\text{def}}{=} c \mid z \mid (e + e) \mid (e - e)$, where $z \in Z$ and $c \in \mathbb{Z}$. We use E_Z to denote the set of all possible expressions over Z. For an expression e, let $\mathsf{var}(e)$ denote the set of variables in e. Given a set of expressions E, we also use $\mathsf{var}(E)$ to denote the set of all variables appeared in E, i.e., $\mathsf{var}(E) = \bigcup_{e \in E} \mathsf{var}(e)$. A *guard* over Z is defined recursively by the following rules: $g \in \mathsf{G}_Z \stackrel{\text{def}}{=} \text{true} \mid v < v \mid v = v \mid v > v \mid g \wedge g$, where $v \in Z \cup \mathbb{Z}$. We use G_Z to denote the set of guards over Z. A *guarded expression* over Z is a pair $(g, e) \in \mathsf{G}_Z \times \mathsf{E}_Z$.

---

[2] http://hadoop.apache.com.
[3] http://spark.apache.com.

A *valuation* ρ of Z is a function from Z to $\mathbb{Z}$. The value of an expression $e \in \mathsf{E}_Z$ under a valuation ρ over Z, denoted by $\llbracket e \rrbracket_\rho$, is defined recursively in the standard way. Let ρ be a valuation of Z and g be a guard in G_Z. Then ρ satisfies g, denoted by $\rho \models g$, iff g is evaluated to true under ρ. We say that a guard g is *satisfiable* if there exists a valuation ρ satisfying g.

Definition 28 (Streaming numerical transducers). *A streaming numerical transducer (SNT) S is a tuple $(Q, R, X, \delta, q_0, O)$, where Q is a finite set of states, R is a finite set of* control registers, *X is a finite set of* data variables, *δ is the set of transitions, $q_0 \in Q$ is the initial state, O is the output function, which is a total function from Q to $2^{\mathsf{G}_R \times \mathsf{E}_{R \cup X}}$, i.e. $O(q)$ for $q \in Q$ is a finite set of guarded expressions over $X \cup Y$ where the guards only put constraints on R. In addition, a distinguished register* cur $\notin R$ *is used to denote the data value in the current position. For convenience, let $R^{\odot}$ denote $R \cup \{$cur$\}$.*

The set of transitions δ comprises the tuples (q, g, η, q'), where $q, q' \in Q$, g is a guard over $R^{\odot}$, and η is an assignment function which is a partial function from $R \cup X$ to $\mathsf{E}_{R^{\odot} \cup X}$ such that for each $r \in \mathrm{dom}(\eta) \cap R$, $\eta(r) \in R^{\odot}$. Informally, η maps a data variable to an expression over $R^{\odot} \cup X$ and a control register to either cur *or another control register. We write $q \xrightarrow{(g,\eta)} q'$ to denote $(q, g, \eta, q') \in \delta$ for convenience. Moreover, we assume that an SNT S is* deterministic. *That is, (1) for each pair of distinct transitions originating from q, say (q, g_1, η_1, q_1') and (q, g_2, η_2, q_2'), it holds that $g_1 \wedge g_2$ is unsatisfiable, (2) for any state $q \in Q$ and each pair of distinct guarded expressions (g_1, e_1) and (g_2, e_2) in $O(q)$, it holds that $g_1 \wedge g_2$ is unsatisfiable.*

Semantics of SNTs. The semantics of an SNT S is defined as follows. A *configuration* of S is a pair (q, ρ), where $q \in Q$ and ρ is a valuation of $R \cup X$. An *initial* configuration of S is (q_0, ρ_0), where ρ_0 assigns zero to all variables in $R \cup X$. A sequence of configurations $\mathcal{R} = (q_0, \rho_0)(q_1, \rho_1) \ldots (q_n, \rho_n)$ is a *run* of S over a data word $w = d_1 \ldots d_n$ iff there exists a *path* (sequence of transitions) $P = q_0 \xrightarrow{(g_1, \eta_1)} q_1 \xrightarrow{(g_2, \eta_2)} q_2 \ldots q_{n-1} \xrightarrow{(g_n, \eta_n)} q_n$ such that for each $i \in [n+1]$, $\rho_{i-1}[d_i/\mathsf{cur}] \models g_i$, and ρ_i is obtained from ρ_{i-1} as follows: (1) For each $r \in R$, if $r \in \mathrm{dom}(\eta_i)$, then $\rho_i(r) = \llbracket \eta_i(r) \rrbracket_{\rho_{i-1}[d_i/\mathsf{cur}]}$, otherwise $\rho_i(r) = \rho_{i-1}(r)$. (2) For each $x \in X$, if $x \in \mathrm{dom}(\eta_i)$, then $\rho_i(x) = \llbracket \eta_i(x) \rrbracket_{\rho_{i-1}[d_i/\mathsf{cur}]}$, otherwise, $\rho_i(x) = \rho_{i-1}(x)$. We call (q_n, ρ_n) the *final configuration* of the run. In this case, we also say that the run $\mathcal{R}$ follows the path P. We say that a path P in S is *feasible* iff there exists a run of S following P. Given a data word $w = d_1 \ldots d_n$, if there is a run of S over w from (q_0, ρ_0) to (q_n, ρ_n) and there exists a guarded expression $(g, e) \in O(q_n)$ such that $\rho_n \models g$, then the output of S over w, denoted by $S(w)$, is $\llbracket e \rrbracket_{\rho_n}$. Otherwise, $S(w)$ is undefined, denoted by $\bot$.

Example 19 (SNT for max). The SNT $S_{\max}$ for computing the maximum value of an input data word is defined as $(\{q_0, q_1, q_2\}, \{\mathsf{max}\}, \varnothing, \delta, q_0, O)$, where the set of transitions δ and the output function O are illustrated in Fig. 9 (here $R = \{\mathsf{max}\}$, $X = \varnothing$, and $\mathsf{max} := \mathsf{cur}$ denotes the assignment of cur to the variable max).

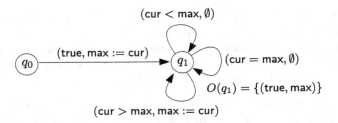

Fig. 9. The SNT $\mathcal{S}_{\max}$ for computing the maximum value

We focus on three decision problems of SNTs defined as follows: (1) *Commutativity*: Given an SNT $\mathcal{S}$, decide whether $\mathcal{S}$ is commutative, that is, whether for each data word w and each permutation w' of w, $\mathcal{S}(w) = \mathcal{S}(w')$. (2) *Equivalence*: Given two SNTs $\mathcal{S}, \mathcal{S}'$, decide whether $\mathcal{S}$ and $\mathcal{S}'$ are equivalent, that is, whether over each data word w, $\mathcal{S}(w) = \mathcal{S}'(w)$. (3) *Non-zero output*: Given an SNT $\mathcal{S}$, decide whether $\mathcal{S}$ has a non-zero output, that is, whether there exists a data word w such that $\mathcal{S}(w) \notin \{\bot, 0\}$.

Theorem 25 ([CSW16, CLTW16]). *The commutativity, equivalence, and non-zero output problem of SNTs can be decided in exponential time.*

In [CSW16, CLTW16], Theorem 25 was proved as follows:

1. The commutativity problem of SNTs is reduced to the equivalence problem of SNTs in polynomial time, which can be further reduced to the non-zero output problem of SNTs in polynomial time.
2. Then it is shown that the non-zero output problem of SNTs can be decided in exponential time, by extending Karr's algorithm for computing affine relationships in affine programs [MS04].

Further Reading. Recently, Neven et al. proposed variants of register automata and transducers as formal models for the distributed evaluation of relational algebra on relational databases in MapReduce framework [NSST15]. They introduced three models and investigated the expressibility issues.

10   Conclusion

This chapter has provided a tutorial and survey on the state of the art of automata models and logics to reason about the behaviour of software systems which embrace data values from an infinite domain. We have presented the models with different mechanisms to deal with infinite data values, register automata (and related logics), data automata (and related logics), pebble automata, and symbolic automata and transducers. In addition, we included two application-oriented sections, on formal models to reason about programs manipulating dynamic data structures and for the static analysis of data-parallel programs respectively. For these two sections, we presented separation logic with data constraints, logic of graph reachability and stratified sets, streaming transducers, and streaming numerical transducers. For each model, we introduced the basic definitions, used some examples to illustrate the model, and stated the main theoretical properties of the model.

For the perspectives of this field, in our opinion, researchers should strengthen the connections of the models with applications to better motivate, or to achieve greater impact of, their work. In particular, symbolic automata and transducers, separation logic with data constraints, and streaming numerical transducers are the formalisms that are better motivated by applications. These formalisms are still the research focus in the verification and database community. In addition, in order to produce practical tools to solve industrial-scale problems, there are still various challenges, and interested readers are encouraged to work on, and contribute to, this promising field.

Acknowledgments. Taolue Chen is partially supported by EPSRC grant (EP/P00430X/1), European CHIST-ERA project SUCCESS, ARC Discovery Project (DP160101652), Singapore MoE AcRF Tier 2 grant (MOE2015-T2-1-137), NSFC grant (No. 61662035), and an oversea grant from the State Key Laboratory of Novel Software Technology, Nanjing University (KFKT2014A14). Fu Song is partially supported by Shanghai Pujiang Program (No. 14PJ1403200), Shanghai ChenGuang Program (No. 13CG21), and NSFC Projects (Nos. 61402179, 61532019 and 91418203). Zhilin Wu is partially supported by the NSFC projects (Nos. 61100062, 61272135, 61472474, and 61572478).

References

[AC10] Alur, R., Cerný, P.: Expressiveness of streaming string transducers. In: Proceedings of the 30th Conference on Foundations of Software Technology and Theoretical Computer Science (FSTTCS), Leibniz International Proceedings in Informatics (LIPIcs), vol. 8, pp. 1–12 (2010)

[AC11] Alur, R., Cerny, P.: Streaming transducers for algorithmic verification of single-pass list-processing programs. In: Proceedings of the 38th Annual ACM SIGPLAN-SIGACT Symposium on Principles of Programming Languages (POPL), pp. 599–610 (2011)

[ACW12] Alur, R., Cerný, P., Weinstein, S.: Algorithmic analysis of array-accessing programs. ACM Trans. Comput. Log. **13**(3), 27 (2012)

[AD12] Alur, R., D'Antoni, L.: Streaming tree transducers. In: Czumaj, A., Mehlhorn, K., Pitts, A., Wattenhofer, R. (eds.) ICALP 2012. LNCS, vol. 7392, pp. 42–53. Springer, Heidelberg (2012). doi:10.1007/978-3-642-31585-5_8

[ADGT13] Alur, R., Durand-Gasselin, A., Trivedi, A.: From monadic second-order definable string transformations to transducers. In: Proceedings of the 28th Annual ACM/IEEE Symposium on Logic in Computer Science (LICS), pp. 458–467 (2013)

[AGH+14] Antonopoulos, T., Gorogiannis, N., Haase, C., Kanovich, M., Ouaknine, J.: Foundations for decision problems in separation logic with general inductive predicates. In: Muscholl, A. (ed.) FoSSaCS 2014. LNCS, vol. 8412, pp. 411–425. Springer, Heidelberg (2014). doi:10.1007/978-3-642-54830-7_27

[AHJ+13] Abdulla, P.A., Holik, L., Jonsson, B., Lengal, O., Trinh, C.Q., Vojnar, T.:
Verification of heap manipulating programs with ordered data by extended
forest automata. In: Proceedings of the 11th International Symposium on
Automated Technology for Verification and Analysis (ATVA), pp. 224–239
(2013)

[BBL09] Bansal, K., Brochenin, R., Lozes, E.: Beyond shapes: lists with ordered
data. In: de Alfaro, L. (ed.) FoSSaCS 2009. LNCS, vol. 5504, pp. 425–439.
Springer, Heidelberg (2009). doi:10.1007/978-3-642-00596-1_30

[BCO05] Berdine, J., Calcagno, C., O'Hearn, P.W.: Symbolic execution with separation logic. In: Yi, K. (ed.) APLAS 2005. LNCS, vol. 3780, pp. 52–68.
Springer, Heidelberg (2005). doi:10.1007/11575467_5

[BDES09] Bouajjani, A., Drăgoi, C., Enea, C., Sighireanu, M.: A logic-based frame-
work for reasoning about composite data structures. In: Bravetti, M.,
Zavattaro, G. (eds.) CONCUR 2009. LNCS, vol. 5710, pp. 178–195.
Springer, Heidelberg (2009). doi:10.1007/978-3-642-04081-8_13

[BDES12] Bouajjani, A., Drăgoi, C., Enea, C., Sighireanu, M.: Accurate invariant
checking for programs manipulating lists and arrays with infinite data. In:
Chakraborty, S., Mukund, M. (eds.) ATVA 2012. LNCS, vol. 7561, pp.
167–182. Springer, Heidelberg (2012). doi:10.1007/978-3-642-33386-6_14

[BDM+11] Bojanczyk, M., David, C., Muscholl, A., Schwentick, T., Segoufin, L.: Two-
variable logic on data words. ACM Trans. Comput. Logic 12(4), 27 (2011)

[BFGP14] Brotherston, J., Fuhs, C., Gorogiannis, J.N., Perez, A.N.: A decision procedure for satisfiability in separation logic with inductive predicates. In:
Proceedings of the 29th Annual ACM/IEEE Symposium on Logic in Computer Science (LICS) (2014)

[BKLT13] Bojańczyk, M., Klin, B., Lasota, S., Toruńczyk, S.: Turing machines with
atoms. In: Proceedings of the 28th Annual ACM/IEEE Symposium on
Logic in Computer Science (LICS), pp. 183–192 (2013)

[BL12] Bojanczyk, M., Lasota, S.: An extension of data automata that captures
XPath. Log. Methods Comput. Sci. 8(1), 1–28 (2012)

[BMS+06] Bojanczyk, M., Muscholl, A., Schwentick, T., Segoufin, L., David, C.: Two-
variable logic on words with data. In: Proceedings of the 21th IEEE Symposium on Logic in Computer Science (LICS), pp. 7–16 (2006)

[Boj13] Bojańczyk, M.: Modelling infinite structures with atoms. In: Libkin, L.,
Kohlenbach, U., de Queiroz, R. (eds.) WoLLIC 2013. LNCS, vol. 8071, pp.
13–28. Springer, Heidelberg (2013). doi:10.1007/978-3-642-39992-3_3

[BS10] Björklund, H., Schwentick, T.: On notions of regularity for data languages.
Theor. Comput. Sci. 411(4–5), 702–715 (2010)

[BSSS06] Bojańczyk, M., Samuelides, M., Schwentick, T., Segoufin, L.: Expressive
power of pebble automata. In: Bugliesi, M., Preneel, B., Sassone, V.,
Wegener, I. (eds.) ICALP 2006. LNCS, vol. 4051, pp. 157–168. Springer,
Heidelberg (2006). doi:10.1007/11786986_15

[Büc60] Büchi, J.R.: Weak second-order arithmetic and finite automata. Z. Math.
Log. Grundl. Math. 6, 66–92 (1960)

[Büc62] Büchi, J.R.: On a decision method in restricted second-order arithmetic.
In: Proceedings of the 1960 International Congress for Logic, Methodology
and Philosophy of Science, pp. 1–11. Stanford University Press (1962)

[CDNQ12] Chin, W.-N., David, C., Nguyen, H.H., Qin, S.: Automated verification
of shape, size and bag properties via user-defined predicates in separation
logic. Sci. Comput. Program. 77(9), 1006–1036 (2012)

[CDOY11] Calcagno, C., Distefano, D., O'Hearn, P.W., Yang, H.: Compositional shape analysis by means of bi-abduction. J. ACM **58**(6), 26:1–26:66 (2011)

[CHO+11] Cook, B., Haase, C., Ouaknine, J., Parkinson, M., Worrell, J.: Tractable reasoning in a fragment of separation logic. In: Katoen, J.-P., König, B. (eds.) CONCUR 2011. LNCS, vol. 6901, pp. 235–249. Springer, Heidelberg (2011). doi:10.1007/978-3-642-23217-6_16

[CHSW15] Chen, Y.-F., Hong, C.-D., Sinha, N., Wang, B.-Y.: Commutativity of reducers. In: Baier, C., Tinelli, C. (eds.) TACAS 2015. LNCS, vol. 9035, pp. 131–146. Springer, Heidelberg (2015). doi:10.1007/978-3-662-46681-0_9

[CJL+08] Chaiken, R., Jenkins, B., Larson, P.Å., Ramsey, B., Shakib, D., Weaver, S., Zhou, J.: SCOPE: easy and efficient parallel processing of massive data sets. PVLDB **1**(2), 1265–1276 (2008)

[CK98] Cheng, E.Y.C., Kaminski, M.: Context-free languages over infinite alphabets. Acta Inf. **35**(3), 245–267 (1998)

[CLTW16] Chen, Y.-F., Lengal, O., Tan, T., Wu, Z.: Equivalence of streaming numerical transducers (2016). (manuscript)

[CSW16] Chen, Y.-F., Song, L., Wu, Z.: The commutativity problem of the MapReduce framework: a transducer-based approach. In: Chaudhuri, S., Farzan, A. (eds.) CAV 2016. LNCS, vol. 9780, pp. 91–111. Springer, Cham (2016). doi:10.1007/978-3-319-41540-6_6

[D'A12] D'Antoni, L.: In the maze of data languages. CoRR, abs/1208.5980 (2012)

[DA14] D'Antoni, L., Alur, R.: Symbolic visibly pushdown automata. In: Biere, A., Bloem, R. (eds.) CAV 2014. LNCS, vol. 8559, pp. 209–225. Springer, Cham (2014). doi:10.1007/978-3-319-08867-9_14

[DG04] Dean, J., Ghemawat, S.: MapReduce: simplified data processing on large clusters. In: Proceedings of the 6th Symposium on Operating System Design and Implementation (OSDI), pp. 137–150 (2004)

[DHLT14] Decker, N., Habermehl, P., Leucker, M., Thoma, D.: Ordered navigation on multi-attributed data words. In: Baldan, P., Gorla, D. (eds.) CONCUR 2014. LNCS, vol. 8704, pp. 497–511. Springer, Heidelberg (2014). doi:10.1007/978-3-662-44584-6_34

[DL09] Demri, S., Lazic, R.: LTL with the freeze quantifier and register automata. ACM Trans. Comput. Log. **10**(3), 16:1–16:30 (2009)

[DOY06] Distefano, D., O'Hearn, P.W., Yang, H.: A local shape analysis based on separation logic. In: Hermanns, H., Palsberg, J. (eds.) TACAS 2006. LNCS, vol. 3920, pp. 287–302. Springer, Heidelberg (2006). doi:10.1007/11691372_19

[DV14] D'Antoni, L., Veanes, M.: Minimization of symbolic automata. In: Proceedings of the 41st Annual ACM SIGPLAN-SIGACT Symposium on Principles of Programming Languages (POPL), pp. 541–554 (2014)

[DV15] D'Antoni, L., Veanes, M.: Extended symbolic finite automata and transducers. Form. Methods Syst. Des. **47**(1), 93–119 (2015)

[Elg61] Elgot, C.: Decision problems of finite automata design and related arithmetic. Trans. Am. Math. Soc. **98**, 21–52 (1961)

[ESW15] Enea, C., Sighireanu, M., Wu, Z.: On automated lemma generation for separation logic with inductive definitions. In: Finkbeiner, B., Pu, G., Zhang, L. (eds.) ATVA 2015. LNCS, vol. 9364, pp. 80–96. Springer, Cham (2015). doi:10.1007/978-3-319-24953-7_7

[Fig12] Figueira, D.: Alternating register automata on finite words and trees. Log. Methods Comput. Sci. **8**(1), 1–43 (2012)

[FV98] Fülöp, Z., Vogler, H.: Syntax-Directed Semantics - Formal Models Based on Tree Transducers. Monographs in Theoretical Computer Science. An EATCS Series. Springer, Heidelberg (1998)

[FV14] Fülöp, Z., Vogler, H.: Forward and backward application of symbolic tree transducers. Acta Inf. **51**(5), 297–325 (2014)

[Gal85] Gallier, J.H.: Logic for Computer Science: Foundations of Automatic Theorem Proving. Harper & Row Publishers, Inc., New York (1985)

[GCW16] Gu, X., Chen, T., Wu, Z.: A complete decision procedure for linearly compositional separation logic with data constraints. In: Olivetti, N., Tiwari, A. (eds.) IJCAR 2016. LNCS (LNAI), vol. 9706, pp. 532–549. Springer, Cham (2016). doi:10.1007/978-3-319-40229-1_36

[GKS10] Grumberg, O., Kupferman, O., Sheinvald, S.: Variable automata over infinite alphabets. In: Dediu, A.-H., Fernau, H., Martín-Vide, C. (eds.) LATA 2010. LNCS, vol. 6031, pp. 561–572. Springer, Heidelberg (2010). doi:10.1007/978-3-642-13089-2_47

[GKS12] Grumberg, O., Kupferman, O., Sheinvald, S.: Model checking systems and specifications with parameterized atomic propositions. In: Chakraborty, S., Mukund, M. (eds.) ATVA 2012. LNCS, vol. 7561, pp. 122–136. Springer, Heidelberg (2012). doi:10.1007/978-3-642-33386-6_11

[GKS13] Grumberg, O., Kupferman, O., Sheinvald, S.: An automata-theoretic approach to reasoning about parameterized systems and specifications. In: Hung, D., Ogawa, M. (eds.) ATVA 2013. LNCS, vol. 8172, pp. 397–411. Springer, Heidelberg (2013). doi:10.1007/978-3-319-02444-8_28

[GKS14] Grumberg, O., Kupferman, O., Sheinvald, S.: A game-theoretic approach to simulation of data-parameterized systems. In: Cassez, F., Raskin, J.-F. (eds.) ATVA 2014. LNCS, vol. 8837, pp. 348–363. Springer, Heidelberg (2014). doi:10.1007/978-3-319-11936-6_25

[GS92] German, S.M., Sistla, A.P.: Reasoning about systems with many processes. J. ACM **39**(3), 675–735 (1992)

[HHR+12] Habermehl, P., Holík, L., Rogalewicz, A., Šimáček, J., Vojnar, T.: Forest automata for verification of heap manipulation. Form. Methods Syst. Des. **41**(1), 83–106 (2012)

[HLL+16] Hofman, P., Lasota, S., Lazić, R., Leroux, J., Schmitz, S., Totzke, P.: Coverability trees for petri nets with unordered data. In: Jacobs, B., Löding, C. (eds.) FoSSaCS 2016. LNCS, vol. 9634, pp. 445–461. Springer, Heidelberg (2016). doi:10.1007/978-3-662-49630-5_26

[HU79] Hopcroft, J.E., Ullman, J.D.: Introduction to Automata Theory, Languages, and Computation. Addison-Wesley, Reading (1979)

[IJS08] Ihlemann, C., Jacobs, S., Sofronie-Stokkermans, V.: On local reasoning in verification. In: Ramakrishnan, C.R., Rehof, J. (eds.) TACAS 2008. LNCS, vol. 4963, pp. 265–281. Springer, Heidelberg (2008). doi:10.1007/978-3-540-78800-3_19

[Kar16] Kara, A.: Logics on data words: expressivity, satisfiability, model checking. Ph.D. thesis, TU Dortmund University (2016). https://eldorado.tu-dortmund.de/bitstream/2003/35216/1/Dissertation.pdf

[KF94] Kaminski, M., Francez, N.: Finite-memory automata. Theor. Comput. Sci. **134**(2), 329–363 (1994)

[KST12] Kara, A., Schwentick, T., Tan, T.: Feasible automata for two-variable logic with successor on data words. In: Dediu, A.-H., Martín-Vide, C. (eds.) LATA 2012. LNCS, vol. 7183, pp. 351–362. Springer, Heidelberg (2012). doi:10.1007/978-3-642-28332-1_30

[KT06]   Kaminski, M., Tan, T.: Regular expressions for languages over infinite alphabets. Fundam. Inform. **69**(3), 301–318 (2006)

[KT10]   Kaminski, M., Tan, T.: A note on two-pebble automata over infinite alphabets. Fundam. Inform. **98**(4), 379–390 (2010)

[LSC16] Le, Q.L., Sun, J., Chin, W.-N.: Satisfiability modulo heap-based programs. In: Chaudhuri, S., Farzan, A. (eds.) CAV 2016. LNCS, vol. 9779, pp. 382–404. Springer, Cham (2016). doi:10.1007/978-3-319-41528-4_21

[LTV15] Libkin, L., Tan, T., Vrgoc, D.: Regular expressions for data words. J. Comput. Syst. Sci. **81**(7), 1278–1297 (2015)

[MP71]   McNaughton, R., Papert, S.: Counter-Free Automata. MIT Press, Cambridge (1971)

[MPQ11] Madhusudan, P., Parlato, G., Qiu, X.: Decidable logics combining heap structures and data. In: Proceedings of the 38th Annual ACM SIGPLAN-SIGACT Symposium on Principles of Programming Languages (POPL), pp. 611–622 (2011)

[MR11a] Manuel, A., Ramanujam, R.: Class counting automata on datawords. Int. J. Found. Comput. Sci. **22**(4), 863–882 (2011)

[MR11b] Mens, I.-E., Rahonis, G.: Variable tree automata over infinite ranked alphabets. In: Winkler, F. (ed.) CAI 2011. LNCS, vol. 6742, pp. 247–260. Springer, Heidelberg (2011). doi:10.1007/978-3-642-21493-6_16

[MRT14] Murawski, A.S., Ramsay, S.J., Tzevelekos, N.: Reachability in pushdown register automata. In: Csuhaj-Varjú, E., Dietzfelbinger, M., Ésik, Z. (eds.) MFCS 2014. LNCS, vol. 8634, pp. 464–473. Springer, Heidelberg (2014). doi:10.1007/978-3-662-44522-8_39

[MS04]   Müller-Olm, M., Seidl, H.: A note on Karr's algorithm. In: Díaz, J., Karhumäki, J., Lepistö, A., Sannella, D. (eds.) ICALP 2004. LNCS, vol. 3142, pp. 1016–1028. Springer, Heidelberg (2004). doi:10.1007/978-3-540-27836-8_85

[NO79]   Nelson, G., Oppen, D.C.: Simplification by cooperating decision procedures. ACM Trans. Program. Lang. Syst. **1**(2), 245–257 (1979)

[NSST15] Neven, F., Schweikardt, N., Servais, F., Tan, T.: Distributed streaming with finite memory. In: Proceedings of the 18th International Conference on Database Theory (ICDT), pp. 324–341 (2015)

[NSV01] Neven, F., Schwentick, T., Vianu, V.: Towards regular languages over infinite alphabets. In: Sgall, J., Pultr, A., Kolman, P. (eds.) MFCS 2001. LNCS, vol. 2136, pp. 560–572. Springer, Heidelberg (2001). doi:10.1007/3-540-44683-4_49

[NSV04] Neven, F., Schwentick, T., Vianu, V.: Finite state machines for strings over infinite alphabets. ACM Trans. Comput. Log. **5**(3), 403–435 (2004)

[ORS+08] Olston, C., Reed, B., Srivastava, U., Kumar, R., Tomkins, A.: Pig latin: a not-so-foreign language for data processing. In: Proceedings of the ACM SIGMOD International Conference on Management of Data (SIGMOD), pp. 1099–1110 (2008)

[PWZ13] Piskac, R., Wies, T., Zufferey, D.: Automating separation logic using SMT. In: Sharygina, N., Veith, H. (eds.) CAV 2013. LNCS, vol. 8044, pp. 773–789. Springer, Heidelberg (2013). doi:10.1007/978-3-642-39799-8_54

[PWZ14] Piskac, R., Wies, T., Zufferey, D.: Automating separation logic with trees and data. In: Biere, A., Bloem, R. (eds.) CAV 2014. LNCS, vol. 8559, pp. 711–728. Springer, Cham (2014). doi:10.1007/978-3-319-08867-9_47

[Rey02] Reynolds, J.C.: Separation logic: a logic for shared mutable data structures. In: Proceedings of the 17th IEEE Symposium on Logic in Computer Science (LICS), pp. 55–74 (2002)

[RISK16] Reynolds, A., Iosif, R., Serban, C., King, T.: A decision procedure for separation logic in SMT. In: Artho, C., Legay, A., Peled, D. (eds.) ATVA 2016. LNCS, vol. 9938, pp. 244–261. Springer, Cham (2016). doi:10.1007/978-3-319-46520-3_16

[Sch65] Schützenberger, M.P.: On finite monoids having only trivial subgroups. Inf. Control 8(2), 190–194 (1965)

[Seg06] Segoufin, L.: Automata and logics for words and trees over an infinite alphabet. In: Ésik, Z. (ed.) CSL 2006. LNCS, vol. 4207, pp. 41–57. Springer, Heidelberg (2006). doi:10.1007/11874683_3

[SG87]   Sistla, A.P., German, S.M.: Reasoning with many processes. In: Proceedings of the 2nd Symposium on Logic in Computer Science (LICS), pp. 138–152 (1987)

[SRW02] Sagiv, M., Reps, T., Wilhelm, R.: Parametric shape analysis via 3-valued logic. ACM Trans. Program. Lang. Syst. 24(3), 217–298 (2002)

[SW14]   Song, F., Wu, Z.: Extending temporal logics with data variable quantifications. In: Proceedings of the 34th International Conference on Foundation of Software Technology and Theoretical Computer Science (FSTTCS), pp. 253–265 (2014)

[SW16]   Song, F., Zhilin, W.: On temporal logics with data variable quantifications: decidability and complexity. Inf. Comput. 251, 104–139 (2016)

[Tan10] Tan, T.: On pebble automata for data languages with decidable emptiness problem. J. Comput. Syst. Sci. 76(8), 778–791 (2010)

[Tan13] Tan, T.: Graph reachability and pebble automata over infinite alphabets. ACM Trans. Comput. Log. 14(3), 19 (2013)

[Tan14] Tan, T.: Extending two-variable logic on data trees with order on data values and its automata. ACM Trans. Comput. Log. 15(1), 8 (2014)

[TSJ+09] Thusoo, A., Sarma, J.S., Jain, N., Shao, Z., Chakka, P., Anthony, S., Liu, H., Wyckoff, P., Murthy, R.: Hive - a warehousing solution over a mapreduce framework. PVLDB 2(2), 1626–1629 (2009)

[TW68]   Thatcher, J.W., Wright, J.B.: Generalized finite automata theory with an application to a decision problem of second-order logic. Theory Comput. Syst. 2, 57–81 (1968)

[VB11a] Veanes, M., Bjørner, N.: Foundations of finite symbolic tree transducers. Bull. EATCS 105, 141–173 (2011)

[VB11b] Veanes, M., Bjørner, N.: Symbolic tree transducers. In: Clarke, E., Virbitskaite, I., Voronkov, A. (eds.) PSI 2011. LNCS, vol. 7162, pp. 377–393. Springer, Heidelberg (2012). doi:10.1007/978-3-642-29709-0_32

[VB15]   Veanes, M., Bjørner, N.: Symbolic tree automata. Inf. Process. Lett. 115(3), 418–424 (2015)

[VB16]   Veanes, M., Bjørner, N.: Equivalence of finite-valued symbolic finite transducers. In: Mazzara, M., Voronkov, A. (eds.) PSI 2015. LNCS, vol. 9609, pp. 276–290. Springer, Cham (2016). doi:10.1007/978-3-319-41579-6_21

[VBNB14] Veanes, M., Bjørner, N., Nachmanson, L., Bereg, S.: Monadic decomposition. In: Biere, A., Bloem, R. (eds.) CAV 2014. LNCS, vol. 8559, pp. 628–645. Springer, Cham (2014). doi:10.1007/978-3-319-08867-9_42

[VD16]   Veanes, M., D'Antoni, L.: Minimization of symbolic tree automata. In: Proceedings of the 30th IEEE Symposium on Logic in Computer Science (LICS) (2016)

[Vea13] Veanes, M.: Applications of symbolic finite automata. In: Konstantinidis, S. (ed.) CIAA 2013. LNCS, vol. 7982, pp. 16–23. Springer, Heidelberg (2013). doi:10.1007/978-3-642-39274-0_3

[VHL+12] Veanes, M., Hooimeijer, P., Livshits, B., Molnar, D., Bjørner, N.: Symbolic finite state transducers: algorithms and applications. In: Proceedings of the 39th ACM SIGPLAN-SIGACT Symposium on Principles of Programming Languages (POPL), pp. 137–150 (2012)

[Via09] Vianu, V.: Automatic verification of database-driven systems: a new frontier. In: Proceedings of the 12th International Conference on Database Theory (ICDT), pp. 1–13 (2009)

[vL90] van Leeuwen, J. (ed.): Handbook of Theoretical Computer Science. Formal Models and Semantics, vol. B. Elsevier and MIT Press, Amsterdam and Cambridge (1990)

[vNG01] van Noord, G., Gerdemann, D.: Finite state transducers with predicates and identities. Grammars 4(3), 263–286 (2001)

[VW86] Vardi, M.Y., Wolper, P.: An automata-theoretic approach to automatic program verification (preliminary report). In: Proceedings of the 1st Symposium on Logic in Computer Science (LICS), pp. 332–344 (1986)

[Wat96] Watson, B.W.: Implementing and using finite automata toolkits. Nat. Lang. Eng. 2(4), 295–302 (1996)

[Wu11] Wu, Z.: A decidable extension of data automata. In: Proceedings of the 2nd International Symposium on Games, Automata, Logics and Formal Verification (GandALF), pp. 116–130 (2011)

[Wu12] Wu, Z.: Commutative data automata. In: Proceedings of the 26th International Workshop, 21st Annual Conference on Computer Science Logic (CSL), pp. 528–542 (2012)

[WVS83] Wolper, P., Vardi, M.Y., Sistla, A.P.: Reasoning about infinite computation paths. In: Proceedings of the 24th Annual Symposium on Foundations of Computer Science (FOCS), pp. 185–194 (1983)

[Zar03] Zarba, C.G.: Combining sets with elements. In: Dershowitz, N. (ed.) Verification: Theory and Practice. LNCS, vol. 2772, pp. 762–782. Springer, Heidelberg (2003). doi:10.1007/978-3-540-39910-0_33

Author Index

Printed in the United States
By Bookmasters